The News Service of Florida's
POLITICAL ALMANAC OF FLORIDA 2014

Who lives where in Florida, what do they care about and how do they vote?

DAVID ROYSE

PUBLISHED BY THE NEWS SERVICE OF
FLORIDA, TALLAHASSEE, FLA.

COVER DESIGN AND MAPS: JASON JONES

ISBN: 13: 978-0615978260

NEWS SERVICE
FLORIDA

The Political Almanac of Florida is published by The News Service of Florida, Tallahassee, Fla., Ruth Herrle, Publisher.

The News Service of Florida provides subscribers daily, online, news coverage of the Florida Legislature, the executive branch, and the courts from Tallahassee. The News Service, which started in 2008, has quickly become an authoritative, up-to-the-minute, non-partisan chronicler of Florida's government and political scene. It is widely trusted and used by those who need up-to-date information from the Capitol. Every major newspaper in Florida subscribes, as well as individuals and firms who need daily information on state government and politics.

To subscribe, or for a free trial, go to www.newsserviceflorida.com

The News Service of Florida
336 E. College Ave., Suite 304, Tallahassee, Fla.
32301
850-580-8090

Table of Contents

SPECIAL THANKS

This almanac wouldn't have been possible without the commitment of the owners of the News Service of Florida, Craig Sandler, Russel Pergament and Stephen Cummings, and News Service publisher Ruth Herrle. My deepest thanks for buying into this idea and seeing it through. Thanks must go also to Jim Saunders, the editor of The News Service for taking on more work as I contemplated this project, and eventually left the newsroom to do it. Jim also offered constructive thoughts on parts of the book and encouragement. And thanks to Jason Jones for his work on the maps used in this book and designing the cover.

Several people deserve mention for contributing in ways large and small to the creation of the almanac. First, Lance deHaven Smith and Tom Fiedler, who compiled the original Almanac of Florida Politics in the 1990s, and Michael Barone and Grant Ujifusa, whose Almanac of American Politics was also a model. Several people were consulted on this project, either to contribute their thoughts on a particular area of Florida, or to check what I wrote or proof read sections.

Thanks to Bill Kaczor, Dara Kam, Scott Maxwell, Bob Shaw, Bill Rufty, Buddy Nevins, Christian Sachleben, Jeremy Wallace, Mitch Stacy, Brian Crowley and Nancy Klingener for sharing their knowledge of Florida communities. Thanks also for thoughts on politics from Steve Schale, Kartik Krishnayer, David Johnson and numerous operatives and analysts, both Republican and Democrat who have spelled out for me through the years the way things work. Thanks to Colin Hackley and Laura Sullivan for helping with art. Also, thanks to Steve Wilkerson of the Florida Cable Television Association for our thoughtful discussions about Florida politics over the years. And finally, and most especially, thanks to my wife, Jessica Bishop-Royse, for her support.

INTRODUCTION

Many political operatives and observers believe
demography is destiny in politics, and the
results of the 2012 presidential election in
Florida, along with the electoral realities of
legislative politics in the state bear this out, at
least to some degree. Who lives in a particular
area appears to dictate, largely, who can get
elected there. There is no question that voters
do take into account things that candidates say
when running for office - see Gov. Rick Scott's
performance, for example, in otherwise
conservative areas that typically back
Republicans, but had lots of state workers who
were wary of his anti-government rhetoric in
2010. But generally, as the country and state
have gotten more hyper-partisan, people have
tended to vote fairly predictably in ways that
correlate somewhat reliably with their ethnicity,
national origin, religious background, age,
gender, income and education level and the
degree to which they live in a rural, suburban or
urban area. These things are not permanently
static. We're witnessing a change right now, for
example, as young Cuban-Americans are
starting to vote for Democrats, after years when
Cubans voted solidly Republican. But overall,
demography predicts voting very well.

Of course people also vote based on
partisanship. For years, Florida lawmakers drew
districts that clearly favored one party or the
other as part of the redistricting process.
Technically, that's no longer allowed under the

constitution, but unless you can divine what's in the mind of a lawmaker, there's no way to ever know whether they have "gerrymandered" a district to favor one party or the other - you can only know whether elections do indeed favor one party or the other.

The way we all choose to live makes political demography even more useful in predicting. That's because in American society in the early 21st Century, there's a clear self-segregating phenomenon in how most of us choose where to live. Liberal, hippy-types (not all liberals are hippy-types, but just go with me on the example) drive certain kinds of vehicles, want their kids to go to certain kinds of schools, and eat at certain restaurants - and they tend to look to live in neighborhoods where they can do that comfortably with like-minded people. Likewise, conservative evangelicals tend to live around other conservative evangelicals, Mexican-Americans around other Mexican-Americans, and union card-carrying pipefitters tend to live down the street from union-member plumbers, iron workers or truck drivers. Elderly retirees in Florida cluster together - whether it's in the old-people-only cities like The Villages or Sun City Center or the condo towers of Broward and Palm Beach counties. And we all know about ethnic areas, the "black neighborhoods," or Hispanic ones. You can find many posts on real estate web sites by people seeking to know what ethnic groups live in a neighborhood they're considering. People want to live places where others are like them, and want the same things. That could be low taxes, safe public parks, good schools, a choice of kosher delis and synagogues, or just plain tolerance of something like their sexual orientation, their accent or their skin color.

This book looks at the state by each of its 120 new state House districts as created by the Legislature after the 2010 Census and first used in the election cycle of 2012. In that context, it tries to paint a demographic and political portrait of each district. We chose House districts because counties and Senate districts are so much larger and often more diverse. Also, if the reader is interested in who lives in a particular Senate district, or county, and what the issues are there, the information can be gleaned by looking at the House districts that are within the larger jurisdiction in combination.

Understanding who the people are, politically and otherwise, who live in Florida's House districts is not just a way to make a prediction on who might win a given election. It also gives a better understanding of why the Legislature does what it does - who various members represent, or in other words, who sends them to Tallahassee to do their bidding. And in having a sense of that, along with some of the history of the areas they represent, one may be able to get a clearer understanding of the political and policy decisions made by lawmakers.

When designing this almanac, we also decided to include short biographical information about each of the members of the House, because it seemed that a full picture of a particular district should include information about what kind of people the voters there have elected beyond the mere fact of the representative's party affiliation.

NOTES ON DATA

Much of the data referred to in this book, from median incomes to percentages of people of a given national origin, to the outcomes of previous elections can be found by the reader online somewhere with a little work, or at the most, a few phone calls and a request for a spreadsheet. But this book attempts to put that information together in a way that paints a contextual picture. Much of the information, including the racial breakdown, the percentage of Hispanics in a district, housing occupancy, median age, and gender breakdown, comes from the Legislature itself. Far more of the information included here comes from the U.S. Census or the Census Bureau's American Community Survey, which posts information online, though not by state House district. For some data, we had to match districts with other areas that correspond, such as Census tracts and blocks, cities, counties and zip codes. Median household and family incomes by Census tract all come from the American Community Survey, American Economic Surveys and other data from the Census. Some economic data, including information on employers and types of jobs in a given area, also come from the University of Florida's Bureau for Economic and Business Research and various state agencies like the Department of Economic Opportunity. The Jewish Databank's Jewish Population of the United States was used throughout to determine numbers of Jewish residents in a given area. It is cited, the first time, but is the basis for all estimates of Jewish population, unless otherwise noted. Data on religious identification and the numbers of churches of a given denomination in an area came from the Census Bureau's 2012 Statistical Abstract, the Association of Religion Data Archives, and the Pew Research Religion and Public Life Project, among other sources. Some real estate web sites were also used to get a sense of the property values in certain areas. Information about past elections, with the exception of the 2012 presidential race, comes from the state Division of Elections.

For an estimate of how many votes Barack Obama and Mitt Romney got in each district in 2012, the precinct vote totals from each county supervisor of elections were used, and in most cases simply matched up with the districts in which those precincts sit. The reason we characterize those figures as estimates is that in some counties, precincts are split - with some voters in one House district and some in another, and there's no way to know how that breaks down. Those cases are relatively few though, and in all cases, the estimates were matched up with those made by political operatives, and our results are identical or very close.

For the more qualitative and descriptive

elements in the overviews of each district, driving through the area was the preferred method of research. In many cases, I was familiar with an area from having been there to cover a story (or multiple stories) during several years covering news in Florida. Some areas were easy to describe because I've lived there, vacationed there, or, in one case, my parents live there now. I asked people I know to describe their neighborhoods, and their neighbors. I also relied on the descriptions of certain areas from other reporters and writers who know the state or part of it well, either by talking to them for this project, or by finding the descriptions in earlier works, primarily in news stories that have been published in recent years. In some cases, I referred to books, particularly for historical information. In some cases where there is more information that could be of interest to the reader, I have included footnotes. In cases where the information is widely available, I did not include any citation. In any cases in which there is something misrepresented, if it's not cited to some other source, it's my own mistake.

In the data section, the party registration figures are from the end of 2012, though most county elections supervisors update that information regularly and put it on their websites. The data on ethnicity is for voting age population only, not the entire district population.

This project owes a debt of gratitude to the Almanac of Florida Politics, published in the late 1990s, which looked at the politics of each county, and which, while now dated in such a fast growing state, still informed the writing here. I also must acknowledge the Almanac of American Politics, published every two years by Michael Barone and Grant Ujifusa and the National Journal. Its Congressional district-by-district look at the country is a model for the Florida book and was valuable contextually as well. Barone's work, in particular, on elections, voting patterns and electoral demographics through various works, is essential to anyone wanting to understand the American political landscape.

David Royse, 2014

HOUSE DISTRICT 1
PENSACOLA, NORTH ESCAMBIA

COUNTIES: Escambia

RATING: Solid Republican

LOWER ALABAMA: CHURCH ON SUNDAY, GO NAVY AND ROLL TIDE

Escambia County, Florida's westernmost county, up against the Alabama line, is culturally, and in many ways politically, more like Alabama than much of Florida. It's in the central time zone, it hasn't voted for a Democratic presidential candidate since John F. Kennedy, and the Rev. Jerry Falwell once called Escambia "the most conservative county in America." That's probably not entirely true today – Mitt Romney got about 62 percent of the vote here, less than in some neighboring areas just to the east – but it's still a place full of flags (American and Confederate), churches, the Navy, and conservative voters. "To call Escambia County a Republican stronghold is like calling Tiger Woods a decent golfer," Tampa Bay Times reporter Adam Smith wrote in a 2004 piece. [1] Geographically, it's far-removed from much of Florida – more than 10 hours by car from Miami if there's no traffic. When people here think of going to the big city nearby, they're thinking of New Orleans or Birmingham and on SEC football game days, Roll Tide is just as prevalent here as a Gator chomp.

The 2012 redistricting split Escambia County and Pensacola into two districts, with District 2 in the south including downtown and historic Pensacola, Gulf Breeze and the barrier island beaches, and District 1 to the north and west, taking in the suburban and rural parts of the county.

While much of Pensacola, including the naval air station that gives the city a central part of its identity, is in House District 2 to the south, parts of House District 1 certainly are Navy suburbs. The district includes Ferry Pass, Ensley, Cantonment, Northwest and West Pensacola, mostly working class areas where lots of military personnel also live. The district also includes the small town of Century, a majority African-American town on the Alabama border.

---

[1] Adam Smith, "Panhandle Residents Never Waver from Bush." *St. Petersburg Times.* 10 August 2004.

WHO LIVES HERE?

In addition to its large military presence, the district is mostly white (68 percent to about 23 percent black) and the Hispanic flavor of the state as a whole is largely absent in this district (less than 4 percent). The area is financially fairly stable - about 70 percent of residents live in an owned home. And, not surprisingly, in a place with many military personnel and in a district that includes one of the state's 12

universities, the University of West Florida, the district is youngish. The largest four-year age group is 20-24 year olds, who account for 8.8 percent of the population, and the median age in the district is 37.4, slightly under the state median age of 40.7.

POLITICAL ISSUES AND TRENDS

The area is deeply religious, and generally, social conservatives get elected here –although the party registration figures may not give the impression of a GOP fortress. Only about 45 percent of voters are registered Republicans, with another 15 percent in no party, though most of those no party voters are also very conservative. Many of the Democrats, who make up 37 percent of the electorate, also vote for Republicans. Mitt Romney in 2012 and Rick Scott in 2010 both won the district by about 25 percentage points, and Democrats didn't field a candidate for the district's state House seat in 2012.

This is unquestionably part of the old South. Many voters here were Democrats just two generations ago (the county sent Democrat Earl Hutto to Congress for 20 years and former Democrat W.D. Childers, who later became a Republican, to the state Senate) and religious-based social conservatism, along with a strong pro-military, pro-defense current, are the main factors behind Republican votes.

The district is represented by Rep. Clay Ingram, R-Pensacola. Ingram, a former teacher who played football for Florida State University, was elected in 2010 and faced no opposition in 2012. Ingram serves as chairman of the Government Operations Appropriations Subcommittee. In 2013 Ingram passed legislation to boost penalties for trespassing in school zones, an effort to curb gang activity, and has sponsored legislation banning "bath salts," sold as hallucinogenic drugs. He has voted with his Republican colleagues on high profile issues, including bills involving gun rights, taxes and abortions.

DISTRICT 1 STATS

Registration (Book closing, 2012)
Republicans 45.6 percent
Democrats 37 percent
NPA 15 percent

Voting-Age Population (2010 Census): 121,724
White (Non-Hispanic) 71.3 percent
Black 19.8 percent
Hispanic 3.8 percent

Median Age: 37.4

Men 48.6 percent
Women 51.4 percent

2012 PRESIDENT
Mitt Romney 62.2 percent, Barack Obama 36.4
percent (Estimated) *

2012 STATE HOUSE
No race. Rep. Clay Ingram re-elected without
opposition in general or primary.

2010 GOVERNOR
Rick Scott 58.9 percent, Alex Sink 35.6 percent

2008 PRESIDENT
John McCain 61.9 percent, Barack Obama 36.8
percent

---

* All calculations of the vote tally for the 2012
presidential election in the precincts of a particular
House district are estimates, though many will be
exact. Some aren't exact because precincts are split
between House districts.

HOUSE DISTRICT 2
PENSACOLA AND GULF BREEZE

COUNTIES: Escambia, Santa Rosa
RATING: Solid Republican

NAVY TOWN

Pensacola is a Navy town, above all else. The Navy has been here since the 1820s - the U.S. Navy anyway; the Spaniards first thought the area good for a naval outpost back in the 1550s. But ever since President John Quincy Adams signed off on construction of a Navy yard, through use as a base from which to fight slave traders and pirates, through possession by the Confederate Navy, up to its 20th Century fame as the "cradle of Naval aviation,"

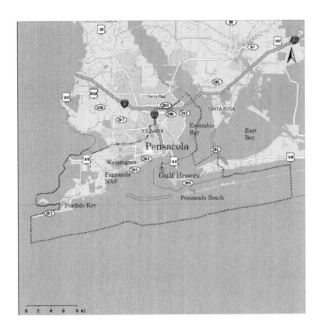

Pensacola has been defined in part by the Navy's presence. Today, the Pensacola area is home to more than 24,000 uniformed military personnel and about 80,000 jobs in Escambia and Santa Rosa County are related to the armed services. Add in thousands of military retirees who return to or remain in the area and you have a place with a heavy military culture. That, of course, manifests itself in the politics here - the whole area is strongly conservative and votes overwhelmingly Republican. House District 2 includes much of the city of Pensacola, including the entire downtown area and Southeast Pensacola, the Bayou Chico area to the southwest of downtown, Warrington, the Pensacola Naval Air Station, Perdido Key, and across Pensacola Bay, Gulf Breeze, Oriole Beach and Pensacola Beach.

WHO LIVES HERE?

Demographically, House District 2 is a near twin of neighboring District 1. It's mostly white (about 70 percent of the voting age population), about 20 percent black, and less than 5 percent Hispanic. Median household incomes are mixed, from over $80,000 a year, well above the state median of $47,827, near the beach, to about $25,000 closer to downtown Pensacola, just over half the state median. The median age is just over 38, a little lower than the state average, mostly because of a high number of Navy personnel.

POLITICAL ISSUES AND TRENDS

About 45 percent of voters here are registered Republicans and about 35 percent Democrats, but Republican candidates typically win by closer to 20 percentage points. The Pensacola area shifted along with much of the rest of the South in the 1980s and 1990s, going from a Dixiecrat stronghold to reliably Republican area.

Democrat Virginia "Ginger" Bass (later Ginger Whetherell, who served as secretary of the Florida Department of Environmental Protection) represented part of Pensacola in the House through most of the 1980s, but during that decade, local voters also elected Republican Tom Banjanin at a time when Escambia County included House Districts 1, 2 and 3. At the time, Pensacola Democrat W.D. Childers (who would later switch parties) represented the area in the Senate and Democrat Earl Hutto was the region's congressman – though voters here were voting for Republican presidential candidates through the 1970s and '80s. Locally, Pensacola still elected Democrats in the 1980s and '90s - Democrat Buzz Ritchie represented part of Pensacola in the House from 1988 to

1998, during a time when Republican gains in north and central Florida put the GOP in control of the Legislature. He was followed in the seat briefly by his ex-wife, DeeDee Ritchie, also a Democrat. But registration had shifted in the 1980s, with Ronald Reagan inspiring a number of white Southern Democrats to register as Republicans, and by the early 1990s, many of them were running for office in the Panhandle and winning. Hutto narrowly won re-election in the early 1990s and retired before the '94 election, to be replaced in Congress by Republican Joe Scarborough. And in 1990, when DeeDee Ritchie decided to run for a state Senate seat, Holly Benson won the Pensacola-based seat (then HD 3), becoming the first Republican to represent that district. Since Benson left to take an administration position, the district has remained Republican, represented by Clay Ford, and now Mike Hill, the only African-American Republican currently in the Legislature.

When he won a special election in 2013, Hill became the first African-American Republican from a Panhandle district in the modern Legislature. Hill is the founder of the "Northwest Florida Tea Party," and was elected easily, defeating Democrat Jeremy Lau by 16 points. Hill is a State Farm agent, and a graduate of the U.S. Air Force Academy. He ran on a platform of limiting government, lowering taxes and reducing regulatory burdens on business. He has also pledged to try to roll back license fees that were increased a few years before he was elected. The 2014 session will be his first.

DISTRICT 2 STATS

Registration (Book closing, 2012)
Republicans 44.6 percent
Democrats 35.4 percent
NPA 17.1 percent

Voting Age Population (2010 Census): 122,970
White (Non-Hispanic) 70.1 percent
Black 20 percent
Hispanic 4.8 percent

Median Age: 38.2

Men 50.2 percent
Women 49.8 percent

2012 PRESIDENT
Mitt Romney 58.4 percent, Barack Obama 40.2
percent (Estimated*)

2012 STATE HOUSE
Rep. Clay Ford faced only write-in opposition.
Ford died in office in March, 2013 and was
replaced by Republican Mike Hill, who won a
special election in June, 2013, defeating
Democrat Jeremy Lau, 58 percent to 42
percent.

2010 GOVERNOR
Rick Scott 55.7 percent, Alex Sink 39.5 percent

2008 PRESIDENT
John McCain 57.6 percent, Barack Obama 41.2
percent

HOUSE DISTRICT 3
SANTA ROSA, NORTH
OKALOOSA

COUNTIES: Santa Rosa, Okaloosa
RATING: Super Republican

PANHANDLE GOP FORTRESS

Across Escambia Bay from Pensacola, Highway 90 runs through Pace and Milton, which, while typical Southern small towns, are also now bedroom communities for Pensacola. They're in Santa Rosa County, which also includes Navarre, a beach community on a peninsula that juts out through East Bay and into Pensacola Bay. The county's other main community, Gulf Breeze, is in neighboring House District 2. Navarre bumps up against

Eglin Air Force Base, which takes up most of the southeastern quadrant of the county. Navarre also runs up against Hurlburt Field, another Air Force facility, though it's next door in House District 4. But the two facilities make this community home to a large number of Air Force personnel and retirees who often stay in the area. The Navy also has a presence right in the middle of the district, where Naval Air Station Whiting Field sits just outside Milton.

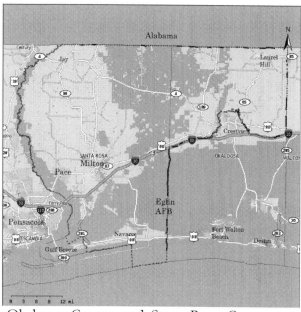

Okaloosa County and Santa Rosa County are first and third in the state in the defense industry's impact on the local economy. A 2013 state report puts the defense impact on the gross county product at 65 percent in Okaloosa County and 33 percent in Santa Rosa. The northern part of Santa Rosa County is rural, with much of it taken up by the Blackwater River State Forest. In northwest Santa Rosa County, one finds the tiny town of Jay, home of the Jay Peanut Festival, and the unincorporated farming area known as Chumuckla. Peanuts and cotton are a small part of the state's overall farm economy, but Santa Rosa County is often the state's top cotton producing county and the second largest peanut producing county. Jay has two cotton gins – possibly the only ones in Florida. Santa Rosa County also has had an oil industry since the 1970s, when the Jay Field was discovered – at that time the largest discovery east of the Mississippi. While most of the crude has been drilled out, people here have benefitted for decades from mineral rights, some of them collecting thousands of dollars a month in royalties and made millionaires, and it helped fund the county for a couple decades. At one point in the early 1980s, about 20 percent of Santa Rosa County's revenue was a result of the oil drilling. While the boom is over, exploration and drilling continues in the area. House District 3 also includes roughly the northern half of Okaloosa County, generally north of Interstate 10 and north of Crestview, which is in neighboring District 4. It's an almost entirely rural area with a few very small population areas like Baker and Laurel Hill (where the high school teams are the Hoboes, a nod to Laurel Hill's railroad-related history.)

WHO LIVES HERE?

This is a Super Republican district, where voters give GOP candidates 40 and 50 percentage point wins over Democrats, who often don't even contest local elections. The district is about 85 percent white, and while the Hispanic population nearly doubled between

2000 and 2010, it remains miniscule – less than 5 percent. Black residents make up just under 6 percent. The area is heavily Baptist and Evangelical – with the largest number of churches being Southern Baptist, followed by other Evangelical Protestant churches and Pentecostal congregations. The population in the district is stable – most families have been here for a couple of generations, and nearly 80 percent own their home. The area near Eglin Air Force Base has a population that, naturally, is a little less stable, but a lot of veterans either stay or return to the area when they retire. About 3 percent of Santa Rosa workers are military personnel, while about 12 percent of workers in Okaloosa County are active military, though many of those are likely living in neighboring House District 4. Household incomes in both Santa Rosa and Okaloosa counties are above the state median, in the mid-$50,000s.

POLITICAL ISSUES AND TRENDS

District 3 is the place in Florida where 2012 GOP presidential candidate Mitt Romney did the best, picking up 76.5 percent of the vote to just 22 percent for President Obama (though the 55 percentage point difference was far from the most lopsided: Obama won several districts by much more, including five districts the president won by more than 70 percentage points.) HD 3 also gave Republican Rick Scott his largest margin of victory in the 2010 governor's race. Scott got 69.4 percent of the vote here, more than 45 points ahead of Democrat Alex Sink. Democrats didn't bother to put up a state House candidate in 2012. The super Republican nature of this district looks unlikely to change significantly anytime soon. If anything, recent elections seem to show an increasing strength in Republican votes, with Romney doing a little better than Scott, and Scott doing better than presidential candidate John McCain in 2008. You have to go back to 1992 to find a Democratic House candidate who won in Santa Rosa County. At the time, the county included part of House District 1, where Democrat Bo Johnson of Milton – who was speaker-designate that year - won with 63 percent of the vote. But even then, the shift to becoming a GOP county was on. Johnson's little-known opponent, Republican Zina Steinsiek got nearly 40 percent of the vote, and the voters in the other House district that at the time included part of Santa Rosa County, HD 4, elected Republican James Kerrigan.

Rep. Doug Broxson, R-Midway, hasn't been out front on many highly controversial issues in the Legislature since his election in 2010, having said at the time he was mainly running to represent local people on more parochial issues. In his first term much of Broxson's attention was on helping constituents deal with the aftermath of the 2010 Deepwater Horizon oil spill and navigate the claims process related to it. During his campaign, Broxson also cited rising health care costs as a major problem he hoped the Legislature would take on. Broxson filed legislation in 2013 that would have encouraged additional oil and gas exploration in the Blackwater River State Forest, but he withdrew the bill, saying he got a lot of pushback from environmentalists and wasn't convinced that the district supported the measure.

DISTRICT 3 STATS

Registration (Book closing, 2012)
Republicans 57.7 percent
Democrats 23.2 percent
NPA 16.2 percent

Voting Age Population (2010 Census): 120,717
White (Non-Hispanic) 86.2 percent
Black 5.9 percent
Hispanic 3.6 percent

Median Age: 38.9

Men 50.5 percent
Women 49.5 percent

2012 PRESIDENT
Mitt Romney 76.5 percent, Barack Obama 22 percent (Estimated*)

2012 STATE HOUSE
Rep. Doug Broxson, R-Midway, faced only write-in opposition

2010 GOVERNOR
Rick Scott 69.4 percent, Alex Sink 23.8 percent

2008 PRESIDENT
John McCain 74.4 percent, Barack Obama 24.3 percent

HOUSE DISTRICT 4
THE EMERALD COAST

COUNTIES: Okaloosa

RATING: Super Republican

THE MOST REGISTERED REPUBLICANS

House District 4 is the most Republican district by registration in the state. Just under 58 percent of registered voters at the end of 2012 were Republicans - and in this area, a lot of Democrats vote for GOP candidates as well, giving Democrats almost no hope of winning here. Democrats make up just over 20 percent of the electorate, a tiny bit more than no party voters, who are about 19 percent.

Most of the physical geographic area of District 4 is within the enormous Eglin Air Force Base, the largest military installation in the United States. It's been one of the Air Force's key bases since World War II, when it was one of the places Lt. Col. Jimmy Doolittle trained his B-25 crews for the 30 seconds over Tokyo bombing raid. Eglin is huge, occupying more than 720 square miles in parts of three counties. It's a high tech base, with its main wing responsible for the development and testing of air-delivered weapons.

The district, however, is much more than runways, test labs and bombing ranges. It has

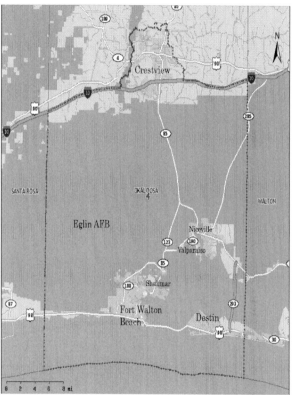

four main population centers: the military-heavy town of Fort Walton Beach; the upscale vacation town of Destin; the bayside hamlets of Valparaiso and Niceville; and the inland city of Crestview, on the north side of Eglin along Interstate 10.

The economy is strong in Okaloosa County, which was buffered against the worst of the recession by its reliance on military jobs. The unemployment rate was just 4.8 percent in the Crestview/Fort Walton/Destin area in May of 2013, third lowest in the state and well below the state rate of 7.1 percent that month. One of the big concerns in recent decades has been growth, and the problems that come with it, including traffic and increasing need for services. But perhaps most concerned about growth in the area is the military. New high rises and more people change what the Air Force liked about this area in the first place - a remote place to test aircraft and weapons. Ironically, the military, while responsible for bringing so many people here, is also one of the main forces seeking to limit its growth.

WHO LIVES HERE?

There is obviously a large military presence in District 4, particularly in the Fort Walton Beach area, which, in addition to being near Eglin, is right up against Hurlburt Field. A 2002 University of West Florida report that pinned military employment in Okaloosa County at 24,000, noted that made the military 20 times the size of the next largest employer in the county. Nearly one in three of the active duty military personnel stationed in Florida are in the county. Another 20,000 or so jobs in the area are related to the military's presence. The district is 75 percent white, 11 percent black and about 7 percent Hispanic, and the median age is 37.7, slightly under the state median. There are military families throughout the district, including a heavy presence in Crestview and Niceville in addition to Fort Walton.

Besides being home to a huge number of Air Force personnel, the area also has one of the nation's highest concentrations of military retirees. The Department of Defense's count of military retirees in the three western Panhandle counties of Florida, including Okaloosa, in 2012 was 32,633, behind only the San Antonio, Texas and San Diego, Calif. areas and about the same as the area in North Carolina near Fort Bragg and Camp Lejeune.

POLITICAL ISSUES AND TRENDS

Okaloosa County is often referred to as one of the most conservative places in the country, and Rick Scott beat Alex Sink in the 2010 governor's race here by 45 percentage points. Remarkably, this was once "yellow dog Democrat" country, typical of the Old South, with no Republicans to be found. That was long ago turned on its head. Back in 2000, Tom Fiedler quoted a former Okaloosa school superintendent, Pledger Sullivan, saying so. "You could take a hog, paint an R on it, turn it loose in the Yellow River Swamp, and it will get 15,000 votes," Sullivan said. Fiedler wrote that the Air Force helped drive the change: civic-minded Air Force wives bolstered the local GOP starting in the 1970s to counter what they saw as a good old boy Democratic stranglehold on local politics. [1] The district continues to be reliably conservative, and shows no sign of changing. "Well, three things are certain in

---

[1] Tom Fiedler and Lance deHaven-Smith, Almanac of Florida Politics 2000 (Political Guides, Inc., 1999), 667.

Panhandle politics," said the seat's current holder, Rep. Matt Gaetz, R-Fort Walton Beach. "The sun rises in the east, it sets in the west, and the most conservative candidate wins." [2]

It would be hard to discuss politics and Crestview without mentioning longtime former Congressman Robert "Bob" Sikes, who represented the area in Congress from 1941 to 1979. Sikes gets much of the credit for Eglin becoming the behemoth it is, and was the original politician known as the "He-Coon." The name was later bestowed on Gov. Lawton Chiles, who mentioned the old "cracker" term for a wily male raccoon in a debate. Sikes was the son of a Confederate soldier, and a newspaperman by trade, known for steering projects back to his district.

In the recent political history of the Destin area, the big story is the rise and fall of former House Speaker Ray Sansom, who never got to preside over a full session of the Legislature, having been forced to step down shortly after becoming speaker. As budget chairman earlier, Sansom, R-Destin, had helped put money in the budget for a building at Northwest Florida State College that later was alleged to have been a gift for a contributor who planned to use it for an airplane hangar. Sansom then took a job with the college. Sansom was hounded over the controversy after he officially became speaker in November of 2008. He stepped down as

[2] Lauren Sage Reinlie, "Rep. Matt Gaetz to run for father's state Senate seat." *Northwest Florida Daily News.* 13 May, 2013.

speaker before the start of the 2009 session and later resigned his seat. He was charged criminally, but prosecutors dropped all charges, clearing Sansom of criminal wrongdoing.

Gaetz was elected in a 2010 special election to fill Sansom's seat. He beat four others, including former legislator Jerry Melvin, in the GOP primary and then defeated Democrat Jan Fernald 66 percent to 34 percent to take the seat just a couple weeks before the end of the 2010 session. Gaetz, an attorney, is the son of Sen. Don Gaetz, who was in the Senate at the time his son was elected, though not yet Senate president. The younger Gaetz, who was once an intern in the Florida House, is planning to run for his father's Senate seat, open in 2016.

In the House, Gaetz has never shied away from controversy, and is often one of the most vocal proponents on the conservative side in committee and floor debates. He drew some criticism for his staunch defense of the state's "stand your ground" self-defense law when he said he wouldn't change "one damn comma" of the law that was under fire in the wake of the acquittal of neighborhood watch volunteer George Zimmerman in the shooting of Trayvon Martin. Gaetz, who was chairman of the House Criminal Justice Subcommittee, drew praise, though, for allowing a debate and a vote by the panel on a bill to abolish the death penalty in Florida. The bill had been filed for several years but never got a hearing. The bill died on the subcommittee vote, but backers said they appreciated the chance to have the debate. During the same session, Gaetz successfully sponsored another bill aimed at speeding up death penalty appeals. Gaetz was one of two House members who voted against 2013 legislation that would have allowed children of undocumented immigrants to get driver's licenses. The bill was later vetoed by Gov. Rick Scott.

DISTRICT 4 STATS
Registration (Book closing, 2012)
Republicans 57.9 percent
Democrats 21.4 percent
NPA 18.9 percent

Voting Age Population (2010 Census): 123,651
White (Non-Hispanic) 78.3 percent
Black 9.6 percent
Hispanic 6.3 percent

Median Age: 37.7

Men 50.4 percent
Women 49.6 percent

2012 PRESIDENT
Mitt Romney 72.7 percent, Barack Obama 25.7 percent (Estimated*)

2012 STATE HOUSE
No Race. Rep. Matt Gaetz, R-Fort Walton Beach, re-elected with no primary or general election opposition.

2010 GOVERNOR
Rick Scott 69 percent, Alex Sink 24 percent

2008 PRESIDENT
John McCain 70.9 percent, Barack Obama 27.9 percent

HOUSE DISTRICT 5
MIDDLE PANHANDLE

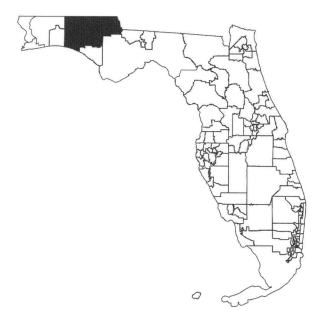

COUNTIES: Walton, Holmes, Washington, Bay, Jackson

RATING: Super Republican

FRIED GREEN TOMATOES MEETS THE TRUMAN SHOW

The broad Fifth District – stretching across four-and-a-half Panhandle counties – has two distinct and different cultures: the rural Old South of most of the district in contrast to the magazine-cover New South beach towns like Seaside, Grayton Beach, Santa Rosa Beach, and Rosemary Beach along the Walton County Gulf coast. While most of Destin is in the neighboring Fourth District, the east end of what many think of as Destin - actually

Miramar Beach - is in House District 5. The town is home to Sandestin, a lush, upscale seaside golf resort. Most of the district's population is either in that affluent coastal strip, or in a ribbon of small, county seat towns along Interstate 10: DeFuniak Springs, Bonifay, Chipley, and Marianna.

Farming is still a top industry in the inland part of the district: Jackson County, along the Alabama and Georgia borders, is the state's

leading peanut, soy bean and corn producing county and vies with Santa Rosa as the top cotton producing county.

Timber is also a big industry in the region - Walton and Jackson counties are both in the top 10 in the state in acres of timberland, and Jackson is one of the top log producing counties in the state.

Another major industry in the district is prisons: Corrections officer is the most common occupation in Jackson County among males, with one in ten men in the county employed in one of the three state prisons in the county, the federal prison in Marianna or the private prison in Graceville. The district also includes major prisons in Holmes, Washington and Walton counties, each of which employs about 300.

House District 5 is home to the Wausau Possum Festival, in the tiny Washington County crossroads town of about 400 people. The town, which calls itself the Possum Capital of the World, has a monument to the marsupial, which is credited with helping people here survive the Great Depression by being plentiful, and easy to catch and, if not easy, at least possible, to eat. Politicians from all over the region - and many candidates for statewide office as well - have endured the indignity of posing for pictures holding up a squealing possum by the tail, or making a strange face when tasting the greasy possum meat between asking for votes at the annual festival.

WHO LIVES HERE?

The rural areas and small towns in the inland portion of the district are predictably super-conservative, propelling Republican candidates here to 40 point wins - despite a nearly even party registration. The area along the coast has most of the more liberal voters - a number of artists have moved to the towns on the Walton County coast, bringing their more liberal voting tendencies, for example, but there aren't enough progressive voters to come anywhere near to matching the number of die-hard conservatives in the area. The district is 80 percent white, about 14 percent black and 4 percent Hispanic, and lots of people here are regular church goers, mostly Baptist and Evangelical. Median family incomes vary, with families in Miramar Beach having incomes over $80,000, and families in similarly-sized Marianna having a median income about half that, right around $42,000.

POLITICAL ISSUES AND TRENDS

In the early 2000s, Republican Party Chairman Al Cardenas and then-Lt. Gov. Frank Brogan got on a charter bus and rode through this area, hitting picnics, barbecues, town squares and country stores in towns like Chipley and Bonifay. Their mission was to convince some of the many registered Democrats in the area to change their party, given the fact that so many of them voted regularly for Republican candidates anyway. Today, Republican registration is much higher than it was then - but still right about even with Democrats - amazing considering Mitt Romney won the district by about 47 percentage points and Rick Scott by nearly 30 points. This is one of the last hold-outs in north Florida for old time Democratic Party members who vote for Republicans in statewide and national races. Even at the local level, the Democratic Party is far less relevant than it once was - the party didn't put up a candidate in 2012 to challenge Republican Rep. Marti Coley, R-Marianna.

Coley never had any intention of being in the Legislature. But when her husband, then-

Rep. David Coley, died in office in 2005, she decided to seek his seat in a special election, saying that "having the opportunity to serve in his seat and finish his term and continue his legacy and honor him is something that is very important to me and to my children." Coley, a former high school English teacher, switched to the college level and has taught at Chipola College for two decades. She has chaired the committee that writes the PreK-12 education budget, and been a vocal advocate for avoiding deep cuts to education spending during the economic downturn, while pushing for more spending in other years. Coley supported teacher merit pay legislation, ending tenure for public school teachers. She has also been an advocate for the Bankhead-Coley research program, a cancer research program named in part for her husband, and also has been a leader in a fight against septic tank inspections, because of the cost to many of her constituents. During the last redistricting, Coley was drawn into the same district as Rep. Brad Drake, R-Eucheeanna. But with Coley one of the most widely respected and well-liked members of the House, Drake decided not to seek re-election, allowing Coley to run without having to face another incumbent. Coley easily defeated Danny Glidewell of DeFuniak Springs in the 2012 GOP primary and beat no party candidate Travis Pitts in the general election by 46 points.

DISTRICT 5 STATS

Registration (Book closing, 2012)
Republicans 43.3 percent
Democrats 43.2percent

NPA 11.9 percent

Voting Age Population (2010 Census): 125,985
White (Non-Hispanic) 80 percent
Black 13.6 percent
Hispanic 3.7 percent

Median Age: 41

Men 53.1 percent
Women 46.9 percent

2012 PRESIDENT
Mitt Romney 72.9 percent, Barack Obama 25.8
percent (Estimated*)

2012 STATE HOUSE
Rep. Marti Coley, R-Marianna, 72.9 percent,
Travis W. Pitts, NPA, 27.1 percent

2010 GOVERNOR
Rick Scott 61.8 percent, Alex Sink 32.6 percent

2008 PRESIDENT
John McCain 71.3 percent, Barack Obama 27.3
percent

HOUSE DISTRICT 6
PANAMA CITY

COUNTIES: Bay

RATING: Super Republican

TEN MONTHS CONSERVATIVE, TWO MONTHS OF CRAZY

House District 6 takes in the Panama City area, including the city itself, the largest between Pensacola and Tallahassee, spring break haven Panama City Beach, Tyndall Air Force Base, the towns of Laguna Beach and Mexico Beach on either side of Panama City, and the suburban area inland from the city, including Southport and Lynn Haven. The area has a lot of tourists and is well-known for its long strip of beachfront shops, restaurants and bars that serve the tourists - but it actually has one of the more diversified economies of the many beach communities this size.

WHO LIVES HERE?

The area is probably best known as a vacation spot, with hundreds of thousands of visitors a year hitting the area's beaches, and spring breakers practically taking over the city in March. But during the rest of the year, Panama City's vibe is actually the opposite of what it is during the notoriously rowdy spring

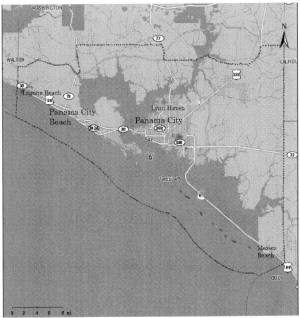

break period - it's a family-oriented, church-going town, mostly. And, while about a quarter of the people here work in tourism-related businesses or retail, there's much more to the local economy than mini-golf, fishing charter boats and seafood restaurants.

Just under 10 percent of workers here are military or civilian employees of the federal government. Tyndall Air Force Base is Bay County's largest employer, with more than

7,200 military and civilian personnel. The city is also home to the Naval Support Activity facility, a major Navy research base that is also one of the city's largest employers, with nearly 3,000 military and civilian personnel. Eastern Shipbuilding is one of the biggest civilian employers here in an area that has a significant blue collar industrial economy. There's been shipbuilding here for a long time - some of the Liberty Ships that helped win World War II were built and launched in Panama City. Another large category of employment here is typical of places that are home to lots of families: 20 percent of workers are employed in education, health care or social services. About 10 percent of workers here are employed in construction. Though building was mostly idled during the recession, the population in Bay County has continued to grow through the years, and large timber holders like the former St. Joe Company are converting land to new housing.

In part because it can get cold in north Florida, the Panhandle Gulf coast has typically been less attractive to retirees than South Florida, though there are retirement communities here. Like its Gulf coast neighbors to the west, the area attracts a number of often younger military retirees, thanks in part to the military's presence. Still, the median age is below that of the state as a whole. The median family income for the county as a whole is just under $60,000, right about the state average. The district is 81 percent white, 11 percent black and just 4 percent Hispanic.

POLITICAL ISSUES AND TRENDS

Registered Republicans dominate the political landscape here, making up just 50 percent of the electorate to just 31 percent who register as Democrats and about 17 percent who register with no party. The district votes overwhelmingly for Republicans, though like everywhere else in the Panhandle that's a recent phenomenon. Before current Rep. Jimmy Patronis, the seat was held by Allan Bense, who served as House speaker from 2004 to 2006. But Bense was the first Republican elected to the seat, having replaced Democrat Scott Clemons, who held the seat through most of the 1990s. Through the 1980s, the seat was held by Democrat Ron Johnson. But as elsewhere, these were socially conservative Democrats: pro-gun, tough-on-crime, and usually pro-development.

The district voted for Mitt Romney for president in 2012 by more than 40 points over President Obama, and for John McCain in 2008 by about the same margin. The last Democratic presidential candidate to win Bay County was Jimmy Carter, who narrowly edged Gerald Ford by about 2 percentage points in 1976. In 2012, Patronis faced no general election opposition.

Panama City was represented in the Senate for most of three decades by the legendary Dempsey Barron, a conservative Democrat who was one of the most powerful men in the state during his time in the Legislature. He was elected to the House in 1956 and in 1960 to the Senate, where he served until 1988, including a stint as Senate president in 1975 and 1976.

Patronis' family owns the landmark Captain Anderson's Restaurant in Panama City so in that way he represents well many of his constituents, a large percentage of whom work in some way in the hospitality industry in the tourism-dependent Panama City area. When Panhandle businesses that rely on tourists were hit hard by the Deepwater Horizon spill-induced slowdown, Patronis understood it as well as anyone. (Being involved in a seafood restaurant he also understood well the effect of the spill on consumers' fears about the safety of fish harvested from the Gulf, which badly hurt the seafood industry in the region.) Patronis has been a reliable Republican vote on most issues, though he did buck his party's establishment in being an early supporter of Rick Scott for governor in 2010, when most GOP elected officials were backing Bill McCollum. Patronis has also worked across the aisle, for example joining Senate Democratic Leader Nan Rich in sponsoring legislation to make it easier for families to enroll their children in KidCare, the subsidized health insurance program for children. Patronis had planned to seek a Senate seat after being forced to leave the House in 2014 due to term limits. But in 2013, Patronis said he was dropping out of consideration for the Senate seat, leaving Rep. Matt Gaetz a likely easy path to the Republican nomination. Patronis said he wanted to spend more time with his young family, and re-focus on the restaurant. Patronis is chairman of the House Economic Affairs Committee.

DISTRICT 6 STATS

Registration (Book closing, 2012)
Republicans 49.8 percent
Democrats 31.2 percent
NPA 16.7 percent

Voting Age Population (2010 Census): 124,614
White (Non-Hispanic) 81 percent
Black 10.6 percent
Hispanic 4.2 percent

Median Age: 39.4

Men 49.5 percent
Women 50.5 percent

2012 PRESIDENT
Mitt Romney 70.5 percent, Barack Obama 28.1
percent (Estimated*)

2012 STATE HOUSE
No race. Rep. Jimmy Patronis, R-Panama City,
re-elected with no primary or general election
opposition

2010 GOVERNOR
Rick Scott 65.7 percent, Alex Sink 29 percent

HOUSE DISTRICT 7
FORGOTTEN COAST, BIG BEND

COUNTIES: Calhoun, Franklin, Gulf,
Jefferson, Lafayette, Leon, Liberty, Madison,
Taylor, Wakulla
RATING: Leans Republican

ONCE YELLOW DOG, THEN BLUE DOG
DEMOCRAT, NOW REPUBLICAN

Rural North Florida voters for generations
elected conservative Democrats to the
Legislature, but the GOP over the last decade
or so has made in-roads, convincing more and
more Blue Dog Dixiecrats who have long voted
for Republicans on the national ticket to choose
the Grand Old Party down the ballot, too.

The massive House District 7, from Gulf
County to Madison County, is a poster child

district for this phenomenon. Some of the area before redistricting was represented by Democrat Leonard Bembry, who often voted with Republicans, but the new district was won by a Republican, Monticello nurseryman Halsey Beshears. One of the candidates who lost to Beshears in the GOP primary is another example of the area's political transition in the 1990s and 2000s: Jamey Westbrook, a former peanut farmer, used to be a Democrat when he was in the Legislature in the 1990s, but ran in 2012 as a Republican. And another former representative of part of the area was Will Kendrick, who also switched from Democrat to Republican. It's difficult to compare the area to former districts, pre-redistricting, however. The current HD 7, which includes all or parts of nine counties, covers at least a share of what used to be six different House seats.

WHO LIVES HERE?

The district is mostly rural, with some areas that have become Tallahassee bedroom communities thrown in - but is hard to pigeon hole. That's because it's such a big district - stretching from seafood industry towns like Port St. Joe, Apalachicola and East Point in the southwest of the district and the heavily forested timber lands of Calhoun and Liberty counties in the northwest to the fast-growing Tallahassee suburb of Wakulla County, and the horse farms around Monticello in the middle, to the farming area around Madison in the east. Jefferson County is home to many state workers who commute to Tallahassee, but otherwise is mostly farm land, including a number of horse farms. Ted Turner has a plantation home in Jefferson County. While much of Jefferson County has a genteel feel, Madison County – also very rural – is more historically hardscrabble. It was in the "Jellyroll" community on the outskirts of tiny Greenville in Madison County where R&B legend Ray Charles was raised.

The district also curves around the Big Bend of Florida, south through the paper mill town

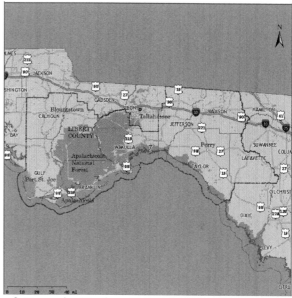

of Perry in Taylor County, and down to the town of Steinhatchee, a little coastal hamlet that's literally at the end of the road tucked away from just about everywhere else. Many of these towns are home to people whose families have lived there for generations.

Wakulla County, just south of Tallahassee, has been one of the fastest growing counties in the state, with newcomers arriving in the last couple decades to take advantage of cheap real estate near the Gulf but just outside the capital city. The county, however, still has many residents whose families have been on the "Forgotten Coast" for a century or more. Drive through Crawfordville or Sopchoppy and you'll notice one of a few surnames seem to be on just about every third mailbox or business, the names of families who settled the area and whose descendants still live here: Posey, Walker, Roddenberry, Barwick, Crum, and a few others.

Apalachicola, likewise, has undergone some demographic change, though looking at the historic homes there you may not guess it. Once almost entirely a fishing and oystering village, the town, while still retaining a working seafood industry, has transformed itself into a touristy beach, bed and breakfast town that's now home to far more artists than would seem probable in such a small community. Gulf County has also seen a massive change in the last quarter century. Its principal city, Port St. Joe, was once a paper mill town. The mill closed in the late 1990s, forcing the town to remake itself, with tourism also on its agenda.

POLITICAL ISSUES AND TRENDS

Because of the size of the district, there's a pretty broad range of interests for anyone trying to court voters here - but a couple stand out. The first is anything affecting state workers and other government employees. According to the Census Bureau, the district has the third-lowest percentage among all House seats of people working for private businesses. That means, lots of people here work for the government, from those working for state agencies in Tallahassee to forestry workers and lots of prison guards, and that means protecting state workers is a primary concern. Privatization of prisons in the area - an idea that was pushed by Republicans - has been opposed by Beshears, who ran ads when he ran for the seat promising to look out for government workers, a contrast with the government-bashing typical of state GOP candidates. He also said that if prisons are going to be closed, they should be closed elsewhere, where there are more job opportunities. State lockups are the only large employer in some towns in the district. Prisons in the area include Calhoun, Franklin, Gulf, Jefferson, Liberty, Madison, Mayo, Taylor, and Wakulla Correctional Institutions. While the district does take in a large swath of western Leon County, which includes the capital city, it's a lightly populated area compared to the two neighboring districts in the county. Still, plenty of state workers who toil in the government buildings of Tallahassee also commute from Wakulla and Jefferson counties, which are included in HD 7, and a few even drive in from Liberty and Taylor counties - also in the district.

Another major concern here in the district is the water flow and health of the Apalachicola River and the bay of the same name, an issue that aligns seafood workers with environmentalists and is probably the top concern of those in Franklin County. The river has its start as the Chattahoochee River north of Atlanta in the Blue Ridge Mountains, and flows right through the Atlanta metropolis -

where it provides much of the drinking water. That has drawn consternation in north Florida, where river flows downstream in the Florida Panhandle have been reduced because of increasing use of water as Atlanta has sprawled. Lower water flows have devastated the Apalachicola Bay area's oyster industry, a problem compounded by drought. Oysters depend on the flow of fresh water into the bay and the mix of fresh and salt water it produces. The dispute has resulted in lawsuits and efforts in Congress to solve the problem of how the water is best apportioned.

The aforementioned shift from a bastion of the old Democratic Party, the pre-Civil Rights era party of the poor South, to a solid Republican stronghold is another ongoing trend here, though it merely mirrors what's happened politically in most of the Southeast over the last four decades or so. Most of the counties in the district show the trend – with the exception of the liberal island of Leon County. The district remains overwhelmingly Democrat by registration – 63 percent to 27 percent for Republicans, but votes for Republican candidates at the presidential level, while splitting lower down the ballot.

Wakulla County, just south of Tallahassee, is a good example of this ticket splitting from election to election, or even in the same year. It's a demographically changing place, adding more Democratic outsiders. But it still is a place where national Republicans can now take votes for granted, though Democrats still have a chance if they're conservative or the Republican isn't well-liked. In 2010, Mitt Romney easily won Wakulla, getting 63 percent of the vote, Republican Marco Rubio had no trouble winning the U.S. Senate race in the county, getting 49 percent of the vote to about 30 percent for no party candidate (and then-Gov.) Charlie Crist, with Democrat Kendrick Meek getting just 20 percent. And Republican Steve Southerland won Wakulla in the local congressional race for District 2, where he unseated Democratic incumbent Allen Boyd. But Republican Rick Scott – who ran for governor on a platform of shrinking government and with a theme of bashing it – barely bested Democrat Alex Sink in the county, beating her by just 318 votes, likely because of the large number of government employees here. And Democrat Loranne Ausley, running unsuccessfully for state Chief Financial Officer, and in her earlier stint in the Legislature one of the most ardent supporters of state workers, eked out a 0.1 percentage point win over Republican Jeff Atwater in Wakulla, the only county Scott won in which a Democrat Cabinet candidate won. Conservative Democrats – like Sen. Bill Montford of Tallahassee and Bembry, have also been able to win in Wakulla.

The district's House member, Beshears, is solidly conservative on most issues, but has broken with the GOP on a number of matters related to the government workforce - which includes a huge number of his constituents. He has opposed privatizing prisons, fearing layoffs, and has criticized efforts to make changes to the pensions of already-hired government workers. "Government must find ways to cut wasteful spending and abuse but it shouldn't be done at the expense of our state employees," he says on his campaign web site. "We must find the right balance that produces a result that is respectful to both the taxpayer and the employees who serve them." He also is at odds with his party as an opponent of school vouchers, saying poor rural districts need more help, rather than to lose good students, and he crossed the aisle to vote against legislation that would give parents of children in failing schools the ability to recommend a charter school takeover. Beshears also voted against a manufacturing tax break bill because it included a provision creating a new board that would have all the power to decide how to spend money coming to the state as a result of a settlement with BP over the 2010 Gulf oil spill. He is in line with Republican colleagues, however, on gun issues, opposing, for example, any changes to the state's stand your ground self defense law. He is in favor of near-shore oil drilling with safeguards, and has said he won't vote for any tax increases, and that while he'll protect workers, he wants to help find ways to "reduce the size and scope of government."

DISTRICT 7 STATS

Registration (Book closing, 2012)
Democrats 63.3 percent
Republicans 26.5 percent
NPA 8.2 percent

Voting Age Population (2010 Census)
124,335
White (Non-Hispanic) 72.4 percent

Black 21.4 percent
Hispanic 4.4 percent

Median Age: 40.2

Men: 55.6 percent
Women: 44.4 percent

2012 PRESIDENT
Mitt Romney 63 percent, Barack Obama 35.8
percent (Estimated*)

2012 STATE HOUSE
Halsey Beshears, Republican, 60.7 percent,
Robert Hill, Democrat, 39.3 percent0

2010 GOVERNOR
Rick Scott 49.5 percent, Alex Sink 46.1
percent

2008 PRESIDENT
John McCain 62.1 percent, Barack Obama
36.6 percent

HOUSE DISTRICT 8
GADSDEN COUNTY, WESTERN
LEON

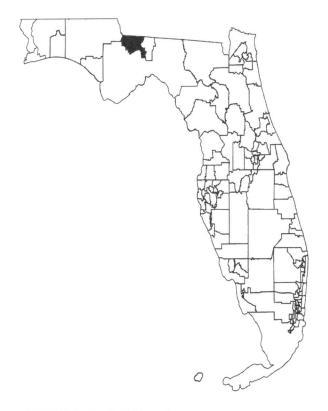

COUNTIES: Gadsden, Leon

RATING: **Super Democrat**

YOUNG DEMOCRATS AND FLORIDA'S MAJORITY BLACK COUNTY

Right next door to the capital city of Tallahassee, one county to the west, is Florida's only majority African-American county, Gadsden County, where 56.7 percent of residents are black. The rural county makes up much of House District 8 geographically, but the district juts into much more densely populated Tallahassee, picking up an area that's mixed in terms of income and race, but, like Gadsden, votes heavily Democratic. This is also the state's youngest district, with a median age of just 26.9 years, one of only two districts in the state with a median age under 30. While the Florida State University campus buildings are in neighboring District 9, the area where many FSU students live, along with nearly all Florida A&M students and many Tallahassee Community College students, is in HD 8. More than 30,000 of the residents in the district, about 1 in 5, is between the ages of 20 and 24. The heavy college student presence makes the Tallahassee part of the district more transient than many other areas. More than half of the homes in the district are rented, rather than owned by the occupants. Only about 10 percent of the residents of the district are over 60. When you cross the Ochlockonee River from relatively urban Leon County into Gadsden County, you might feel you've gone back a half century or so. While Tallahassee is full of bureaucrats, students, lawyers and political operatives, many of them from elsewhere, Gadsden County is populated by a lot of "country" people whose families have been here for generations. Quincy, Gadsden's county seat, is an antebellum post card, where plantation homes and farm fields still dot the landscape.

WHO LIVES HERE?: TALLAHASSEE

While the Gadsden County part of the district is majority black, the African-American presence in the district includes much of the part in Tallahassee as well. The district takes in the historic and mostly black Frenchtown neighborhood northwest of downtown Tallahassee. It also includes south-side Tallahassee neighborhoods around historically black Florida A&M University and off Orange Ave. and Jim Lee Roads, nearly within sight of the Capitol, that are also mostly home to African-Americans. The Tallahassee part of the district also includes the Indian Head Acres neighborhood, just east of the Capitol, a place that's decidedly progressive, known as home to "old hippies" and college professors, and overwhelmingly votes for Democrats. It also includes an area along West Pensacola and West Tennessee Streets that is home to thousands of Florida State University and Tallahassee Community College students – a big part of what makes this the state's youngest House district; and northwest Tallahassee neighborhoods off Old Bainbridge, Hartsfield and Mission Roads, which are politically and racially mixed. The part of the district in Tallahassee includes some areas with relatively low incomes, but also areas with some degree of affluence, including the Myers Park area near the Capitol.

GADSDEN COUNTY

Gadsden County was historically agricultural, with much of its economy tied to shade tobacco. Curing barns, while falling down, can still be seen here. As late as the 1950s, the crop, which was used to make the wrapping for cigars, was the main economic engine here. In fact, Havana, just northwest of

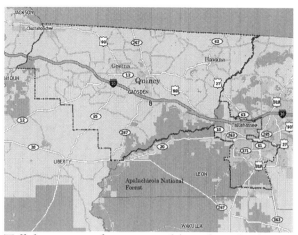

Tallahassee and now a bit of a bedroom community for the capital, was home to Havana cigar tobacco, not the Cuban city with which it shares a name. The county does still have some commercial agricultural producers. A large mushroom grower just resumed production after a shut-down during the recession, and the county is also a significant commercial tomato producer. That agricultural productivity has lured Mexican and Central American farm workers to the area, but Hispanics are less than 10 percent of the population.

While farming was the lifeblood of this region in the past, there are also some people in Quincy whose families are wealthy thanks to a soft drink. More than a century ago, a local banker named Mark "Pat" Munroe got interested in a little Atlanta bottling company that was making a new product called Coca-Cola and bought some stock. He also convinced a lot of local farmers to join him investing in the company, and made several of them millionaires. The Coke millionaires and their offspring have mostly remained in the

Quincy area. Since the decline of shade tobacco in the mid-20th Century, agriculture has been less and less the backbone of the county. Many of its residents now make the short drive on Interstate 10 to Tallahassee to work, and according to the 2010 American Community Survey, only about 4 percent of the workforce here now actually works on a farm. One large employer in the district is Florida State Hospital, a state mental hospital in Chattahoochee. The largest percentage of people in the Gadsden County workforce, about a quarter, work in educational services, health care and social services. Gadsden County has a large percentage of poor people – nearly a quarter of families and 29 percent of all people in the county live below the poverty line. The median household income is a little over $33,000.

POLITICAL ISSUES AND TRENDS

This district has long been safe for Democrats and in drawing it to keep it about half African-American legislators assured it will remain so. Many of the predominantly white areas in the district in Leon County also have large numbers of Democrats. While some of the more conservative white voters in Gadsden County still sometimes register as Democrats, most of them vote for Republicans at the top of the ticket, and sometimes down-ballot, too, but they're a minority of voters here. The newly drawn district lost areas in southeast and southern Leon County and picked up parts of Gadsden County that had previously been lumped in with a more rural district to the south and west. The previous District 8 was also heavily African-American and was represented by Rep. Curtis Richardson, who like the current representative, Alan Williams, is from Tallahassee.

The district surrounds Florida State University, which is in a neighboring district, but includes Florida A&M University, the state's only public historically-black university, and Tallahassee Community College.

Williams, D-Tallahassee, started his political career as an aide to Tallahassee Mayor John Marks, and was heavily involved in local causes before running for the state House when Richardson was term-limited in 2008. He's a Tallahassee native, a graduate of Rickards High and Florida A&M. Williams has been a reliable Democratic vote, and often a spokesman for the party's positions on the floor. He has been one of the leaders of the effort to repeal the "Stand Your Ground" self-defense law in the wake of the George Zimmerman-Trayvon Martin case, and in 2013 was chairman of the Florida Legislative Black Caucus. As a representative of much of the capital city and neighboring Gadsden County, he can be relied on to back state workers on issues that concern them, typically opposing efforts to change their pension benefits and pushing for more pay for government employees. In 2013, Republicans questioned Williams' residency, noting he owns a home that was in the old House District 8, off Buck Lake Rd. in eastern Leon County, but is not in the new district. Williams responded that he owns the home but also owns a home in the current District 8 and lives "in both."

DISTRICT STATS

Registration (Book closing, 2012)
Democrats 69.5 percent
Republicans 14.6 percent
NPA 14.2 percent

Voting Age Population (2010 Census): 125,293
Black 49.4 percent
White (Non-Hispanic) 41 percent
Hispanic 6.7 percent

Median Age: 26.9

Men: 48.4 percent
Women 51.6 percent

2012 PRESIDENT
Barack Obama 76.6 percent, Mitt Romney 22.3
percent (Estimated*)

2012 STATE HOUSE
Rep. Alan Williams, D-Tallahassee, re-elected
with no primary or general election opposition

2010 GOVERNOR
Alex Sink 76.7 percent, Rick Scott 21.3 percent

2008 PRESIDENT
Barack Obama 75.8 percent, John McCain, 23.3
percent

HOUSE DISTRICT 9
TALLAHASSEE, EASTERN LEON COUNTY

COUNTIES: Leon

RATING: Leans Democrat

WHERE THE BUREAUCRACY LIVES

North Monroe St. is the center of Tallahassee - it runs right through the middle of its downtown, and the Capitol building sits on the street. But it is a demographic and psychological divider of the city as well. West of Monroe St. and downtown Tallahassee are the universities, Florida State, and Florida A&M, and neighborhoods lovingly called "student ghettoes," as well as the Tennessee St. strip that has entertained generations of students in the town. Many professionals, including the thousands who work in state government, either graduate from that side of town and move to the eastern half of the city, generally speaking, or if they move to town without having attended one of the big universities, they often go months without setting foot west of North Monroe, except maybe to tailgate, unless they work on the west side. Technically the city's north-south axis is a block or so east (it's called Meridian St. because it is that divide.) And there are exceptions, such as the historically black residential area of Frenchtown, which is on the west side, but generally, Monroe St. is what most people think of as the line between student Tallahassee and grown-folks Tallahassee. The city is roughly divided in half along its north-south centerline for purposes of legislative representation as well - though Monroe St. only serves as the actual border between the city's two House districts, HD 8 and HD 9, for a couple blocks. For the most part, the line separating the two districts juts back and forth across Monroe, a few blocks east of it here a few blocks west of it there - but essentially the city is divided in half in terms of political boundaries with the western half in District 8 and the eastern half and the eastern Leon County suburbs in District 9.

The district runs up to the Georgia border (many Florida residents don't realize it, but Tallahassee is less than 20 miles from the state line) and much of the semi-rural/suburban area northeast of Tallahassee has the aura of Old South gentility. Thomasville Rd., Centerville Rd. and Meridian Rd. run under a canopy of live oaks past old plantation homes as they head toward the Georgia line. Tucked in among the old plantations are the modern subdivisions like the sprawling Killearn, and the wealthy Summerbrooke and Golden Eagle developments, spread out amid golf courses and moss-draped trees. This area is home to many of the state government realm's movers and shakers, the high-powered lobbyists and lawyers who make their living at the Capitol, and those appointed to top government jobs heading state agencies.

WHO LIVES HERE?

Leon County, with about 265,000 people, is young – with a median age of 29.5, tied as the second youngest county in the state after Alachua, home to the University of Florida. The midline county divide is evident in age, too, with a kids vs. grown-up divide between the

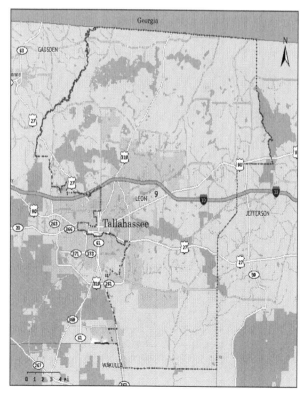

two districts: House District 9 has a median age of 36.3 - a whole decade older than House District 8, the youngest House district in the state. Still, HD 9 is younger than Florida as a whole where the median age is about 40 and places like Charlotte County where it's nearly 55.

The geographical-political division isn't absolute - most of Leon County is overwhelmingly Democratic in representation, and the two sides of town are more similar than not. It's a highly educated county, as unified in its generally progressive, "government is a force for good" world view as in its interest in Florida State football. Tallahassee is, however, still distinctively an Old South capital city - never captured by the Union - and despite the liberal university crowd, has a hint of Dixie, with its moss-draped canopy roads and the drawl of lifelong residents. And while House District 8 next door is majority black, House District 9 is largely white.

POLITICAL ISSUES AND TRENDS

The divide can be seen in looking at election results, with many more people in the eastern half of the county likely to vote for a Republican. President Obama still carried House District 9 in the last presidential election, but winning by only about 6 percentage points, compared to the 54 point walloping the president gave Mitt Romney in neighboring House District 8 to the west. John McCain also ran respectably in the district, getting 46 percent of the vote to just 53 percent for Obama in 2008. And a little-known

Republican, Bradley Maxwell, managed to get nearly 40 percent of the vote in the most recent state House race as well, while losing to incumbent Rep. Michelle Rehwinkel Vasilinda, D-Tallahassee. Democrat Alex Sink won easily here in the last governor's race, but Republican Rick Scott was talking quite a bit about shrinking the big employer in town, state government. Democrats outnumber Republicans in Leon County 2-1, and local Republicans have never gained much of an organizational foothold. But the right GOP candidate could probably win in House District 9. In 2008, former NFL and Florida State football star Peter Boulware ran as a Republican for the District 9 seat - before redistricting - and lost to Democrat Rehwinkel Vasilinda by just a few hundred votes out of more than 80,000 cast, even though she had strong local name recognition as well. But typically, even conservative politicians here have a better bet running as Democrats in the mode of the city's state senator, Bill Montford, a Democrat who sometimes crosses the aisle to vote with Republicans.

Rehwinkel Vasilinda benefitted from two well-known names when running for the House District 9 seat in 2008 after Loranne Ausley was term-limited. Rehwinkel, from her first marriage, is the name of a longtime family in the Tallahassee area. And her current husband, Mike Vasilinda, is the dean of the Tallahassee press corps as a TV reporter who has covered the Capitol since the early 1970s. His work is for several TV station clients, including one in Tallahassee, so viewers in the area may have at least been a little familiar with his wife's name. Still, she barely won the seat in her initial election, having to overcome Boulware's even better known name - and winning by just a half a percentage point. Since winning the seat and re-election twice, Rehwinkel Vasilinda has been a reliable Democratic vote, and has been unafraid to push some liberal issues in the Republican-dominated Legislature that have gone nowhere. For example, Rehwinkel Vasilinda, a staunch anti-death penalty voter, has filed legislation to outlaw the death penalty, but hasn't managed to get the bill through a single committee. She was, however, the only Democrat to vote for a bill in 2009 that could have permitted new near-shore oil drilling off the Florida coast, saying it was a chance for economic development during a recession - and that it was a pragmatic opening for more discussion of renewable energy in an overwhelmingly Republican body. The bill died in the Senate, but the vote drew criticism, and it was a major issue for a Democratic primary opponent, Rick Minor, in 2010, though Rehwinkel Vasilinda easily defeated Minor with nearly 70 percent of the vote. Rehwinkel Vasilinda has also been a vocal advocate in the Legislature for alternative, renewable energy. She has been a full time faculty member at Tallahassee Community College since 1989, and is a lawyer. She is the ranking member of the Finance and Tax Subcommittee.

DISTRICT 9 STATS

Registration (Book closing, 2012)
Democrats 47.7 percent

Republicans 34.8 percent
NPA 14.9 percent

Voting Age Population (2010 Census): 124,130

White (Non-Hispanic) 75.2 percent
Black 15.6 percent
Hispanic 4.8 percent

Median Age: 36.3

Men: 48.4 percent
Women 51.6 percent

2012 PRESIDENT
Barack Obama 52.1 percent, Mitt Romney 46.6
percent (Estimated*)

2012 STATE HOUSE
Rep. Michelle Rehwinkel Vasilinda, D-
Tallahassee, 61.7 percent, Bradley Maxwell,
Republican, 38.3 percent

2010 GOVERNOR
Alex Sink 62.1 percent, Rick Scott 35.8 percent

2008 PRESIDENT
Barack Obama 53 percent, John McCain, 46
percent

HOUSE DISTRICT 10
NORTH CENTRAL FLORIDA:

COUNTIES: Suwannee, Columbia, Hamilton, Baker, Alachua

RATING: Solid Republican

RURAL NORTH FLORIDA ARCHETYPE

The Suwannee River winds lazily south from the Georgia border roughly dividing northwest Florida from northeast Florida, and also creates the western border of House District 10. The district is bisected into eastern and western halves by Interstate 75, and split into northern and southern halves by Interstate 10. The main city in the district is Lake City, the seat of Columbia County. Other towns include Live

Oak, Jasper, Fort White, High Springs and Macclenny. Much of the district is unpopulated - including all of the Osceola National Forest. The area, along the Florida-Georgia border, has much more in common culturally with Dixie than with peninsular Florida and a Miami Herald columnist, the late Al Burt, called the area "Florgia." The district includes all of Hamilton, Suwannee, Columbia and Baker counties, and a sliver of Alachua County.

WHO LIVES HERE?

This district is the archetype of the rural, relatively poor parts of north Florida. Suwannee, Columbia and Baker counties are all below the state median in income, while Hamilton County is one of the poorest, just one of three Florida counties with a per capita annual income below $20,000 (the other two are Union and Lafayette, both in neighboring House districts.) The median family income in

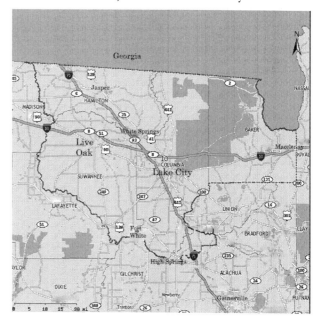

Hamilton County is just under $47,000 a year, and more than 20 percent of the county's residents received food stamps or supplemental nutritional program assistance within the previous year. (In the Hamilton County seat of Jasper, the food stamp recipient percentage jumps to 37.4 percent.) With that poverty comes other bleak statistics. House District 10 may have the highest teen birth rate in the state. The top two counties in Florida in that statistical category are Baker and Hamilton, both more than double the state average. Suwannee and Columbia County also rank about double the state average in teen births, 13th and 15th in the state respectively.

The district is about 77 percent white and 17 percent black. About 5 percent of the voting age population is Hispanic - with a large number of Latinos having migrated to the Live Oak area to work for the Pilgrim's Pride chicken plant. The plant employs more than 1,000 people, is Suwannee County's largest employer, and a major reason the county's population is 10 percent Hispanic and about 5 percent Mexican.

For the most part, as the income figures would suggest, most of the people here are working middle class, with large numbers employed in trucking, warehouse work, and industrial jobs. The biggest industry in Hamilton County, for example, has long been phosphate mining - at one point in the late 1970s, the mining gave the county about 40 percent of its revenue. The biggest employer in the county is the Canadian company Potash

Corp., which operates a phosphate mine and two chemical plants near White Springs, employing about 700 people - roughly 7 percent of Hamilton County's workforce. The biggest private employer in Baker County is a 900-employee Wal-Mart distribution center - and this area has long been a transportation hub, sitting near the intersection of two major interstates, and not far from a third, I-95 along the east coast. Its location along I-10 also gives residents in Baker County another option - many of them make the half hour commute into Jacksonville to work.

Healthcare is also a significant white collar and blue collar employer in the district. The largest employer in Lake City is the VA hospital for veterans, which provides more than 1,000 jobs. And in Baker County, one of the major political battles of recent years was over the county's overall largest employer, Northeast Florida State Hospital, during the deep budget cuts of the 2008-2011 recession. Pre-redistricting, Baker County was part of a more northeasterly district that surrounded Jacksonville, and was represented by Rep. Janet Adkins, R-Fernandina Beach, who spent a considerable amount of time trying to prevent the mental hospital from being privatized to save money. Ultimately, the state retained the hospital, which employs over 1,000 people, and is the largest state-owned psychiatric care facility for civilly committed people in Florida.

POLITICAL ISSUES AND TRENDS

This is another district where registered

Democrats outnumber Republicans (by about 10,000 voters) but GOP candidates win easily, particularly at the state and national level. Both Mitt Romney and John McCain defeated Barack Obama by nearly 40 percentage points here, and Rick Scott won by nearly 25 points. Democrats didn't contest the seat in the House in 2012 either.

But, conservative Democrats can win here. In the late 1990s and early 2000s, Democrat Richard Mitchell of Jasper represented some of this area in the Senate, and was one of is more liberal members, when looking at votes. Before redistricting, much of the area was part of House District 11, which the current HD 10 representative, Republican Liz Porter, won in 2010, unseating incumbent Democratic Rep. Debbie Boyd 54 percent to 40 percent (though the race may not have been as close if a third party "Tea Party" candidate hadn't siphoned off 6 percent of the votes.) But in 2008, Boyd beat Porter 36,892 votes to 36,713 votes after a manual recount. Boyd had won in a similarly close race in 2006 by about 500 votes over Republican David Pope, and not so much has changed in the intervening years to suggest that Democrats are finished in this region.

The area around Lake City has a troubled past, racially. It was an early hotbed of Ku Klux Klan activity, and several black political leaders were murdered here during the reconstruction years. Broader changes in racial attitudes, and generations of new people moving in, however have eased much of that tension, according to local leaders. For years, the power structure in the area was entirely white, but that's changed in the last decade, with black officials more likely now to be elected to local offices.

Porter, R-Lake City, has made protection of water for farm use and eco-tourism, both big in her area, a top concern. In 2012 she sponsored legislation, eventually signed by the governor, dealing with water supply plans and water flow policy, and in part encouraging more cooperation between water management districts on regional issues. She also was an opponent of proposed federal rules on nutrient levels in Florida fresh-water bodies, siding with the state, which proposed its own rules. As vice chair of the Education Committee, Porter also backed legislation, eventually signed by the governor, that gives local school districts the ability to do their own approval of instructional materials, rather than requiring them to participate in a state process. She sponsored the bill with Democratic Sen. Bill Montford. Porter has sponsored anti-abortion legislation to require women seeking first trimester abortions to first have an ultrasound shown to them, which passed in 2011, the only bill she sponsored that year to become law. She was a sponsor of the sales tax holiday bill in 2012, and has pushed legislation putting additional records requirements on animal shelters in an effort to reduce euthanasia, Porter, who works in medical billing, is vice chair of the Education Committee and vice chair of the Economic Development and Tourism Subcommittee and in 2011 was named deputy majority whip. She is a former Columbia County commissioner.

DISTRICT 10 STATS

Registration (Book closing, 2012)

Democrats 48.9 percent
Republicans 37.9 percent
NPA 10.4 percent

Voting Age Population (2010 Census)
120,635
White (Non-Hispanic) 76.5 percent
Black 16.5 percent
Hispanic 5 percent

Median Age: 39.6

Men: 52.1 percent
Women: 47.9 percent

2012 PRESIDENT
Mitt Romney 69.3 percent, Barack Obama
29.7 percent (Estimated*)

2012 STATE HOUSE
No race. Rep. Liz Porter, R-Lake City, re-
elected with no primary or general election
opposition

2010 GOVERNOR
Rick Scott 59.2 percent, Alex Sink 36.4
percent

2008 PRESIDENT
John McCain 68.6 percent, Barack Obama
30.2 percent

HOUSE DISTRICT 11
JAX BEACHES, NASSAU COUNTY

COUNTIES: Nassau, Duval
RATING: Solid Republican

BACK WOODS, COASTAL AFFLUENCE

House District 11 forms a sort of arch around the east, north and far northwest sides of Jacksonville. It is really three distinct areas: On the east side, it includes the beach towns of Jacksonville Beach, Neptune Beach and Atlantic Beach adjacent to the city. Northeast of Jacksonville, across the Nassau County line, the district includes the golf course and resort-covered retirement and vacation haven of Amelia Island and the town of Fernandina Beach at the north end of the island. The third distinct section of the district stretches inland from the Amelia River through a rural buffer that runs between Jacksonville's north side and the Georgia line. That area, in Nassau County, includes the tiny towns of Yulee, Callahan and

Hilliard. Much of inland Nassau County is timberland.

The district also includes the huge Naval Station Mayport, which sits where the St. Johns River empties into the Atlantic, and is the third largest Naval facility in the United States. Mayport is home base to about 5,500 military personnel, with many of them likely to be more conservative voters - though their impact is spread among a few northeast Florida House

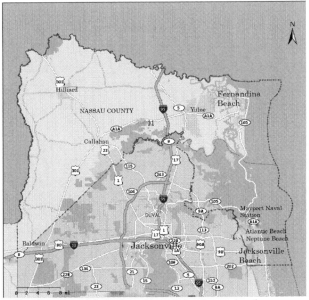

districts in which they live. The base is also one of the area's largest employers, with more than 6,000 civilian personnel as well.

WHO LIVES HERE?

Amelia Island is an upscale resort community - the type of festivals on the island may give a hint of its character: some of the big ones include the Jazz Festival, the Chamber Music Festival and the "Concours d'Elegance," kind of a beauty pageant for luxury cars. There are seven golf courses on the small island, along with several seaside resorts. It has a thriving arts community, and author John Grisham is among a handful of celebrities with property on the island (Pete's Bar and the Sea Turtle Inn in Neptune Beach are featured in Grisham's The Brethren). The island is also home to plenty of well-off retirees. The median age in Fernandina Beach is 50 - well above the state median.

While many on the island are wealthy, there is a blue collar economy as well. The RockTenn paper mill, the second largest containerboard producer in North America, is in Fernandina Beach and employs more than 400. A Rayonier wood cellulose fibers mill in Fernandina Beach employs another 280. Many who work at those facilities live farther inland, closer to Yulee, because of high property values on the beach. Fernandina and Yulee - which is connected to the sea by a series of bays and streams - have a long-established seafood industry as well, with generations of people in the two towns having worked on shrimp boats or processing shrimp.

The beaches - Jacksonville Beach, Atlantic Beach and Neptune Beach - are independent of Jacksonville, which is otherwise consolidated with Duval County. The three communities each have their own personality, but all three have more low-rise development, including single family homes, than the high rise condos of many other major beach towns. All three are full of relatively young professionals - these are communities with lots of people in their 30s and 40s mostly, many of them commuting to Jacksonville during the day, some heading up to

Mayport where they work for Uncle Sam. Jacksonville Beach is known, in part, for its night life - young professionals move to the area to be close to restaurants and bars, in addition to the beach. Atlantic Beach and Neptune Beach to the north of Jax Beach, are quieter, with less nightlife. The beaches are relatively affluent, with a median household income right around $60,000, well above the state median. Whites make up more than 90 percent of the population in Jacksonville Beach and Neptune Beach and about 83 percent in Atlantic Beach (which is about 10 percent African-American.)

As the home port for about 5,500 Navy personnel, the area is also home to a large number of Navy retirees. However, while some do live near the base on the beaches and therefore in HD 11, more live farther inland where housing is cheaper, with a large number living in neighboring House District 12 in eastern Jacksonville. Hilliard, in western Nassau County, is home to the Federal Aviation Administration's Jacksonville regional Air Route Traffic Control Center, which tracks planes between airports. With the Navy and the FAA, in addition to local agencies, more than 15 percent of workers in Nassau County are employed by the government.

The district is about 85 percent white and the median age is about 40. The median household income in Nassau County is just under $60,000 and the median family income about $66,000. Just under 10 percent of the population lives below the poverty line. The population here is generally stable, with the exception of the Navy families, who are more likely to be short-time residents. Nearly 80 percent of people in Nassau County own their home. Many of the homes that aren't family-owned homes are rental properties near the beach.

POLITICAL ISSUES AND TRENDS

Slightly over half of voters here are registered Republicans, and judging by recent performance many of the nearly 20,000 no-party voters (about 17 percent) also vote for GOP candidates. The area is fairly culturally conservative, and gives mainstream Republican candidates huge wins. Mitt Romney got nearly 70 percent of the vote in the district, and Republican Janet Adkins got about the same in the state House race. Rick Scott in 2010 and GOP presidential candidate John McCain in 2008 got just under 70 percent.

There's nothing to suggest that top of the ticket Democrats would do well here anytime soon if sheer demographics are the main factor in a race. Like elsewhere in north Florida, that's a new phenomenon. As recently as 2000, Nassau County was represented in the House by Rep. George Crady, D-Yulee, who had been in office since the late 1970s. Crady was a classic conservative Democrat, however, having often voted with Republicans.

Rep. Janet Adkins, R-Fernandina Beach, is chairwoman of the House K-12 Subcommittee, which handles most substantive legislation dealing with schools. She's a major backer of school choice, and a reliable proponent of legislation aimed at helping alternatives to traditional public schools, such as charter schools. She has sponsored legislation aimed at providing taxpayer dollars for capital projects for charter schools, which can't use new property tax levies for building. Before she was elected to the House, Adkins was an elected member of the Nassau County school board from 1998 to 2008. Adkins is also a reliable vote for reducing taxes and regulations in line with the Republican caucus in general. She's also in line with GOP colleagues on lawsuit rules and gun ownership rights, and is anti-abortion. In 2010, she sponsored a bill that would have required government employers to check immigration status, required driver license applicants to prove legal status and created a state police hotline for people to report illegal immigrants. The bill also would have prevented illegal immigrant children from attending public K-12 schools or prekindergarten, and required the Lottery to check the immigration status of winners. The bill failed. During the 2013 session, Adkins pushed a proposal that would have required body mass index testing for firefighters, but it also failed. She also successfully sponsored legislation to remove the word "retarded" from state laws, substituting "intellectual disabilities."

During Adkins' first two terms in the Legislature she represented a district that stretched farther west, including Baker County, and was heavily involved in a fight to keep the North Florida State Hospital open. Adkins, a full-time legislator, was elected in 2008, and re-elected in 2010 and 2012. She was an advocate before that, though, having worked in the early 2000s to push for passage of legislation (later signed into law by Gov. Jeb Bush) to strengthen local school advisory councils.

DISTRICT 11 STATS

Registration (Book closing, 2012)
Republicans 51.6 percent
Democrats 27.9 percent
NPA 16.6 percent

Voting Age Population (2010 Census): 123,593
White (Non-Hispanic) 84.8 percent
Black 7.6 percent
Hispanic 4.3 percent

Median Age: 39.9

Men 50.5 percent
Women 49.5 percent

2012 PRESIDENT
Mitt Romney 69.9 percent, Barack Obama 29 percent (Estimated*)

2012 STATE HOUSE
Rep. Janet Adkins, R-Fernandina Beach, 71.8 percent, Dave Smith, Democrat, 28.2 percent.

2010 GOVERNOR
Rick Scott 64.6 percent, Alex Sink 32.4 percent

2008 PRESIDENT
John McCain 67 percent, Barack Obama 32 percent

HOUSE DISTRICT 12
JACKSONVILLE, ARLINGTON, SOUTHSIDE

COUNTIES: Duval
RATING: Solid Republican

THE FIRST COAST

They call the Jacksonville area and northeast Florida "The First Coast" - and the oldest permanent European settlement down in St. Augustine is well known and part of the reason. But there's also a reason St. Augustine's historical significance has to be qualified with "permanent." About a year before St. Augustine was settled, a group of French Huguenots started a settlement at Fort Caroline, on the south bank of the Saint Johns River just a bit upriver from today's Mayport Naval Station, and not far from the future site of downtown Jacksonville. The 1564 settlement was the first French colony in the present-day United States, though it was demolished a short time later by the Spaniards who settled down the coast and claimed Fort Caroline was a staging base for pirates (it probably was).

The area that now makes up House District 12, between downtown Jacksonville and the Intracoastal Waterway, has obviously changed

considerably in the intervening 450 years or so, becoming a saw mill community in the 19th Century and then a heavily developed residential neighborhood after World War II. Development picked up especially after the 1953 construction of the Matthews Bridge across the Saint Johns River, linking the area east of the river to downtown Jacksonville. That made Arlington the fastest growing part of Jacksonville in the 1950s and 1960s. While the neighboring district that includes downtown Jacksonville, HD 13, reaches across the river to Old Arlington, the eastern reaches of the neighborhood, are in HD 12. East Arlington remains a high growth area - nearly doubling in population since 1990. The district, made up of mostly well-off white collar neighborhoods, is bounded on the north by the St. Johns River and on the south by Butler Blvd., near the University of North Florida, which is part of the district.

WHO LIVES HERE?

The area overall is mostly white collar, generally well-off and made up of lots of young families and singles - the median age here is a youthful 33.8. Mean incomes are fairly high, with most families in the $70,000 range, with higher incomes along the river and the river's Mill Cove in the north of the district. The median dips to the mid-$40,000s in the Census tract near the University of North Florida because of the large number of students, which also contributes to keeping the median age in the district low. The district population counting all ages is about 64 percent white, 16 percent black, and 10.5 percent Hispanic. Jacksonville also has the largest concentration of Filipino-Americans in the state, about 25,000, in part due to Mayport Naval base (and American sailors who married spouses from the Philippines.)

Although Mayport itself is in neighboring House District 11, a number of Navy personnel assigned to the station live throughout the

Jacksonville area, including HD 12. The Jacksonville area also is home to a huge number of Navy retirees.

POLITICAL ISSUES AND TRENDS

Duval County has traditionally been a Republican stronghold, though in recent years Democrats have increased registration in the area and over the last couple of decades some affluent white voters who are more likely to vote Republican have fled to neighboring St. Johns County, which has a reputation for having particularly good schools. While Democrats are clearly making gains in the county as a whole (Mitt Romney got just 51 percent of the vote in Duval County in 2012 and Democrat Alvin Brown was elected mayor), House District 12 on Jacksonville's east side is still a place where Republicans will easily win elections. Romney won the district's precincts by 20 percentage points - nowhere near as much as in neighboring House District 11, but still an easy win. HD 12 also gave Republican Rick Scott 60 percent of the vote in the 2010 governor's race, and Democrats didn't put up a candidate to run against Republican state Rep. Lake Ray in 2012. Ray defeated Green Party candidate Karen Morian by nearly 40 percentage points. The small number of minorities and the general relative affluence of the area keep it demographically a Republican lock, even though the district is seven years younger than the state median, and younger voters are more likely to vote Democratic. Some of the younger voters in this area, however, are military families, and that presence boosts Republican votes.

Ray, R-Jacksonville, has generally avoided the spotlight of major controversial issues in the Legislature, focusing instead mostly on more mundane legislation that is nonetheless important to someone, often local officials. For example, Ray passed a bill in 2013 that made changes to the way local governments implement their transportation concurrency plans, and he has also pushed, so far unsuccessfully, for local governments to be able to create "freight logistics zones," to be able to get incentives, and for tax credits for manufacturers that use Florida ports. In 2013 Ray was also the House sponsor of successful legislation aimed at boosting use of natural gas in car and truck fleets by exempting it from the fuel tax for the next five years. Ray, a former Jacksonville city council member, has also been a major booster of the Jacksonville port, and pushed for its expansion. He is the president of the First Coast Manufacturing Association, but before that was an engineer with a company that works on port design.

Ray is reliably with his Republican legislative colleagues on nearly every issue, and was also nearly completely in line with the pro-business lobbies, including Associated Industries and the Florida Chamber, breaking with each of them only once in the 2013 session. Ray was also highly marked by the fiscally conservative Americans for Prosperity, although he broke with AFP when he voted for some hometown economic incentives, backing a proposal to give tax breaks for renovations at Everbank Field in

Jacksonville and improvements at Daytona International Speedway. Ray is chairman of the Joint Legislative Auditing Committee, and vice chairman of the Transportation and Economic Development Appropriations Subcommittee and the Transportation and Highway Safety Subcommittee.

DISTRICT 12 STATS

Registration (Book closing, 2012)
Republicans 40.4 percent
Democrats 39.7 percent
NPA 16.7 percent

Voting Age Population (2010 Census): 116,646
White (Non-Hispanic) 64.7 percent
Black 22.3 percent
Hispanic 7.3 percent

Median Age: 35

Men 48.3 percent
Women 51.7 percent

2012 PRESIDENT
Mitt Romney 56.9 percent, Barack Obama 41.9 percent (Estimated*)

2012 STATE HOUSE
Rep. Lake Ray, R-Jacksonville, 68.3 percent, Karen Morian, Green Party, 31.7 percent.

2010 GOVERNOR
Rick Scott 56.9 percent, Alex Sink 40.2 percent

2008 PRESIDENT
John McCain 56.7 percent, Barack Obama 42.4 percent

HOUSE DISTRICT 13
DOWNTOWN JAX, OLD
ARLINGTON, SOUTHBANK

COUNTIES: Duval

RATING: Solid Democrat

IN THE SHADOW OF JACKSONVILLE'S NEW IDENTITY

Jacksonville, it could be said, is Florida's business center. Although Miami and Tampa could make a good claim in recent years as the center of corporate Florida, Jacksonville remains the state's boardroom capital, in part because Miami and Tampa are so diverse - Miami is more a trendy tourist town and also could be thought of more as the capital of Latin America, while the Tampa-St. Petersburg area has its retirees. Jacksonville, while it also has the

Navy, has mostly been for decades a town of everyday people going to work.

It is a diverse workforce - for years a blue collar mainstay dominated by paper mills, the railroad, and a huge port, but later becoming a corporate haven as well. Not just home to the railroad yards, it was home to the railroad company headquarters, with CSX one of the dominant companies here. (It used to be joked that in a town that was home to such a big railroad company, the local newspaper never reported that a train hit a car. The car always hit the train.) For years, there was also the paper industry, which gave Jacksonville a reputation as a place that could be a bit foul smelling when the wind was right. But insurance company and bank offices in the St. Johns River might be thought of now as the icon of Jacksonville, more than the paper mills and factories of the last century. It's also a major health care center, with nationally-known hospitals and health insurers. And now, the city's downtown skyline is probably what most people think of when they think of Jacksonville - unlike Miami where people are more likely to think of South Beach, and the Tampa-St. Pete area, where people might think of retirees sitting on downtown benches, or watering the lawn in front of their manufactured home.

Many of these corporate offices of downtown Jacksonville are in House District 13. But the district also takes in the majority African-American and relatively poor neighborhoods immediately to the north and west. The district also crosses the river to the

Southbank area and picks up the historic and trendy San Marco neighborhood, with its high-end boutique shops, historic homes and swanky condos on the river. Also on the south side of the river, the district includes the St. Nicholas neighborhood, with its stately mansions and two of the Jacksonville area's top private schools, Bishop Kenny and Episcopal. Back on the other side of the river, just west of downtown, is the neighborhood that was the historic center of black culture in Jacksonville,

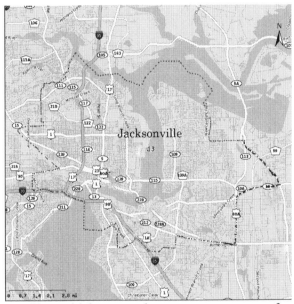

LaVilla, which started out as a town for African-Americans in the 1860s. While LaVilla's Ashley St. corridor was a must-stop for many black entertainers in the pre-Civil Rights era, the neighborhood declined as an entertainment center in the 1960s and 1970s, and has struggled since. The district also includes the African-American neighborhood of Mixon Town.

WHO LIVES HERE?

This is a starkly bifurcated district, with the St. Johns River splitting it in two both physically and economically. The district is centered on downtown Jacksonville, and the poor, mostly black neighborhoods bordering downtown. For the most part, wealthy people work in this part of Jacksonville - but they don't live here. The median family income in this area is a dismally low $29,000 a year, unemployment was very high here during the recession, and 45 percent of the people in the area's main zip code, 32202, are below the poverty level. In sharp contrast, when you cross the Fuller Warren, Acosta or Main St. Bridges to the other side of the St. Johns River, you enter the fashionable San Marco neighborhood and its well-off neighbor St. Nicholas. In this area, the median family income is over $55,000, and fewer than 20 percent are below the poverty level. One real estate marketing web site describes San Marco as being home to "single professionals, young married couples, gays and lesbians, creative types and artists." With the part of the district north and west of the river being mostly black, and the part east and south of the river heavily white, the district ends up being split, with 53 percent of all residents being black and 40 percent white. Among those of voting age, the district is 50 percent black and 41 percent white. The voting age population is 6 percent Hispanic, with the largest portion of the Latino population being Puerto Rican.

POLITICAL ISSUES AND TRENDS

The urban core of Jacksonville was the second area in the state to break the white stranglehold on legislative districts that existed before majority African-American districts were created, sending Jacksonville dentist Arnett Girardeau to the House in 1976, even before redistricting created boundaries favoring black candidates. (The first area to elect black lawmakers was Miami, which sent Joe Kershaw and Gwen Cherry to Tallahassee earlier.) Ever since the redistricting after the 1980 Census, Jacksonville has had two House districts in which African-Americans were the dominant demographic - although in this district the voting age black population comes in at just a shade under 50 percent, while about 41 percent of the voters here are white. The district is comfortably in the Democratic camp in terms of registration and performance, with Democrats making up 60 percent of the electorate to 23 percent for Republicans, and another 14 percent have no party affiliation.

As you would expect, Barack Obama won easily here in both his presidential elections, though Mitt Romney and John McCain both managed to get about 32 percent of the vote. Republicans didn't run a candidate for the state House in 2012, giving Rep. Reggie Fullwood automatic re-election. The district had to be changed fairly significantly during the 2012 redistricting. Fullwood's old District 15 had 20 percent fewer voters than were needed to make up a properly sized House district.

Fullwood, the head of an affordable housing real estate development organization, was elected to the Legislature in 2010 and re-elected with no opposition in 2012. The Jacksonville native was the youngest city councilman in the history of the city when he was elected to the council in 1999. He was re-elected to that post in 2003 and was twice chairman of the council's Finance Committee. In the House, Fullwood sponsored legislation seeking to guarantee that children born in the United States and raised in Florida could get in-state college tuition even when their parents are in the country illegally. The measure failed, but the change was later made as the result of a court case.

Fullwood was the House sponsor in 2013 of a measure aimed at expanding punishments for cyberbullying, a bill that passed both chambers unanimously and was signed into law by the governor. Fullwood first tried to get to the Legislature in 2006, challenging then Rep. Audrey Gibson in the Democratic primary, but losing. He succeeded her in 2010 when Gibson was elected to the Senate, and got 67 percent of the vote in the general election against Republican Randy Smith. Fullwood was fined $1,220 by the House in 2011 for failing to register to vote in his district for 15 days after he was elected. According to a consent decree, Fullwood had moved to the district in time, but hadn't gotten his voter registration changed.

DISTRICT 13 STATS

Registration (Book closing, 2012)
Democrats 60.3 percent
Republicans 23.2 percent
NPA 14.2 percent

Voting Age Population (2010 Census):
119,339
Black 49.9 percent
White (Non-Hispanic) 40.8 percent
Hispanic 6.2 percent

Median Age: 35.7

Men 48.6 percent
Women 51.4 percent

2012 PRESIDENT
Barack Obama 67 percent, Mitt Romney 32.1
percent (Estimated*)

2012 STATE HOUSE
No race. Rep. Reggie Fullwood, D-
Jacksonville, re-elected with no primary or
general election opposition

2010 GOVERNOR
Alex Sink 61.7 percent, Rick Scott 35.6
percent

2008 PRESIDENT
Barack Obama 66.9 percent, John McCain
32.4 percent

HOUSE DISTRICT 14
JACKSONVILLE NORTHSIDE

COUNTIES: Duval

RATING: Solid Democrat

JACKSONVILLE'S MOST DEMOCRATIC NEIGHBORHOODS

House District 14 includes the Northside of Jacksonville, an economically and racially mixed area stretching north of the Trout River out past Jacksonville International Airport. The district also includes closer-in areas to the northwest of Jacksonville, off Lem Turner Rd., including several almost entirely African-American neighborhoods, including some, like the Ribault neighborhood, that have some of the poorest Census tracts in the state. In addition to Ribault, neighborhoods in this near northwest side of Jacksonville area that are in the district include Riverview, Osceola Forest and Sherwood Forest. The district then curves around Jacksonville in the very lightly populated area west of I-295, taking in all the area of northwestern Duval County out to the Nassau County line. In the south, the district includes close-in neighborhoods to the southwest of downtown Jacksonville including Lackawanna, Edgewood, Normandy and

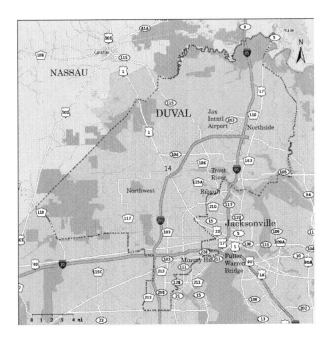

Hillcrest, all near the river. Murray Hill, another neighborhood in that part of the district, is becoming a trendy neighborhood, drawing young families into historic homes.

WHO LIVES HERE?

Overall, the district is pretty diverse, economically and racially. It's about 53 percent black and 39 percent white with a wide-range of incomes, from relatively well-off young families in the Murray Hill neighborhood and other areas in the southern part of the district, to average to upper income, working families in the Northside area, to very poor families in some areas around the Trout River. Much of the far northern and western part of the district has an almost rural feel, while closer in, it has a very urban vibe. The area around the airport, including the Oceanway area, is seen as being ripe for upscale development with the economic rebound, in part because of the success of a major new shopping complex called River City Marketplace. The most densely populated parts of HD 14, however, are the poorest areas, those closest in to the city's core. The Ribault neighborhood has a median household income of just over $20,000 a year and many here live below the poverty line.

POLITICAL ISSUES AND TRENDS

This is Jacksonville's most reliably Democratic district, but it's still only about 62 percent Democrats by registration. Democratic candidates don't have to worry though - Barack Obama won the district by more than 30 points in 2008 and 2012, Democratic gubernatorial candidate Alex Sink got 64 percent of the vote here. The area's House member, Rep. Mia Jones, didn't draw a Republican challenger and defeated a Libertarian candidate 79 percent to 21 percent. In addition to the majority of voters being black, many of the white voters are working class, including union members who vote for Democrats. Because the area reaching out to the edge of Duval County on the west and north is less developed, growth hasn't been the major issue here that it is in many other parts of the state, though with newer developments north of Jacksonville near the airport, some expect that will soon become a concern. Improving health care and public education resonated well for Jones in her election campaigns, particularly with the area's poor residents.

Jones started her career in community work in the Office of Equal Employment under Jacksonville Mayor Ed Austin and then worked for the Duval County schools, where she was involved in minority hiring. In 2003, Jones was elected to the Jacksonville City Council, representing many of the Northside neighborhoods she now represents in the Legislature. During her time on the Council she sought to boost the neighborhood economically and she served on the council until 2008, when she ran for the legislative seat being vacated by Rep. Terry Fields because of term limits. Jones narrowly defeated fellow city council member Pat Lockett-Felder in the Democratic primary and then easily won the general election, defeating Republican Sarah Lovett with 74 percent of the vote. She was unopposed for re-election in 2010 and easily defeated Libertarian Jonathan Loesche in 2012.

Jones sought the votes of her Democratic House colleagues to be the party's floor leader starting in 2014, but lost by one vote to Rep. Darryl Rouson of St. Petersburg, who was himself later replaced by Rep. Mark Pafford before leading the caucus during a session. Jones also served for a time as chairwoman of the Legislative Black Caucus. Jones has been one of several Democrats who have called for changes to the state's "Stand Your Ground" defense law, and was also a vocal proponent of the state accepting federal Medicaid expansion money to cover more people under the Affordable Care Act. Jones also sponsored legislation seeking to repeal a law allowing counties to run their own juvenile detention facilities, a measure that has so far failed to pass.

Jones is in line with her Democratic colleagues on typically partisan issues. She is in favor of abortion rights, tends to oppose expansions of gun rights, and is generally a strong advocate for public schools and teachers. Jones filed legislation for the 2014 session seeking to give judges more discretion in certain criminal sentences, a measure she also filed in 2013 that died in committee. She also filed legislation in 2013 seeking to require insurers to cover certain telemedicine costs, a bill seeking to soften "zero tolerance" policies in schools to have them only apply to threats of violence, a bill requiring health education in the schools and a bill seeking to mandate certain nutritional requirements in child care facilities. All of her bills in 2013 failed to make it out of committee. In 2012, she filed a bill seeking to increase the required minimum number of daily hours of care in nursing homes, a measure that also failed.

DISTRICT 14 STATS

Registration (Book closing, 2012)
Democrats 61.8 percent

Republicans 22.7 percent
NPA 13.2 percent

Voting Age Population (2010 Census):
114,782
Black 50 percent
White (Non-Hispanic) 42.8 percent
Hispanic 4.1 percent

Median Age: 35.8

Men 47.5 percent
Women 52.5 percent

2012 PRESIDENT
Barack Obama 65.6 percent, Mitt Romney
33.6 percent (Estimated*)

2012 STATE HOUSE
Rep. Mia Jones, D-Jacksonville, 78.7 percent,
Jonathan Loesche, Libertarian, 21.3 percent

2010 GOVERNOR
Alex Sink 63.6 percent, Rick Scott 33.9
percent

2008 PRESIDENT
Barack Obama 65.8 percent, John McCain
33.5 percent

HOUSE DISTRICT 15
JACKSONVILLE WESTSIDE

COUNTIES: Duval

RATING: Leans Republican

SINGIN' SONGS ABOUT THE SOUTHLAND

Jacksonville's Westside has been slower to develop than most of the rest of the metro area and suburban neighborhoods have only recently started to crop up outside of the wrap-around I-295. But the city's suburbs are now starting to extend into an area on the western fringes of Duval County that in a few places is still woodsy. House District 15 starts at the western Duval County line, includes the Baldwin area, and runs through the area known as Westside all the way to the St Johns River, forming its eastern boundary. The district takes in the southwestern corner of Duval County, and runs up to the Fuller Warren Bridge on the southwest side of downtown Jacksonville. A big part of the district is the Cecil Commerce and Industrial Park, the site of the former Cecil Field Naval Air Station. The center now is home to several industrial and office tenants, and about 2,000 people work there, though the city has struggled to attract one major mega employer at the park. On its eastern edge, the district also includes one of Jacksonville's wealthiest neighborhoods, Ortega.

WHO LIVES HERE?

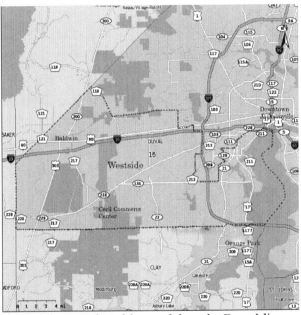

While mostly white and largely Republican, the district does have a sizeable number of African-Americans, who make up a quarter of the district's population and 22 percent of its voting age population. Another 7.3 percent of the voting age people in the district are Hispanic, and 5 percent are Asian.

The median household income varies a bit across the district, ranging from a well below average $40,000 a year in some neighborhoods in the far western part of the district to the mid $50,000s, right around the state median household income, in the middle before dropping back to just around $50,000 a year in the eastern part. Then at the very eastern end of the district is Ortega, its streets lined with multimillion dollar homes, and its riverfront dotted with yachts. The neighborhood, on a peninsula sticking into the river, is among the wealthiest in the area.

But overall, those who live here on Jacksonville's Westside are middle class. A lot are white collar workers, though, and more than 80 percent have at least some college education. About two-thirds of people here own their own home, and most are part of relatively young families. The median age is 35, younger than the state median, and more than 35 percent of households in the district have children under 18 living in them.

In the eastern part of the district near the river are Lake Shore Middle School, formerly Lake Shore Junior High, and Robert E. Lee High School, where members of what would become Lynyrd Skynyrd met and started playing music. While it is more diverse now, the district remains the kind of place where you're likely to hear Free Bird coming from the stereo in the pickup truck next to you at the red light.

POLITICAL ISSUES AND TRENDS

At the top of the ticket the district votes reliably, but not overwhelmingly Republican. While Mitt Romney and John McCain won here by double digits in the last two presidential elections, Barack Obama got over 40 percent of the vote both times. Rick Scott also won the district, getting 57 percent of the vote, and Republican Rep. Daniel Davis faced no opposition in 2012 from the Democratic Party (or anyone else.)

Davis, who isn't seeking re-election in 2014, was elected to the House in 2010 and re-elected in 2012 after sitting on the Jacksonville city council from 2003-10, serving as the council's president in 2007-08. Davis ran and served as a pro-business Republican, closely allied with the Jacksonville business community and generally supporting what was good for corporate Jacksonville.

In 2013, Davis pushed into law a measure to make it harder to "steal houses" by using adverse possession, putting additional requirements into law before someone can assume ownership of a home by essentially squatting in an abandoned - usually foreclosed - home and paying the taxes on it. In line with the business community, Davis has been, during his time in the Legislature, a supporter of tax breaks for the Jacksonville Jaguars, saying the team boosts Jacksonville's image. Overall, Davis has voted in line with his Republican colleagues on social issues as well, and has been a vocal supporter of anti-abortion legislation. He also supported the teacher merit pay bill that ended tenure-based pay for public school teachers, one of the more high profile pieces of legislation to become law during his tenure.

DISTRICT 15 STATS
Registration (Book closing, 2012)
Republicans 40.4 percent

Democrats 39.7 percent
NPA 16.7 percent

Voting Age Population (2010 Census):
116,646
White (Non-Hispanic) 64.7 percent
Black 22.3 percent
Hispanic 7.3 percent

Median Age: 35

Men 48.3 percent
Women 51.7 percent

2012 PRESIDENT
Mitt Romney 56.9 percent, Barack Obama
41.9 percent (Estimated*)

2012 STATE HOUSE
No race. Rep. Daniel Davis, R-Jacksonville,
faced no primary or general election
opposition.

2010 GOVERNOR
Rick Scott 56.9 percent, Alex Sink 40.2
percent

2008 PRESIDENT
John McCain 56.7 percent, Barack Obama
42.4 percent

HOUSE DISTRICT 16
JACKSONVILLE SOUTHSIDE, MANDARIN

COUNTIES: Duval
RATING: Solid Republican

JACKSONVILLE'S PINSTRIPED CLASS

The Southside of Jacksonville, south and east of the Saint Johns River, includes relatively affluent neighborhoods along the river, like Miramar, Lakewood and San Jose. Historic Mandarin, along the river south of the city, was once home to Harriet Beecher Stowe, the author of Uncle Tom's Cabin, who charged visitors to show them her home. Now, it's a quiet upscale residential area of high end single family homes and apartment and condo complexes. The district goes south to Julington Creek, and continues east, past I-295 nearly to the Intracoastal Waterway. Huge expanses of the eastern-most portion of the district are undeveloped.

WHO LIVES HERE?

The upper middle class families and young professionals of Jacksonville live here. Median household incomes (including singles living alone) top $50,000 and median family incomes are well over $60,000, making this area more affluent than the state as a whole. The mean family income is close to $90,000 in the San Jose area, although about 10 percent of the population in the district does live below the poverty line. Mandarin's largest Census Tract

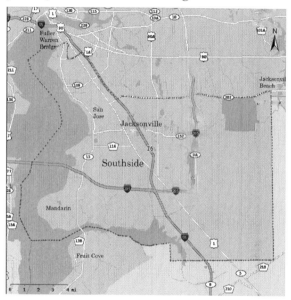

has a very high median household income, over $100,000. About a third of the households in the district are families with children under 18, while only about 20 percent include people 65 and older. The median age in the district is young - 36.5. House District 16's voting age population is 73 percent white, 11 percent black and about 7 percent Hispanic. Many residents work in Jacksonville's downtown office buildings, for insurance, banking and financial companies, or defense and aerospace companies, among others. Some of the Navy personnel who work at nearby Mayport also call this district home - particularly in the more affordable apartment and condo developments.

POLITICAL ISSUES AND TRENDS

Like much of Duval County, this district is solidly Republican, in registration and performance. The GOP counts just under half of registered voters, with about 31 percent registered as Democrats, and 18 percent with no party affiliation. More of those NPA voters side with Republicans when they go in the booth. Republican candidates John McCain in 2008, Rick Scott in 2010 and Mitt Romney in 2012 got 62 percent, 61 percent and 63 percent of the vote here, respectively. There doesn't appear to be much movement, or any trend toward notable change, and demographic patterns in northeast Florida have fluctuated much less than in other parts of the state, so this district appears likely to remain solidly Republican for the foreseeable future.

Rep. Charles McBurney, a political activist and former prosecutor, was elected to the House in 2007 in a special election when Rep. Mark Mahon was appointed to a judgeship. McBurney had sought the seat in 2000 but lost in the Republican primary to Mahon. In 2007, McBurney defeated Jacksonville City Councilman Lad Daniels in the GOP primary, and then easily beat Democrat Debra Jahns-Nelsen. McBurney came into the Legislature just as lawmakers were starting to deal with the downturn in the economy, and among the first things he had to think about was cutting the budget. "My constituents are not clamoring for new taxes or fees," he told the Florida Times-Union about how he might approach that task.

Another issue McBurney cited when he campaigned was civics education, lamenting the fact that many students can't name the branches of government. He filed a proposal to require civics education that failed in 2008 and 2009 but finally became law in 2010. Also during his tenure, McBurney successfully sponsored legislation to protect consumers from being caught off guard by automatic contract renewals for certain services such as lawn maintenance. In 2011, McBurney sponsored a proposed constitutional amendment to require state Senate confirmation for Supreme Court justices and appeals court judges. Though his original proposal stalled, the idea passed in a companion measure and the issue eventually showed up on the ballot as Amendment 5 in 2012. Voters, however, rejected it.

McBurney has been a solidly reliable GOP vote, and has been rewarded with committee assignments on the "majors," including the appropriations, education and judiciary committees, and was named chairman of the Justice Appropriations Subcommittee, a good fit for a former prosecutor.

McBurney's name came up in connection to controversy when in 2013 a Florida Highway Patrol trooper gave McBurney a citation for not having insurance - allegedly to save McBurney from getting a more expensive speeding ticket. But McBurney complained about the insurance ticket, saying he did have insurance - and disputed the claim that he was speeding.

McBurney's complaint led to the firing of the trooper. McBurney is the stepson of former House Speaker William V. "Bill" Chappell, Jr., a Democrat, who led the House in 1962 and 1963 and later was a 10-term Congressman.

DISTRICT 16 STATS

Registration (Book closing, 2012)
Republicans 47.4 percent
Democrats 31.3 percent
NPA 17.6 percent

Voting Age Population (2010 Census):
122,729
White (Non-Hispanic) 73.4 percent
Black 11 percent
Hispanic 7.8 percent

Median Age: 37.9

Men 48 percent
Women 52 percent

2012 PRESIDENT
Mitt Romney 62.6 percent, Barack Obama
36.3 percent (Estimated*)

2012 STATE HOUSE
No race. Rep. Charles McBurney, R-
Jacksonville, faced no primary or general
election opposition.

2010 GOVERNOR
Rick Scott 60.5 percent, Alex Sink 36.6
percent

HOUSE DISTRICT 17
ST. AUGUSTINE, NORTHERN ST. JOHNS

COUNTIES: St. Johns
RATING: Super Republican

THE OLDEST EUROPEAN-AMERICAN CITY, GOLF COURSES AND RETIRED TYCOONS

By the time the Pilgrims arrived in what would become Massachusetts in the 1620s, most of the original inhabitants of the nation's true first city of St. Augustine had died of old age and the second and third generations of colonists were running the city. St. Augustine was settled in 1565 by Spanish Admiral Pedro Menendez de Aviles, a full 55 years before the Mayflower arrived, and more than 40 years before the Virginia Company developed Jamestown. Every year as the nation mimics the pilgrims' Thanksgiving feast of turkey, some the residents of St. Augustine might remember that the actual first Thanksgiving feast was a half century earlier, in 1565 where the Spanish ate cocina stew with the Timucuan Indians. The city would come to be the capital of Spanish Florida for 200 years, and St. Augustine continues to celebrate itself as the nation's oldest city - and its most notable feature is its historic charm. It has preserved its Spanish colonial-era old town with coquina-walled buildings, narrow streets and the oldest wooden schoolhouse in America. The Castillo de San Marcos, the 17th Century fort, is the oldest masonry fort still in existence in the United States. The preservation of the city's Spanish history gives the town a feel of authentic oldness that's rare in most of Florida.

The northern part of House District 17 might be best looked at geographically by pointing out where the rough, the fairways and the water hazards are. To call the district a giant golf course would be going too far, but not by a whole lot. From the Ponte Vedra Inn and Club and the Marsh Landing Country Club in the north, through an area that includes TPC Sawgrass, with its iconic island 17th hole, right into St. Augustine, home to the World Golf Village Resort, and its World Golf Hall of Fame, this is an area of doglegs, bunkers and argyle socks. The PGA headquarters is even in this district.

Inland, the district stretches to the St. Johns River, including Fruit Cove and the new planned community of Nocatee. The northern part of the district is generally thought of as part of suburban Jacksonville, while St. Augustine, though certainly within commuting distance of Jacksonville, has its own separate identity, rooted partly in its distinction as the birthplace of the European colonization of the state. St. Augustine is home to Flagler College, a liberal arts college right in the historic old party of the city.

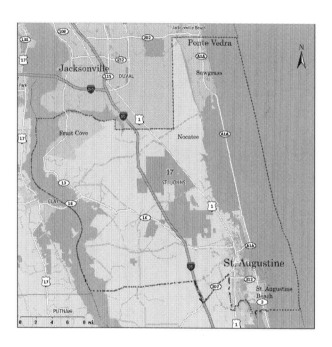

WHO LIVES HERE?

House District 17 is one of the wealthiest districts in Florida, and the term "country club Republican" would be a good one if you had to come up with an archetype for the area's residents. In the 2000 Almanac of Florida Politics, Tom Fiedler called Ponte Vedra "a magnet for retired and semi-retired corporate tycoons," and it's not just that town that makes this one of the highest income areas in the state. Fruit Cove is wealthy, with a median household income just under $100,000, and a large number of people in the town's workforce are in finance, insurance and real estate. Even in St. Augustine, the "poor" part of the district, the median family income is about $55,000, just below the state median family income of about $57,000, but hardly among the poorest. St. Johns County overall is the wealthiest county in the state, according to the University of Florida Bureau of Economic and Business Research. It has a median household income over $60,000, well above the state median of about $48,000, and almost $10,000 a year higher than the next wealthiest, Nassau. The voting age population of the district is 87 percent white, 5 percent black, and 5 percent Hispanic.

POLITICAL ISSUES AND TRENDS

St. Johns County is one of the reddest counties in the state in terms of performance, even though just a little over half of voters are registered Republicans. In 2010, when the Daily Caller ranked America's "most conservative friendly counties" in the whole country, St. John's was No. 38 on the list, behind only Nassau (No. 21) and Clay (No.14) among Florida counties. [1] John McCain nearly doubled Barack Obama's vote total in House District 17. Mitt Romney, did even better, crushing Obama as he did in other very wealthy

---

[1] Chris Palko, "America's Top 20 conservative-friendly counties." *The Daily Caller.* 19 March, 2010.

parts of the state, getting about 70 percent of the vote to 30 percent for Obama. Republican Rick Scott won in this district by more than 30 percentage points, and while he faced a no party opponent, Rep. Ron Renuart had no opposition from the Democratic Party in 2012.

Renuart, an osteopathic doctor and military field surgeon in the Florida Army National Guard who served tours in Iraq and Afghanistan, was elected to the House in 2008. As the representative of one of the most Republican performing areas in the state, he has been a solid vote for GOP priorities in the House.

As a physician, Renuart came to the Legislature and immediately began trying to carve out a niche as a healthcare legislator. In his first session all of his substantive bills were health and medicine related: he filed a bill to give sovereign immunity to emergency health care providers, a bill to let some students use a certain pancreatic enzyme supplement in school, a measure seeking state coverage of myotubular myopathy, a bill creating a prescription drug donation program for the prison system, and a bill dealing with where EMS responders take cardiac patients. All of those bills that first session failed to pass. Renuart saw the pancreatic enzyme bill pass in his second session in 2010, and broadened his bill filing to include a measure dealing with annual leave for National Guard personnel, an idea that was part of companion legislation that passed in 2010. Renuart pushed another Guard-friendly bill to passage in 2011, preventing Guard members' activation status or deployment from being used against them to change a child custody or visitation rights agreement. In 2012, Renuart sponsored and passed a bill requiring high school sports authorities to develop rules and policies related to head injuries, probably Renuart's signature legislation of his tenure.

DISTRICT 17 STATS

Registration (Book closing, 2012)
Republicans 54.1 percent
Democrats 24.4 percent
NPA 18.2 percent

Voting Age Population (2010 Census): 120,029
White (Non-Hispanic) 86.9 percent
Black 5.2 percent
Hispanic 4.7 percent

Median Age: 41

Men 48.7 percent
Women 51.3 percent

2012 PRESIDENT
Mitt Romney 69 percent, Barack Obama 30.1 percent (Estimated*)

2012 STATE HOUSE
Rep. Ron "Doc" Renuart, R-Ponte Vedra Beach, 72.5 percent, Rebecca "Sue" Sharp, NPA, 27.5 percent

2010 GOVERNOR
Rick Scott 64.2 percent, Alex Sink 32.8 percent

2008 PRESIDENT
John McCain 65.9 percent, Barack Obama 33.1 percent

HOUSE DISTRICT 18
NORTHERN CLAY COUNTY

COUNTIES: Clay
RATING: Solid Republican

REPUBLICAN NAVY FLIER SUBURB

District 18 stretches from the middle class Jacksonville suburb of Orange Park, following Blanding Blvd. and Doctors Lake down through the Lakeside area and around the lake into the affluent suburb of Fleming Island. The district stretches west into the sparsely populated northwest of Clay County - much of which is taken up by Jennings State Forest. In the southern part of the district is Middleburg, a town of suburban/country blend that is one of Jacksonville's farthest out bedroom communities to the south.

WHO LIVES HERE?

When released Vietnam prisoner of war John McCain returned to the United States after more than 5 years in the "Hanoi Hilton," he came back to his home in Orange Park. He and his family had lived there before he went to Vietnam, along with other Navy families stationed, like McCain, at Naval Air Station Cecil Field in southwest Jacksonville.[1]

He would later write of Orange Park as a particularly close-knit community that took care of his family while he was held captive. Orange Park was then, as it is now, a middle class

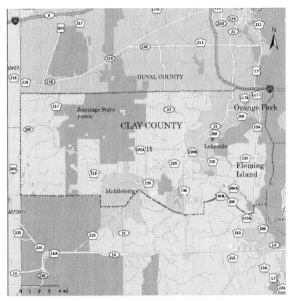

suburb of nice homes, mostly white and like the rest of suburban Jacksonville, relatively conservative in outlook. Cecil Field is closed now, but Naval Air Station Jacksonville is just north of Orange Park, along the river, making this area popular still with Navy families.

---

[1] Robert Timberg, *The Nightingale's Song.* (Simon & Schuster, 1995.) Also, Alex Leary, "John McCain: From Orange Park to White House?" *St. Petersburg Times,* 19 July, 2008.

The median household income in Orange Park is about $47,000 - almost exactly the state median. Incomes go up as you head farther out, getting close to the $70,000s in Lakeside and jumping in Fleming Island to over $100,000. The voting age population is about 78 percent white, 10 percent black and 7 percent Hispanic.

POLITICAL ISSUES AND TRENDS

The heavy military presence is just one thing that keeps this area conservative. Like most of suburban Jacksonville, Orange Park and Fleming Island were sleepy, small, Southern towns a generation ago. Like most of the South, this area has, generally within that generation, shifted from a general affiliation with the Dixiecrat wing of the Democratic Party to a solid Republican stronghold. The district's registered voters are now 55 percent Republicans, and just 24 percent Democrats, with 18 percent in neither major party. There's nothing demographically that would suggest that will change anytime soon. Former Orange Park resident McCain won the district's precincts in the 2008 presidential race by more than 40 percentage points, and Mitt Romney in 2012 and 2010 Republican gubernatorial candidate Rick Scott did about the same.

Former Clay County commissioner and Orange Park mayor Travis Cummings was elected to the House in 2012, after being the only one to qualify. In his first session, Cummings sponsored a proposed sales tax rebate for improvements at the Jacksonville Jaguars' Everbank Field, but the bill died without a final vote. Cummings did manage as a freshman to pass a bill tightening record-keeping rules for check-cashing businesses. Cummings also sponsored successful legislation to boost record keeping on animal shelter euthanasia. He got a bill through the House offering health insurance subsidies to low income residents as an alternative to expanding Medicaid, but couldn't get House and Senate versions lined up.

DISTRICT 18 STATS

Registration (Book closing, 2012)
Republicans 55.1 percent
Democrats 23.9 percent
NPA 18.1 percent

Voting Age Population (2010 Census): 112,715
White 77.5 percent
Black 10 percent
Hispanic 7.3 percent

Median Age: 36.9
Men: 48.8 percent
Women 51.2 percent

2012 PRESIDENT
Mitt Romney 71.5 percent, Barack Obama 27.2 percent (Estimated*)

2012 STATE HOUSE
No race. Travis Cummings, R-Orange Park, faced no primary or general election opposition

2010 GOVERNOR
Rick Scott 69.5 percent, Alex Sink 27.4 percent

2008 PRESIDENT
John McCain 70.5 percent, Barack Obama 28.6 percent

HOUSE DISTRICT 19
INLAND NORTHEAST AND THE
IRON TRIANGLE

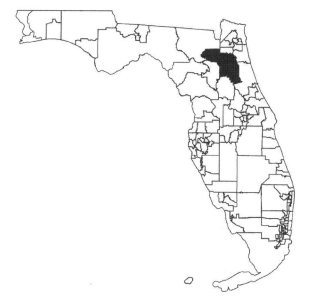

COUNTIES: Union, Bradford, Putnam, Clay
RATING: Solid Republican

METAL PRISON BARS AND METAL
WORKERS

House District 19 sprawls across three
northeast Florida counties and half of a fourth,
running nearly 100 miles along Highway 100
and U.S. 17 from near Lake Butler in Union
County, not too far from the Georgia border,
to Crescent City, not far from Daytona Beach.
It's an enormous district geographically, but
fairly similar demographically, full of mostly
white, working class people living in small
towns and along rural back roads, far from the
glitz and beaches of the Florida travel
brochures. In between Lake Butler and

Crescent City are Starke, in Bradford County; Green Cove Springs, the county seat of Clay County, and Keystone Heights in southern Clay County; and Interlachen and Palatka in Putnam County. Also in the southern part of House District 19 is the upper part of Lake Ocklawaha, also known as the Rodman Reservoir, one of the state's most controversial water bodies in recent years. The Ocklawaha River was dammed in 1968 to create the lake as part of an effort to create the Cross-Florida Barge Canal, linking the Gulf to the Atlantic. The canal project was canceled officially in 1990, though work had stopped in the early 1970s mainly because of environmental concerns. The Rodman Reservoir has become a hugely popular fishing spot in inland northeast Florida, and an economic driver in Putnam County. Environmentalists, though, have continued to push to "free the Ocklawaha" by removing the dam and restoring the river's natural flow, but have faced opposition from advocates for the lake as a fishing spot.

THE IRON TRIANGLE

If you put the entire population of Union County inside Ben Hill Griffin Stadium down the road at the University of Florida, you'd still have 73,064 empty seats. And not everyone of the roughly 15,000 people in Union County would likely be allowed to attend a football game, anyway. More than 4,000 of that number are behind bars at Union Correctional Institution near Raiford, formerly known as "The Rock," or at the Prison Reception and Medical Center in Lake Butler. While Union County isn't Florida's smallest county, if you take away the prisoners, it becomes one of the most sparsely populated.

Leave Raiford by State Road 16 and in a few minutes you'll drive across the line into Bradford County and pass Florida State Prison. This area is known as the "Iron Triangle" and it houses most of the state's most dangerous prisoners. The prisons, taken together, are among the largest employers in the area- Union C.I. has nearly 800 staff, and two nearby prison medical center and reception complexes even more. Together, the Union County Department of Corrections facilities employ more than 15 percent of the county's non-incarcerated population. Florida State Prison and Florida State Prison West in Bradford County employ more than 700 people in Bradford County, which has a workforce of about 12,000, making the prison system the largest employer there, as well.

SOUTHERN CLAY, PUTNAM COUNTIES

The rest of the district is also mostly rural, except for the manufacturing center of Palatka. In the northern tip of the district, Middleburg, which most would consider Jacksonville's farthest-out southern suburb, does reach down across the border from HD 18 into this district, and Green Cove Springs, which also serves as a far-out Jacksonville bedroom community for some, is also in this district. But both are more small-town/rural in character than big city suburban, and Green Cove Springs may be best known as home to an agricultural operation, Gustafson's Farm. It's one of the largest privately-owned dairy farms in the southeast and a familiar brand throughout the state, with its picture of the elderly couple that started the farm (Mama and Papa Gus) on all its milk cartons.

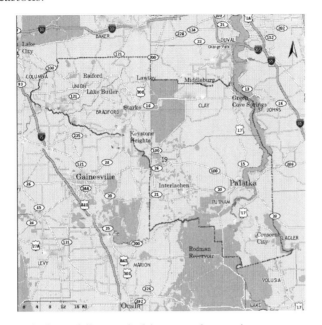

Palatka, while nestled in a rural area, is a rare thing in Florida, a small industrial city. A large Georgia-Pacific paper mill in the city makes paper for the Quilted Northern and Brawny brands, among others, and typically employs 1,000 to 1,500. Veritas Steel (formerly PDM Bridge) has a fabrication plant in Palatka where huge sections of steel bridge are fabricated, assembled and painted. There are also two power plants in the area, a large plant that makes gypsum wallboard for the construction industry, and a shipbuilder, St. Johns Shipbuilding, which builds steel tugboats, barges, ferries, cargo ships and other steel ocean going ships in Palatka. Nearly 1 in 5 workers in Palatka is employed in the manufacturing sector - more than three times the average percentage in Florida - and Putnam County may be the most industrialized rural county in the state. There's also a prison in Putnam County, and Palatka has a hospital that employs more than 500.

WHO LIVES HERE?

For years, prison work was economic salvation in this rural area without many other jobs - though the timber industry has survived and still is another large employer. While corrections officers don't make much, it was long thought of as a secure job with decent benefits, and a good retirement plan that you could get without going to college. Recently, that notion has been cracked, if not shattered, as lawmakers facing budget deficits have sought to close prisons, and make changes to state pension plans.

Except for the fact that so many people are prison guards, the area is otherwise typical of most other rural, counties in the American South: deeply conservative, while coming in below average in income and many typical measurements of socio-economic status. Per capita income in Union county is below $15,000 a year, less than half the 2011 state per capita income of $39,636. In Bradford County, despite having a few more private employers in mining and retail, as well as a local branch of the Shands Hospital system, the per capita income is just $17,000. Median family incomes in this area are below $50,000 a year. More than 18 percent of the population in both Bradford and Union counties is below the poverty line. In addition to being poor, educational attainment here is fairly low - fewer than 10 percent have a Bachelor's degree and about 25 percent don't have a high school diploma.

At the other end of the district, around Palatka, the workforce is similarly blue collar, but many here wear hardhats instead of prison guard browns. People here are welders working on bridges and ships, paper millworkers, truckers and machinists. Timber and agriculture also provide some jobs in Putnam County, which is part of a large fern growing region, and also has some potato and cabbage farms. While the area has decent paying jobs, they're subject to the whims of the economy. And overall, incomes here are below the state average, with the median family income in Putnam County just over $42,000 a year.

The total population of House District 19 is 76 percent non-Hispanic white, about 16 percent black, and just 5 percent Hispanic. Much of the district's African-American population is concentrated in Palatka, where in the city itself, black residents make up half the population, outnumbering whites. Across the river, East Palatka, also in HD 19, is about 62 percent white and 33 percent black.

POLITICAL ISSUES AND TRENDS

This remains one of those Old South anomaly districts - where Democratic registration continues to be strong but everybody votes for Republicans, at least in legislative, statewide and national races. Democrats outnumber Republicans 43 percent to 41 percent and another 14 percent aren't in either party. But all four counties are solidly Republican at the top of the ticket. In 2012,

Mitt Romney got 73.8 percent of the vote in Union County, about 71 percent in Bradford, 73 percent in Clay County and 62 percent of the vote in Putnam County. Other recent presidential elections had similar results.

The 2010 governor's race was a bit of an outlier, though, because of the huge number of prison guards here. The Police Benevolent Association, which at the time represented corrections officers, backed Democrat Alex Sink and ran ads claiming Rick Scott's state government budget cutting plans included closing prisons. The ad said Scott's plan would "cut Florida's prison budget in half, close prisons, and release tens of thousands of prisoners early..." Scott never actually proposed closing prisons, specifically, though he did propose cutting the Corrections budget by $1 billion and alluded to possible pay cuts for guards. That was probably enough to cost him lots of votes in places like Union and Bradford counties, and other places with lots of prison workers. Scott barely won Union County, with 1,781 votes to 1,667 for Sink, and while he got 60 percent of the vote in Bradford County that's a big drop off from the county's support of Republicans in presidential races. Overall, Scott won this district with about 62 percent of the vote, which while low compared to other races, is still an easy win.

There hasn't even been a Democrat on the ballot for a House seat in Union County since 2000. That year, however, the Democratic candidate for then-House District 12, Bobby Hart, won Union County, though he lost the overall race to Republican Aaron Bean in the district, which included four other more northeastern counties. Clay and Putnam counties are also staunchly conservative, and Democrats don't stand much chance there either. Rick Scott got 70 percent of the vote in the 2010 governor's race in Clay County, and 60 percent in Putnam.

Architect Charles Van Zant of Keystone Heights in Clay County was elected to the House in 2008 and after re-election in 2010 was re-elected again in 2012 to represent the current House District 19. Van Zant's son, Charles Jr., is superintendent of schools in Clay County.

In the House, Van Zant may be best known for being one of the House's most stridently religious conservatives. He has a master's in divinity, and also received a doctorate in theology from Western Baptist Seminary in Havana, Cuba, while on a Baptist preaching and humanitarian aid mission to the country. As an architect, he donates much of his time to designing churches, seminaries, homeless shelters and orphanages. And in the House and in campaigns, he often cites religion as his motivator. He is among the most strident abortion opponents in the House, and in 2013 sponsored a bill prohibiting sex-selective or race-selective abortions. The measure passed the House, but the Senate and House never agreed on a final version. Van Zant, who is white, accused Planned Parenthood and other abortion providers of a willful genocide on the African-American population, alleging that abortion providers put clinics intentionally in black neighborhoods. "Without the Nazi holocaust, without the Ku Klux Klan, Planned

Parenthood and other abortionists have reduced our black population by 25 percent since 1973," Van Zant said on the floor, angering some black members.

Van Zant also filed legislation in 2013 that essentially sought to outlaw abortion, which would have served as a challenge to Roe v. Wade had it passed in its original form. In 2012, Van Zant was the sponsor of a bill that became law that allowed local school boards to adopt policies that would allow students to deliver "inspirational messages," including prayers, at school events at which attendance was required. Van Zant has been staunchly opposed to any expansion of gambling, and ardently pro-gun. Van Zant was also the House sponsor of a controversial 2009 bill to allow near-shore oil drilling, saying it would help reduce dependence on foreign oil. That effort lost traction after the 2010 Deepwater Horizon oil spill. Van Zant also is a supporter of keeping the Rodman Dam and reservoir in place.

DISTRICT 19 STATS

Registration (Book closing, 2012)
Democrats 43.3 percent
Republicans 40.7 percent
NPA 13.7 percent

Voting Age Population (2010 Census): 120,969
White (Non-Hispanic) 78.3 percent
Black 14.5 percent
Hispanic 5.4 percent

Median Age: 41.8

Men 52.3 percent

Women 47.7 percent

2012 PRESIDENT
Mitt Romney 68.1 percent, Barack Obama 31.1
percent (Estimated*)

2012 STATE HOUSE
No race. Rep. Charles Van Zant, R-Keystone
Heights, faced no primary or general election
opposition

2010 GOVERNOR
Rick Scott 61.5 percent, Alex Sink 34.7 percent

2008 PRESIDENT
John McCain 65.9 percent, Barack Obama 33
percent

HOUSE DISTRICT 20
GAINESVILLE-OCALA

COUNTIES: Alachua, Marion
RATING: Solid Democrat

YOUTH, ETHNICITY MAKE DISTRICT A DEMOCRATIC LOCK

The sorority and fraternity houses in the shadow of UF's Swamp are a couple minutes by car, but a world away from the eastside of Gainesville, majority black and mostly low-income. And the eastside's urban landscape is a century away from the rural paradise evoked in Marjorie Kinnan Rawlings' The Yearling, and has little in common with the post card fences lining the horse farms in the rolling hills of northwest Marion County. Yet they're all lumped together in the diverse House District 20 running from the edge of the UF campus and its futuristic high tech spinoffs to the farm country near Ocala, much more evocative of the past.

The district includes the eastern part of Gainesville, east of NW 13th St., and east of the University of Florida campus, but very close to it. It includes downtown Gainesville, and all of eastern Alachua County out to the Putnam County line, including the town of Hawthorne. The district also wraps around the south of Gainesville, including the Alachua County towns of Archer and Micanopy, and into Marion County. There it dips down into Ocala, taking in roughly the northwestern quadrant of the city. The area northwest of Ocala includes part of Marion County's horse country, with thoroughbred farms like Bridlewood and others making parts of this area look more like Kentucky than Florida.

In between Gainesville and Ocala are miles of rolling farmland and the area known as Paynes Prairie, a state preserve, and the Cross Creek area, which was home to Rawlings and

the setting for *The Yearling*. To the southwest of Gainesville, the district includes the small town of Archer, for many years home to Blues-Rock legend Bo Diddley.

WHO LIVES HERE?

The eastside of Gainesville is where most of the city's African-American population lives, though District 20's voting age population is majority white, at about 56 percent, with 31 percent of the voting age population African-American. Another 8 percent is Hispanic. There's also a heavy concentration of black residents around Reddick in Marion County. The district also includes the part of Ocala west of 441 and south of Silver Springs Blvd. that is home to a large African-American community. That area is also very poor, with a median household income just over $15,000.

While UF is mostly in neighboring District 21, thousands of students live in House District 20, which runs right up against the campus. The school's sororities and fraternities are in an area just east of SW 13th St., putting them in this district. That large number of students is a major factor in making District 20 the fifth youngest House district in the state, with a median age just under 31. That also makes this a district with a relatively high educational attainment level, though it's offset by a relatively low education level in some of the poorer neighborhoods of the city's eastside. Gainesville as a whole is a very educated city - Forbes put it on a list of the "smartest cities" in America.

But African-American leaders have often

wondered whether the growth that has come from the city's reputation as an intellectual incubator filters to the eastside. That part of Gainesville has continued to have struggling schools, and dealt with higher crime and drug problems, while the city as a whole is often cited as being among the favorites of the "creative class." While unemployment in Gainesville never got as high as many other places during the recession, it was worse in the poorer eastside than the city as a whole. The area just east of the university has an extremely low median household income of just $15,000 - one of the lowest in the state - though that's in part because of the students.

POLTICAL ISSUES AND TRENDS

While not a majority-minority district, HD 20 is drawn in a way - with a large contingent of young students combined with a high number of African-Americans - that make it a near lock for Democrats. The district's precincts are 55 percent Democrat and just 23.5 percent Republican, with nearly another 20 percent having no party affiliation. Barack Obama won here by about 30 percentage points in both 2008 and 2012, and Alex Sink did the same in the 2010 governor's race.

Rep. Clovis Watson, elected in 2012 with only write-in opposition in the general election, was the Gainesville city manager from 2002 to 2009 and a former police officer in Alachua. In 2006, Watson switched to the Republican Party, but then in 2008 he switched back - saying he'd made a mistake. Watson only filed two bills in his freshman term, but managed to pass one, a bill increasing penalties for making false police reports. The other said that legislators' district aides should have preference in hiring for state jobs when the lawmaker leaves office. For the 2014 session, Watson is sponsoring a proposed constitutional amendment on restoration of civil rights for ex-felons, and a bill requiring a unanimous jury recommendation for a death sentence, rather than a majority vote.

DISTRICT 20 STATS

Registration (Book closing, 2012)
Democrats 55 percent
Republicans 23.5 percent
NPA 18.9 percent

Voting Age Population (2010 Census): 115,237
White (Non-Hispanic) 56.2 percent
Black 30.7 percent
Hispanic 7.7 percent

Median Age: 30.9

Men: 48.6 percent
Women 51.4 percent

2012 PRESIDENT
Barack Obama 64.7 percent, Mitt Romney, 33.5 percent (Estimated)*

2012 STATE HOUSE
Clovis Watson, Democrat, faced only write-in opposition

2010 GOVERNOR
Alex Sink 62.8 percent, Rick Scott 29.1 percent

2008 PRESIDENT
Barack Obama 65.8 percent, John McCain 32.7 percent

HOUSE DISTRICT 21
UF TO NATURE COAST

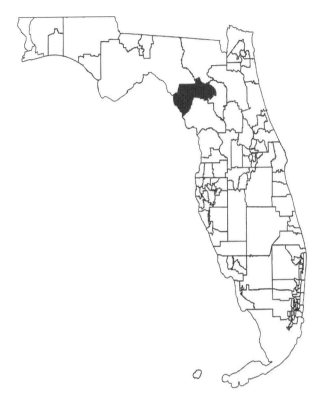

COUNTIES: Alachua, Gilchrist, Dixie

RATING: Swing District

TINY TOWNS, GRADUATION GOWNS

Of all of Florida's House districts, HD 21 is among the most up-in-the-air. The Political Hurricane Blog called this mix of college-urban and rural worlds "the purest of toss-up seats in the state."[1] The district includes the western half of Gainesville, including the University of

---

[1] The Political Hurricane. *State House Capsules*. (Online, 12 October, 2012) http://thepoliticalhurricane.com/2012/10/30/state-house-capsules-rest-of-state/

Florida, western parts of the city of Alachua, a small part of High Springs, and most of western Alachua County. That's where most of the district's population lives. Then, it goes west through one of the few areas in Florida largely untouched by the last half century's unbelievable growth.

From Gainesville the district runs west to the Gulf, in an area usually

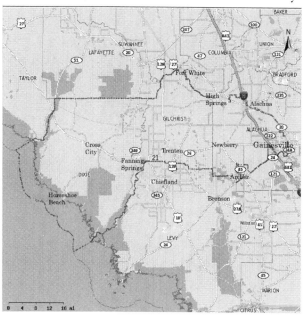

thought of as the northern part of the "Nature Coast." This is about as rural and off the beaten path as one can get - and locals generally like it that way. In addition to western Alachua County, it includes all of rural Gilchrist and Dixie counties. Newberry, Trenton, Bell and Cross City, all small crossroads towns, are in the district, and the district line runs right through another small town, Fanning Springs. The Gulf coast in this area is not the Gulf coast of Sarasota or Destin. No beachfront resorts, no fancy marinas. It includes the town of

Suwannee, and the tiny hamlet of Horseshoe Beach, but otherwise is nearly uninhabited.

WHO LIVES HERE?

Near the university, this district includes students. Most of the campus is in this district, and Alachua County Census Tract 10, the area including the University Park and College Park neighborhoods adjacent to campus, is decidedly young - with about half of the area's residents between the ages of 20 and 24. An incredible 70 percent of the population of that area is under 40. The median age in the district as a whole is 34.2. The student-heavy area around the university gives way going north and northwest to the Brywood, Fox Grove and the Meadows area, and neighborhoods where median household incomes shoot up into the $80,000 range. The suburban area to the west is similarly affluent. Naturally, the farther away from the university you get, the less tied to it the people are, and the less likely they are to be progressive transplants from somewhere else, and the more likely they are to be traditional Southern conservatives.

The change is pretty dramatic across the county line. In the 2000 Almanac of Florida Politics, Tom Fiedler called Gilchrist County "deliberately agrarian, a place of farms, mobile homes on dirt roads, horse and cattle ranches...." and it remains that today. [2] The median family income in Gilchrist County is $42,617, well below the state median and one in five families lives below the poverty line. There

---

[2] Fiedler and deHaven Smith, Pg. 375.

aren't any large private employers here and many people commute to Gainesville to work.

Hardly anyone lives in Dixie County, more than half of which is covered by timberland. While Florida as a whole has a population density of 350 people per square mile, in Dixie County there are 23 people per square mile. The economy in Dixie County is reliant on just a few employers as well - and the Georgia Pacific sawmill in Cross City has been idle since 2007.

The district is mostly white, about 76 percent, just under 10 percent black and a little over 8 percent Hispanic.

POLITICAL ISSUES AND TRENDS

While it is the District 20 in the eastern part of Alachua County, including the heavily black east side of Gainesville, and a large student and faculty population that solidify Gainesville as an island of blue in a sea of Republican red in north Florida, this district also has plenty of Democratic voters, particularly in Gainesville. But unlike eastern Alachua, this area also has swaths of conservative Republican voters to balance out the liberals, making this the interesting swing district it is. Democrat Alex Sink won here in the 2010 governor's race, by about eight percentage points. But Mitt Romney won here in 2012, barely, with about 51 percent of the vote. Barack Obama had won the district in 2008 - though again, just barely, with 50.1 percent of the vote. And voters in House District 21 sent Rep. Keith Perry, a Republican, to Tallahassee.

Many of the Democratic votes in this district

come from Gainesville, and particularly the student-heavy areas around the University of Florida campus. The younger voters were a big anchor of the Obama coalition, and in this area, places like Alachua County Precincts 5 and 26 just north of the university, Obama got more than 60 percent of the vote to about 30 percent for Romney. Obama won in the affluent suburbs to the west of the university too, getting more than 60 percent in some precincts, but with closer margins in others, such as Precinct 40, where Obama beat Romney just 53 percent to 45 percent. Generally, as you get farther away from Gainesville, with its more progressive, university-influenced culture, Republican identification increases. By the time you get to the quasi-rural suburban town of Newberry, west of Gainesville, Republican voting is the norm. Romney won the two Newberry precincts, getting more than double Obama's vote total in one, and winning the other 57 percent to 40 percent. Gilchrist and Dixie counties aren't even a contest - Romney got 75 percent of the vote in Gilchrist County and just under that in Dixie County.

For Perry, winning here was impressive. Although he was an incumbent, the new district's reach into Gilchrist and Dixie counties put Perry on the ballots of voters who didn't know him, with his previous district stretching instead from Alachua into Levy and Marion counties. And the district was 44.5 percent Democrats by voter registration and 34.2 percent Republican in 2012. But Perry defeated Democrat Andrew Morey of Gainesville, getting 57 percent of the vote in 2012, despite the district voting for Barack Obama over Mitt Romney by about 4 percentage points.

Perry, a contractor and Gainesville native, was first elected to the House in 2010. Perry tried for three years to get legislators pass a bill to create background screening requirements for non-teachers who work on school grounds, such as construction workers, finally getting the measure passed in 2013. Also in 2013 Perry was a co-sponsor of a bill repealing the Florida Renewable Fuel Standard Act, which had required blended gasoline containing 10 percent ethanol. He also successfully pushed legislation increasing the licensing requirements for boarding schools.

DISTRICT 21 STATS

Registration (Book closing, 2012)
Democrats 44.5 percent
Republicans 34.2 percent
NPA 18.8 percent

Voting Age Population (2010 Census):
128,894
White (Non-Hispanic) 77.6 percent
Black 8.4 percent
Hispanic 7.8 percent

Median Age: 41.8

Men 49.2 percent
Women 50.8 percent

2012 PRESIDENT
Mitt Romney 51.1 percent, Barack Obama 47.1 percent (Estimated*)

2012 STATE HOUSE

Rep. Keith Perry, R-Gainesville, 56.7 percent,
Andrew Morey, Democrat, 43.3 percent

2010 GOVERNOR
Alex Sink 52.1 percent, Rick Scott 44.3 percent

2008 PRESIDENT
Barack Obama 50.1 percent, John McCain 48.2
percent

HOUSE DISTRICT 22
NATURE COAST, SOUTHWEST
OCALA

COUNTIES: Levy, Marion
RATING: Solid Republican

OLD FOLKS AT HOME (WAY DOWN UPON THE SUWANNEE RIVER)

House District 22 includes all of Levy County, along what is known as the "Nature Coast" between the historic Suwannee River and Withlacoochee Bay, and runs inland into Marion County, including roughly the southwest quadrant of the city of Ocala. The district includes the heavily developed area south and southwest of Ocala, including Marion Oaks and the On Top of the World retirement area before heading into Dunellon. The Levy County part of the district includes the city of Chiefland and the towns of Bronson and Williston, the island town of Cedar Key, and at the southern edge of the district along the Withlacoochee River, the adjoining towns of Inglis and Yankeetown.

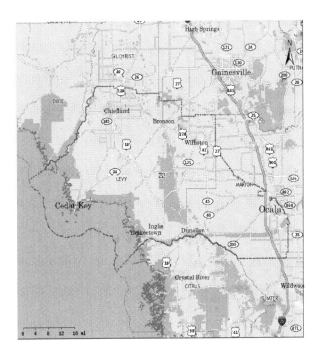

WHO LIVES HERE?

There is a sizable population of people who live in Levy County and southwest Marion who are refugees from the urban landscape of the rest of Florida. They've moved here to escape the perceived rising crime, hectic pace and demographic change in the places they've come from - Gainesville, Tampa, Orlando, even Fort Lauderdale and Miami. They're looking for a quieter, country life, moving to a mobile home near Williston, or oceanfront shack on Cedar Key, or a horse farm or golf course community south of Ocala. The district is older, with a median age just under 50 - skewed by large numbers of retirees. Many of Levy County's kids go off to college, and don't return to raise their families because of a lack of jobs. A chance at getting a few more high wage jobs was lost recently when Duke Energy scrapped plans to build a nuclear power plant in Levy County.

While it's bigger, Ocala is also kind of sleepy - a haven for retirees where voters have been ambivalent about new ideas and growth, a place with a much more laid back pace than other Florida cities, leading some locals to call it "Slowcala." As you head southwest out of Ocala on State Road 200, you pass On Top of the World, a 55-and-up only "active-adult" community that has been on lots of "best places to retire" lists and other developments that are mostly home to the older set. Because of the lower cost of living than in retirement communities near the coasts, many middle class retirees come here, and some come here to get more space, buying houses instead of condos or mobile homes.

The district is about 75 percent white, just under 10 percent black and about 13 percent Hispanic. People here have modest incomes generally, but there are pockets of affluence, particularly in some of the Marion County retirement communities. But for the most part, the people who move here to live out their days slowly are more of the camper set, rather than the pampered set.

POLITICAL ISSUES AND TRENDS

Republicans Mitt Romney and Rick Scott won in 2012 and 2010 here by more than 15 percentage points, and Democrats didn't put up a candidate for state House in 2012, allowing Marion County Commissioner Charlie Stone to walk into the seat. Registration is 42 percent Republican, 38 percent Democrat and 15 percent no party.

Stone served eight years on the Marion County Commission before running unopposed for the newly drawn District 22 seat when the area's previous representative, Keith Perry, lost the Marion and Levy parts of his old district and ran in District 21. Stone said he wanted to concentrate on job creation, keeping the budget from growing too much and protecting central Florida's water supply. During his first session, Stone, president of a petroleum product company, successfully sponsored legislation to create a new specialty license plate to help Masonic homes but was unsuccessful with a proposal to limit the ability of state and local governments to buy land for conservation purposes. He also sponsored a bill that would have given the governor more say over the list of candidates from which he chooses new judges, an effort that was criticized by Democrats as a court-stacking move, and which failed to become law.

DISTRICT 22 STATS

Registration (Book closing, 2012)
Republicans 41.8 percent

Democrats 37.7 percent
NPA 14.8 percent

Voting Age Population (2010 Census):
125,768
White (Non-Hispanic) 78 percent
Hispanic 11.2 percent
Black 8.2 percent

Median Age: 49.1

Men 48 percent
Women 52 percent

2012 PRESIDENT
Mitt Romney 58.7 percent, Barack Obama 40.2
percent (Estimated*)

2012 STATE HOUSE
No Race. Charlie Stone, R-Ocala, faced no
primary or general election opposition

2010 GOVERNOR
Rick Scott 54.1 percent, Alex Sink 40.3 percent

2008 PRESIDENT
John McCain 56.1 percent, Barack Obama 42.4
percent

HOUSE DISTRICT 23
EASTERN MARION COUNTY

COUNTIES: Marion

RATING: Solid Republican

CULTURALLY CONSERVATIVE, OLD FLORIDA

House District 23 includes eastern Ocala and eastern and northeastern Marion County, out to the Putnam, Volusia and Lake County lines. More than half of the geographic area of the district is in the Ocala National Forest and sparsely populated. To the southeast of Ocala, the district includes the quasi-rural suburbs of Silver Springs Shores and Belleview.

WHO LIVES HERE?

This is conservative, small-town America, with one illustration of the political sentiment here being choices made at the ballot box. Eastern Ocala and Marion County have for the last several years strongly backed social conservatives like the district's current House member, Dennis Baxley, former head of the state Christian Coalition and one of the most prominent conservatives in the House. Baxley is a prominent Southern Baptist, and while Marion County isn't as religious as the state or nation as a whole in terms of regular religious adherents, it is strongly Baptist. There are 70 Southern Baptist congregations, by far the most of all denominations, in Marion County, accounting for about 20,000 church goers. The broader category of "evangelical protestant," which includes Southern Baptists, is the largest self-identified group of all those who say they are religious in Marion County, accounting for about 60,000 people. [1] Voters here have elected Baxley going back more than a decade. He served in the House from 2000 to 2007, left, and then was elected again in 2010. In the intervening period, voters here elected another staunch social conservative, Kurt Kelly.

District 23 is about 80 percent white, about 8 percent black and 8 percent Hispanic. While not very diverse compared to a lot of other areas of the state, it's less homogenous than it was a decade ago, when non-Hispanic whites made up 86 percent of the population. Most of the non-white growth in the district over the decade has been in the Hispanic community,

---

[1] Association of Religion Data Archives, Marion County, Florida Religious Traditions 2010 (Online, 2010.)
http://www.thearda.com/rcms2010/r/c/12/rcms2010_12083_county_name_2010.asp

which has obvious political implications, though growth in Democratic-leaning voters wouldn't appear to be fast enough to threaten the district's strong Republican lean anytime soon.

The median family income in Marion County as a whole is just under $40,000, well below the state median. In HD 23, income levels get a bit higher going south and east of downtown Ocala, with median family incomes getting into the low $50,000s and farther east into the $60,000s. But to the north and northeast, north of East Silver Springs Blvd., median incomes plummet into the very poor low to mid-$20,000s. Overall, yearly median family incomes throughout most of the district are modest - in the $30,000 to $45,000 range.

The area does have a fair number of retirees, though southwest Ocala, in neighboring District 22, is home to the majority of the area's retirement communities. The area along U.S. 27 heading south toward The Villages, does have a number of retirement areas. About 28 percent of the district's population is aged 60 and over, and the district's median age is 44.

POLITICAL ISSUES AND TRENDS

The area shows no signs of being anything but solidly Republican for the near-term future, with growth in Hispanic population the long-term wildcard. The GOP has a comfortable voter registration advantage of 10,000 voters over the Democratic Party, and the recent trend is going the right way for Republicans, with Mitt Romney winning by a bit more than 20 percentage points in the 2012 presidential election, bettering the victory margins of around 17 points enjoyed by gubernatorial candidate Rick Scott in 2010 and presidential candidate John McCain in 2008. Baxley didn't face any opposition in 2012, and both senators whose districts overlap this House district, Sen. Dorothy Hukill in Senate District 8 and Sen. Alan Hays in District 11, are Republicans who were easily elected.

Baxley, a funeral director by profession, is one of the most prominent Republicans in the House, and a respected voice on the conservative side of a number of issues. But he is probably best known as the sponsor of the original Stand Your Ground self defense law during his first run in the House, and its most vocal defender amid recent scrutiny over its application. Baxley carried - and argued vehemently for - the 2005 bill that extended the state's "castle doctrine." That doctrine says a person's home is their castle, and they have no duty to retreat in the face of a threat when they're in their own home. The 2005 law extended that idea out into public spaces, saying that when threatened, someone has no duty to retreat, and may "stand their ground," and fight force with force. Baxley was successful, and Florida was the first state to pass such a law.

Baxley left the Legislature in 2007 to run for the Senate, but lost in a Republican primary to Charlie Dean of Inverness, who went on to win the seat. Baxley then took a job as the director of the Christian Coalition of Florida, and later left that job to help Marco Rubio in his U.S. Senate campaign.

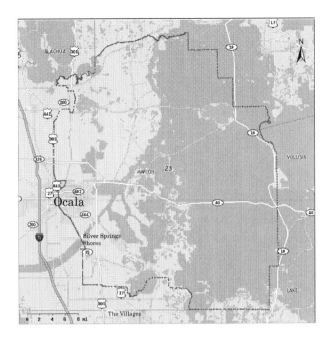

In 2010, when Kelly, Baxley's successor in then-House District 24, left the House to make an unsuccessful bid for Congress, Baxley decided to make a run to return to his old seat in the House. Baxley was elected in District 24 in 2010, and faced no opposition for another term, this time in the redrawn District 23, in 2012.

During his second tenure in the Legislature, the stand your ground law came into sharp focus again, after the shooting of an unarmed teen by a neighborhood watch volunteer, George Zimmerman, in Sanford. While the stand your ground law wasn't the reason Zimmerman was acquitted, it was invoked in a new debate over who may shoot whom that arose out of the teen's death. Baxley stood by the law, but sat on a panel that looked at whether changes were needed. Ultimately, no major changes were suggested or made.

Baxley came in for criticism from the left when Barack Obama was running for election the first time, in 2008. Baxley, who was out of the Legislature at the time, said Obama's childhood in the Muslim country of Indonesia was "pretty scary," because there was, Baxley said, an "active movement by radical Muslims to occupy us." [2]

When he ran to return to the House, however, Baxley said the economy was his main focus, not the socially conservative issues that he was known for championing during his first tenure in the House. The reason, Baxley said, was that the Ocala area happened to have one of the highest unemployment rates. But he also said he had hoped to be involved in measures aimed at reducing abortions, as well. In his time in the House, Baxley has backed measures aimed at preventing doctors from asking patients whether they have guns in their homes, requiring drug tests for welfare recipients and is always an ardent supporter of anti-abortion measures. Baxley also was the sponsor in 2011 of House Bill 1355, a broad elections bill that critics said ultimately made it harder for some people to vote. The measure required provisional ballots for people who had to change their address at the polls, and put new restrictions on groups that register voters, among other things. It also created the panel that set Florida's 2012 presidential primary date.

---

[2] Beth Reinhard. "Christian Leader Calls Obama 'Scary' ..." The Miami Herald Naked Politics Blog (Online, 10 September 2008
http://miamiherald.typepad.com/nakedpolitics/2008/09/christian-leade.html)

Baxley, who is chairman of the Judiciary Committee, has a self-described "penchant for issues that are colorful" and acknowledges he enjoys pushing political "hot potatoes." Baxley said in September 2013 that he will seek the seat being vacated by Dean, who will face term limits in 2016.

DISTRICT 23 STATS

Registration (Book closing, 2012)
Republicans 45 percent
Democrats 35.2 percent
NPA 15.4 percent

Voting Age Population (2010 Census): 121,630
White (Non-Hispanic) 82.2 percent
Black 7.8 percent
Hispanic 7.6 percent

Median Age: 44.2

Men 48.2 percent
Women 51.8 percent

2012 PRESIDENT
Mitt Romney 60.1 percent, Barack Obama 38.6 percent (Estimated*)

2012 STATE HOUSE
No race. Rep. Dennis Baxley, R-Ocala, faced no primary or general election opposition

2010 GOVERNOR
Rick Scott 55.9 percent, Alex Sink 38.6 percent

2008 PRESIDENT
John McCain 57.9 percent, Barack Obama 40.8 percent

HOUSE DISTRICT 24
MATANZAS TO ORMOND

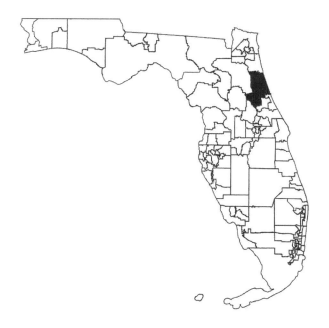

COUNTIES: St. Johns, Flagler, Volusia
RATING: Leans Republican

ONCE FAST-GROWING REGION NOW
JOBLESS CAPITAL (OR BEACHES,
FERNS, POTATOES, AND NUDISTS)

House District 24 runs from just south of
St. Augustine along the St. Johns and Flagler
County coasts to Ormond-by-the-Sea, just over
the line in Volusia County. In the north, the
district runs inland to the Putnam County line
picking up the tiny potato farming town of
Hastings in St. Johns County. Farther south, in
the middle of the district, is the large planned
town of Palm Coast and Flagler Beach, and
going inland, adjacent to Palm Coast, the

Flagler County seat of Bunnell. In the south, the district crosses into Volusia just enough to pick up neighborhoods in Ormond-by-the-Sea, but stops short of Ormond Beach. Inland, the southern part of the district goes west to Lake George and picks up the small town of Pierson, the "Fern Capital of the World," (and the Sunny Sands Nudist Resort), and in the southwest corner of the district, De Leon Springs. The fern industry is a major employer in the southwestern part of the district, with

ferneries lining the sides of U.S.17 in and around Pierson.

Palm Coast was the model town of sorts for Florida's planned communities of the second half of the 20th Century. It was developed by ITT Corp., the parent company of the old Levitt development company that gave America Levittown, N.Y., Levittown, Pa., and Levittown, N.J. Palm Coast was developed in the early 1970s, though it wasn't incorporated until 1999.

For much of the first decade of the 2000s, before the recession, surrounding Flagler County was consistently one of the fastest growing places in Florida. The county's population grew at an astonishing clip in those years, going from just under 50,000 people in 2000 to more than 90,000 by 2008. New businesses and homes seemingly appeared every day.

But when the recession came, the building bubble here popped, and the county became known for skyrocketing unemployment. By 2009, there were foreclosed homes all over the county, and nobody was building new ones. With so many people having moved here to take part in the building boom, the lack of construction was a disaster. Flagler routinely was at the top of the unemployment statistics through the recession, with the jobless rate around 16 percent, well above the statewide rate. [1] New building permits went from more than 4,000 in 2004 to about 300 a year during the recession. Near the end of 2013, the unemployment rate in Flagler County was still over 9 percent, lagging in its recovery far behind the state as a whole, which had a jobless rate just above 6 percent at the time. During the recession, the county's workforce got smaller,

---

[1] Kathleen Haughney, "Economic Snapshot, Flagler County," The News Service of Florida, 19 August 2009. Also, Jim Stratton, "In Flagler, Jobs Crashed with Housing Collapse," *Orlando Sentinel*, 6 February, 2013.

with many of the construction workers who had lived on the boom a half decade earlier leaving for elsewhere. About 20 percent of the homes in House District 24 are vacant. While nearly half of those empty houses are un-rented vacation homes, that's another problem in an already struggling area.

St. Johns County, by contrast, has had a relatively low unemployment rate - and had one of the lowest jobless rates in the state in late 2013. St. Johns hadn't seen the same type of growth as Flagler, and the county wasn't so deeply tied to construction, so the fall wasn't so far.

The stretch of coastline between St. Augustine and Daytona Beach isn't particularly reliant on tourism - most of the coastal communities in this area are small, and heavily residential. There's some tech industry in the Palm Coast area - media services company Palm Coast Data is a large employer in the district. Otherwise, the district's workforce is primarily involved in education, social services, health care, retail, and management. Ten-year-old Florida Hospital Flagler in Palm Coast - necessitated in the early 2000s by the county's heavy growth, employs about 1,000 people. The school system and the city of Palm Coast are among the largest employers in the district. In Flagler Beach, there's a factory that makes Sea Ray boats that employs several hundred, but overall, there's little heavy industry in the area.

Inland, there's a significant agricultural economy - though it accounts for a tiny percentage of the district's workforce. The sign at the edge of the little town of Hastings says it's "Florida's Potato Capital," but in truth, the spud industry here has seen far better days. Hundreds of potato farmers have sold their land or diversified and the packing plants are mostly idled. [2] Pierson is best known as the center of a major fern producing area, and that industry is the main employer in and around the town.

WHO LIVES HERE?

A decade ago Flagler County was full of carpenters, drywall hangers, electricians and other construction industry workers riding the building frenzy. Many have moved. The Census 2012 population estimates reflected an exodus of young families from Flagler County. The migration was enough to increase the county's median age by nearly two years between 2010 and 2012. [3] With the departure from Flagler County of so many construction workers who left looking for new opportunities, one in three Flagler County residents, and one in three residents of District 24, is now over 60. The district's median age of just under 49 years puts it in among the oldest third of districts in the state. About 40 percent of households here include someone over 65.

The inland farming areas, particularly around Pierson, are where much of the district's

[2] Abby Goodnough. "Hastings Journal; Florida's Potato Country Makes a Low-Carb Move," *The New York Times*. 8 August, 2004.

[3] Andrew Gant. "Census: Volusia, Flagler Aging Faster than Florida." *The Daytona Beach News-Journal*. 12 June, 2013.

Hispanic population lives. More than half of Pierson's 2010 population of about 1800 is Hispanic, mostly fern farm workers, and mostly of Mexican origin. The number of immigrants in the country illegally is thought to be high in the area - so the number of uncounted Hispanics may be much higher than the 1,000 or so officially recorded in the community. 4

POLITICAL ISSUES AND TRENDS

Republicans have won the precincts in HD 24 by about 15 percentage points in recent top of the ticket elections, with Mitt Romney winning in 2012, getting about 57 percent of the vote to 42 percent for Barack Obama - and Rick Scott winning the governor's race here by around the same margin in 2010.

But it's clear that the right Democrat could win in this district - and it nearly happened in the 2012 House race. Flagler County Commissioner Milissa Holland lost by about two percentage points, about 1,900 votes out of 63,000, to Republican Travis Hutson. About 60 percent of the district's voters are in Flagler, where Holland was well known from serving several years on the commission, and for being the daughter of James F. Holland, one of the founding fathers of Palm Coast. Holland won the Flagler County precincts by more than 10 percentage points. Hutson is from St. Johns County, and while his name was familiar because of his real estate business, he was not

---

[4] For more on Mexicans in the Pierson area, see: John Pemberton, "Mexican Workers are Making an Impact on Agricultural Towns Such as Fern Growing Pierson," *Florida Times-Union*, 11 March, 2001.

as well known as Holland in the most heavily populated parts of the district. But Hutson outraised Holland by quite a bit, which helped him raise name recognition.

Flagler and Volusia counties also appear to be trending to the GOP. In the two counties as a whole, voters went for Obama in 2008 but Romney in 2012, and Flagler County saw a Democratic voter registration advantage switch to a GOP advantage, with about 25,300 Republicans and 23,700 Democrats at the end of 2013. With both counties getting older, it's no surprise they'd get a bit more Republican. The question remains whether the slight growth in Hispanic population will continue, and if so, if it will create new Democratic voters and offset the aging of the area.

The Republican majority is fairly close in the Volusia County part of the district - about 7,600 Republicans to 5,200 Democrats, with about 3,700 non-party voters. That part of the district is nearly all white and more than a third of the voters in that part of the district are aged 66 and up.

A good part of the district was formerly in House District 20, which was represented for eight years by St. Augustine Republican Bill Proctor. District 24, as newly drawn, is the first district in decades to be centered on Flagler County, which hasn't been home to a House member since William Littledale Wadsworth served in the House in 1966. [5]

---

[5] Florida House of Representatives, "People of Lawmaking in Florida 1822-2008."

Hutson, of Elkton, first drew attention as a candidate, when he was one of the top fundraisers among newcomers. During his first session in the House, in 2013, he carried a bill backed by big retail chains like Walgreens that would allow more pharmacy technicians to work under the supervision of one pharmacist. The bill would have increased the maximum from three to six, but the bill died in committee. Hutson passed one bill, a measure making clarifications to the law about what physical therapists are allowed to do. Hutson was also one of a handful of Republicans who opposed a bill that would have given parents of children at failing schools the ability to call for the school to be taken over by charter school companies. While the measure passed in the House, it died in the Senate.

DISTRICT 24 STATS

Registration (Book closing, 2012)
Republicans 40.2 percent
Democrats 31.9 percent
NPA 23 percent

Voting Age Population (2010 Census): 127,516
White (Non-Hispanic) 81.8 percent
Black 7.8 percent
Hispanic 7.8 percent

Median Age: 48.4

Men: 48.4 percent
Women: 51.6 percent

VOTING PERFORMANCE

2012 PRESIDENT

Mitt Romney 56.9 percent, Barack Obama 42.1 percent (Estimated*)

2012 STATE HOUSE
Travis Hutson, Republican, 49.5 percent, Milissa Holland, Democrat, 47.2 percent, Michael Cornish, NPA, 3.3 percent

2010 GOVERNOR
Rick Scott 55.2 percent, Alex Sink 40.8 percent

2008 PRESIDENT
John McCain 53.2 percent, Barack Obama 45.6 percent

HOUSE DISTRICT 25
DAYTONA AREA BEACHES, PORT ORANGE

COUNTIES: Volusia

RATING: Leans Republican

BREAKERS AND BIKERS

The heart of House District 25 is the famous part of Daytona Beach, the barrier island strip of sand running from the gilded age playground of Ormond Beach in the north, past the famous Daytona Beach boardwalk, through Daytona Beach Shores and down the coast to Ponce Inlet. On the mainland, in the north it includes parts of Ormond Beach, and in the south, Port Orange and New Smyrna Beach.

This is the Daytona Beach of Spring Break, with the hard-packed sand beach covered every March by college kids and events hosted by

MTV. While iconic as a spring break destination, it's not as big as it once was. As the annual bacchanal grew, pumped up by TV programs featuring semi-famous entertainers and scantily clad co-eds, locals got more and more wary of it, and by the 1990s area officials were trying to quiet the party down a bit. That pushed some of the big spring break productions to places like Panama City, though Daytona Beach remains a popular spring break destination.

Other big events still bring massive numbers of tourists here. Local officials and businesses welcome Bike Week, an annual gathering that started in the 1930s when motorcycle racing was held on the beach itself. Motorcycle enthusiasts from around the country now descend on the area for the 10-day festival each year. Racing cars is a big part of what made this community famous - though the races moved off the beach in the 1950s to the speedway, which is inland, in neighboring District 26. Still, when there are big races at the track, the crowd spills out to the beach as well.

Going south, the high rise hotels of Daytona Beach give way to a quieter beach around Ponce Inlet, where there are no big hotels, just condos, rental homes, low-slung mom and pop motels, marinas and Florida's tallest lighthouse. Farther south, the district ends at New Smyrna Beach, a vacation resort town of about 20,000. It's much more low key than neighboring Daytona Beach. On the mainland in the southern part of the district is Port Orange, a haven for retirees where 16 percent of the population is over 70 and more than 30 percent

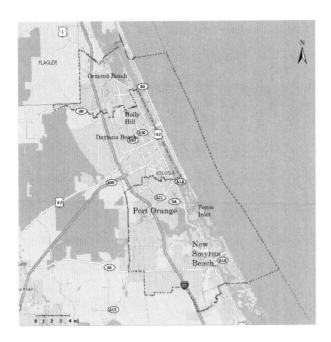

is over 60. Port Orange is also home, however, to a number of suburban families who live in neighborhoods of single family homes.

WHO LIVES HERE?

At about 90 percent, this is one of the whiter districts in the state, with about 4 percent of the total district population Hispanic and just 3.6 percent black. The voting age population is 91 percent white, the third highest of all the districts. It's ironic because Port Orange has an important African-American history, having started as a haven for former slaves after the Civil War. But the agricultural economy that sustained those emancipated slaves didn't last, and neither did the working people who descended from those first families. Today, this area surrounding Daytona Beach is known far more as a place for vacationers and retirees than workers.

And that also makes this one of the older

districts in the state, one of just 10 districts with a median age over 50. Nearly 35 percent of the population in the district is over 60, and another 16 percent are in their 50s.

This is not a playground for the rich. Normally, neighborhoods near the ocean are home to the wealthy, but that's not the case in the Daytona area. Even on the barrier island that includes the world famous beach, median incomes are in the $30,000s and $40,000s, below the state average. Most of the Census tracts in the district have median household incomes slightly below or slightly above the state median, with the exception of the Ponce Inlet area, which is fairly affluent, with a median household income over $70,000.

POLITICAL ISSUES AND TRENDS

Republicans have a slight registration majority in House District 25, about 39 percent to 34 percent at the end of 2012. But the 23 percent of voters with no party affiliation appear to be swinging this district a bit more toward GOP candidates. Mitt Romney beat Barack Obama by more than 10 percentage points here. That's an improvement over 2010 when Republican gubernatorial candidate Rick Scott beat Democrat Alex Sink in the district by 8.5 percentage points - and a considerable improvement for the GOP over 2008 when John McCain beat Obama by less than 3 percentage points. The old north Volusia district before redistricting, HD 26, had been trending Republican slightly for a few years as well.

It's hard to say whether something is

changing demographically in Volusia County that would make it trend more Republican - though the county did get slightly older between 2010 and 2012, which tends to improve Republican performance. It's also possible that support for Obama among no party voters simply dropped off, and enthusiasm for Obama among Democrats may have been lower than in 2008. Local Democrats didn't put the question to the test in the House race in 2012, sitting out the race and leaving Republican Dave Hood to face off against no party candidate Christina Spencer-Kephart.

Hood, a former Ormond Beach mayor and city commissioner, won easily, defeating Spencer-Kephart by more than 20 points, 61 percent to 39 percent. While generally supporting his party, Hood wasn't out-in-front on ideological issues during his first session, and on at least one occasion joined Democrats in backing one of their signature issues. Hood was one of just three Republicans, along with Rep. Holly Raschein, and Rep. Heather Fitzenhagen, who attended a news conference in support of a bill banning workplace discrimination based on sexual orientation.

Hood saw one of his top priorities pass, a measure allowing homeowners to rent out their home for up to 30 days a year without losing their homestead exemption. Hood was also the sponsor of the Department of Law Enforcement's legislative package, which made a number of technical changes dealing with missing persons reports, background checks by local government agencies and registration of sex offenders.

DISTRICT 25 STATS

Registration (Book closing, 2012)
Republicans 38.9 percent
Democrats 34.2 percent
NPA 23.8 percent

Voting Age Population (2010 Census): 130,766
White (Non-Hispanic) 90.9 percent
Hispanic 3.5 percent
Black 3 percent

Median Age: 50.6

Men: 48.4 percent
Women: 51.6 percent

2012 PRESIDENT
Mitt Romney 54.8 percent, Barack Obama 42.8
percent (Estimated*)

2012 STATE HOUSE
Dave Hood, Republican, 61.3 percent,
Christina Spencer-Kephart, NPA, 38.7 percent

2010 GOVERNOR
Rick Scott 52.2 percent, Alex Sink 43.7 percent

2008 PRESIDENT
John McCain 50.8 percent, Barack Obama 48
percent

HOUSE DISTRICT 26
CENTRAL VOLUSIA

COUNTIES: Volusia

RATING: Solid Democrat

NASCAR WORKS HERE, BUT DOESN'T NECESSARILY LIVE HERE

Early in the 20th Century, somebody thought the hard-packed sand near Daytona Beach would be a good place to see how fast cars could go. Beach racing went on there for the next half century, until a mechanic named Bill France built a big new speedway out west of town in 1955 to run the cars on the concrete. That started stock car racing's transformation from rural past-time to multi-billion dollar international enterprise, a change in which Daytona played the pivotal role.

The Speedway is this district's big moneymaker, and brings millions of tourists here each year. But this isn't really that much of a "NASCAR district." It's a little like the crowds at the races - mostly white, and generally speaking, not wealthy. But the area is less white than the racing crowd, and a little poorer. The people who live around here are also a lot younger than your average stock car racing fan - and as long as you're not looking in the grandstand during the Daytona 500, you'll find lots of Democrats in this area.

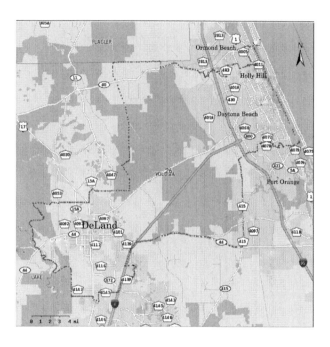

In addition to mainland Daytona Beach, the district also includes all or parts of South Daytona, DeLand and Orange City.

WHO LIVES HERE?

Despite the stereotype of NASCAR as a poor man's sport, the crowd at the Speedway on race day is likely to be more affluent than the track's neighbors. Several Census tracts in Daytona Beach proper (on the mainland) have median household incomes below $30,000 a year (while nearly half of stock car racing fans make more than $50,000, according to NASCAR). In the area just east of the track, around Bethune-Cookman University, an area with lots of non-working students, the median household income drops to under $20,000. The district is also more ethnically and racially diverse than your average stock car racing crowd, though it's still largely white. The city of Daytona Beach has had a large African-American population from its earliest days, and today is more than 35 percent African-American. But the district as a whole has a black population of a little over 20 percent, with whites making up 70 percent. (To keep the comparison going, NASCAR says its fan base is 80 percent white.) This is one of a small number of Florida House districts with a white majority and a black House member, in this case, Rep. Dwayne Taylor. DeLand, which is the major population center in the western part of the district, also has a fairly large African-American population of nearly 20 percent. The major difference between this district's biggest industry and its residents is age. NASCAR fans are on average in their early 50s, a decade older than the median age of 40.5 in House District 26.

POLITICAL ISSUES AND TRENDS

Another way in which House District 26 breaks with the NASCAR fan base is in political outlook. Stock car racing fans are 50 percent more likely to be registered as Republicans than Democrats, but this is a solidly Democratic district. Barack Obama won by more than 20 points here in 2008, though he slipped some in 2012. And Democrat Alex Sink won the district's precincts in the 2010 governor's race by 12 points. Registration also solidly favors Democrats, who make up 46 percent of voters to 29 percent for Republicans and 23 percent in neither party.

Taylor was a Daytona Beach city commissioner from 2003 to 2008 before he was elected to the Legislature when former Rep. Joyce Cusack was term limited out. He has made collective bargaining and public pension issues one of his top concerns, having been a firefighter and served as a police and fire pension board trustee. Taylor is a supporter of government employees, having regularly pushed for pay raises for state workers, and has been an outspoken critic of proposals that could make it harder for people to vote. Taylor generally votes with his Democratic colleagues.

DISTRICT 26 STATS

Registration (Book closing, 2012)
Democrats 45.8 percent
Republicans 28.6 percent
NPA 22.5 percent

Voting Age Population (2010 Census): 124,948
White (Non-Hispanic) 69.8 percent
Black 20.6 percent
Hispanic 6.9 percent

Median Age: 40.5

Men: 49.6 percent
Women: 50.4 percent

2012 PRESIDENT

Barack Obama 55 percent, Mitt Romney 43.6 percent (Estimated*)

2012 STATE HOUSE
No race. Rep. Dwayne Taylor, D-Daytona Beach, faced no primary or general election opposition.

2010 GOVERNOR
Alex Sink 53.5 percent, Rick Scott 41.4 percent

2008 PRESIDENT
Barack Obama 60.1 percent, John McCain 38.6 percent

HOUSE DISTRICT 27
SOUTH VOLUSIA: DELTONA, DEBARY

COUNTIES: Volusia

RATING: Swing District

DISTRICT SWINGS, BUT BEAT IS MORE AND MORE SALSA

This immense district, which on a map kind of looks like a tornado, stretches from far inland DeBary, which is on a straight line above Orlando, to the coast south of New Smyrna. The district also sticks down - the funnel part of this giant storm cloud - in a way that would seem odd, because in doing so it only picks up a few sparsely populated areas around Lake Harney. But the funnel is merely following the county line, picking up a part of Volusia County that sticks weirdly southward, wedging in between Seminole County to the west and Brevard to the east.

The district includes Deltona, the largest city in Volusia County, and one of two major inland population centers in the county (the other is DeLand in neighboring District 26). It also includes Deltona Lakes and Osteen in the west. The middle of the district is a rarity in Florida: a huge expanse of mostly undeveloped area. Between Interstate 95 and the coast, the district includes the town of Edgewater, and the tiny community of Oak Hill.

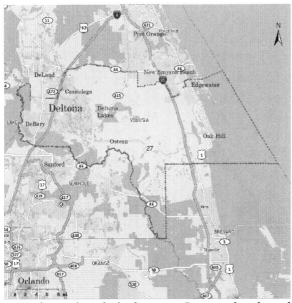

Deltona is relatively new. It was developed in the early 1960s as a master-planned retirement community, but the lots were very cheap - and sold at $10 down, and $10 a month by Mackle Brothers, which was also developing in Southwest Florida (see House District 75). While Deltona was a retirement town at first, Orlando was growing outward toward the area. As real estate prices skyrocketed in the Orlando area, middle class and less affluent residents were pushed farther and farther away from the city. With cheap real estate in the Deltona area, which was right on Interstate 4, the town mushroomed, essentially becoming an exurban bedroom community, and quickly overtaking more established Daytona in population. The change was dramatic - the median age in the Deltona area in 1970 was 62. By 1990, it was 35. The massive growth in the area led residents to incorporate as the city of Deltona in 1995.

WHO LIVES HERE?

As it is in so many places around Florida, the growing Hispanic population is the other big demographic story here. The district's Latino population is 20 percent, up from 11.5 percent in 2000. Most of that growth is in Deltona, where Puerto Ricans, mostly ones who were priced out of closer-in Orlando suburbs, stared moving in large numbers in the 1990s. Deltona is now over 30 percent Latino, and about 20 percent Puerto Rican.

While Deltona was a place where working people moved seeking affordability, incomes in the area are right around the state median. In most of the Census tracts around the district, median household incomes are in the high $40,000s and low-to-mid $50,000s.

POLITICAL ISSUES AND TRENDS

Hispanics in the Deltona area started gaining political power about a decade after they began moving there in large numbers. Residents made Joe Perez the first Hispanic on the Deltona city commission in 1995, and he was followed by David Santiago, now the district's House member, who was elected to the commission in 2003. While Santiago is a Republican, exit polling shows most Hispanics in the state, especially non-Cuban Hispanics, voted for Democrats. This district has trended a bit toward the GOP, but if the Latino growth continues, it may swing back the other way.

For the moment, however, the political trend in this district, as it appears to be in Volusia County at large, is toward the Republican Party. Barack Obama won here in 2008, but Mitt Romney won narrowly in 2012. Also in 2012, Frank Bruno, considered one of the Democrats' strongest state Senate candidates, lost a race in this area to Republican Rep. Dorothy Hukill. In between the two presidential years, Republican Rick Scott edged Democrat Alex Sink in the 2010 governor's race here. Santiago won the House seat in 2012 by more than 9 percentage points but Democrat Phil Giorno was a late replacement on the ballot for Dennis Mulder, who dropped out of the race because of family concerns. Volusia County traditionally has been a swing area of the state. Before she was elected to the Senate, Hukill represented much of southern Volusia in the House, but her predecessor, Suzanne Kosmas was a Democrat.

Santiago moved to the area in the early 1990s, and worked in insurance and real estate before his current career as a financial adviser specializing in helping military veterans. In the House, he has been an advocate for veterans, and in his first session, Santiago sponsored a bill that will waive certain health care profession licensing fees for veterans. Santiago has also been a supporter of tax rebates for improvements at the Daytona Speedway. He is a vocal backer of more school choice, but was one of just seven House Republicans who voted against a bill that would allow parents to vote to have charter school companies take over their kids' failing schools. Mostly, though, Santiago took up relatively non-controversial issues in his first legislative session.

DISTRICT 27 STATS

Registration (Book closing, 2012)
Democrats 37.4 percent
Republicans 33.3 percent
NPA 25.8 percent

Voting Age Population (2010 Census): 120,909
White (Non-Hispanic) 73.4 percent
Hispanic 17.8 percent
Black 6.4 percent

Median Age: 42.5

Men: 48.6 percent
Women: 51.4 percent

2012 PRESIDENT
Mitt Romney 50.9 percent, Barack Obama 48.4 percent (Estimated*)

2012 STATE HOUSE
David Santiago, Republican, 54.8 percent, Phil Giorno, Democrat, 45.2 percent

2010 GOVERNOR
Rick Scott 48.5 percent, Alex Sink 46.3 percent

2008 PRESIDENT
Barack Obama 52.3 percent, John McCain 46.4 percent

HOUSE DISTRICT 28
ORLANDO SUBURBS: SANFORD, WINTER SPRINGS, OVIEDO

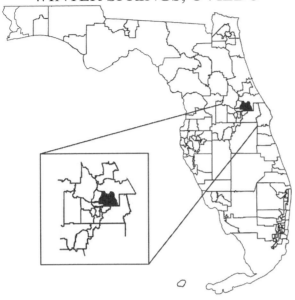

COUNTIES: Seminole
RATING: Leans Republican

ONCE CELERY COUNTRY, NOW AFFLUENT SUBURBIA

At the far end of the commute through the northern suburbs of Orlando, you get to Sanford, which developed not as a bedroom community, but a city in and of itself. The town started as a shipping terminus for produce, and for a while was one of the largest points of departure for citrus heading north by train and steamboat on Lake Monroe and the St. Johns River. While the citrus industry eventually moved farther south, out of the reach of the cold, Sanford would become known as the center of a celery growing region, and for nearly a century was often called "Celery City." Agriculture dominated the northern part of

Seminole County well into the 20th Century.

But after World War II - and especially after the arrival of Disney World, Orlando began its seemingly inexorable march outward, gobbling up land for housing and hotels. Its suburbs creeped northward through Seminole County, and eventually linked up with Sanford, which some now see as a just far-enough away bedroom community for the area's major city.

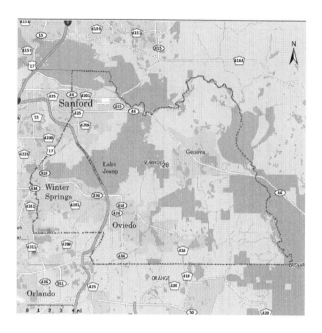

Sanford, was mostly known in recent decades as the home of Orlando's second international airport, the arrival point for hundreds of thousands of tourists coming to the Orlando area, many on smaller, niche airlines and tourist charters. The city drew unwelcome attention in 2012 when 17-year-old Trayvon Martin was shot by neighborhood watch volunteer George Zimmerman, in a case that opened up questions of racial stereotyping and an examination of Florida's gun and self defense laws. The actual incident, though, took place in the western part of the city, in House District 29.

Lake Jesup separates Sanford from the district's other two large communities, the affluent suburbs of Winter Springs and Oviedo. Both are communities of about 30,000 that run nearly indistinguishably together, and are the kinds of places that show up in magazine lists of the "best places to live," "best places to raise kids," and "top towns for families." Both are relatively quiet - the most exciting thing generally going on involves the fact that wild chickens famously roam Oviedo's downtown. Winter Springs wants to become a magnet for high tech businesses, citing a blossoming local "technology corridor," that links the city to the University of Central Florida, and Orlando's Lake Nona bioscience cluster.

Politically, while Oviedo was home to recent House Speaker Tom Feeney, it is probably better known as the town where former Florida Republican Party Chairman Jim Greer was deputy mayor before he was plucked from obscurity by Charlie Crist to serve as the statewide party boss. Greer later pleaded guilty to money laundering and fraud in connection with a scheme in which he steered party money to a company he owned.

WHO LIVES HERE?

While the population of Sanford is 30 percent black, the influence of its African-American community in the Legislature is diluted, split as it is into two districts. That gives District 28 a voting age population just under 10 percent black, and neighboring District 29 a similar percentage. House District 28 is about 70 percent non-Hispanic white and about 15 percent Latino, with Puerto Ricans being the largest single Hispanic group.

Mostly, the district is made up of families with kids, with 37 percent of households in the district having at least one child under 18 living in the house. Another 22 percent of the homes here have at least one person over 65, but the elderly make up a small part of the overall population, right around 10 percent.

The people who live in the southern part of District 28 are pretty well-off. Winter Springs touts itself in business recruiting brochures as "home to young, affluent, well-educated, professional families," a claim generally borne out by Census data. Winter Springs and Oviedo are both much more affluent than the state as a whole, and even Seminole County. The Census tracts in the two cities have median incomes ranging from the $70,000s to over $90,000. The northern area in the district, in the city of Sanford, is poorer. Many Census tracts in that part of the district are right around or slightly below the statewide median in income, and the central part of the city, between downtown and Lake Monroe, is extremely poor with a median household income of just $16,000 a year.

POLITICAL ISSUES AND TRENDS

In Seminole County, 2012 marked several setbacks for Republicans, but this district in the eastern part of the county was an exception, providing a strong counterweight for the GOP against Democratic inroads elsewhere. While

Democrats Mike Clelland and Karen Castor Dentel picked up House seats for their party in other Seminole County districts, Mitt Romney won in District 28, as did incumbent Republican Rep. Jason Brodeur. Romney appears to have improved slightly on the GOP's showing in the district as well, drawing more of the vote percentage than John McCain did in 2008 and outperforming Rick Scott in the 2010 governor's race.

Brodeur was first elected to the House in 2010 and re-elected in 2012 by more than 30 points over a Libertarian challenger, with no Democrat in the race. Brodeur, a staunch "limited-government" style Republican whose job is president of the Seminole County Regional Chamber of Commerce, is the chairman of the House Health Innovation Subcommittee. In the House, Brodeur has probably been most controversial as the sponsor of legislation in 2011 that restricts ways in which doctors can talk to their patients about the presence of guns in a home. The "Firearm Owners Protection Act," was declared unconstitutional by a South Florida judge, and in 2013 the case was on appeal. Brodeur has also been a strong advocate of cutting taxes, and made an effort in 2012 to expand the homestead tax exemption, though the bill died. He also was chairman of the House Government Operations Subcommittee in 2013 that wrote legislation to shift future state employees into a 401 (k)-style retirement plan. In 2014, Brodeur was a sponsor of legislation that would steer state tax dollars to help Daytona International Speedway make upgrades.

DISTRICT 28 STATS

Registration (Book closing, 2012)
Republicans 40.5 percent
Democrats 33.5 percent
NPA 23.1 percent

Voting Age Population (2010 Census): 120,940
White (Non-Hispanic) 71.1 percent
Hispanic 14.4 percent
Black 9.9 percent

Median Age: 37.6

Men: 48.8 percent
Women: 51.2 percent

2012 PRESIDENT
Mitt Romney 55.5 percent, Barack Obama 44.5
percent (Estimated*)

2012 STATE HOUSE
Rep. Jason Brodeur, R-Sanford, 66 percent,
Franklin Perez, Libertarian, 34 percent

2010 GOVERNOR
Rick Scott 51.2 percent, Alex Sink 45 percent

2008 PRESIDENT
John McCain 51.1 percent, Barack Obama 47.9
percent

HOUSE DISTRICT 29
NORTH ORLANDO SUBURBS - SEMINOLE COUNTY

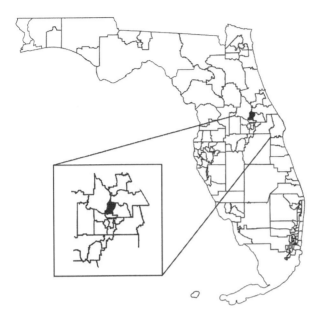

COUNTIES: Seminole
RATING: Leans Republican

THIS IS THE 'BURBS

Welcome to Suburbia. The modern American suburban experience is encapsulated in the northern suburbs of Orlando, up Interstate 4 in western Seminole County communities like Longwood, Lake Mary and Heathrow. That includes all that's bad about suburbia: commuters packed onto the highway to and from downtown Orlando and jammed up on the other roads too, the cookie-cutter apartment and condo complexes. And all that's good: high-rated schools of which locals are really proud, low crime, nice homes and a lack of concrete. "Lots of open space, birds and alligators," is part of what Orlando Sentinel political columnist Scott Maxwell thinks of when asked what's in Seminole County.

The Sentinel back in 2003 described Seminole County as a "huge expanse of Leave-it-to-Beaver suburbia," though noting that officials were hoping to lure jobs to the area so suburbanites wouldn't have to commute to Orlando. (Traffic here is so bad, that officials not long ago asked to be considered a special case for road help because of "transportation

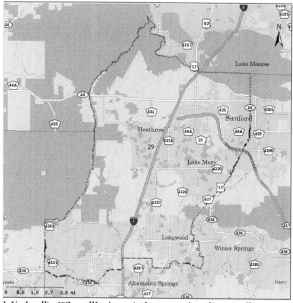

blight.") The "bring jobs to the 'burbs" effort was working - office complexes were popping up here, and there was talk that it would soon eclipse downtown Orlando - at least until the recession slowed the growth some.

The district also includes the western part of Sanford. Though Sanford is about 30 percent African-American, the population is split between Districts 29 and 28, making each about 10 percent black. It was in a western neighborhood of Sanford in this district in 2012 where a young black man, Trayvon Martin, was shot by a neighborhood watch volunteer, leading to a new discussion of Florida's gun and self defense laws, but also a re-examination of what it means to be black in mostly white suburbia.

While blacks are a minority here, Sanford has had a significant African-American population since absorbing the former black community of Goldsboro in the early 20th Century. The city is part of another footnote in the nation's rocky racial history. In the late 1940s, the Brooklyn Dodgers had used Sanford for spring training for their minor league players assigned to Triple A Montreal, while the big league team trained in Daytona Beach. But when Jackie Robinson showed up for spring training in 1946, the mayor told the team that they wouldn't be able to train there because of Robinson and another black player the Dodgers were considering, John Wright. The Dodgers moved minor league training to Daytona Beach.

WHO LIVES HERE?

When asked to describe Seminole County, Maxwell thought, in addition to bird and alligators, of affluent, gated communities and Republicans, and there are plenty of both of those in House District 29, too. The wealth starts almost exactly at the line separating this district from the poorer (and more Democrat-voting) district to the south, House District 30. For example, if you are in Seminole County Census Tract 220.01 in HD 30, the people around you have a median household income of $28,242, nearly half the statewide median. But if you walk across S. Ronald Reagan Blvd.

or North St., into Census Tract 215.04, in House District 29, the median household income jumps to $70,357. Surrounding Census tracts in District 29 all have median incomes in the high $60-thousands, and low-$70,000s in Longwood. Going west, the incomes go even higher, into the mid-and high-$80,000s in Wekiva Springs. North of there, in the woodsy neighborhoods nestled among the country clubs on the east bank of the Wekiva River, the median household income rises to an astoundingly high $180,000 a year. Overall, the district is likely among the wealthiest in the state. The district's voting age population is nearly 70 percent non-Hispanic white, about 14 percent Hispanic and 11 percent black.

POLITICAL ISSUES AND TRENDS

The impression that this area is full of Republicans is accurate as well. Registered Republicans outnumber registered Democrats in the district 41.5 percent to 33 percent, and Mitt Romney beat President Obama in the 2012 presidential election in these precincts by 10 percentage points. In that same election of 2012, however, a Democrat won the district's House seat. The question arose as to whether the election of Rep. Mike Clelland, D-Lake Mary, was an anomaly because of some well-publicized problems of Republican incumbent Chris Dorworth, or part of a larger trend away from GOP dominance. The former appears more likely - Romney won the district by about the same margin as Republican Rick Scott in the 2010 governor's race and actually did a couple percentage points better than GOP presidential candidate John McCain did in 2008.

Seminole County transformed, as did so many places in Florida, during the last quarter of the 20th Century, from an old-fashioned rural place where people were Southern Democrats to a much more diverse suburban county where conservatives began voting for the Republican Party. This middle part of the county is among the most solidly Republican areas in the northern Orlando suburbs - with Democrats clustered mostly in Sanford to the north, and farther south in the county in parts of Altamonte Springs and other places along the Orange County line.

Dorworth had been in line to be speaker of the House before he was ousted by Clelland. Dorworth faced questions about his own personal spending and behavior, as his house went into foreclosure, and the media revealed he had a number of unpaid tolls. He also appeared to underestimate Clelland, who as a former firefighter and a union leader was backed by firefighter friends who worked neighborhoods for him. Clelland's brother is president of the Orlando firefighters union and helped mobilize volunteers. Also, Clelland may have gotten some coat-tail effect from Obama, even though Romney won the district - Democratic turnout was higher than it otherwise may have been.

Clelland is a union lawyer for first responders and before becoming a lawyer he was a Longwood firefighter in this district for 26 years, rising to battalion chief.

Clelland's win as a Democrat in a strongly Republican district was the upset of 2012 among Florida races, and knowing that

Republicans outnumber Democrats in his district Clelland has pledged to try to reach across the aisle to find common ground with the GOP. He was one of just a few Democrats to vote against trying to get the Legislature to hold a special session on the Stand Your Ground law, a move reflecting the sentiment in the district. Clelland called during his campaign for more attention to the needs of public education and criticized the GOP-led Legislature's cutting of spending on schools and changes to public employee retirement fund rules. Clelland was endorsed by just about every public employees union and many other organized labor organizations.

During his first session in the House, Clelland failed to pass any legislation. Among the unsuccessful bills he sponsored was a measure to require the state to implement national Common Core standards for schools, an ethics bill that would have expanded the powers of the Commission on Ethics and required more reporting of interests by lawmakers, and a measure to create a special Lottery scratch-off game with the sale proceeds to benefit breast cancer research. For 2014, Clelland filed a bill to ban the trade of shark fins, sometimes harvested for sale in Asia where they're used in soup. Clelland got a political science degree at the University of Central Florida. He then got his law degree at night at Florida A&M's Orlando law school while still working as a fireman.

DISTRICT 29 STATS

Registration (Book closing, 2012)

Republicans 41.5 percent
Democrats 33 percent
NPA 22.6 percent

Voting Age Population (2010 Census): 121,258
White (Non-Hispanic) 69.1 percent
Hispanic 14.4 percent
Black 11.1 percent

Median Age: 38.9

Men: 48.2 percent
Women 51.8 percent

2012 PRESIDENT
Mitt Romney 54.2 percent, Barack Obama 43.9
percent (Estimated*)

2012 STATE HOUSE
Mike Clelland, Democrat, 50.1 percent, Rep.
Chris Dorworth, R-Lake Mary, 49.9 percent
after a recount

2010 GOVERNOR
Rick Scott 53.3 percent, Alex Sink 43.1 percent

2008 PRESIDENT
John McCain 52.4 percent, Barack Obama 46.7
percent

HOUSE DISTRICT 30
NORTHERN ORLANDO SUBURBS

COUNTIES: Orange, Seminole
RATING: Swing District

SUBURBAN EVERY-DISTRICT

This district directly north of Orlando includes a ribbon of typical, mostly white suburbs along the Interstate 4 corridor as it goes north out of Orlando. The area, which straddles the Orange-Seminole County line, is dominated by Altamonte Springs, which sprawls seamlessly into the other towns here, and which the Orlando Sentinel more than a decade ago called "the prototype of a city without a center." In many ways, it looks like the rest of suburban Orlando, with strip malls, big box stores, and wide, traffic-choked streets. There are plenty of nice subdivisions that get greener the farther you get from Orlando. One exception to the vibe is Eatonville, six miles north of Orlando. One of the first all-black towns in the country to be incorporated after slavery, had its early days profiled in the novel *Their Eyes Were Watching God* by Zora Neale Hurston, who grew up in Eatonville. It is proud of its history and resistant to being overrun by the rest of suburban Orlando. [1] The district also includes all or parts of Maitland and Winter Park, Forest City, and Casselberry.

WHO LIVES HERE?

Eatonville, which is still 90 percent African-American, is the exception demographically as well as aesthetically. Most of District 30 is white, but with a growing Hispanic population. The voting age population in the district as a whole is just 12 percent African-American. Non-Hispanic whites make up 66 percent of the voting-age population while the fastest growing group, like everywhere else in the Orlando area, is Hispanics, now at about 17 percent of the voting age population, up from 12 percent a decade ago.

This is a diverse area economically, with Census tracts where half the households are bringing in less than $30,000 a year, and others where half are making over $70,000 - a wide divergence that is likely one of the driving factors making it competitive. Many of the more affluent areas are home to middle and upper income families with kids in school - one reason they move to Seminole County, which has a reputation for decent education.

POLITICAL ISSUES AND TRENDS

---

[1] Damien Cave, "In a Town Apart, the Pride and Trials of Black Life" *The New York Times*, 28 September, 2008

If you plot the median age of all the House districts in Florida and match the plot line with election performance, a striking trend leaps off the chart. In districts where the median age is under 37, it's likely, with only a few exceptions, that Barack Obama won the last presidential election. In districts where the median age is over 37, its likely, again, with a few exceptions, that Mitt Romney won. In places like House District 30, where the median age is 37, well, bets are off. And it turns out this district is the

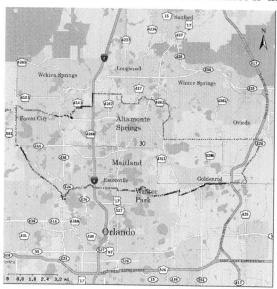

perfect 37-year-old, waffling back and forth on whether it wants to be a young liberal, or a middle aged conservative. The two parties have nearly even registration. Obama won here in 2012 by less than 2 percentage points. The same for Democrat Alex Sink, who was a narrow winner in these precincts in the 2010 governor's race.

Demographic trends appear to be pushing the district slightly more Democratic, no surprise given growth in the Latino population.

Democrats picked up a seat in this district in 2012 when Karen Castor Dentel defeated incumbent Republican Rep. Scott Plakon. The redistricting year had something to do with that, though, as Plakon was running in an area that included new voters who didn't know him. Castor Dentel is a teacher, and this is a district with many young families who have moved here for the schools, and may be presumed to be at least somewhat in line with Democrats on favoring public schools over alternatives. Clearly this moderate county is pro public education - voters here recently easily passed a school tax referendum.

Castor Dentel comes from one of the pre-eminent Democratic political families of Florida. Her sister is U.S. Rep. Kathy Castor, and her mother is former education commissioner and state Sen. Betty Castor. Castor Dentel's father, Don Castor, was a judge and her stepfather, Sam Bell is a former state representative. Castor Dentel was elected to the House in 2012 after campaigning heavily on her experience as a teacher and concern for public schools. She quickly took high profile Democratic priorities, including sponsoring a bill to expand the list of sites for early voting.

But like most Democrats in the Republican-controlled House, she failed to pass any legislation her first year. Most of her efforts involved education, including a bill seeking to make changes to how teachers could be evaluated under the Republican merit pay plan, and a measure setting out new requirements for charter schools. She also filed bills related to waivers from middle school physical education, and allowing additional criteria for setting teacher salary schedules. In 2014, Castor Dentel filed legislation seeking to increase the number of pregnant women who qualify for Medicaid coverage by raising the income threshold. With District 30 seen as a swing district, several Republicans were already lining up in early 2014 to challenge Castor Dentel.

DISTRICT 30 STATS
Registration (Book closing, 2012)
Democrats 37.3 percent
Republicans 36.6 percent
NPA 23.4 percent

Voting Age Population (2010 Census): 100,521
White (Non-Hispanic) 65.7 percent
Hispanic 17.7 percent
Black 12 percent

Median Age: 37.5

Men: 48.4 percent
Women 51.6 percent

2012 PRESIDENT
Barack Obama 49.7 percent, Mitt Romney 48.4 percent (Estimated*)

2012 STATE HOUSE
Karen Castor Dentel, Democrat, 53.1 percent, Rep. Scott Plakon, R-Longwood, 46.9 percent

2010 GOVERNOR
Alex Sink 48.7 percent, Rick Scott 47.5 percent

2008 PRESIDENT
Barack Obama 51.4 percent, John McCain 47.6 percent

HOUSE DISTRICT 31
FLORIDA'S LAKE REGION

COUNTIES: Lake, Orange
RATING: Solid Republican

GOD, GUNS AND GRANDMAS

This immense, but heavily rural district stretches from the far northwestern Orlando suburb of Apopka on its southern edge to a ribbon of small towns nestled among lakes along the west side of the district. The district runs through Zellwood, Mount Dora, Tavares, Eustis and Umatilla. The northern tier of the district is covered by part of the Ocala National Forest and the eastern part of the district includes the Seminole National Forest.

WHO LIVES HERE?

The general picture of the residents of District 31 is of middle income families and retirees, predominantly white, with what could fairly be called "typical" small-town, conservative values. The yards here have

American flags much of the time, not just on the Fourth of July, the driveways have pickup trucks, and the oldest - and probably best known - local business is A.W. Peterson's Gun Shop in Mount Dora. Lots of people in Lake County go hunting. Peterson's opened in Mount Dora in 1953, though it had been around a long time before that. Its new owner, farmer Leighton Baker, moved it to Lake County from Colorado, where A.W. Peterson had opened it in 1886. Leighton Baker's son, Carey Baker, grew up working in the store, and ran it with his brothers before entering politics. He represented this area in the House from 2000-2004 and in the Senate from 2004-2010.

When he first ran for the House, an Orlando Sentinel columnist wrote a story asking whether owning a gun shop would hurt Baker's chances. It actually probably helped him quite a bit. "Lake County, the thinking goes, is politically in tune with the gun-rack-in-the-truck crowd, not the minivan soccer mom set," noted the columnist, David Damron. [1]

The district is heavily religious, with a conservative, protestant predominance. While the district is 73 percent non-Hispanic white, there are areas in and around Apopka where you wouldn't believe that figure. The city, which is in Orange County and partly in neighboring District 45, is more than 20 percent African-American. Starting in the 1940s, the marshy areas on the shores of Lake

---

[1] David Damron, "Does Owning Gun Shop Hurt Candidate? Nope." *The Orlando Sentinel*, 16 July, 2000.

Apopka were drained and turned into "muck farms," full of fertile lake bed soil. Most of the workers who came to the area to work the muck farms were black, though some were also Latino. In the late 1990s, after years of studies that showed serious environmental damage from pesticide use in the area, the state bought the muck farms and shut them down, but many descendants of the people who came to work on them remain.

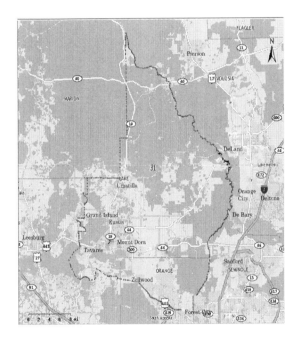

Now, Apopka bills itself as the "Indoor Foliage Capital of the World," with its thriving industry of hundreds of nurseries growing ornamental indoor plants sold around the world. Mexicans and Central Americans work in those nurseries in large numbers, and the city of Apopka is 25 percent Hispanic, with just under 10 percent of the population from Mexico. The racial and ethnic diversity of

Apopka, however, is overshadowed by the large white population in the rest of the district.

A quarter of the people in District 31 are over aged 60 and about 35 percent of households in the area have someone over 65 living in them. Places like Tavares, Umatilla and Eustis have the same problem as lots of small towns that are just a bit outside commuting range to a big city, particularly when the economy takes a downturn. Some number of young people leave and don't come back.

POLITICAL ISSUES AND TRENDS

The district is solidly Republican and shows little sign of that changing. The area is deeply conservative and religious, and it's middle income social conservatives who give the area its Republican character, rather than the corporate wing of the party. Still, Mitt Romney won easily here, as did Rick Scott and John McCain. The area has elected socially conservative Republicans for years. Since Carey Baker left the Senate and returned to serve in county government, voters here have sent Alan Hays, a Umatilla dentist, to the state Senate. He's one of that body's staunchest social conservatives.

Besides the fact that people here will almost assuredly vote Republican, there's another electoral certainty in Apopka: people here will vote for John Land for mayor. Land was first elected to the post in 1949, and has been there almost ever since He sat out one term in the 1960s, but otherwise, he's been returned to office every election year and is now in his 90s. Most Apopka residents have never known another mayor.

Rep. Bryan Nelson, R-Apopka, was first elected in 2006 and will be forced to leave the House in 2014. He most recently served as chairman of the Insurance and Banking Subcommittee, an as an insurance agent, has made property insurance his main focus in the Legislature. Nelson has been heavily involved in efforts to reduce the risk to the state of a big hurricane wiping out the reserves of Citizens Property Insurance. Nelson sponsored legislation over the years aimed at raising rates for Citizens in an effort to restore a private insurance market in the state, including the 2009 legislation that ended a mid-2000s freeze on rate increases for the state-backed company. Nelson also has tried to pass legislation to let school districts sell ads on school buses to raise revenue, but failed to get the Legislature to go along with the idea. Back in 2009 Nelson sponsored a bill to allow universities to build mausoleums on campus to allow alumni to be buried at their old college haunts. A version of the bill eventually became law.

DISTRICT 31 STATS

Registration (Book closing, 2012)
Republicans 44.9 percent
Democrats 32.9 percent
NPA 18.5 percent

Voting Age Population (2010 Census): 123,715
White (Non-Hispanic) 76.8 percent
Hispanic 11.3 percent
Black 9.2 percent

Median Age: 43.4

Men: 48.8 percent
Women 51.2 percent

2012 PRESIDENT
Mitt Romney 57.9 percent, Barack Obama 40.6
percent (Estimated*)

2012 STATE HOUSE
No race. Rep. Bryan Nelson, R-Apopka, faced
no primary or general opposition

2010 GOVERNOR
Rick Scott 55.2 percent, Alex Sink 40.4 percent

2008 PRESIDENT
John McCain 56.8 percent, Barack Obama 42.3
percent

HOUSE DISTRICT 32
LEESBURG, SOUTHERN LAKE COUNTY

COUNTIES: Lake
RATING: Solid Republican

BUCOLIC RURAL COUNTY, RELIABLY CONSERVATIVE

This is quintessential rural Central Florida, dotted with the lakes that draw people here (and gave the county its name) and small towns that feel like they're from a simpler time. If Seminole County to the west is Leave it to Beaver land, Lake County, with its small towns like Clermont, Yalaha and Leesburg, is kind of like Andy Griffith's Mayberry, though with more chain stores and restaurants. In the Whole Foods vs. Cracker Barrel predictor of party affiliation and voting, Lake County is Cracker Barrel America (there's one on U.S. 441 in Leesburg and another in Clermont). More chicken and dumplings than gourmet pot stickers, more sweet tea, than hibiscus green tea.

WHO LIVES HERE?

The little town of Astatula makes it easy to figure out who lives there, by holding something every New Year's Eve called the "Blue Collar Ball Drop." More than one in five workers here works in the non-professional trade and transportation sector, meaning they're service employees like retail shop workers, or they're in the transportation industry, like truckers (one of the largest employers in the district is a trucking company in Okahumpka.) The hospital in Leesburg, the Wal-Mart Supercenter and Publix are the other big local employers here.

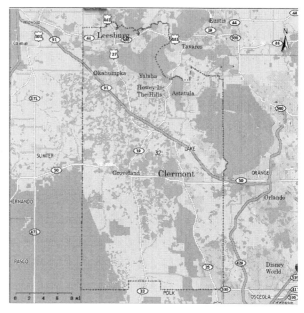

In Leesburg, which is in the northern tip of the district, and in roughly the western half of the rest of the district, most households are earning right around the median state income, or just a little below. Incomes are higher in the eastern part of the district, including Howey-In-The-Hills and the affluent, though sparsely populated area south of there, along the western shore of Lake Apopka. Household incomes in Clermont, in the middle of the district, are also right around the state median. Much of the southern part of the district is rural and lightly populated.

The district's voting age population is about 72 percent white, 13 percent Hispanic and 11 percent black. The median age in the district is just under 43, over the age where it seems Florida voters tend to start being more likely to vote Republican and older than most districts, but not among the very oldest.

POLITICAL ISSUES AND TRENDS

This is unquestionably conservative territory. Lake County hasn't voted for a Democrat in the presidential race since voters here went with FDR in 1944, at the height of World War II, (though Democrat Harry Truman fell short of Republican Thomas Dewey in 1948 in Lake County by only 100 votes.) If it weren't for the fact that Democratic U.S. Rep. Corrine Brown's majority black Congressional district has to cut through the unpopulated Ocala National Forest part of Lake County to link Jacksonville to Orlando, the county would only have one elected Democrat, Elections Supervisor Emogene Stegall. In addition to all the local officials, the county's senators, Dorothy Hukill and Alan Hays are both conservative Republicans, as are its three House members, Bryan Nelson, Larry Metz and Marlene O'Toole, and its other two members of Congress, Dan Webster and Rich Nugent. Mitt

Romney won in the district by a comfortable seven percentage points over Barack Obama in the 2012 presidential election, and Republican Rick Scott won by a similar margin in the 2010 governor's race.

Democrats didn't put up a candidate against Rep. Larry Metz, R-Yalaha, in 2012. Metz, an attorney, is chairman of the Civil Justice Committee. It's in that capacity that Metz has taken on the two issues for which he is probably best known in the House. He's one of the House Republicans' top experts on tort reform. Metz pushed a bill changing the standards for admissibility of expert witness testimony in civil cases, for example, getting it through the House for two years before finally getting it through the Senate in 2013. The other legislation to which Metz has become closely linked is a perennial effort to state in law that decisions by judges must comply only with protections afforded by the U.S. legal system, an effort to prohibit the inclusion of principles from foreign legal systems when working out disputes such as divorces or child custody. Metz was also a sponsor in 2013 of legislation aimed at reducing the role of the Florida High School Athletic Association.

DISTRICT 32 STATS

Registration (Book closing, 2012)
Republicans 42 percent
Democrats 34.7 percent
NPA 19.6 percent

Voting Age Population (2010 Census): 120,674
White (Non-Hispanic) 72.1 percent
Hispanic 13.5 percent

Black 10.5 percent

Median Age: 42.9

Men: 48.6 percent
Women 51.4 percent

2012 PRESIDENT
Mitt Romney 55.5 percent, Barack Obama 42.9
percent (Estimated*)

2012 STATE HOUSE
No race. Rep. Larry Metz, R-Yalaha, faced no
primary or general opposition.

2010 GOVERNOR
Rick Scott 54.7 percent, Alex Sink 41.1 percent

2008 PRESIDENT
John McCain 54.2 percent, Barack Obama 45
percent

DISTRICT 33
THE VILLAGES AND SUMTER COUNTY

COUNTIES: Sumter, Lake, Marion
RATING: Solid Republican

WORLD WITHOUT CHILDREN

There are a few clichés about statewide and national campaigning in Florida. Candidates always hit the condos in Broward. They go to the Versailles Restaurant in Little Havana. And for the last decade or so, they make sure they stop by The Villages. The community south of Ocala spreads through three counties and is home to more than 50,000 people. The craziest thing about the place is that two decades ago it barely existed. In 2000, about 8,000 people lived there. By 2010, its population had increased more than 500 percent and it now holds the distinction of being the largest gated 55-and-over community in the world. The

Villages is geographically huge as well, sprawling between the Florida Turnpike and U.S. 441 and between Leesburg and the southern suburbs of Ocala. Besides The Villages, District 33 includes the adjacent town of Lady Lake and nearby Fruitland Park. It also includes Wildwood, known to many Florida drivers as either the first exit or the last on the Turnpike. Farther south in Sumter County the district includes Coleman, home to a federal prison, Bushnell , which is the Sumter County

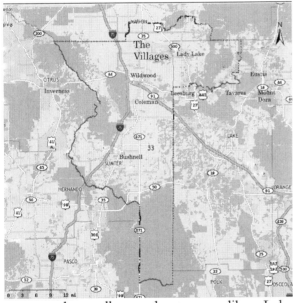

seat, and small, rural, towns like Lake Panasoffkee, Sumterville, Center Hill and Webster.

Because residents must be at least 55 to live in The Villages proper, this can be a strange place - a whole town where the kids are only visitors. Author Andrew Blechman wrote a book about The Villages called "Leisureville," with the subtitle: "Adventures in a World Without Children."

WHO LIVES HERE?

Usually when someone refers to a place as being home only to "old white people," they're speaking figuratively. Not here. Old, of course is relative - and many here keep plenty active, tooling around on golf carts, hitting the links, and, according to some articles about the dating scene here, hitting on each other. White isn't so relative. While the district as a whole is almost 15 percent non-white, the district's largest population center, The Villages, is nearly all white.

"Older" Americans are the most obvious demographic standout in this district. But with a median age of 61.1, it's actually only the second oldest House district in the state, with the average resident nearly two years younger than the average resident of District 91 in Palm Beach County. Still, an incredible 17 percent of the district's residents are over 75, and 43 percent of the district's residents are over 65. The Villages is solidly Republican, and these are true "Reagan Republicans," people who were in their 30s and 40s when they voted for Ronald Reagan. Many are likely also Nixon Republicans and Goldwater Republicans and a few here might have cut their electoral teeth in an election that involved Franklin D. Roosevelt.

The whiteness also is notable in The Villages, which, according to the 2010 Census is 97 percent non-Hispanic white, 1.5 percent Hispanic and 0.6 percent black. The broader district is more diverse, with Hispanics making up 5.5 percent of the population and blacks accounting for 7.6 percent. Much of the district's African-American population is in

Wildwood, which is 21 percent black. The population of the town of Coleman is nearly 40 percent black, but the entire town's population is only about 700.

Median incomes in Sumter County are right around the state median at $47,000 a year per household and $56,000 a year per family. The average annual wage is in the low $30,000s. Major employers in the district include the federal correctional complex at Coleman, the largest employer in Sumter County with just over 1,000 employees. Add a state prison, Sumter Correctional, to that and corrections officer is one of the most common occupations here. Because of The Villages, which seems to be ever growing, the construction industry is also robust here, responsible for about 8 percent of jobs in Sumter County. Other large employers include the school district, a concrete company, a community college, and, of course, the Wal-Mart Supercenter at The Villages. The area is also home to a significant number of health care professionals, at the Villages Regional Medical Center, which sits just inside Sumter County and the huge number of doctors office complexes lining U.S. 441 through adjacent Lady Lake. The Villages draws retirees from across the economic spectrum, some who buy "premier homes," that would fit in nicely in some of the wealthiest suburbs. But many of the retirees here are of modest means, living in the "historic" part of the development in smaller, manufactured homes that are generally inexpensive.

Sumter County can't hold The Villages. The sprawling retirement city has crossed the line to the north into Marion County and the eastern part of The Villages now reaches into Lake County. Lady Lake is also in Lake County, but runs up against The Villages and in many ways is hard to distinguish from its larger neighbor. Lady Lake is even older, on average, than The Villages, with a median age of 66.5, and with 53 percent of residents over age 65.

POLITICAL ISSUES AND TRENDS

This is solidly Republican country, but that is almost entirely due to the emergence of the Villages and other nearby retirement communities as home to large numbers of fiscally conservative retirees. Less than a generation ago, Sumter County was comfortably Democratic, but it began to shift in the 1990s. Democrat Lawton Chiles narrowly beat Republican Jeb Bush in the governor's race in Sumter County in 1994 but Republicans won farther down the ballot in local commission and school board races that year. Similarly, Democrat Bill Clinton edged Bob Dole in Sumter County in 1996, while Democrat Everett Kelly narrowly beat Republican Pamela Bronson in Sumter County in the 1996 race for the House District 42 seat. But by 1998, the tables had turned in Sumter County and Jeb Bush beat Democrat Buddy MacKay in the governor's race - even though MacKay was from nearby Ocala (MacKay also lost his home county of Marion to Bush.) Democrats haven't won a governor's or presidential election in Sumter County since.

It's not completely clear why there are so many Republicans retiring to The Villages, though the community's developer, H. Gary

Morse, is a well-known Republican activist and donor, and some say the community is more friendly to conservatives and Republicans than Democrats. A 2012 story in The Huffington Post about the community's political leanings noted that residents here know that when they buy a home here, some of the money Morse makes from selling it ends up as donations to Republican candidates. And people here talk about a "conservative vibe" that sometimes keeps more liberal retirees from considering moving to the community. "It's definitely a draw - most of my friends are Republicans," a 72-year-old Villages resident was quoted as saying in that story. [1]

Retired IBM executive Marlene O'Toole, a Republican from Lady Lake, and now the chief operating officer of a non-profit group that gives scholarships to at-risk children, was first elected to the House in 2008 and now holds one of the top posts in the House as chairwoman of the Education Committee. In 2013, a top priority for O'Toole was legislation, ultimately passed, that sought to revamp the early learning system, trying to improve the quality of the state's pre-school programs. She also shepherded to passage legislation to provide for faster approval of new nursing home beds in certain places - a bill aimed at helping the Villages.

O'Toole's gotten high marks from all the conservative issue tracking organizations, and predictably low marks from the liberal issue

---

[1] Dave Jamieson. "Villages Democrats Find Second-Rate Citizenry ..." *The Huffington Post.* Nov. 6, 2012.

groups. In 2010, O'Toole won praise from the pro-gun lobby when she sponsored a bill that said guns and ammunition made in Florida wouldn't be subject to federal regulation. The bill died in committee. Her work for the nonprofit group "Take Stock in Children," and simultaneous service on the legislative committee that writes the education budget has raised the most high profile controversy in O'Toole's career. She came in for criticism in 2013 when the group got $9 million in the budget that came out of the education appropriations subcommittee, of which O'Toole was vice chair. O'Toole is paid $50,000 a year by Take Stock for Children, and voted for the budget containing the line item. She also didn't initially disclose the potential conflict. [2]

DISTRICT 33 STATS

Registration (Book closing, 2012)

Republicans 49.2 percent
Democrats 30.9 percent
NPA 15.2 percent

Voting Age Population (2010 Census): 139,794
White (Non-Hispanic) 87 percent
Black 6.8 percent
Hispanic 4.7 percent

Median Age: 61.1

Men: 50.2 percent
Women 49.8 percent

---

[2] Michael Van Sickler, "Florida House Member Finally Discloses ...." *Tampa Bay Times*, 30 November 2013.

2012 PRESIDENT
Mitt Romney 65.9 percent, Barack Obama 33 percent (Estimated*)

2012 STATE HOUSE
Rep. Marlene O'Toole, R-Lady Lake, faced no primary or general election opposition.

2010 GOVERNOR
Rick Scott 61.1 percent, Alex Sink 33.6 percent

2008 PRESIDENT
John McCain 62.5 percent, Barack Obama 36.5 percent

HOUSE DISTRICT 34
CITRUS COUNTY, NORTHWEST HERNANDO

COUNTIES: Citrus, Hernando
RATING: Solid Republican

RETIREES AND MANATEES

Where the spring-fed Crystal River flows out of Kings Bay and into the Gulf of Mexico, warm water (and a protected sanctuary) draws thousands of manatees every winter. The manatees, in turn, draw people. Diving and snorkeling tourists are a mainstay in Crystal River, an otherwise quiet and off-the-beaten path old Florida town. The Gulf here doesn't meet the shore on beaches, but rather in a series of marshy inlets, making this a place that the typical Florida tourist developments bypassed. But its rugged, tied-to-nature vibe still draws hordes of manatee loving visitors, and the area is extremely popular with retirees. House District 34 includes all of Citrus County, including the cities of Crystal River, Inverness and Homosassa, and the sprawling developments of Citrus Springs and Lecanto. It also includes the northwestern quadrant of Hernando County, including North Weeki Wachee.

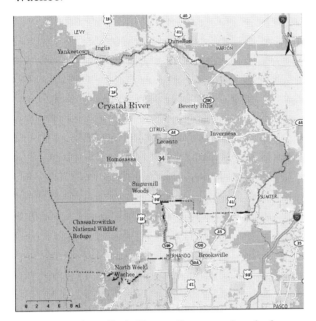

While it's called Citrus County, that industry fled farther south over a century ago. A bad freeze in the late 1800s convinced growers that Citrus County wasn't good for citrus. Timber has been harvested here for a long time - and much of the cedar along the Homosassa River was cut down to make Dixon Ticonderoga pencils. But mostly this is an area fueled by retirees, with a little bit of tourism thrown in. Most of the economy here is related to serving those who retire in the area, from the chain drug stores to the golf courses to the Fat Boys Bar B Q on U.S. 19, and age is the distinguishing characteristic of the populace.

The reliance on retirees has never been

bigger because of a recent change in the local economic landscape. One of the big features of the Crystal River "skyline," visible from U.S. 19 and for years a mainstay of the local workforce, is the Crystal River nuclear power plant. But the plant has been offline since 2009 because of a series of problems, and its owner, North Carolina-based Duke Energy, recently decided to close the nuclear plant permanently. The complex still has four coal-fired generators at Crystal River, though most people don't see coal as the future of energy production in the United States. With 600 full time workers when the nuclear generator was running, the power plant has been Crystal River's largest employer for about three decades, and its jobs are high wage. The company still employs about 350 at the coal generators, and said more than 200 will continue to work at the nuclear plant until it is fully decommissioned.

WHO LIVES HERE?

With half the population over the age of 53, the district is among the oldest in the state, with just six others having a higher median age. Retirees live all over the district, from the suburban-feeling subdivisions around Crystal Springs, Lecanto and Inverness, to the nearly all retirement developments near Weeki Wachee in the southern tip of the district.

The other demographic feature about District 34 that catches the eye is that it's overwhelmingly white. In fact, the district has the second whitest voting age population in the state, and is one of just three where the over-18 population is more than 90 percent white. The district's voting age population is 4.2 percent

Hispanic and 2.5 percent black.

With so many retirees on fixed incomes, House District 34 isn't affluent, with a median household income in Citrus County a bit under $40,000, while the median for the state as a whole is over $47,000. The median family income here is also about $10,000 below the state median.

POLITICAL ISSUES AND TRENDS

This is a strong Republican district, where the brand of conservatism often comes with a large dose of rural libertarianism, a bit of anti-corporate sentiment, and a little bit of environmental conservationist thrown in - though not if it goes too far. It's the area that was home to former Rep. Nancy Argenziano, a firebrand populist who had a mish-mash of political ideology from pro-consumer to environmentalist to a strong libertarian streak that made her a Republican when she was in the Legislature. She drifted away from her party though over a number of issues, including her disdain for big political money in the system. She was often on the outs with its leaders anyway, and tried to run as a Democrat for a congressional seat in 2012. She wasn't allowed to run as a Democrat, though because she didn't register with the party early enough under a new rule. After challenging that rule in court and losing, Argenziano decided to run as an independent in a challenge to incumbent Republican Rep. Jimmie Smith of Inverness - but lost badly.

Smith, too, is a bit of a firebrand, and also reflects well many of the sentiments of the district. Many here cherish traditional values, including hard work, and aren't big fans of the welfare system - and Smith's signature issue, the drug testing of welfare recipients, while proving problematic in a legal sense, plays well back home.

The district has generally given Republicans about 60 percent of the vote recently. While there clearly is at least a bit of an anti-establishment current running through the district, it's not too broadly entrenched. Mitt Romney, the ultimate board room candidate, did just fine in this district, beating Barack Obama in the 2012 presidential count in these precincts by just a bit over 20 percentage points. Smith got just under 60 percent in his race against Argenziano in 2012. Rick Scott, who ran basically as a populist despite spending more than $70 million of his own money, won the governor's race by about 15 points in the district. John McCain also won here by about 15 points in the 2008 presidential race.

For decades one of the major issues here has been balancing the area's natural beauty and environmental character - a big part of what has drawn retirees to live here and what brings in the tourists - with the need for growth to serve the people who have moved in. The area's voters are generally against heavy-handed government regulations, for example, Smith has urged Congress to reconsider a rule that limits boat speeds in Kings Bay, aimed at protecting manatees. But the local business owners who cater to tourists certainly don't want anything to hurt the manatees. And similarly, voters here tend to have anti-tax sentiments, but local officials have often debated sewer and other infrastructure needs to keep the local waters clean.

Smith, who retired from the U.S. Army and went to work as a security guard at the Crystal River power plant, hasn't shied away from hot-button issues since getting elected to the House in 2010. Smith said he got interested in politics when he read a quote from his local state representative, Republican Ron Schultz, who said that Florida didn't have a spending problem, and needed more revenue. Smith, with no political experience or name recognition, challenged Schultz and narrowly won the primary to unseat him. In the House, Smith has been particularly aggressive in trying to curb what he sees as abuses by recipients of government assistance. In addition to pushing for drug testing for welfare recipients, he also has claimed that there is a problem with people on assistance using state help for things besides food. "I don't want you to get a lap dance on my dollar," Smith said on the House floor in 2013. The bill barring use of electronic benefits cards for booze, gambling or strippers, is now law, though critics said it wasn't really a major problem, just red meat for Smith's conservative voters back home. Smith also has pushed legislation requiring drug testing of state employees, a pet measure of Gov. Scott. Smith also sponsored legislation requiring drug felons to undergo treatment before getting temporary cash benefits.

DISTRICT 34 STATS

Registration (Book closing, 2012)

Republicans 43.2 percent
Democrats 33 percent
NPA 20.2 percent

Voting Age Population (2010 Census): 131,684
White (Non-Hispanic) 91.9 percent
Hispanic 4.2 percent
Black 2.5 percent

Median Age: 53.5

Men: 48.5 percent
Women 51.5 percent

2012 PRESIDENT
Mitt Romney 60.7 percent, Barack Obama 40.2 percent (Estimated*)

2012 STATE HOUSE
Rep. Jimmie Smith, R-Inverness, 58 percent, Nancy Argenziano, Independent, 42 percent

2010 GOVERNOR
Rick Scott 54.5 percent, Alex Sink 39.2 percent

2008 PRESIDENT
Barack Obama 58.1 percent, John McCain, 41.3 percent

HOUSE DISTRICT 35
SPRING HILL AND BROOKSVILLE

COUNTIES: Hernando
RATING: Leans Republican

WHO GETS THE MERMAID VOTE?

Conjure up your best images of Florida's boom days after World War II, during the go-go early 1950s when families got in big cars with fins and those Airstream trailers and spent some of America's new wealth driving down U.S. 19 on their way to a Florida vacation. When you think about those images, where everything seemed to be pink and yellow in those first early color photographs, one of the places that's likely to come to mind is Weeki Wachee Springs, a Gulf coast attraction built in 1947 before Florida was full of attractions. The mermaid shows at Weeki Wachee are as kitschy "old Florida" as you can get, and they're the emblem of this part of the Gulf coast. But the park and the town of Weeki Wachee, population 4 people, 15 mermaids, doesn't tell you much about how the other 150,000 or so humans in these parts live day-to-day.

A New York Times Magazine piece from 2013 did accurately capture some of what can be seen in this area between Orlando and the Gulf coast, where the rural landscape starts to bleed into the suburbs of Tampa Bay. The piece mentioned roads lined with "pawn shops looking to buy guns and gold, and billboards with photographs of babies and reminders that 'my heart beat 18 days from conception.' Strip malls were broken up by new town-home complexes, old trailer parks and churches." [1] Much of what could be inferred by the mention of those coded references is that this is conservative, religious, gun-loving, rural America. And it is, at least in the eastern part of the district. District 35 includes the two main population centers of Hernando County, separated by a distinct cultural line.

The part of the district heavy on guns and churches is the eastern part, where you find Brooksville. This part of the district is Old South, with its town square, historic homes, and its Confederate statue.

In western Hernando County, many of the residents are old Yankees. What started as just another planned suburban place for retirees to settle on the outer reaches of the Tampa area grew and grew and grew, and now dwarfs

---

[1] Virginia Sole-Smith, "The Last Mermaid Show," *The New York Times Magazine*, 5 July, 2013.

Brooksville in size. Spring Hill, started in the 1960s as a planned community developed by the Deltona Corp. and the Mackle Brothers, now sprawls from U.S. 19 near the coast almost over to U.S. 41 in the east. Right in the middle is the Suncoast Parkway, which is part of what spurred the growth because it allows commuters to get to Tampa in under an hour. Spring Hill isn't incorporated, but the community has about 100,000 people, making it the dominant community in Hernando County.

On the southern border of the district, just outside of Spring Hill, is Masaryktown, which was founded by Czechs and named after the first president of Czechoslovakia. They initially were citrus farmers, an industry ended in this area by freezes, but the area between Masaryktown and Trilby is an egg farming area now.

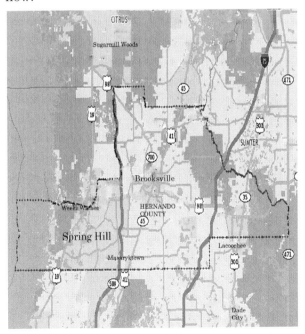

WHO LIVES HERE?

The Mackle Brothers marketed Spring Hill, as they had Deltona on the east coast, by offering low cost property to northerners tired of the winter. Their ads talked a lot about the weather, and featured pictures of people barbecuing. Spring Hill was marketed to active, younger retirees who wanted to still do things, as well as people who weren't yet retired but buying with plans to move down soon. "More than $28,000,000 has been recorded in Spring Hill home and homesite sales in less than 20 months, solid proof that knowledgeable people have put Spring Hill in their plans for today ... and tomorrow," said a 1969 magazine ad for the development. "But your future in Florida, whether scheduled for this year, or several years ahead, must begin right now. Florida is booming, its population exploding. An average of 672 new residents are being added every 24 hours. Spring Hill, just 45 miles north of Tampa and St. Petersburg, combines your investment in Florida with realistic dreams of easy, unhurried Florida living."[2] Spring Hill was also marketed heavily to firemen, police officers and military personnel, many of them likely to retire young.[3]

But as the Sunbelt states, and Florida, in particular, continued to grow, more younger families were finding their way out of the old cities and into the suburbs, and as new highways reached those places, those suburbs

---

[2] Magazine Ad for Mackle Brothers, 1969.

[3] Fiedler, 436.

became more accessible. There was a spike in young families moving to the Spring Hill area after the Suncoast Parkway was built in the early 2000s. With commuting a viable option, developments were built in the area with larger, more expensive homes for young families, rather than just retirees. Still, it's a retiree heavy district, with a median age of about 48, and more than a quarter of the people in the district over 65.

Incomes here are generally a little below the state average, but there are lots of very comfortable middle class people. The area is also getting more affluent. In Spring Hill, the median annual household income in 2000 was just under $33,000. Now, it's almost $42,000. That still puts it squarely in the middle class realm, and there aren't many major employment drivers in the area. Wal-Mart is the largest employer, followed by two area hospitals. Electronics manufacturer Sparton has a plant in Hernando County as well. The district is predominantly white, with the non-Hispanic, white voting age population at 84 percent.

POLITICAL ISSUES AND TRENDS

The mix creates a district that leans Republican, but only slightly. The eastern part of the district includes Old South Democrats who have been voting for Republicans for years based on shared cultural values. But the area where the bulk of the votes are is in the west county, and that's a mixed bag. There are blue collar retirees from the northeast, including old union members, many of whom have remained Democrats. There are also plenty of retirees from the Midwest (along with some from the northeast as well) who are Republicans, though more likely to be fiscal conservatives than the more rural-oriented, social conservatives in the eastern part of the county. That fiscal rather than social conservatism manifested itself in Hernando County's choice of Mitt Romney in the 2012 Republican presidential primary. Romney won the district in the 2012 general election, and Republicans Rick Scott and John McCain won here as well, but none by more than about 8 percentage points.

Rep. Rob Schenck, R-Spring Hill, has made his mark in the Legislature primarily in health care. In terms of long range impact, probably Schenck's biggest achievement was in 2011 as sponsor in the House of the legislation that shifted the Medicaid program to a managed care delivery system statewide. That same year he sponsored a bill that created a statewide drug database to fight prescription drug abuse. During the 2010 and 2011 sessions, Schenck was chairman of the Health and Human Services Committee, putting his stamp on many of the major pieces of health care legislation passed, and rejected, during that time. Schenck also, arguably, had an influence on the current makeup of the Legislature, as co-chairman of the redistricting subcommittee that drew the new House boundaries. Before the 2013 session, Schenck got new duties, giving up the Health Care chairmanship and taking over as Rules chairman, giving him considerable influence over the House's floor agenda. In that role it also fell to Schenck to sponsor a bill for Speaker Will Weatherford in 2013 making major changes to the state's campaign finance laws. He also served as chairman of the Select Committee on Gaming. Schenck is prevented by term limits from running for another term in 2014.

DISTRICT 35 STATS

Registration (Book closing, 2012),

Republicans 39.5 percent
Democrats 37 percent
NPA 19.5 percent

Voting Age Population (2010 Census): 125,778
White (Non-Hispanic) 84.2 percent
Hispanic 9.1 percent
Black 4.7 percent

Median Age: 47.5

Men: 47.6 percent
Women 52.4 percent

2012 PRESIDENT
Mitt Romney 53.5 percent, Barack Obama 45.3 percent (Estimated*)

2012 STATE HOUSE
Rep. Robert Schenck, R-Spring Hill, 55.5 percent, Rose Rocco, Democrat, 44.5 percent

2010 GOVERNOR
Rick Scott 50.8 percent, Alex Sink 43.3 percent

2008 PRESIDENT
John McCain 51 percent, Barack Obama 47.9 percent

HOUSE DISTRICT 36
COASTAL PASCO

COUNTIES: Pasco
RATING: Swing District

GULF COAST SWING DISTRICT

Heading north out of St. Petersburg on U.S. 19, the infamously bad traffic finally begins to thin out after Tarpon Springs, shortly after you cross the Anclote River and then a few blocks later cross into Pasco County. While you're a good 45 minutes out of St. Pete as you enter the town of Holiday, this is still part suburbia, but also a haven for mostly blue collar retirees looking for affordability. U.S. 19 is lined with the entrances to housing subdivisions with names like Country Estates, Siesta Terrace and Holiday Gardens. While not too far from the Gulf, this is not a country club community - the subdivisions are mostly full of small, older, low-cost houses and mobile homes, and the median household incomes in this area are in the

$30,000s, well below the state as a whole. Median home values here are also below average. This is classic Gulf coast Florida in a lot of ways. Turn down a side road and you'll get the old Florida kitsch at places with names like Tiki Village Mobile Home Park, but you'll also find newer condo communities, both archetypes of Florida retirement living.

The district continues north along U.S. 19 and the Gulf Coast, taking in all of New Port

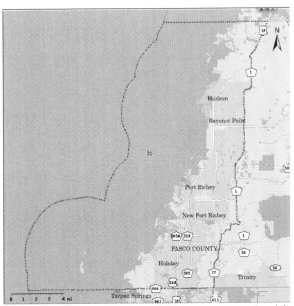

Richey and Port Richey. This area started with dreams of becoming a home to movie stars and film sets in the 1920s, but the idea crashed with the Depression and the area remained a sleepy outpost along the road to St. Petersburg for decades. Growth came in the 1960s and 1970s as the closer-in areas of the Tampa Bay region were built out. In the middle of the district is Jasmine Estates and in the north are Bayonet Point and the town of Hudson.

WHO LIVES HERE?

From Holiday in the south on the Pinellas County line to Hudson in the north this is an area of working class people and retirees with lower incomes. Nearly every Census tract in the district is below the state median in household income, and in many areas the household incomes are in the $20,000s, about half the statewide average. These neighborhoods are home to both blue collar workers and retired blue collar workers. "It's a little bit lower income than some of the other parts of the county," University of South Florida political science professor Susan MacManus told the News Service of Florida when describing the district before the 2013 special election to fill the seat. "Pasco's retirees are not like Sarasota's." [1]

While the district's median age is kept in the 40s by the presence of younger suburban families, about one in three people in District 36 is over the age of 60. You could probably guess that when driving through the area and looking at what's here, like the mobile home communities with perfectly manicured lawns or the five hearing aid stores on U.S. 19 between Holiday and Hudson. Much of the economy here is geared to serve an older population. The list of the 10 largest employers in New Port Richey includes three nursing homes. Among the others: North Bay Hospital, Gulfside Regional Hospice, Madison Pointe Rehab and Nursing Center. Also on the list: Cracker

---

[1] Brandon Larrabee, "Post-Fasano, Dems See Opportunity in Pasco Seat," The News Service of Florida, 13 August, 2013.

Barrel.

The district isn't very diverse racially - it's mostly white, about 85 percent overall, and 88 percent of the voting age population. In the last couple decades Hispanics have spread out from the central urban area around Tampa and into the suburbs. That demographic change has started to reach Pasco County, and House District 36 is nearly 10 percent Latino. There's a larger Hispanic population farther east in Pasco County, in District 38 around Dade City.

POLITICAL ISSUES AND TRENDS

Several demographic and historical trends have come together to make HD 36 an unpredictable swing district. First, the evidence: election results here have swung back and forth. In 2008, Barack Obama won here by almost 6.5 percentage points. Then in 2010, GOP gubernatorial candidate Rick Scott won narrowly amid a national and state GOP wave election. And in 2012, the district swung back, with Obama beating Mitt Romney by a little less than 6 percentage points. The registration is close - about 37 percent Democrat and just over 34 percent Republican. And in 2013, when former Rep. Mike Fasano left the Legislature to become Pasco County's tax collector, the special election to replace him couldn't have been much closer. Democrat Amanda Murphy beat Republican Bill Gunter by just over 300 votes out of about 19,000 cast.

Many middle and lower income workers here, some members of unions, appear to identify with the Democratic Party, as do some working class retirees. But like they have in much of the country, many white working class retirees, particularly from the Midwest and Rust Belt, have come in the last decade to identify culturally more with the Republican Party. Those who have made that shift, and those who haven't, are both here - and are at the heart of the battle for this district. That's where the district's previous House member comes in.

Fasano, the populist Republican who held the seat before Murphy, appealed to both Democrats and Republicans. He was socially conservative - a staunch anti-abortion Catholic, who nearly always ends a conversation with "God bless," and was a hawk on things like government waste. But he appealed to Democrats by looking out for the little guy - and often angered the corporate wing of the GOP. He nearly single-handedly blocked a Republican-led effort to privatize prisons and he was long a harsh critic of insurance companies and utilities. His willingness to stand up to GOP leadership was appreciated by many Democrats, who voted for Fasano. In fact, the Democrats didn't even run a candidate against him when he first sought the District 36 seat after being term limited out of the Senate, despite the fact that Democrats held the registration advantage and Obama had won here in 2008. Older voters loved Fasano - he often took up causes siding with the elderly against companies or government policies. During his eight years representing this area in the Senate, and before that, another long tenure in the House, Fasano was fond of saying his job was to look out for the "seniors and savers" that were his constituents. Fasano stepped down in 2013 when Scott appointed him to replace the Pasco County tax collector, who died. Putting an exclamation point on his maverick, bipartisan reputation, Fasano ended up endorsing the Democrat, Murphy, in the race to replace him.

Murphy, a Raymond James vice president, defeated Gunter in the 2013 special election to replace Fasano, 50.9 percent to 49.2 percent. In addition to doing well among independents, Murphy may have gotten some crossover votes from moderate Republicans - some of the aforementioned northerners who are former Democrats. The daughter of a commercial fisherman, Murphy grew up in Pasco County, and was active in the community before running for office. During her campaign, she said improving education and working to expand Medicaid to cover more people under the Affordable Care Act would be priorities. As most politicians 'must along this part of the Gulf coast, Murphy also pledged to try to keep property insurance rates low. Coastal Pasco has some of the highest sinkhole coverage premiums in the state.

Murphy signed on to co-sponsor legislation to repeal a law that lets power companies charge customers for new power plants before they're built, taking up where Fasano left off on an issue that's highly controversial in this area. The first bill Murphy filed as primary sponsor would provide for a medical alert logo on the driver's license of someone with a medical condition. She also quickly signed on as a co-sponsor of legislation to prohibit workplace discrimination based on sexual orientation.

DISTRICT 36 STATS

Registration (Book closing, 2012),
Democrats 37.3 percent
Republicans 34.4 percent
NPA 21.5 percent

Voting Age Population (2010 Census): 125,696
White (Non-Hispanic) 87.5 percent
Hispanic 7.8 percent
Black 2.2 percent

Median Age: 46.4

Men: 48.2 percent
Women 51.8 percent

2012 PRESIDENT
Barack Obama 51.2 percent, Mitt Romney 46
percent (Estimated)*

2012 STATE HOUSE
Rep. Mike Fasano, R-New Port Richey, faced
only write-in opposition. Fasano resigned in
2013 when he was appointed Pasco County tax
collector.

Special election to replace Fasano, 2013
Democrat Amanda Murphy 50.9 percent,
Republican Bill Gunter 49.2 percent

2010 GOVERNOR
Rick Scott 47.5 percent, Alex Sink 45.7
4percent

2008 PRESIDENT
Barack Obama 52.4 percent, John McCain, 45.9
percent

HOUSE DISTRICT 37
CENTRAL PASCO

COUNTIES: Pasco
RATING: Solid Republican

COMMUTER DISTRICT, VOTES
REPUBLICAN

House District 37 covers the middle part of Pasco County, sandwiched in between two other Pasco County districts to the east and west, and running the full height of the county from its northern border to its southern border. The main population center is the Tampa suburb of Land O'Lakes, but the district also includes Shady Hills in the north and Trinity and Odessa in the south. The district is relatively affluent and, at least in the south, serves mainly as a bedroom community for people who work in Tampa. In fact, about a third of the population of Land O'Lakes leaves the county each day to go to work. The county as a whole sees more than 60,000 of its residents leave every day to go to their job, according to the Census, making it the biggest daily exporter of workers in the state. Thanks to the Suncoast Parkway running through the middle of the district, the commute isn't too bad, though according to the Census more than 20 percent of people in Land O'Lakes commute at least 40 minutes each way and the mean travel time is over a half an hour.

This part of Pasco County has seen rapid growth over the last couple of decades. The district's total population at the 2010 Census was just under 155,000, a pretty big increase over the 94,000 who lived here when the 2000 Census was taken. Land O'Lakes and Pasco County officials are trying to turn the area into more of a workplace, rather than just a bedroom community, encouraging the construction of office space and the moving of white collar jobs from the city out to this

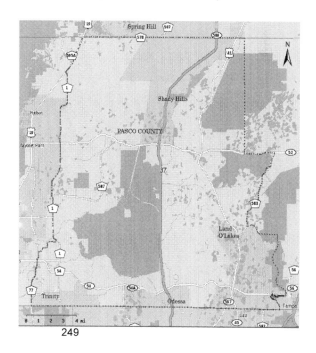

suburban area.

WHO LIVES HERE?

Middle to upper income suburban families live in this swath of Pasco County. Most are likely to own their home and traipse off to Tampa every day for an office job that pays fairly well. About a third of the households here have children under 18 at home, median household incomes are mostly in the $60,000s and $70,000s, well above the state average, and about a third of the residents of this area have at least a bachelor's degree.

The district is 83 percent non-Hispanic white, just under 9 percent Hispanic - with Puerto Ricans being the largest Latino group - and 3 percent black. The Hispanic population, while still small, has grown considerably during the last decade. When the 2000 Census was taken, this same area was 93 percent non-Hispanic white instead of 83 percent, and 4 percent Hispanic.

The district is average in terms of age, with a median of 42.7 and more than half the population in the prime working age range of 25 to 65. With less than 10 percent of the population over 70, the district stands in stark contrast to its neighbor to the west, the coastal Pasco retiree area that makes up District 36.

POLITICAL ISSUES AND TRENDS

Republicans John McCain in the 2008 presidential race and Rick Scott in the 2010 governor's race both got about 53 percent of the vote in this district while Mitt Romney did better with 56 percent in 2012. Republicans outnumber Democrats 42 percent to 32 percent.

The district is, for now, comfortably in Republican hands. If growth in the Hispanic community doubles its size again and the white population doesn't grow as much, it's possible that by 2020 nearly 1 in 5 voters could be Latino, and Democrats could likely close some of the registration and performance gap.

Rep. Richard Corcoran, Republican of Land O'Lakes, represents the area in a state House in which he's been a major behind-the-scenes player, and is expected to become speaker. Corcoran has worked as an advisor to former House speakers Daniel Webster and Tom Feeney, and was chief of staff to Speaker Marco Rubio, so he knows as well as anyone how the House works. After working for Rubio, Corcoran, an attorney, was elected to the House in 2010. When many freshmen lawmakers were trying to learn their way around the Capitol, Corcoran already knew the process well, knew how the budget works, knew the history of the place and many people who work in it.

Corcoran served in 2013 as chairman of two very high profile committees, the Health and Human Services Committee and the Select Committee on the federal health care law. And he has the pledged support of enough House members that he is expected to be named in 2016 to be the speaker of the House starting in the 2017 session.

Corcoran came into office saying he'd hoped to work on property taxes. Before he was elected to the Legislature, Corcoran served on the Taxation and Budget Reform Commission that looked at ideas for changing Florida's tax structure. While he has so far failed to make much headway, if he becomes speaker look for property tax reform to return to the forefront of the House's agenda.

Corcoran also was a major backer of the switch to paying teachers based on merit rather than tenure. He also has been notable as a vocal critic of red light cameras, and a leader of the effort to repeal a law allowing cities to use them to catch light runners. Corcoran told Florida Trend Magazine that the thing he's most passionate about, however, is "systemic, cultural change," around how the Legislature is run. "And the biggest change that I think we all agree on is that the special interests have too much influence," Corcoran told the magazine.[1] Assuming Corcoran holds on to his seat and Republicans hold on to power, he will be the second Pasco County speaker in this decade. Will Weatherford is from eastern Pasco.

DISTRICT 37 STATS

Registration (Book closing, 2012),
Republicans 42.2 percent
Democrats 31.6 percent
NPA 21 percent

Voting Age Population (2010 Census): 120,471
White (Non-Hispanic) 85.2 percent

---

[1] Amy Keller, "Legislative Rookies: Promising New Florida House Members," *Florida Trend*. 15 May, 2012.

Hispanic 8.8 percent
Black 2.9 percent

Median Age: 42.7

Men: 49.1 percent
Women 50.9 percent

2012 PRESIDENT
Mitt Romney 56 percent, Barack Obama 42
percent (Estimated*)

2012 STATE HOUSE
Republican Primary: Rep. Richard Corcoran, R-
Trinity, 83.3 percent, Strother Hammond, 16.7
percent. Corcoran faced no general election
opposition.

2010 GOVERNOR
Rick Scott 53.4 percent, Alex Sink 41.6 percent

2008 PRESIDENT
John McCain 53.7 percent, Barack Obama 45
percent

HOUSE DISTRICT 38
EASTERN PASCO

COUNTIES: Pasco

RATING: Leans Republican

THE AMERICAN DREAM - REACHED BY SOME, SOUGHT BY OTHERS

Eastern Pasco County holds two images of the American Dream. In the area closest to Tampa is the affluent suburb of Wesley Chapel, where it would seem many are living the dream already. They're making $70,000-some-odd and living in showcase homes on cul de sacs backing up to one of the fairways at the Saddlebrook Resort or in relatively new developments with names like Preserve at Quail Woods or Meadow Pointe.

Closer to the north end of the district - though just one exit away on Interstate 75 - is a poverty-plagued place where migrant farm workers have come with faint hope that one day they, or at least maybe their children, might see their own American dream come true - though at the moment most in this community are a long, long away from the beautiful homes of Wesley Chapel. In the Tommytown area of Dade City, there are thought to be perhaps 15,000 migrant farm workers, most Mexican or Central American and dirt poor. The area in some ways isn't much better off than their homelands, and farm worker advocate Margarita Romo, who has worked for decades to better the lives of migrants here, once called Tommytown a "third world country." Much of this population doesn't play into Florida's politics - many of these workers don't have permanent Florida residence, and some are in the county illegally, so most can't vote. But even if it doesn't have much impact on the vote, their presence in eastern Pasco affects the the area, from its schools to its tax base to its real estate market.

In between, both in metaphorical and geographical terms is eastern Pasco's other population center of Zephyrhills. Joke all you want about Florida being just a big retirement home for old Yankees, but Zephyrhills really was that. It started out in the early 20th Century as a retirement village for Union Civil War veterans. The town was mostly a retirement and farming village for years. But after a local man started bottling water from Pasco County's Crystal Springs in the 1960s, the word Zephyrhills would come to be known to many as a brand of bottled water. It's now owned by Swiss giant Nestlé.

Growth has been the defining characteristic of this region, particularly in Wesley Chapel, which sits near the Pasco-Hillsborough county line, within easy commuting distance of Tampa. The now sprawling upscale bedroom community has ballooned in size since 2000.

WHO LIVES HERE?

The socio-economic bookends in the district are stark. Incomes are relatively comfortable, mostly above $65,000, in the west and southwest, including Wesley Chapel, and north of there in the San Antonio community. But on

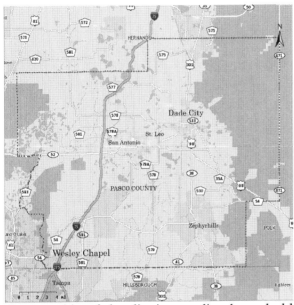

the east side of the district, median household incomes drop by 50 percent or more, with half of households in Dade City bringing in less than $32,000 a year. In Zephyrhills, incomes are mixed, ranging from the $20,000s to the $50,000s. The voting age population is about 73 percent white, 13 percent Hispanic and 7 percent black.

Pasco County was the fastest growing county in the 2000s, and nearly one in three new residents is Hispanic. A county where the

Hispanic population was once mainly the Mexican farm workers in the Dade City area has seen its Latino population broaden, particularly with an increase in Puerto Rican residents. In 2010, a Hispanic Chamber of Commerce was started in Pasco County. Many of these new Hispanic residents are more affluent, and are living in nice, ranch style homes just like the non-Hispanic residents who have moved here in such large numbers.

This is a relatively young district, with half of people here under 42. People in their 30s make up about 12 percent of the population, though more than a quarter are over age 60.

POLITICAL ISSUES AND TRENDS

Like much of Florida, this was almost exclusively Democratic territory fairly recently. A 1954 St. Petersburg Times article recorded the beginning of the change, noting the creation of the East Pasco Republican Club and the beginning of "a serious campaign to create a two-party system of government for Pasco County." It noted that going into the 1954 election there were over a thousand Republicans in Pasco. In 1952 there had been fewer than 500 with over 11,000 Democrats. "Of the county's 27 precincts, only one did not reveal any Republican registration," the article said. "Precinct I, located in the northeast corner of the county, has a registration of 42 Democrats, but no Republicans." [1]

[1] P.D. Loucks, "Pasco County Registration Shows Republican Gains," *St. Petersburg Times*, 18 April, 1954.

Things have changed. Republicans now outnumber Democrats in the county as a whole and in District 38. The early 1990s, when growth in young families in the southern part of the county took off at the same time as a general Florida swing to the GOP, was when Republican registration started getting close. As recently as 1984 Democrats still had a 20,000 voter advantage in Pasco County, but the numbers got closer and closer to even, and in 1998 each party had about 88,000 voters in the county. Republican registration surpassed Democratic registration in 1999 and has been higher ever since. The GOP currently counts about 40 percent of voters in District 38 to 36 percent for Democrats, and 20 percent in neither party. Mitt Romney won here in 2012, Rick Scott in 2010 and John McCain in 2008, though only Scott won by more than 10 percentage points. The district's representative, Republican Will Weatherford, was in line to become speaker in 2012, and was unchallenged.

Weatherford, young, articulate and well-connected, was a rising star in the Legislature as soon as he got elected, being a protégé (and son-in-law) of the popular former House Speaker Allan Bense. Bense had noticed Weatherford, a teammate of Bense's son on the football team at Jacksonville University. "Within a minute after meeting him, I said to myself, 'This guy has got potential,'" Bense recalled in an Associated Press story. [2] Weatherford went to work as Bense's aide, and

[2] Brent Kallestad, "Politics in ... Weatherford's Blood," *The Associated Press*, 26 February, 2013.

eventually married Bense's daughter.

Weatherford came from a political family - his grandmother was a prominent Democrat in Arizona, where she ran for governor in 1986 - and he rose quickly in the House, a trajectory to leadership accelerated by term limits. Weatherford turned 33 just before taking over as speaker in 2012. During his first six years in the Legislature, Weatherford became known in part for an interest in education policy. Weatherford, who was home-schooled, is a backer of school choice, and also had as a pet issue pushing for exploration of a future new state university that would be online only. While backing traditional Republican causes of lower taxes and regulation, Weatherford has also been keenly interested in cleaning up the political process. In addition to poverty, illiteracy and burdensome regulations, Weatherford cited "broken government" as a chief concern when he took over as speaker before the 2013 session. In his first push to fix those kinds of broken systems, Weatherford championed as speaker an overhaul of the campaign finance system and lawmakers obliged. Among the chief aim of the legislation was increasing transparency in political spending. He also pushed to passage, with Senate President Don Gaetz, a major measure seeking to eliminate some of the overt ethics problems that plagued the Legislature in recent years. Weatherford was also faced immediately on taking the speaker's chair with an election problem. Florida was criticized again in 2012, as it had been for more than a decade, for a cumbersome elections process, and

Weatherford acknowledged that the process needed fixing. He oversaw passage of a bill that restored some additional early voting days as part of the fix, a bipartisan move that drew praise from Democrats. Weatherford is term-limited after the 2014 session, but has often been mentioned as a strong candidate for further political service, including frequent suggestions of a future run for governor or U.S. Senate.

DISTRICT 38 STATS
Registration (Book closing, 2012),
Republicans 39.8 percent
Democrats 35.8 percent
NPA 20.4 percent

Voting Age Population (2010 Census): 119,957
White (Non-Hispanic) 76.5 percent
Hispanic 13.1 percent
Black 6.8 percent

Median Age: 41.9

Men: 48.6 percent
Women 51.4 percent

2012 PRESIDENT
Mitt Romney 53.5 percent, Barack Obama 44.4 percent (Estimated*)

2012 STATE HOUSE
No race. Speaker Will Weatherford, R-Wesley Chapel, faced no primary or general opposition.

2010 GOVERNOR
Rick Scott 53.2 percent, Alex Sink 42.3 percent

2008 PRESIDENT
John McCain 53.4 percent, Barack Obama 45.3 percent

HOUSE DISTRICT 39
LAKELAND, NORTHERN POLK, CELEBRATION

COUNTIES: Polk, Osceola

RATING: Solid Republican

SOLID GOP LINK ON I-4 CHAIN

House District 39 is mostly in central and northern Polk County, including Auburndale, Polk City and some neighborhoods north and east of Lakeland, but not most of Lakeland itself. In the far northeast corner of the district, it juts into Osceola County and picks up the Disney town of Celebration, and the area around the southern-most part of the Disney World complex of resorts. This district along the politically crucial Interstate 4 corridor is, in part, defined by that interstate.

Much of Polk County's recent growth is due to its geographic position between Tampa and Orlando. This district just bumps against the suburbs of both, with the northeastern corner of the district hugging the Orange County line and including Celebration, which most think of as part of the Orlando area, and the district's western edge a few minutes from Zephyrhills, a Tampa suburb.

Much of the population in the district lives in what would be considered suburbia, in neighborhoods near Lakeland or Orlando with big box stores and strip malls, though interspersed with areas that remain more rural

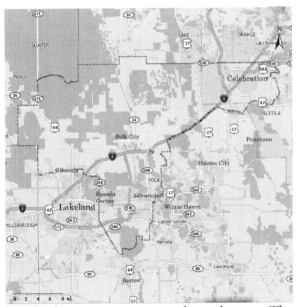

in both appearance and culture. The neighborhoods on the eastern edge of Lakeland, including Combee, Fussels Corner and K-ville, are working-class suburbs that melt into Auburndale, and going southeast toward Winter Haven, in neighboring District 41. Many here commute to work in Lakeland or Winter Haven. K-ville, incidentally, is short for Kossuthville, which was settled in the mid-1920s by families from Hungary, some of whose descendants still live in the area.

At the northeast corner of the district, just inside Osceola County, is a town that builders hoped would remind people of a quainter time, the idealized mid-20th Century town where everyone is friendly and the kids all happy. The town, Celebration, built by Disney in 1994, has white picket fences, and to paraphrase one economist, the people who bought homes here thought, or at least hoped, it had been sprinkled with Pixie Dust. It was part of the New Urbanism movement that sought to restore "old fashioned, small-town" values to communities. The town of about 7,500 people, many of them wealthy retirees, but also some younger families, has a median household income above $90,000 and a median family income above $110,000, both about double the state median.

WHO LIVES HERE?

While "suburban" in the sense that most of the district is outside of, but close to, cities of some size, many parts of the district have more of a rural feel, rather than sprawling suburbs. And the area is generally home to working people of typically modest means. The exception is Celebration, where homebuyers pay a premium for the ambience and the proximity to Walt Disney World, and where the median home value got to a quarter million dollars before the recent crash. But overall, this is a mostly blue collar district, and construction has been one of the biggest employers in the area. So when the bottom fell out of Florida's housing boom in the late 2000s, this area was among many in Florida hit hard by the crisis. The poverty rate in the Polk County suburbs jumped near the end of the decade and areas from Lakeland to Auburndale were full of homes in foreclosure. The Lakeland metro area was one of eight in Florida on the top 10 list for foreclosures in the whole country in March of 2013, and nearly one in three residents of Auburndale lived below the poverty line in 2009. Even Celebration was hit hard by the crisis. In part because the homes were well above average in cost, the foreclosure rate in the storybook town was about double the statewide rate at its worst. [1]

The construction industry remains one of the largest employers in the area, even after the recession, though there are also large numbers of people who work in the hospitality service industry, as would be expected, in the corner of the district near Orlando and Disney. Median incomes in the district are mostly either around the state median, or below it, running from a low median household income of around $25,000 annually - about half the state median - in the Combee area just east of Lakeland to median household incomes in the mid-$40,000s in many other areas, right around the state median. The exception is the aforementioned wealth in Celebration, where many families make well over $100,000 a year. The district's population is largely white - about 76 percent of the total and 73 percent of those of voting age, and about 14 percent Hispanic and 7 percent African-American. Most of the Hispanics are of

[1] Kathleen M. Howley. "Pixie Dust Loses Magic as Foreclosures Slam Utopian Disney Town." Bloomberg News. 13 December, 2010.

Puerto Rican descent, as in the rest of Polk and Osceola counties.

POLITICAL ISSUES AND TRENDS

The Democratic Party was entrenched in Polk County for decades until the great shift of white southerners to the GOP in the 1980s - symbolized here by the area's Congressman, Andy Ireland, who like so many others in this part of the world, also changed his registration from Democrat to Republican. Since then, it has voted solidly for Republicans for president, governor, Congress (Charles Canady for years and then Dennis Ross) and elected GOP candidates locally. Gov. Rick Scott won here by 17 points, and Mitt Romney by about 15. State Rep. Neil Combee won the seat in 2012 by 30 points. There's not much demographic reason to suspect broad movement away from the GOP in the near future, though like everywhere else, the Hispanic population is expected to grow faster than the white population, and that could give Democrats some inroads, though it doesn't appear it would be enough to make the district competitive anytime soon. In 2012, Romney made strong showings in precincts north of Lakeland and between Lakeland and Polk City straddling Interstate 4, including areas along Commonwealth Ave. and near the new Florida Polytechnic University. Romney also won Celebration, and crushed Obama in precincts in the northern end of Auburndale, north of Old Lake Alfred Rd. in the neighborhoods around Lake Ariana and Lake Arietta. Obama ran strongest in the Osceola County parts of the district, particularly in the neighborhoods near Disney, like Osceola

Precinct 101 right along the Orange County line and Precinct 104, a heavily Democratic area right across Poinciana Blvd. from Kissimmee. Obama didn't beat Romney by a lot anywhere in the Polk County part of the district, managing to squeak out wins in just a few precincts, such as in the southern neighborhoods of Auburndale, south of U.S. 92.

The district is home to the new Florida Polytechnic University, which former state Sen. JD Alexander of Lake Wales pushed into existence in 2012, replacing the old University of South Florida-Lakeland.

Combee, R-Polk City, who was a longtime Polk County commissioner before his election to the House, is a rock-solid conservative who went to Tallahassee intending to reduce government regulations, fight tax increases and protect gun rights. He's mostly done that. He's been solidly pro gun, filing legislation for the 2014 session that specifies that firing a warning shot doesn't put someone in danger of a minimum mandatory sentence, which he also filed in 2013 only to see it die between the House and Senate. Combee generally voted with the Republican caucus, including for the 2013 campaign finance overhaul to raise individual contribution limits, supporting legislation to give parents more say in turning failing schools into charter schools (which failed), and the measure outlawing Internet cafes. Combee, who is in agribusiness and real estate, was elected in 2012, after a bizarre failure to qualify for a House run in 2010. That year, Combee had planned to challenge Rep.

Kelli Stargel, R-Lakeland, in the primary, but when he filed his qualifying paperwork, he paid a fee that was one penny short. His check was for $1,781.81, but the qualifying fee was $1,781.82. The Division of Elections didn't contact him to tell him about the shortfall in time, and Combee was disqualified.

DISTRICT 39 STATS

Registration (Book closing, 2012)
Republicans 38.1 percent
Democrats 35.7 percent
NPA 22.6 percent

Voting Age Population (2010 Census) 119,224

White (Non-Hispanic)   76.7 percent
Hispanic 13.1 percent
Black 7.3 percent

Median Age: 40.5

Men 49.8 percent
Women 50.2 percent

2012 PRESIDENT
Mitt Romney 57.1 percent, Barack Obama 41.3 percent (Estimated)*

2012 STATE HOUSE
Neil Combee, Republican, 64.8 percent, Carol Castognero, NPA, 35.2 percent

2010 GOVERNOR
Rick Scott 56 percent, Alex Sink 39.1 percent

2008 PRESIDENT
Barack Obama 69.7 percent, John McCain 29.6 percent

HOUSE DISTRICT 40
LAKELAND

COUNTIES: Polk
RATING: Leans Republican

I-4 IN FLUX

Since its settlement in the 1870s and a big growth boom in the1920s, Lakeland has been a center for industries in the immediate surrounding area: citrus, cattle and phosphate mining. But unfortunately for boosters of Lakeland as a place with its own identity, its location halfway between two of Florida's megacities, Orlando and Tampa, is starting to redefine the city, and may be central to its future identity. The two giant neighboring cities have almost grown together, meeting in the middle at Lakeland.

The city remains far more than a bedroom community for commuters to the two bigger cities nearby - there's still phosphate mining nearby and the Mosaic company is a major employer in Polk County. Lakeland is also home to the Publix Supermarket Chain's headquarters. But many of the largest employers relate simply to serving people who live there, from hospitals, to the local school system and local government, to the retail outlets that serve a major residential area.

House District 40 includes the Greater Lakeland area, including the city itself, the

Gibsonia area north of town, the Winston area west of town, down to Lakeland Heights in the south and Highland City in the southeast, and east to take in part of Crystal Lake.

WHO LIVES HERE?

A growing Hispanic population has cut into the white majority in this district, though Latinos are still outnumbered by both blacks and whites. Still, the growth is what is most noticeable about the demographics of the area.

In 2000, Hispanics made up 7 percent of the population, by the 2010 Census they made up more than 11 percent. The district also has a significant black population of nearly 18 percent (about 15 percent of the voting age population). By decade of age, the largest group of people in the district are those in their 50s.

The inner city of Lakeland is poor, with median incomes in some Census tracts below $20,000 a year and most below $30,000 a year. The areas to the south, particularly outside the Polk Parkway corridor and in Lakeland Heights, have much higher median incomes, ranging from around $50,000 to into the $80,000s. The median age in the district is just over 38, slightly above the mark where districts become more likely to vote Republican.

POLITICAL ISSUES AND TRENDS

This district for now remains one that leans toward the GOP, having voted for Republicans Mitt Romney, John McCain, Rick Scott and for state House, Seth McKeel. But with blacks and Latinos together now making up more than 30 percent of the population, and more of the younger population, this district is ripe for a shift. A large percentage of the Republicans in Lakeland are senior citizens, giving further cause to believe the district may become friendlier to Democrats in the coming decade. It's something that's happening all over Polk County, though the huge Hispanic growth seen in the county as a whole isn't being seen as much in Lakeland itself. While Republicans have gotten elected here recently, the shift in registration has lagged with some here still registering as Democrats, as their "Old South" parents and grandparents did, but voting for Republicans.

McKeel, as chairman of the House Appropriations Committee, is the second most powerful member of the House after the speaker. McKeel came into the job at a lucky time, as he and subcommittee chairmen and members got to craft a House budget in 2013 that was the first in years to grow, following several years of recession that blasted holes in the budget. He was deputy majority leader in 2009 and 2010, as well as chairman of the State Affairs Committee. McKeel, who helps run a family real estate management company, is a former Lakeland city commissioner. He was elected to the commission at age 24 and served from 2000-2005, before getting into the race for the then-House District 63 when Dennis Ross ran for Congress in 2006. McKeel faced a Democrat, James Davis, who had the same name as the Democratic candidate for governor that year, Jim Davis. Nationally, Democrats did well in 2006, riding war fatigue and some high profile Republican scandals. The combination of a strong Democratic turnout and the possibility for confusion over the Davis name had McKeel worried, but he won easily with 60 percent of the vote. (Charlie Crist beat gubernatorial candidate Jim Davis that year.) "I'm the other guy who beat Jim Davis," McKeel told The Associated Press. [1] In 2010, McKeel sponsored legislation that re-created

---

[1] The Associated Press, "Davis 'two-time loser,'" 8 November, 2006.

fundraising committees that had been abolished in the past, authorizing legislative leaders to large amounts of money into individual legislative races through "affiliated political committees." The measure passed, but was vetoed by Gov. Charlie Crist.

DISTRICT 40 STATS

Registration (Book closing, 2012),

Democrats 39.9 percent
Republicans 38.5 percent
NPA 18.5 percent

Voting Age Population (2010 Census): 119,242
White (Non-Hispanic) 70.1 percent
Black 15.4 percent
Hispanic 11.4 percent

Median Age: 38.6

Men: 47.9 percent
Women 52.1 percent

2012 PRESIDENT
Mitt Romney 54 percent, Barack Obama 44 percent, (Estimated*)

2012 STATE HOUSE
Rep. Seth McKeel, R-Lakeland, 64 percent, Lillian Lima, NPA, 36 percent

2010 GOVERNOR
Rick Scott 53.2 percent, Alex Sink 42.3 percent

2008 PRESIDENT
John McCain 52.4 percent, Barack Obama 46.4 percent

HOUSE DISTRICT 41
CENTRAL, EASTERN POLK
COUNTY

COUNTIES: Polk

RATING: Swing District

HISPANIC GROWTH MAKES AREA
MORE COMPETITIVE

During the run up to the 2012 election, political analysts and demographers warned that some areas were notably different than just a few years ago and it would mean changes in the electoral landscape. The big change: huge increases over the last decade in the number of Hispanic voters. There are several representations of the phenomenon in Florida, including in Lake and Osceola counties on either side of Orlando. The Hispanic population in the state as a whole grew 57 percent during the last decade, compared to 18 percent growth overall. But in few places does the change seem more likely to have a major impact on future elections than in Polk County.

The huge, land-locked county between Tampa and Orlando, long known as home to vast expanses of citrus groves, saw its Hispanic population more than double over the last decade, and the percentage of Hispanics also nearly double, now making up just under 18 percent of the county's population. As Polk County has been one of the epicenters of the state's Hispanic growth, House District 41 in central, eastern and northeastern Polk County, is a major thrust of the county's new influx of Latinos. The district's population is now just a bit under 20 percent Hispanic, up from just over 12 percent in the same areas in the 2000 Census. And notably, Democrats now outnumber Republicans in House District 41 by about 4,000 voters, or 5 percentage points. With Hispanic growth here expected to continue, Democrats have a chance in this slightly Republican-performing district.

WHO LIVES HERE?

While Polk County has long had a noticeable population of Hispanic farm workers, mostly from Mexico, much of the growth in the last decade in Polk County has been due to Puerto Ricans moving to the area - many from neighboring parts of Central Florida, and many of them educated professionals. And most significantly for political observers, because they're more educated - and because Puerto Ricans are U.S. citizens - they are more likely to vote than some other Latino groups. And though they tend to vote Democratic, they're not a lock for either party. Because some of them are moving from the Orlando area - and there's a large Puerto Rican community already very well established in neighboring Osceola County to the east - many of the arrivals are living in the eastern part of the county, including in the areas making up House District 41. Haines City's population is now 40 percent Hispanic, and may reach half in the coming decade. The small town of Davenport, also in

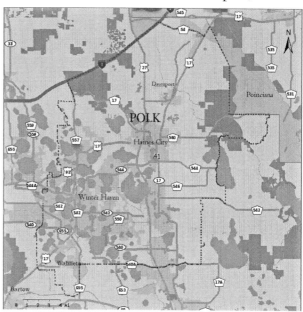

the district, is already more than 40 percent Hispanic. When drawing the new political boundaries in 2012, lawmakers split the only community in Polk County that is majority Hispanic. The unincorporated hamlet of Wahneta, south of Winter Haven, is more than 60 percent Hispanic. The new House map puts a little over half of Wahneta's homes in District 41 and the others in House District 56 to the southwest. Most of Wahneta's residents are farm workers originally from Mexico.

The heavy Hispanic presence in the eastern part of the district is balanced by the western part being mostly white. Winter Haven, in the southwest corner of the district is just 12 percent Hispanic, 56 percent white, and 29 percent black. Lake Alfred, on the west side of the district is also heavily white. Incomes in the district vary quite a bit, from in the mid-$30-thousands, well below the state average, in Haines City, to right around the state median in Winter Haven.

POLITICAL ISSUES AND TRENDS

Polk County for many years, like most of the South, produced and helped elect conservative Democrats. Florida political legends Spessard Holland and Lawton Chiles, both Democrats, were from Polk County - though farther west around Lakeland and Bartow respectively, and the Winter Haven area later gave the state Democrat Rick Dantzler, who served in the Senate and was Buddy MacKay's running mate in his unsuccessful 1998 gubernatorial bid.

But after the 1980s and 1990s shift of the South, especially rural and small-town white Southerners, to the GOP, Polk County mostly matched that trend, sending Republicans like Adam Putnam, JD Alexander and Marty Bowen to Tallahassee. Bowen, a citrus grower from Haines City, had represented much of the area now making up HD 41 from 2000 to 2008. But the part of the county now in District 41 has been seeing signs for a few years that Democrats could again get votes here. In 2008, when Bowen left because of term limits, Rep. John Wood, R-Winter Haven, was elected to then-House District 65 by fewer than 3,000 votes, a little over 3 percentage points, over Democrat Bob Hagenmaier. That same year, Republican presidential candidate John McCain won the precincts now in District 41 by a tally of 49.7 percent to 49.2 percent, - almost a tie vote.

Even though registration now favors Democrats in the district, in the last few years, Republicans have done a little better - Wood won easily in 2010 and Republican Rick Scott won the governor's race in the district that year by about 8 percentage points over Alex Sink. In 2012, Wood defeated Democrat Karen Cooper Welzel 51.5 percent to 48.5 percent, close but not like McCain's razor-thin win four years earlier. Mitt Romney also got around 53 percent of the vote here in 2012, and Obama dropped off in support in 2012 from his first run. But with Democrats targeting Hispanics in registration drives and policy, the truly astonishing figure for political watchers to consider is the University of Florida's Bureau of Business and Economic Research's projection for Hispanic growth in Polk County. From the 2011 figure of just under 110,000, the county's Latino population is expected to be well over 150,000 by 2020, and to have more than doubled to about 240,000 by 2035.

Wood, elected narrowly in 2008 when Rep. Marty Bowen was term-limited from being re-elected to then-House District 65, has made insurance one of his main issues in Tallahassee, even though he doesn't serve on the Insurance Committee. Wood, who has one of Florida's largest private insurance companies, State Farm Florida, in his district in Winter Haven, has particularly been a vocal advocate for shrinking the state-backed Citizens Property Insurance Company as it has grown to be Florida's largest property insurer. He sponsored the 2013 House version of a Citizens Property Insurance overhaul that included creation of a clearinghouse to help private companies take out policies and an effort to raise Citizens rates to levels more comparable to the private market.

Wood, who earned a degree in economics from Columbia University, is a staunch fiscal conservative, and even rejected for himself the Legislature's health and life insurance benefits, which he says saves taxpayers $10,000 a year. He got the highest grade possible from the Florida Chamber, voting with the chamber on every bill the group tracks. He is a reliable Republican vote on business and economic matters, such as supporting legislation to make changes to state pensions and efforts to cut taxes, and on gun rights. Wood also typically sides with insurance companies on cost issues, opposing coverage mandates, for example. He also has supported efforts to require drug testing of convicted drug felons before they can receive state benefits, and limits on where food stamp benefits could be used. Wood has also opposed all claims bills in the House, saying the way lawmakers decide to compensate some people for injuries and not others is unfair to those who don't have the ability to navigate the legislative process. The Polk County native is a real estate attorney and home builder.

DISTRICT 41 STATS

Registration (Book closing, 2012)
Democrats 41.1 percent
Republicans 36 percent
NPA 19.8 percent

Voting Age Population (2010 Census)
120,257
White (Non-Hispanic) 65.9 percent
Hispanic 16.6 percent
Black 15 percent

Median Age: 42.1

Men 48.5 percent
Women 51.5 percent

2012 PRESIDENT
Mitt Romney 52.9 percent, Barack Obama
45.5 percent, (Estimated*)

2012 STATE HOUSE
Rep. John Wood, R-Winter Haven, 51.5
percent, Karen Cooper Welzel, Democrat,
48.5 percent

2010 GOVERNOR
Rick Scott 51.5 percent, Alex Sink 43.5
percent

2008 PRESIDENT
John McCain 49.7 percent, Barack Obama
49.2 percent

HOUSE DISTRICT 42
SOUTHEAST POLK, EASTERN OSCEOLA

COUNTIES: Polk, Osceola

RATING: Swing District

A PUERTO RICAN, A COWBOY AND A RETIRED MAILMAN WALK INTO A BAR

Like District 41 next door, House District 42 has more Democrats than Republicans, barely, but some of them are old-South Democrats who vote GOP, and Republican candidates have been able to win here in recent years, though in very close races. With the large area south of Orlando having seen its Hispanic population - in particular its Puerto Rican population - grow immensely in the last decade and more, the whole region is getting more Democratic, as its original white, and mostly rural, conservative - and older - Republican population dwindles as a percentage. The most recent House district map packed most of those Hispanics into House District 43, a majority Hispanic district to the northwest of here that centers on Kissimmee and now appears to be a lock for Democrats. But even in doing so, significant numbers of Hispanics remained in a few neighboring districts, including HD 42, increasing the number of Democratic voters in those districts as well. This wasn't an overwhelmingly Republican area to begin with, thanks in part to northern retirees, and so with the surge in Puerto Rican voters, the district has become extremely competitive. Barack Obama and Mitt Romney basically tied here, and Obama won the district by less than a percentage point in 2008. Republicans have managed to just hold on to the district in the House, but Hispanic population growth is expected to outpace non-Hispanic growth in the coming decade, putting the district even more in play for Democrats.

The district covers all but the northwest corner of Osceola County, and includes St. Cloud - but most of the southern and eastern parts of the county are rural and lightly populated - with many areas home to more cattle than people. The county has the second most beef cows in Florida, just behind Okeechobee County. Osceola is also one of just eight Florida counties with more than 300,000 acres or more of farm or ranch land (Polk County next door, parts of which are also in HD 42, is one of the others.) St. Cloud and surrounding Osceola County are a mash-up of old and new, rural and urban Florida. The quaint, historic downtown is like so many others in the state, the usual mom-and-pop stores and small eateries giving it a classic small-town feel, along with the ranchers driving into town in their pickups, wearing cowboy hats and boots. Drive just a few minutes outside of town to the south or east and you're surrounded by hammock and marshes - and the many lakes that also bring fishermen and boaters to the area on the weekends. Yet the

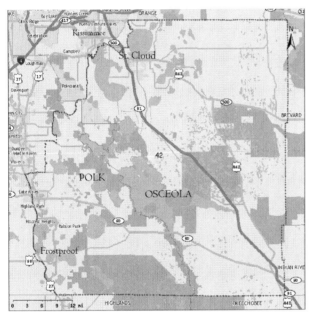

town sits right off of Florida's "Main Street," the Florida Turnpike, and within minutes residents here can be dodging tourists in Orlando, or they can just drive up U.S. 192 heading out of town, past miles of strip malls, motels and kitsch as it goes through Kissimmee on the way to Walt Disney World.

To the southwest of St. Cloud, the district crosses the county line to take in nearly the southeastern quadrant of Polk County. It picks up neighborhoods at the south end of Poinciana, which is partly in neighboring HD 43. The Polk County part of the district also includes the towns of Lake Wales and Frostproof.

WHO LIVES HERE?

Neither snow nor rain nor heat nor gloom of night will keep some residents of the area from playing shuffleboard. District 42 is home to hundreds of retired mail carriers and other federal workers, many from major northern cities like Kansas City, Cleveland, or New York. Nalcrest is an odd little development southeast of Lake Wales that is home almost entirely to retired postal service employees. Nalcrest comes from the acronym for the National Association of Letter Carriers, the union for city postal workers, which opened the retirement community in the early 1960s. One mile east is Lakeshore, which used to be called FedHaven, also established in the '60s as a retirement community for federal government employees.

These aren't the only retirement communities in the district - just two that are easy to pigeonhole demographically. Thousands of retirees live in southeastern Polk County, many in retirement communities like Saddlebag Lake and Towerwood, though some of them are non-voters because they're seasonal residents (the Saddlebag Lake homeowners association holds an annual picnic in Ontario, Canada, where many of its residents spend the summer.) In all, just under 28 percent of the district's population is 55 or over.

While 25 percent of the district's population is Hispanic, and many of those are Democratic voters, and another 10 percent are African-American, who also typically vote for Democrats, the district voting age population is more than 62 percent white. While the majority of those white voters are classic, small-town or rural, conservatives who vote Republican (even if some of the older ones remain registered Democrats) some percentage of white voters here do vote for Democrats. That's where Nalcrest and a number of other retirement communities come in - with many of those voters having been blue collar northerners in their younger days. This coalition of Democratic retirees and Puerto Ricans are what make the district so competitive.

Most of the Latino population in the district is in the St. Cloud area, which was about 19 percent Hispanic in the 2010 Census. Frostproof, in Polk County, is also heavily Hispanic, more than 30 percent, but the population of the town is tiny, only a bit over 3,000. Lake Wales, also in Polk County, is home to a significant portion of the district's African-American population. While only 10 percent of the entire district's voting age population, black residents make up almost 30 percent of the population in Lake Wales, about double the state percentage. The district is expected to get more Hispanic over the coming decade. While significantly larger, the white population of the district is older than the Latino population, and there is less net in-migration to the area by white people than by Hispanics.

While St. Cloud is relatively typical in terms of income - with annual household income in the high $40,000s, parts of the Polk County part of the district are poorer. The median household income in Lake Wales is only in the mid $30,000s, well below the state median of about $45,000.

POLITICAL ISSUES AND TRENDS

This mostly rural area for years was part of House and Senate districts that were represented by ranchers and farmers, men (almost all of them) like Irlo "Bud" Bronson Jr. of Kissimmee and his father, Irlo Bronson, Sr., The elder Bronson, though he was founder of the Florida Cattlemen's Association, and its president for years, played a major role in changing the character of the area when he sold the land that would become Walt Disney World for about $100 an acre. Until the late 20th Century, most, like both Bronsons, were conservative Democrats like those in most of the South. Bud Bronson, Jr., reflected the broader shift of rural conservative whites to the GOP when he switched to the Republican Party late in his legislative career after several cycles of very narrow wins as a Democrat. Starting in the 1990s, Republicans were elected to represent the area in the Legislature, including Bud Bronson's cousin, Charles Bronson, who grew up on the family ranch near St. Cloud. By the time he was elected to the Senate, he had moved to neighboring Brevard County, but his district included parts of Osceola County now in House District 42. From the Polk County part of the district came Republican JD Alexander of Frostproof, who came from a citrus farming and ranching family.

But the area never fully became a Republican stronghold. While Republicans won elections, and in some cases easily, registration remained in favor of Democrats, and when voters cast ballots for the first time in the newly drawn district in 2012, Republican Mike La Rosa eked out a 529 vote win over Democrat Eileen Game, and La Rosa lost the Polk County precincts by a couple thousand votes. That election, however, was likely an anomaly, because La Rosa was a latecomer to the contest, having to be recruited at the last minute to run for the seat after Rep. Mike Horner, R-Kissimmee, was caught up in a prostitution scandal and dropped out of the race. La Rosa ran a real estate company in Celebration, which isn't in the district, and Horner's name was on the ballot, not La Rosa's. Clearly Republicans can win here by wider margins: Republican Rick Scott beat Democrat Alex Sink in the precincts in House District 42 by 10 percentage points. But with the surge in Hispanics registering as Democrats, it doesn't take too many of the white voters to give Democrats a shot here, as evidenced by the fact that Barack Obama got about 49 percent of the vote in the district's precincts in both 2008 and 2012.

Real estate broker La Rosa was chosen by Republicans to replace Horner in the race for House District 42 about a month before the 2012 election when Horner unexpectedly dropped his re-election bid in the midst of a prostitution scandal. La Rosa had the handicap of having Horner's now scandal-plagued name on the ballot, which couldn't be changed so late in the election season. But La Rosa defeated Game of Frostproof 50.4 percent to 49.6 percent, keeping the seat in GOP hands.

La Rosa, the son of a Cuban immigrant, lived as a child in Miami but moved to Osceola County at age 15. Later, he his brother Joe started a successful real estate firm. His short campaign focused on economic recovery and bringing jobs to the state and after his election, which surprised many political watchers, La Rosa was appointed vice chairman of the Energy and Utilities Subcommittee. He managed to pass several bills in his first session, though none particularly controversial. Probably his most high profile legislation dealt with school emergencies, a bill that passed in the wake of the Newtown, Conn., school shooting. The law requires emergency response agencies to notify private schools of emergencies in some cases, sets out some policies for notifying school district personnel of emergencies, and provides for schools to have epinephrine pens on hand. Another successful bill softened regulations on mortgage brokers, and another required state agencies to report data on energy consumption and costs. He also successfully sponsored a bill related to condo or community associations, dealing with how records must be kept and putting in place some ethics rules for association officers. La Rosa got high rankings from the business community and voted with the Republican majority on high profile legislation.

DISTRICT 42 STATS

Registration (Book closing, 2012)
Democrats 39.9 percent
Republicans 34.4 percent
NPA 22.5 percent

Voting Age Population (2010 Census) 115,872
White (Non-Hispanic) 62.2 percent
Hispanic 24.8 percent
Black 10.1 percent

Median Age: 38.7

Men 49.5 percent
Women 50.5 percent

2012 PRESIDENT
Mitt Romney 50 percent, Barack Obama 49
percent, (Estimated*)

2012 STATE HOUSE
Mike La Rosa, Republican, 50.4 percent, Eileen
Game, Democrat, 49.6 percent

2010 GOVERNOR
Rick Scott 52.7 percent, Alex Sink 42.7 percent

2008 PRESIDENT
John McCain 49.7 percent, Barack Obama 49.1
percent

HOUSE DISTRICT 43
KISSIMMEE, POINCIANA

COUNTIES: Osceola
RATING: Solid Democrat

PUERTO RICO NORTH, DISNEY SOUTH

Who lives in District 43? Well, Snow White and Prince Charming for starters. Every day, they join Tinkerbelle and maybe a guy who drives Space Mountain or some other ride on a drive up Poinciana Blvd. to Kissimmee, take a left and head to their jobs at Disney World. When combined with all the people at on and off-site hotels, restaurants and other businesses reliant on tourists headed to the park, Disney has to be responsible for the majority of jobs in this region southwest of Orlando.

But this district, running from Poinciana in the southwest through Kissimmee and Buena Ventura Lakes to the northeast, has another major demographic: Puerto Ricans. When Tom Fiedler wrote a chapter on Osceola

County in his 2000 Almanac of Florida Politics, he titled it "Se Habla Disney World," and that would work just as well today - only more so. The huge influx of mostly Puerto Rican Hispanics had begun when Fiedler's book was written at the dawn of the millennium. From a political standpoint, however, it matured in the last decade. During the last election, the "Puerto Rican vote" in central Florida was written about more than the "retiree vote," or the "Jewish vote," and even rivaled the numerous stories about the "youth vote."

The two groups, Disney employees - called "cast members" at the park - and Puerto Ricans, overlap some. In fact, Disney is one of the reasons Puerto Ricans came here in the first place. Disney recruited them to work at Walt Disney World because the park needed Spanish speaking employees to accommodate a growing number of Spanish speaking visitors - and Puerto Ricans are already U.S. citizens. Osceola County Commissioner, and former state legislator, John Quinones is an example of that overlap - he moved to the area as a teen from Puerto Rico, and worked his way through college at Disney's Frontierland. Once the community was established, it became a natural destination for other Puerto Ricans moving to the mainland, and for New York Puerto Ricans to escape the cold. Buenaventura Lakes was marketed heavily on Spanish-language media in New York, and a sales office was opened in Puerto Rico. Radio stations here broadcast in Spanish, there are Puerto Rican restaurants, branches of Puerto Rican banks, even campuses of Puerto Rican colleges.

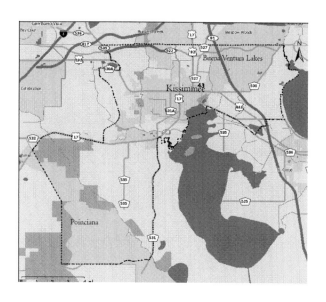

WHO LIVES HERE?

Disney cast members tend to be younger than average, and while some do make a career of it, for many it is a job to get through college, or a stepping stone to something else. Some of the jobs pay very well, but most of the front line park employees, the costumed cast members, the food service people and the ride operators for example, make not much more than minimum wage. The per capita income in Poinciana and Kissimmee are about the same – right around $17,600 a year, in Buenaventura Lakes it is a little lower. In addition to Disney employees, many residents of the area work in the hundreds of chain hotels and restaurants along Irlo Bronson Memorial Highway going right through the middle of Kissimmee, adding to the number of people getting by on relatively low service industry wages.

The Puerto Rican community is fairly diverse, however. While some of that community is lumped in with others who work in low-wage service industry jobs, others are more highly paid. The Puerto Ricans in the area, particularly the second-generation born in Florida, tend to be more educated than many other Latino immigrants, and in the 2000s, more than half of the Puerto Ricans in central Florida were in white collar jobs.

One of the reasons the Puerto Rican community in this part of Osceola County has gotten so much attention is the speed with which it has grown. In the 1970s, there were only a few hundred Puerto Rican people here, but during the 1990s, Florida passed New Jersey to become the state with the second largest Puerto Rican population, after New York, and Osceola County and neighboring Orange County (which includes Orlando) surpassed the Bronx in New York as the top two destinations for migrating Puerto Ricans. [1] And in the 2000s, the percentage of Puerto Ricans in Florida grew 75 percent - and they now account for more than 27 percent of the population of Osceola County.

The change in character in the area happened so fast, it's caught many non-Latinos off guard. That sentiment was captured by Tampa Bay Times political reporter Adam Smith in a story in 2012: "This used to be an old cow town, but it's completely changed today," said house painter J.R. Hatchett, a third-

---

[1] Jorge Duany, "Puerto Ricans in Orlando and Central Florida," University of Puerto Rico, Rio Pedras, (Online, 2006.
http://www.latinamericanstudies.org/puertorico/Puerto _Ricans_in_Orlando.pdf)

generation Osceola County resident and one of the few non-Hispanics living in and around the Buenaventura Lakes area sometimes dubbed Little Puerto Rico. "There are almost no good ol' boys left around here. Back in 1984, my high school had maybe 20 Spanish kids out of at least 1,500. Today the school has almost no white students." [2] For Osceola High School in Kissimmee, that wouldn't quite be the case, though by comparison with two decades ago, it may seem so. The school's student body was 64 percent Hispanic in 2013.

POLITICAL ISSUES AND TRENDS

At the beginning of the 2000s, Bronx-born Tony Suarez was the only Puerto-Rican-American in the Legislature, and though he would later leave the Democratic Party (and the Legislature), Suarez, as the only Democratic Hispanic in the Legislature was a harbinger of the party's rising fortunes in the "Disney suburbs" south of Orlando. In 2012, much was written about Puerto Ricans, and many non-Cuban Hispanics in general, being part of a swing demographic that both parties were trying to woo, but the evidence is that the majority have supported Democratic candidates. There are a number of Republicans in central Florida of Puerto Rican descent, including Quinones, now an Osceola County commissioner. But region-wide, Puerto Ricans voted for Barack Obama over Mitt Romney - the Bendixen and Amandi polling firm put

[2] Smith. "Growing Puerto Rican Population Near Disney Will Be Critical in Picking a President," *Tampa Bay Times*, 30 June, 2012.

Obama's support among Puerto Ricans statewide at 83 percent, almost as much as black voters.[3]

While the degree is new, Democrats have won among Puerto Ricans for more than a decade. The demographic gave Al Gore 60 percent of the presidential vote in 2000, and favored John Kerry by a 2-1 margin in the 2004 presidential race. More recently, voters here sent state Sen. Darren Soto, a Democrat who is half Puerto Rican, to Tallahassee. But in the months leading up to the 2012 election, the shift gained particular momentum with Democrats targeting Puerto Ricans hard. Democrat Ricardo Rangel got nearly 70 percent of the vote in the district in the 2012 House race, and President Obama even more - just under 74 percent of the vote in the district, so it seems the area is fairly comfortably in the Democratic column. Registration is as well - with Democrats claiming just under 50 percent of registered voters in 2012 to less than 20 percent for Republicans. Also, the Latino population in central Florida continues to grow, something that doesn't portend well for Republicans, as growth among whites in the area has stagnated. But Puerto Ricans will vote for GOP candidates, as is evidenced by the elections of local officials like Quinones - and in 2002, exit polling showed Puerto Ricans voted for Jeb Bush over Democrat Bill McBride in the governor's race. Notably, though, Bush spoke fluent Spanish, was

---

[3] Beth Reinhard. " Exit Polls Suggest Seismic Shift in Florida," *National Journal*, 9 November, 2012.

married to a Mexican woman, and frequently tried to appeal to Hispanic voters.

Ricardo Rangel, a native of the Bronx, N.Y., and a U.S. Army veteran, was elected to the House in 2012 in the newly drawn Hispanic majority district, and though most of those Hispanics in the district are from Puerto Rico, Rangel is the son of Ecuadorian immigrants. Before running himself, Rangel worked on campaigns, including working on Puerto Rican outreach for John Kerry's 2004 campaign. Before his election, Rangel also spent much of his time working with community organizations, including United We Paint, which rehabs homes in poor communities, and Big Brothers/Big Sisters.

In 2013 Rangel filed legislation seeking to lock in qualifying scores for Bright Futures scholarships in an effort to avoid a scheduled toughening of the standards, but his bill died in committee. He also filed legislation seeking to ban the use of solitary confinement on juveniles, another measure that failed to make it to the floor, and a bill that would have required annual mental health screenings for members of the National Guard before and after deployments, but that measure also failed to get a final vote. During his campaign, Rangel also said he wanted to increase funding for veterans' mental health, and boost Bright Futures spending, possibly with an Internet sales tax. [4]

---

[4] Further Reading: Meyerson, Harold. "Will Puerto Ricans Push Obama Over the Top," *The American Prospect*, 26 October 2012; Allen, Greg. "One Way Tickets to Florida: Puerto Ricans Escape Island Woes,"

DISTRICT 43 STATS

Registration (Book closing, 2012)
Democrats 49.3 percent
NPA 29.2 percent
Republicans 19.3 percent

Voting Age Population (2010 Census) 116,050
Hispanic 54.9 percent
White (Non-Hispanic) 28.6 percent
Black 12 percent

Median Age: 34.1

Men 48.9 percent
Women 51.1 percent

2012 PRESIDENT
Barack Obama 73.9 percent, Mitt Romney 25.3
percent (Estimated*)

2012 STATE HOUSE
Ricardo Rangel, Democrat, 67.7 percent, Art
Otero, Republican, 32.3 percent

2010 GOVERNOR
Alex Sink 62 percent, Rick Scott 34.5 percent

2008 PRESIDENT
Barack Obama 69.7 percent, John McCain 29.6
percent

National Public Radio, 5 February, 2013; "Puerto
Rico's 79th Municipality?: Identity, Hybridity and
Transnationalism Within the Puerto Rican Diaspora in
Orlando," Doctoral Dissertation in Geography by Luis
Sanchez, Florida State University, 2008.

HOUSE DISTRICT 44
DISNEY WORLD'S DISTRICT

COUNTIES: Orange
RATING: Swing District

THE HAPPIEST PLACE ON EARTH

Walt Disney died in 1966. So it was a bit strange and sort of futuristic, when in 1967 Disney appeared - on film - to testify before the Florida Legislature about his plans for a utopian residential development in Central Florida, a place called the Experimental Prototype Community of Tomorrow, or EPCOT, for short. It would be a "planned, controlled community," Disney said, and a way to showcase American industry and values. In this new world built out of the cattle pastures of central Florida, "there will be no slum areas because we won't let them develop," Disney said. Disney officials got the Legislature to give the company unfettered control over an area southwest of Orlando through the creation of the Reedy Creek Improvement District. But the utopian town never really developed as planned, and the company shifted its focus to creating massive theme parks where the happy world would exist only for visitors escaping their real world lives in real world towns.[1]

There indeed are no slums in Disney World, but while the arrival of "The Mouse" in Orlando did dramatically change the local economy, it proved insufficient for eliminating all social woes. There remains plenty of poverty in the Orlando area, but there's no question that the underpinning of the entire economic structure of central Florida, and some would say the social fabric as well, is tied to Disney and the region full of theme parks that followed the Magic Kingdom, as this area gave itself over to tourism as its central reason for being.

There are other industries. Orlando has successfully tied itself to the nearby Space Coast and pushed to develop a defense and aerospace industry. The entertainment vibe of a town built on theme parks combined with the space-related technology have also made Orlando a hotbed in the video gaming industry.

---

[1] For a critique of the political vision of Disney, see Stephen Fjellman, *Vinyl Leaves, Walt Disney World and America* (Westview Press, 1992). Also: Richard E. Foglesong, *Married to the Mouse: Walt Disney World and Orlando* (Yale University Press, 2001). For historical discussion of Disney's arrival in Florida: Steve Mannheim, *Walt Disney and the Quest for Community*, (Ashgate Publishing, 2002).

In an area surrounded by retirees, health care is big business, and the city has staked part of its economic future on developing a new cluster of life science related research facilities. Shopping has also become an industry, with retailers taking advantage of the arrivals of tens of millions of tourists to promote buying things, particularly at a discount, as a separate vacation activity in itself. But ultimately, Orlando and surrounding Central Florida are probably tied to the theme parks irrevocably. Without theme parks, there is almost no Orlando.

Central Florida is not the tourism capital of the state. It is the tourism capital of the planet. The Orlando area was expecting more than 50 million visitors in 2013, and they were expected to pump billions into the economy. Nearly 400,000 people in the Orlando area attribute their jobs to tourism, much of which all goes back to the theme parks, which likely wouldn't be here without the pioneering park built by Disney. Disney itself employs more than 60,000, though most of the park's workers live farther south, between the park and Kissimmee.

Whatever one's feelings about the fantasy world created by Disney, and whatever one's beliefs on whether it is a utopian world or a dystopian one, there's no escaping its result is a job and cold hard cash for many people in Central Florida. A headline on an editorial in the Orlando Sentinel in 1966 predicted the degree of the change, which would seem possible only through some sort of fantasy sorcery: "Walt Disney to Wave His Magic

Wand Over Us," the headline read. [2]

Much of the southwestern quadrant of House District 44 is taken up by Walt Disney World properties. Walt Disney World Resort covers 40 square miles - almost half as many as the city of Orlando's 102 square miles. In addition to the theme parks, like the Magic Kingdom, Animal Kingdom and others, the properties include the adjacent resorts and golf courses. Even without Disney World, District 44 would still probably draw more tourists than many other entire counties. Just up Interstate 4 from Disney, still in the district, is Sea World, and just north of that, still in the district, Universal Studios Orlando Theme Park.

Most of the northern part of the district is made up of wealthy suburban neighborhoods, including Windermere, and the Doctor Phillips area.

WHO LIVES HERE?

During park hours you'll find the Disney cast - Mickey Mouse, Mulan, Peter Pan and the others - in this district. But like Cinderella, many of them are out of here when the ball closes down. They take their carriages to less pricey neighborhoods, mostly to the south in places like Kissimmee and Poinciana. (See District 43).

There are some who work in the tourism industry here, and District 44 is a lot younger than the state as a whole. It's median age of just

[2] "Walt Disney to Wave His Magic Wand Over Us,"
The Orlando Sentinel, 24 October, 1966.

35.3 puts it in the youngest quarter of House districts and a half decade younger than the state median.

The district is also wealthier and a little whiter than the state as a whole. The Census Tract that includes Disney World has a median income just under $60,000 and there's a narrow strip of the district east of I-4 that's full of people who work in the tourism and service industries and where median household

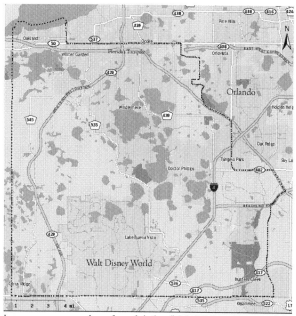

incomes are in the high $30,000s. But aside from those two areas, this is a very affluent district. The lake-dotted area north of Disney, between the park and the Turnpike, is one of the region's wealthiest areas, including Windermere, Doctor Phillips, and Gotha. Most of the Census tracts in the district have median incomes over $90,000 and many of them are over $100,000. The district's overall population is 61 percent non-Hispanic white, 10 percent black, and 17 percent Hispanic.

Republican presidential candidate Mitt Romney improved slightly on John McCain's very narrow win over Barack Obama in this district. Obama lost to McCain in 2008 by less than 2 percentage points. But that was a huge Democratic year, and two years later, in a very strong year for the GOP nationwide, the district swung back to looking more solidly Republican, with Rick Scott winning in the governor's race in the district by almost 10 points over Alex Sink. But in 2012, the pendulum swung back the other way and Romney beat Obama by less than 6 points, making this a narrowly Republican-leaning district. Registered Republicans outnumber Democrats here by about 7 percentage points.

Political analyst and blogger Dave Trotter, who has lived in this district, noted that in the 1990s, this area was part of one of the strongest Republican districts in Florida. Now, it has a high number of no party voters, who are voting for Republicans generally. Trotter believes many are moderate, Republican-leaning voters who have stopped identifying with a rightward moving party, but still vote for many GOP candidates. In addition to the moderates voting for Republicans, however, the district also is in a church-going area, where a strong network of churches tend to boost religious conservative candidates. [3]

---

[3] Dave Trotter, "House District 44 Special Election," *The Florida Squeeze Blog* (Online, 26 January, 2014, http://thefloridasqueeze.com/2014/01/26/house-district-44-special-election-district-overview/)

As with so many other districts in central Florida - and as with quite a few in the state as a whole - the Hispanic population grew dramatically here in the last decade, going from about 11 percent in 2000 to 17 percent in 2010, or from about 1 in 10 people to nearly 1 in 5. Nearly half of those Latinos are "other," Hispanics, meaning not Mexican, Cuban or Puerto Rican. In addition to those mostly South American and Central American immigrants, about 40 percent of the Latinos here are Puerto Rican. While leaning Republican, this is a district just a couple percentage points away in recent elections from looking more like a swing district. If Hispanics continue to move here, depending on the degree to which they continue to vote for Democrats, this is one district that could swing to the other party by the next presidential election.

The district's most recent representative, Steve Precourt,, resigned from the House in early 2014 to pursue a job with the Orlando-Orange County Expressway Authority. The general election to replace Precourt was set for early 2014.

DISTRICT 44 STATS

Registration (Book closing, 2012)
Republicans 39.1 percent
Democrats 32.2 percent
NPA 25.8 percent

Voting Age Population (2010 Census): 120,020
White (Non-Hispanic) 62.2 percent
Hispanic 17.1 percent
Black 8.5 percent

Median Age: 35.3

Men: 48.4 percent
Women 51.6 percent

2012 PRESIDENT
Mitt Romney 52.5 percent, Barack Obama 46.6
percent, (Estimated*)

2012 STATE HOUSE
No race. Rep. Steve Precourt, R-Orlando, faced
no primary or general election opposition.
Precourt resigned in early 2014. A special
election was set for April 18, 2014 to replace
him.

2010 GOVERNOR
Rick Scott 53.4 percent, Alex Sink 44 percent

2008 PRESIDENT
John McCain 50.7 percent, Barack Obama 48.8
percent

HOUSE DISTRICT 45
ORLANDO, OCOEE, WINTER GARDEN, PINE HILLS

COUNTIES: Orange

RATING: Solid Democrat

FROM OUT OF THE MUCK, A DEMOCRATIC FORTRESS

House District 45 hugs the eastern shore of Lake Apopka, running from Winter Garden in the southwest corner of the district, east through Ocoee toward heavily African-American areas northwest of Orlando, including the northern and western parts of the Pine Hills area. In the northern part of the district are Paradise Heights, and South Apopka. The district is one of two predominantly black Orlando-area districts.

WHO LIVES HERE?

The district's population is 42 percent black, 33 percent non-Hispanic white and 19 percent Hispanic, overall. The voting age population is closer to even: about 39 percent black, 37 percent non-Hispanic white, and 18 percent Hispanic. District 45 includes the area right up against the eastern shore of Lake Apopka, where, starting in the 1940s, the marshy land was drained and turned into "muck farms," full of fertile lake bed soil. Most of the workers who came to the area to work the muck farms were black, though some were also Latino. In the late 1990s, after years of studies that showed serious environmental damage from pesticide use in the area, the state bought the muck farms and shut them down. South Apopka, the part of the Apopka area that's in District 45, is more than 65 percent black.

Like nearly everywhere else in central Florida, there has been growth in the percentage of Hispanics here in the last decade, though not to the degree it's been seen in other areas. The 19 percent Hispanic population is up from 15 percent in 2000, nearly a third larger over the decade. Apopka, the southern parts of which are in the district, is also the "Indoor Foliage Capital of the World," with hundreds of nurseries growing ornamental indoor plants. It is home to thousands of Mexicans and Central Americans who work in those nurseries in large numbers, making the city of Apopka 25 percent Hispanic, with about 7 percent of the population from Mexico. During the last couple of decades, large numbers of Puerto Rican families have moved to the western suburbs of Orlando, and those of Puerto Rican descent now make up a slightly larger share of the Hispanic population than Mexicans.

This is a young district, with nearly half of households in the area having children under 18 living in them, and a low median age of just 34. Kids make up the two largest four-year age groups in the district, with 15- to 19-year-olds and 10- to 14-year-olds together making up more than 15 percent of the population.

POLITICAL ISSUES AND TRENDS

As would be expected given the demographics, the district is solidly in the Democrat camp, with Barack Obama having won here by more than 35 percentage points in 2012. Democrats hold a registration advantage in the district of 30 percentage points and Democrat Alex Sink won the district's precincts in the governor's race in 2010 by 25 points

Nothing here suggests any major changes demographically or politically in the immediate future.

The district is represented by Rep. Randolph Bracy, who was elected in 2012. Bracy, the director of business development for a charter school, has been generally a quiet go-along kind of lawmaker so far in his short career, but he's had two particularly controversial tutors. Bracy previously worked for Sen. Gary Siplin, who managed to sidestep all sorts of accusations and difficulties in several years in the state House and Senate. Bracy also worked for one of the most controversial Democrats in Congress, U.S. Rep. Alan Grayson. He got his start, though, as a campaign adviser to former Orange County Commissioner Homer Hartage, and has also worked for former Orange County Commissioner Bill Segal.

Bracy's most high profile bill in his first session was a measure intended to help young, undocumented immigrants get driver's licenses, under the federal deferred-action process, which allows certain undocumented immigrants under 30 to remain in the country for two years. Gov. Rick Scott vetoed the bill. Bracy also filed a bill seeking to prevent credit card solicitations on college campuses, but the measure failed.

DISTRICT 45 STATS

Registration (Book closing, 2012)
Democrats 53.9 percent
Republicans 23 percent
NPA 21 percent

Voting Age Population (2010 Census): 112,443
Black 39.4 percent
White (Non-Hispanic) 37.2 percent
Hispanic 18 percent

Median Age: 33.9

Men: 48 percent
Women 52 percent

2012 PRESIDENT
Barack Obama 67.5 percent, Mitt Romney 31.6 percent (Estimated*)

2012 STATE HOUSE
Randolph Bracy, Democrat, 69.4 percent, Ronney Roger Oliveira, Republican, 30.6 percent

2010 GOVERNOR
Alex Sink 61.3 percent, Rick Scott 36 percent

2008 PRESIDENT
Barack Obama 66.1 percent, John McCain 33.4 percent

HOUSE DISTRICT 46
WEST ORLANDO

COUNTIES: Orange
RATING: Super Democrat

NOT THE ENCHANTED KINGDOM

It may be a small, small world, but the poverty-stricken, mostly minority neighborhoods west of downtown Orlando are a big, big world away from the Enchanted Kingdom. This is gritty, real-world Orlando, with nothing in common with the fantasyland image sold by the community as a whole to millions of tourists who never intentionally see this area. The western neighborhoods of Orlando, starting downtown and including the Holden-Parramore neighborhood, before running northwest to Pine Hills, and southwest to Camelia Gardens and Tangelo Park are also among the most heavily Democratic neighborhoods in the state. And, unlike much of transient Orlando, where most people are from somewhere else, these neighborhoods have deep roots - although they're also seeing new immigrants arriving.

They're part of HD 46, an area where President Obama got more than 80 percent of the vote in 2012 and Democrat Alex Sink got 78 percent in the 2010 governor's race. The Parramore neighborhood, adjacent to downtown Orlando, is the hub of the city's African-American community, and has long been a lock for Democrats. Parts of this district struggle with high crime - several references to Pine Hills in press accounts note that some locals call it "Crime Hills." Do a Google search for news stories about what's happening in Pine Hills and you'll get to several pages before you find one not about a crime. It is one of the most pressing problems in the area - it's been heavily targeted by the Orange County Sheriff's Office for reduction in crime, but it remains a top concern of many who live here. Brownfields are also a concern, as they are in many blighted urban areas, and local officials have sought federal help in cleaning them up. Contaminated sites are the legacy of one-time small-industrial land use in the area, which now includes a number of abandoned gas stations, dry cleaning facilities and even landfills.

WHO LIVES HERE?

Pine Hills, Orlovista and Holden-Parramore - all areas around State Road 50, or West Colonial Dr., - are majority black. Pine Hills, split between HD 46 and neighboring District 45 to the north, is formerly a bedroom community for Martin Marietta employees that changed demographically in the 1980s and '90s. Now, it's relatively diverse: about 70 percent black and with a large Caribbean population, including a burgeoning community of Haitians. The area is also now home to large numbers of Vietnamese, Korean and Cambodian immigrants. In the southwest corner of the district, Tangelo Park is almost 90 percent black. The voting age population in the district as a whole is 52 percent black, 23 percent white and 21 percent Hispanic. Three percent are Asian. The largest group of Hispanics in the district are of Puerto Rican descent, many of whom vote Democratic, as do most, by far, of the African-Americans in the district. The median household income in most of the area is in the low $30,000s, well below the statewide average.

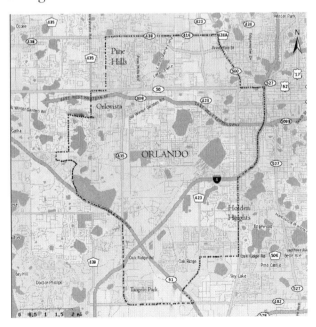

POLITICAL ISSUES AND TRENDS

Orange County as a whole has trended Democratic for a couple of decades with Bob Dole in 1996 the last presidential candidate to win in the county - and that was only by a few hundred votes over Bill Clinton. For most of those years since though, wins in Orange County were marginal for Democrats, with vote totals between the two parties pretty close until 2008 when the Obama machine won big in the county, driven by huge margins in these energized, mostly African-American, largely poor, neighborhoods west of downtown Orlando. As elsewhere in central Florida, increasing numbers of Puerto Rican voters - many moving here from New York, also helped drive the margins higher for Democrats in the last decade or so. Following Obama's 65 point win in 2008 over John McCain, his campaign turned out big numbers again in 2012 in District 46, beating Mitt Romney by nearly 70 percentage points.

Even before what is believed to have been a registration surge during the first Obama campaign, political participation in Orlando's black community was already mature - with many African-American families having lived in the same area for several generations. As longtime residents of an area that has boomed with newcomers moving in around them who take some time to become politically involved, the black community in Orlando has developed its own machine of sorts, apart from the broader Democratic politics, similar to the way Jewish voters have created a machine in South Florida. "African-American politics in Orange

County is just as strong as the machine politics of Chicago," wrote Democratic strategist Dave Trotter in The Political Hurricane Blog in 2012. "Therefore, most of the voters in the district already know who they are voting for before the election. This makes it very hard for any outsider to win an election. If one is in the political machine, they will have success. If not, they will just simply fade away." [1]

When Bruce Antone beat out four other Democrats in the 2012 primary it sealed a win for him in House District 46 that meant a return to the Legislature after a six year absence. Antone served in the House previously from 2002 to 2006 representing then-District 39 before leaving to make an unsuccessful run at the Orange County commission. During his first stint in the Legislature, Antone's most compelling proposal was likely a bill to raise lawmaker salaries from $30,000 a year to $50,000. It was a proposal that had no chance in the election year of 2006, but Antone filed it as a protest of sorts against a Legislature that is increasingly open only to the rich who can afford to take much of the year away from a day-job. He also filed unsuccessful legislation during his first term that would have required written policies on police chases.

---

[1] Dave Trotter. *Understanding the I-4 Corridor...Orange County: Inevitably Democratic.* (Online, 2012 http://thepoliticalhurricane.com/2012/09/22/understanding-the-i-4-corridor-part-iii-orange-county-inevitably-democratic/#more-4542)

Antone, who has a degree in electrical engineering, said early in his new term that he plans to make his mark mostly by trying to get items into the budget for his community in an effort to create jobs in west Orlando. Antone has said that getting money in the budget back in 2006 for a program to train teachers to work in underprivileged neighborhoods was one of his biggest accomplishments during his earlier term. It was a one-year appropriation, but it's an idea he may try to resurrect now that he's back. [2] In 2013, Antone pushed legislation to overhaul the Stand Your Ground self defense law, which was unsuccessful, but he has filed a bill for 2014 that requires guidelines for neighborhood crime watch programs, also a reaction to the George Zimmerman-Trayvon Martin shooting case in central Florida. The measure also makes other changes to self defense and justifiable use of force laws.

DISTRICT 46 STATS

Registration (Book closing, 2012)
Democrats 64.7 percent
NPA 22 percent
Republicans 11.8 percent

Voting Age Population (2010 Census) 116,996
Black 50.2 percent
White (Non-Hispanic) 23.2 percent
Hispanic 21.2 percent

---

[2] Giunta, Eric. "Bruce Antone, Returning Freshman ...." *Sunshine State News*, 21 February 2013.

Median Age: 30.7

Men: 49.7 percent
Women 50.3 percent

2012 PRESIDENT
Barack Obama 82.4 percent, Mitt Romney 17
percent (Estimated*)

2012 STATE HOUSE (Democratic primary)
Bruce Antone 35.6 percent, Pam Powell, 28.6
percent, Three other candidates combined for
35.9 percent; Antone faced no general election
opposition.

2010 GOVERNOR
Alex Sink 78.9 percent, Rick Scott 18.9 percent

2008 PRESIDENT
Barack Obama 82.6 percent, John McCain 17
percent

HOUSE DISTRICT 47
EAST ORLANDO

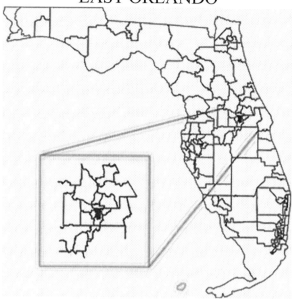

COUNTIES: Orange
RATING: Swing District

ORLANDO'S 'OTHER' DOWNTOWN

When people think of Orlando, the word "downtown," doesn't usually come to mind unless they're thinking of Downtown Disney. But while it may be firmly planted in the American mind as a sprawling vacation land - and it is that - Orlando is still a major American city that needs government offices, banks, hospitals, and it actually does have a business community. While much of the business of Orlando is, like the city as a whole, spread out in clusters around the area, there are office towers forming a central business district in downtown Orlando. The downtown business district is partly in HD 47, though Interstate 4 runs through the middle of it, and is also the district dividing line, putting some of the downtown area in neighboring District 46.

Orlando's downtown is more residential than many other cities' downtown areas, with condo towers part of the skyline, and it quickly fades into regular residential neighborhoods. Tens of thousands of people actually live in the area considered "downtown Orlando." Some of the city's trendiest residential areas are near the city center, including the areas known as Uptown and "bohemian" Lake Ivanhoe to the

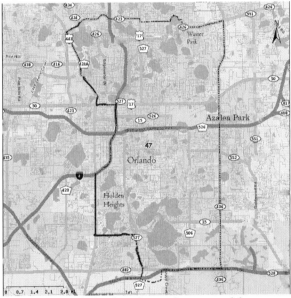

north, areas full of antique shops, and home to some of Orlando's gay community. Farther northwest is the College Park neighborhood, home to large numbers of young professionals. Thornton Park to the east is another close-in trendy residential area, the kind of place where locally owned businesses host art shows and "wine walks."

At the north end of the district is Winter Park, started as a resort community by wealthy industrialists from New England over a century ago. Winter Park is sometimes called the first planned community in Florida (though several other cities and towns claim that too.) Winter Park remains upscale and affluent. It is also home to Rollins College (one of the few schools with a varsity water skiing team, and the only one whose mascot is the Tars), and the area near the school is predictably young. Between downtown and Winter Park is another trendy mixed business-residential area known as Mills 50/ViMi, which includes the city's "Little Saigon," area of restaurants and businesses owned by Orlando's Vietnamese population.

South of downtown, the district includes the Holden Heights area, and several relatively affluent neighborhoods in the Edgewood , Conway, and Belle Isle areas.

WHO LIVES HERE

Many of the residents of this district are young - in fact the largest decade group is people in their 20s, who make up 16.5 percent of the population. People in their 30s make up another 15 percent. These are professional, affluent young people, however. Most of the Census tracts in the district have median household incomes higher than the state median, many of them in the $60,000s. As would be expected in a younger area, it has a higher than usual percentage of people renting, rather than owning their home. Nearly half the households in the district pay rent, rather than a mortgage.

The district is heavily white, 71 percent, but has a growing Hispanic population of 18 percent, up from 13 percent a decade ago.

POLITICAL ISSUES AND TRENDS

This is a marginally Democratic performing district, but Republicans hold a slight registration advantage and recent elections have been extremely close. The median age in the district fits right in with this fence-sitting area: at just under 39, the district is right on the point in the age graph where voting tendencies start going GOP. Districts younger than this one tend to vote Democrat, districts older tend to vote Republican, and districts with lots of people in their late 30s, or equal numbers older and younger, have a hard time making up their mind. Barack Obama won here by about 3 percentage points in both his elections, and state Rep. Linda Stewart defeated former Rep. Bob Brooks by about 5 points in 2012. In between, Democrat Alex Sink also won here by about 5 points.

Stewart was on the Orange County Commission for eight years, from 2002 to 2010, before running for the House seat when former Rep. Scott Randolph, also a Democrat, decided not to seek re-election.

During her first session, Stewart filed the first school safety legislation after the school shooting at Newtown, Conn. that killed 20 children and six adults. Stewart filed two bills, one that would expand the area where guns are prohibited to 500 feet around a school and one that would earmark taxes collected on sales of guns and ammo to pay for school guidance services and other school safety needs. Both bills died in committee. Stewart also has sought, so far unsuccessfully, to let counties increase their local car rental taxes if voters approve.

Another bill filed by Stewart that failed to pass would have authorized same-sex domestic partners to qualify as covered dependents in the state group insurance program.

DISTRICT 47 STATS

Registration (Book closing, 2012)
Republicans 38 percent
Democrats 36.5 percent
NPA 22.9 percent

Voting Age Population (2010 Census): 130,207
White (Non-Hispanic) 73.1 percent
Hispanic 16.3 percent
Black 6.3 percent

Median Age: 38.8

Men: 49.5 percent
Women 50.5 percent

2012 PRESIDENT
Barack Obama 50.9 percent, Mitt Romney 47.8 percent (Estimated*)

2012 STATE HOUSE
Linda Stewart, Democrat, 52.4 percent, Bob Brooks, Republican, 47.6 percent

2010 GOVERNOR
Alex Sink 50.9 percent, Rick Scott 45.6 percent

2008 PRESIDENT
Barack Obama 50.9 percent, John McCain 48.3 percent

HOUSE DISTRICT 48
SOUTH AND EAST ORLANDO

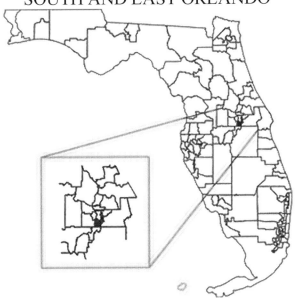

COUNTIES: Orange
RATING: Solid Democrat

ORLANDO'S HISPANIC DISTRICT

House District 48 is one of two districts in central Florida that are at least 50 percent Hispanic by population, and the only one in Orange County. The district achieves the high Hispanic percentage by being an odd "J" shaped district that goes from northeast of downtown Orlando down to the Osceola County line and then curves around the south side of Orlando and juts back up to the area south of downtown. The district includes the area around Orlando International Airport, including the Taft area, Pershing and Azalea Park - unofficially known as Little San Juan - north of the airport, and in the west the area along South Orange Blossom Trail and the Sky

Lake area. The airport itself is also within District 48.

WHO LIVES HERE?

The total population of District 48 is about 56 percent Hispanic, with a third of the district's residents of Puerto Rican descent. The voting age population is about 53 percent Hispanic, which of course means that nearly half the district isn't, making this a fairly diverse area. The district is about 30 percent non-Latino white and about 6 percent black - 13 percent if you include Hispanic blacks. The district also has a fairly substantial Asian population of 5 percent.

Many of the Puerto Ricans in this district didn't move here from the island, but from New York, which has long had the country's largest Puerto Rican community, and from which a number have moved to the Orlando area over the last couple of decades. (See House District 43)

While the area is diverse, Census data show a strong clustering of Latinos in these areas south and east of the city, and the district winds through the area to pick up those neighborhoods. It includes the eastern part of Azalea Park, which is about 40 percent Hispanic and a major center of the area's Puerto Rican community, Meadow Woods, near the airport, which has a Latino population above 60 percent, and the area along South Orange Blossom Trail known as Sky Lake, which is more than half Hispanic. Overall, this is a new phenomenon. A quarter century ago,

323

there would have been no way to create a majority Hispanic House district in Orange County, which saw its Latino population increase 83 percent between 2000 and 2010 according to the Pew Hispanic Center - a much larger growth rate among Latinos than Miami-Dade, Broward or Palm Beach counties.

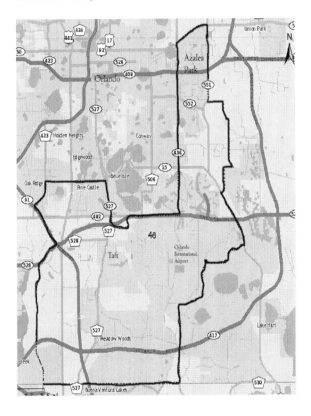

The district is also mixed economically, with the Meadow Woods area, for example, having a median household income right around the state average, but some poor areas like the Ventura neighborhood north of the airport where median household incomes dip below $30,000. It also has areas that are relatively affluent, like in the southwestern corner of the district where most neighborhoods have incomes in the $50,000s and in some places medians rise into the $70,000s. But overall, the district is certainly more middle/working class than affluent. This is also one of the youngest districts in Florida, with a median age just under 34. Only eight districts have a lower median age.

POLITICAL ISSUES AND TRENDS

While the people here may not all know it as they go about their daily lives, this area is at the hot center of state and national politics. "Orlando, ground zero for Florida's rapidly expanding Latino population," proclaimed CNN in 2012.[1] The same article noted that Barack Obama's win in Orange County in 2008 signaled a change in politics here, one that had to take account of the surging Hispanic vote. The county was an up-for-grabs battleground until that year, when Obama won by 85,000 votes over McCain. Before that, it had been decided by fewer than 6,000 votes in presidential elections going back to the 1990s. In 2010, Democratic gubernatorial candidate Alex Sink carried Orange County by 30,000 votes, a much bigger margin than 2006 Democratic gubernatorial candidate Jim Davis.

While much of the growth in Democratic registration and performance in the Orlando area has been due to new African-American voters, nearly a third of the population growth in the region over the decade of the 2000s has

---

[1] Peter Hamby, "Latino Boom Makes Orlando Proving Ground for Obama," *CNN* (Online, 21 June, 2012, http://www.cnn.com/2012/06/21/politics/florida-hispanic-vote/)

been because of new Puerto Rican residents in the area. When also considering new growth in non-Puerto Rican Hispanic population, including Colombians and central Americans, it's easy to see why political operatives are so interested in this area.[2]

District 48 has been at the vanguard of that rising Democratic performance in Orange County. The registration doesn't make it clear - about 47 percent of voters here are registered Democrats, and about 30 percent are no party voters, while 20 percent are Republicans. But those no party voters are clearly siding with Democrats, giving Obama wins of near 40 percentage points in both his elections. Alex Sink won the district by about 26 percentage points. Republicans didn't run a candidate for the district's House seat in 2012.

Like many of his constituents, the representative of District 48, Bronx-born Victor Torres, is of New York-Puerto Rican heritage. He's a labor activist, and before moving to Florida, was a New York City transit detective. Torres walked into his legislative seat

---

[2] For a pre-2012 election analysis of changing voting patterns in the Orlando area, see: Steve Schale "Orlando Rising," (Online, 15 April, 2012, http://steveschale.com/blog/2012/4/15/orlando-rising.html); See also, DaveTrotter. *Understanding the I-4 Corridor...Orange County: Inevitably Democratic.* (Online, 2012 http://thepoliticalhurricane.com/2012/09/22/understanding-the-i-4-corridor-part-iii-orange-county-inevitably-democratic/#more-4542)

unopposed. There was no incumbent - much of the area in the new District 48 was part of the old District 49, which had been represented since 2007 by Democrat Darren Soto, who was also of Puerto Rican descent, and who left the House in 2012 to run for the Senate. After moving to Florida from New York, Torres worked driving a bus for Lynx - the central Florida public transit system. He told The Orlando Sentinel that he wanted to serve in Tallahassee as a representative of the people who rode the bus: the hotel maids, resort gardeners, and restaurant workers. [3] Before he ran, Torres had been active in labor and grass roots politics, volunteering on campaigns, including that of his stepdaughter, Amy Mercado, who unsuccessfully challenged then-House Speaker Dean Cannon for his legislative seat in 2010.

During his first session in 2013, Torres was a vocal backer, along with other Democrats in the House, of expanding Medicaid to cover people who will require health coverage under the Affordable Care Act, an idea the Legislature declined to go along with. All five bills Torres filed in the 2013 session died without becoming law. Among the bills he sponsored was a measure that would have required charter schools to pay employees the same as local traditional public schools pay and a bill that sought to force Florida to request federal money to help out people in foreclosure.

DISTRICT 48 STATS

---

[3] Dan Tracy, "Lynx Bus Driver on Road to Tallahassee as lawmaker," *The Orlando Sentinel,* 24 July, 2012.

Registration (Book closing, 2012)

Democrats 46.7 percent
NPA 31.6 percent
Republicans 19.9 percent

Voting Age Population (2010 Census) 116,536
Hispanic 53 percent
White (Non-Hispanic), 30.4 percent
Black 10 percent

Median Age: 33.7

Men: 48.7 percent
Women: 51.3 percent

2012 PRESIDENT
Barack Obama 68.1 percent, Mitt Romney, 30.9
percent (Estimated)*
*Note: Orange County has several "sub-
precincts" and doesn't report data on vote
totals by jurisdiction smaller than precinct level.
Some estimates have Obama having won this
district by a slightly higher margin based on exit
polling or demographic calculations.

2012 STATE HOUSE
Victor Manuel Torres, Jr., Democrat, elected
with no opposition

2010 GOVERNOR
Alex Sink 61 percent, Rick Scott 35.1 percent

2008 PRESIDENT
Barack Obama 68.2 percent, John McCain, 31.1
percent

HOUSE DISRICT 49
NORTHEASTERN ORLANDO, UCF

COUNTIES: Orange
RATING: Solid Democrat

GO GOLDEN KNIGHTS - THE UCF SEAT

House District 49 includes an area north and east of downtown Orlando going out University Blvd. to the University of Central Florida and the area around it - a big reason this is the second youngest district in the state. The district also follows Colonial Blvd. east through Union Park to the University Park area south of UCF, and includes the area east of downtown north of Curry Ford Rd. On his website, the current House member for District 49, Joe Saunders, acknowledges the huge influence of the university on the area, calling it "the UCF seat."

WHO LIVES HERE?

College students. The standout demographic feature of District 49 is that nearly one in five people here is between the 20 and 24 years old, and the second biggest group, another 11 percent, is in the 15 to 19-year-old range. The district's median age of just under 28 makes it the second youngest House district in the state, behind the district in Tallahassee where many Florida State and Florida A&M students live.

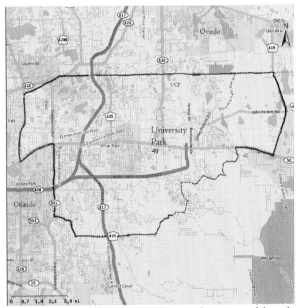

UCF has more than 60,000 students, making it the largest university in Florida and the second biggest in the country. The area also is home to some of the thousands of faculty and just south of the university campus is the Central Florida Research Park, which draws "creative class" people to the area each day to work - and a number of them live here, adding to what gives this district its progressive character and strong Democratic performance.

The voting age population is just over half

white, but also is 30 percent Hispanic and 9.5 percent black. The Census tracts to the immediate south of the university have relatively low median incomes (lots of students), but the tract that includes the university and the area to its east is very affluent, with a median household income above $75,000. Generally, the district is middle income, with lots of Census tracts with median household incomes in the $40,000s, right around the state median.

POLITICAL ISSUES AND TRENDS

Not surprising in an area that includes the second largest university in the United States, there's a strong progressive lean in this district, that also makes it unsurprising that this would be one of the districts that recently sent the first two openly gay legislators to Tallahassee. The district is just under 40 percent Democrat by registration, with no party voters and Republicans nearly even at 29.5 percent and 28.6 percent respectively. Saunders, a Democrat elected in 2012, won by about 12 percentage points here, while Barack Obama won the district by about 20 percentage points over Mitt Romney in 2012 and John McCain in 2008 with a campaign that targeted young people.

Youth is a fairly good indicator of voting preference at the presidential level in Florida. The nine youngest House districts were all won by Obama, and he beat Romney by more than 30 percentage points in seven of them and by more than 20 in eight of them. The age at which it appears more likely that someone lives in a district that will vote for Romney is 37. There are 34 districts with a median age under

37. Obama won 26 of them, Romney won seven and one was essentially a draw. For districts with a median age above that, it becomes far more likely that Romney won the district.

Orange County as a whole has trended Democratic for a couple of decades, and the last Republican presidential candidate to win the county was Bob Dole in 1996. Obama increased the Democratic success here, though, mobilizing the county's black vote and drawing on large increases in the number of Puerto Rican voters. If the demographics of District 49 are what makes it likely to vote Democrat, don't count on a major change. The age range in this district is heavily influenced by the University of Central Florida and isn't likely to change anytime soon.

Given the degree to which this district is the way it is because of college students, it's fitting that Saunders is a graduate of UCF and got his start in politics as a community organizer on the university's campus. After graduation, Saunders began working with Equality Florida, the gay rights organization, and gained a lot of political experience leading a campaign against Amendment 2 in 2008. The amendment banned same sex marriages and civil unions in Florida, and passed 62 percent to 38 percent.

In his 2012 run for the House seat, Saunders was a strong fundraiser, and defeated Republican Marco Pena - also a former student leader at UCF - 56 percent to 44 percent. In his first session Saunders was a primary sponsor of a bill to bar discrimination based on sexual orientation, a measure that died in committee. He also sponsored legislation on charter schools, foreclosure relief, extracurricular activities for virtual school students, voter registration and a bill that would give parents the right to exempt children who speak other languages from having to participate in the English for Speakers of Other Languages program, all of which failed.

DISTRICT 49 STATS

Registration (Book closing, 2012)
Democrats 39.5 percent
NPA 29.5 percent
Republicans 28.6 percent

Voting Age Population (2010 Census) 128,296
White (Non-Hispanic) 53.6 percent
Hispanic 30 percent
Black 9.5 percent

Median Age: 27.8

Men: 50.3 percent
Women: 49.7 percent

2012 PRESIDENT
Barack Obama 59.4 percent, Mitt Romney 39.1 percent (Estimated*)

2012 STATE HOUSE (Democratic primary)
Joe Saunders, Democrat, 56 percent, Marco Pena, Republican, 44 percent

2010 GOVERNOR
Alex Sink 53.7 percent, Rick Scott 42.7 percent

2008 PRESIDENT
Barack Obama 60 percent, John McCain, 39.3 percent

HOUSE DISTRICT 50
TITUSVILE, ORLANDO'S LAKE NONA AREA

COUNTIES: Orange, Brevard

RATING: Leans Republican

ON THE FRONTIERS OF SPACE AND MEDICINE

Titusville was a sleepy town with a small citrus packing and shipping industry, a few other businesses related to agriculture and the seat of Brevard County's government until the start of the Space Program. (See District 51 for more on that). Once the military started using the mostly desolate area along the coast just east of here, and later began using it to launch rockets into space, Titusville was launched, so to speak, into its modern incarnation. As the military and space-related facilities at Cape Canaveral grew, particularly after President

John Kennedy put the United States on the path to a moon landing, the entire region's economy began to transform. Titusville, which city boosters would begin calling "Space City USA," in the 1960s, had just 2,000 people in 1940. By 1960, there were nearly 6,500 - still small, but triple what the population had been before the war. And then, it really grew. By 1970, more than 30,000 people lived there, a 376 percent increase in the 1960s. By 2010 the population was well over 40,000. Titusville and other mainland Brevard County towns have now grown into one large metro area linking Titusville with Port St. John, Cocoa and Rockledge on the mainland and Merritt Island and Cocoa Beach across the Indian and Banana Rivers.

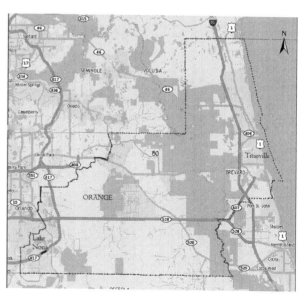

The district also stretches far to the inland southwest of Titusville, all the way to Southeast Orlando, though much of its middle is largely uninhabited forest land. Matching up with the high tech Space Coast area, the Orlando part of this district is also a cluster of "knowledge"

work, centered on the new medical and life sciences park around Lake Nona, which is increasingly being called Orlando's "Medical City." The area is anchored by the University of Central Florida's medical school, the Sanford-Burnham Medical Research Institute, and new veterans' and children's hospitals.

WHO LIVES HERE?

This is a district with some highly educated neighborhoods. There are the doctors who live near Lake Nona. And Brevard County has 48 engineers per 1,000 workers, among the highest percentages in the country and more even than Silicon Valley, though many of those engineers live farther south. Not surprisingly, the district has some fairly affluent areas, with the Census tract around the Lake Nona medical city having a median household income in the $80,000s. The Brevard County part of the district, where the end of the Space Shuttle program has hurt the economy, is less affluent. Household incomes on the outskirts of Titusville are still above the state median, in the high $40,000s and low $50,000s, but drop once you get into the city of Titusville to below $40,000, and in some areas below $30,000. Much of the district is rural, including a sparsely-populated, heavily forested area between the two population centers of the district.

The district is 63 percent non-Hispanic white, and nearly 20 percent Hispanic, mostly people of Puerto Rican descent who live on the eastern edge of Orlando. The district is 10.5 percent black.

POLITICAL ISSUES AND TRENDS

This is a Republican leaning district where GOP candidates have won at the gubernatorial and presidential elections in the most recent cycles, and where the current House seat holder, Tom Goodson, got 53 percent of the vote. But with nearly one in five people of voting age being Hispanic, and a black population of nearly 10 percent, there are Democratic votes to be had here.

The "creative class," made up of the types of knowledge workers you generally find around universities and science and high tech centers like Orlando's new medical city, leans toward voting for Democrats, though not overwhelmingly.[1]

That breaks down, evidently, in a place like the Space Coast, where, clearly, Republicans do better than Democrats, yet where lots of people work in high tech jobs. The likely reason is intuitive - knowledge workers who work for big military contractors are more like an extension of the military vote (and in many cases they're military veterans) and thus are more likely to vote Republican.

As with so many other places in Florida, much of the immediate political trending in this area is probably contingent on the degree of Hispanic growth, particularly in eastern Orlando. Puerto Ricans have shown a tendency recently to favor Democrats, and if the numbers of Latinos grow, so may the

---

[1] Richard Florida, "How the Creative Class is Reshaping America's Electoral Map," *The Atlantic*, 24 September, 2012.

Democratic vote, barring a major shift in allegiance of this critical demographic.

Goodson, a road contractor elected to the House in 2010, is chairman of the Agriculture and Natural Resources Committee in the House and vice chairman of the Economic Affairs Committee. He previously served as chairman of the Canaveral Port Authority.

Goodson has mostly flown below the radar in the House, but in 2011 carried controversial legislation that would have pre-empted to the state the regulation of "wage theft." The bill was aimed at a local ordinance in Miami-Dade County that businesses feared would be adopted elsewhere. The ordinance created a local board to settle wage disputes between workers and contractors. The bill passed the House in 2011 but failed to get a Senate vote. Goodson carried similar bills creating civil causes of action for wage theft in 2012 and 2013 but neither made it out of committee. Much of Goodson's work in the House has been on local bills, dealing with the Space industry or ports, with Brevard County being home to Port Canaveral. In 2013, Goodson, 63, took on "revenge porn." Legislation he sponsored would have toughened penalties for harassment by posting nude pictures of someone without their consent. The bill didn't pass.

DISTRICT 50 STATS

Registration (Book closing, 2012)

Republicans 38.9 percent
Democrats 35.4 percent

NPA 24 percent

Voting Age Population (2010 Census) 120,736
White (Non-Hispanic) 66.2 percent
Hispanic 18.3 percent
Black 9.6 percent

Median Age: 37.2

Men: 50 percent
Women: 50 percent

2012 PRESIDENT
Mitt Romney 52 percent, Barack Obama 46.8
percent (Estimated)*

2012 STATE HOUSE (Democratic primary)
Rep. Tom Goodson, R-Titusville, 53.2 percent,
Sean Ashby, Democrat, 46.8 percent

2010 GOVERNOR
Rick Scott 52.7 percent, Alex Sink 43.1 percent

2008 PRESIDENT
John McCain 53.9 percent, Barack Obama 47.3
percent

HOUSE DISTRICT 51
CAPE CANAVERAL AND THE SPACE COAST

COUNTIES: Brevard

RATINGS: Solid Republican

THE PLACE THAT LAUNCHED THE SPACE PROGRAM

What made Brevard County the urban area it is today was, ironically, its relatively undeveloped character in the late 1940s. The fact that hardly anybody lived in the vast wilderness area around Cape Canaveral made it a perfectly safe place to test missiles and rockets. After World War II, as the U.S. entered the Cold War and began looking to rockets and missiles for weaponry, the military found it was outgrowing its White Sands, New Mexico test range, which was small, and dangerously close to populated areas like El Paso, Texas. The first choice for a site was in Southern California, with a testing range that extended into Baja California, but the Mexican government vetoed that idea (a test missile launched from White Sands in 1947 had crashed into a cemetery in Juarez, Mexico, which may have caused some jitters.)

The Defense Department committee looking for a site then chose the second choice, a barely-inhabited strip of coast line near the Banana River in swampy central Florida. The fact that the area was swamp and farmland, and the coastline undeveloped, was the attraction. The first bridge to the Cape hadn't been built until the 1920s, and the use of much of the land in the area for citrus groves had kept it from being turned into housing. It was also easy to keep the early test missiles more or less secret. While it was hard to hide giant missiles being trucked to the Cape - workers had to actually take down the overhead stop lights to let the trucks pass underneath - the area was so lightly populated, officials don't seem to have worried much about it. Even if the whole town of Cape Canaveral turned up to watch, only a few hundred people would be privy to the military's capability. [1] The isolation was also good for safety in those early years, when about 5 percent of launches ended in an explosion. [2] But the facility's birth would change the area

[1] Colin Burgess, *Freedom 7, The Historic Flight of Alan B. Shepard, Jr.,* (Springer International Publishing, 2013), 4. See also Kenneth Lipartito and Orville R. Butler, *A History of the Kennedy Space Center*, (National Aeronautics and Space Administration, 2007).

[2] Lipartito and Butler, 57.

completely.

Blue collar workers were recruited from around the country to come to the Cape to build the facility. Welders, pipe fitters, machinists and heavy equipment operators were nowhere to be found among the tiny local population. Once they moved to central Florida, many of them stayed, finding other space program-related construction work. Initially, many of them had to live elsewhere and commute to the job site, because there was nowhere to live on the Cape or Merritt Island where the space launch operation was being built. Some drove in everyday from Daytona Beach.[3] Eventually, once the facility was up and running, whole new neighborhoods and towns would grow on what would later come to be known as The Space Coast.

The first rocket launch was in July, 1950, when Bumper 8 lit up the Brevard County sky. The day the modern Space Coast really arrived, though, was probably May 5, 1961, the day Alan Shepard climbed into the Freedom 7 Mercury capsule at Launch Complex 5 and was blasted off on an historic 15 minute flight that started the manned Space Age for Americans. Since then, aerospace has made Brevard County a region that is always ranked among the top high tech centers in the United States. More than 20,000 jobs in the area are considered "high tech" at 700-some-odd aerospace and tech-related firms. Brevard County has nearly 50 engineers per 1,000 workers, one of the highest concentrations in the country.

---

[3] Lipartito and Butler, 90-94.

In addition to Cape Canaveral and Merritt Island, District 51 includes Cocoa Beach (where astronaut Tony Nelson and his genie Jeannie lived in the 1960s sit-com *I Dream of Jeannie*, despite the fact that astronauts at the time lived in the Houston, Texas area, where their training center was and only came to the Space Coast for launches.) On the mainland, the district includes Port St. John, Sharpes, Cocoa, Rockledge, and the northern part of Viera.

WHO LIVES HERE?

The average annual salary for Kennedy Space Center on-site workers in 2010 was well over $80,000. [4] The district reflects that, with many Census tracts here having median household incomes above the state average, ranging mostly from the low $50,000s to the $70,000s. The exception is the city of Cocoa where west of U.S. 1 the median income is among the state's lowest, at right around $20,000. Incomes in other areas of Cocoa are higher, but still below the state median.

Many of the jobs at the space center and at the area's military facilities are actually performed by contractors and military and aerospace work makes up a huge segment of the private workforce here. Harris Corp., headquartered in Melbourne, and a supplier of communications and other technology to the military and the civilian aircraft industry is one of the area's largest employers. United Space Alliance, Rockwell Collins, Northrop

---

[4] NASA, "Economic Impact of NASA in Florida, FY 2010."

Grumman, Raytheon, and Lockheed Martin employ more than 1,000 people each in the region. In addition, the usual large employers in any urban area are here, and one of the other major private companies is not aerospace related, it's Health First, which operates four area hospitals and other health care facilities.

The district is older than the state median, with the largest group by decade being people

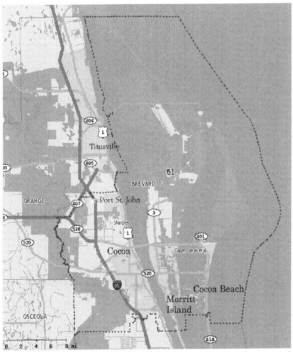

in their 50s, who make up more than 16 percent of the population. The district is nearly 80 percent white, 11 percent black and just 6.5 percent Hispanic.

POLITICAL ISSUES AND TRENDS

As noted in discussion of other Brevard County districts, the "creative class" workers in this area differ from those in many other places, likely because of the nature of the work here.

The Titusville-Melbourne-Palm Bay area is as much a part of the "military industrial complex" as anywhere outside of northern Virginia and there's no question that areas with heavy military influence vote Republican (see the Pensacola area, for example.) While this is a generalization with, undoubtedly some exceptions, engineers who work on Army Apache helicopters for Brevard-based Support Systems, Inc., are far more closely aligned philosophically and politically with the military personnel flying those helicopters than they are with engineering grads designing video games or creating social media startups. That's intuitive - people who work on attack helicopters are likely strongly pro-military, which correlates with voting Republican. But it's also evident from the fact that in many of the places where high tech workers in the military/aerospace industry live, Republican candidates win. The area's low percentage of Hispanic voters and high percentage of white voters keeps the GOP fairly successful, as does the district's age range. In Florida, white people in their 50s are most likely to vote Republican.

Steve Crisafulli, in line to be the next speaker of the House, is the representative of House District 51. Crisafulli, elected in 2008, found himself in line to be speaker starting at the end of 2014 unexpectedly after Rep. Chris Dorworth, who had been in line to follow Speaker Will Weatherford, lost his House seat in the 2012 election. House Republicans then chose Crisafulli, who works in agribusiness and real estate, to replace his classmate. It was a surprise to casual Capitol observers, Crisafulli had generally had a low key four years in the Legislature, largely out of the limelight. He was heavily involved in redistricting, however, and was chairman of the House Agriculture Committee. Crisafulli had also made a mark as a fundraiser – a key attribute for someone whose new job would be helping get Republicans elected to the Legislature. He was one of the top overall legislative fundraisers in the 2011-2012 cycle. Crisafulli had been a bit of a surprise when he was first elected, too, ousting an incumbent, Rep. Tony Sasso, D-Cocoa Beach, in 2008, an achievement made more notable by the fact that Barack Obama won the state that year.

Much of Crisafulli's work in the Legislature has been related to helping the aerospace industry, as might be expected. Crisafulli has also been a key ally of the agriculture industry. Crisafulli also joined with his Space Coast colleague, then-Senate President Mike Haridopolos, to sponsor a relief bill for William Dillon, a Brevard County man who spent 27 years in prison before being exonerated by a DNA test. The measure passed in 2012.

Crisafulli has a political pedigree. He is a cousin of former Gov. Doyle E. Carlton and the grandson of former Supreme Court Chief Justice Vassar B. Carlton.

DISTRICT 51 STATS

Registration (Book closing, 2012)

Republicans 42.7 percent
Democrats 35.7 percent
NPA 17.5 percent

Voting Age Population (2010 Census) 128,426
White (Non-Hispanic) 81.4 percent
Black 10 percent
Hispanic 5.6 percent

Median Age: 45.4

Men: 50.1 percent
Women: 49.9 percent

2012 PRESIDENT
Mitt Romney 55.4 percent, Barack Obama 43.1 percent (Estimated)*

2012 STATE HOUSE (Democratic primary)
No race. Rep. Steve Crisafulli, R-Merritt Island, faced no primary or general election opposition.

2010 GOVERNOR
Rick Scott 53.4 percent, Alex Sink 41.9 percent

2008 PRESIDENT
John McCain 53.9 percent, Barack Obama 44.7 percent

HOUSE DISTRICT 52
MELBOURNE, CENTRAL
BREVARD

COUNTIES: Brevard
RATING: Solid Republican

HERE, IT ACTUALLY IS ROCKET SCIENCE

Melbourne and the area on the beach nearby are a good 20 miles south of the launch facility at Cape Canaveral, but unquestionably and solidly part of the Space Coast and the region's military-industrial-technology economy. Along the Atlantic Ocean, House District 52 includes Patrick Air Force Base, and a branch of Embry-Riddle Aeronautical University. In Melbourne, on the mainland, Brazilian aircraft maker Embraer builds jets, and is building an engineering and technology center. Numerous military contractors are based here. Harris Corp., the military and airline communications technology company that is one of Brevard County's largest employers, is headquartered in Melbourne. So while not home to the Kennedy Space Center itself, this district is in the shadow of the rockets as they sit on the launch pad. In addition to most of Melbourne, District 52 on the mainland includes the southern part of the town of Viera. On the beachside south of Patrick Air Force Base, it includes the communities of Satellite Beach and Indialantic.

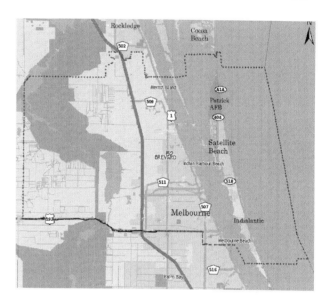

WHO LIVES HERE?

This is a fairly affluent district. As noted in District 51, the average annual salary for Kennedy Space Center on-site workers in 2010 is well over $80,000 and most of the Census Tracts in District 52 have median household incomes well over the state median. In the area between Viera and Melbourne, the median household income is in the $70,000s, and only a few Census tracts here are poor.

This is also a mature district, with the largest

group by age being people in their 50s, who make up more than 15 percent of the population. They're generally professionals, many of them working in high tech industries, for military or space contractors, and the people who make a city run, the teachers, cops, and small business owners. Large numbers of them moved here from somewhere else, many from the northeast, though the region has also seen heavy in-migration from South Florida. The district remains mostly white, with Hispanics making up just 6 percent of the population and African-Americans about 5 percent.

POLITICAL ISSUES AND TRENDS

Like in much of Florida, the demographic and political characteristics of the Space Coast are heavily influenced by relatively new arrivals. In some places around the state it is Latino immigrants, in other areas it is northeastern or Midwestern retirees, who have put their stamp, politically, on an area. In Brevard County, two groups of people who migrated here for work have given the area its political character. One group is people who came to the area because of the military, and an extension of the military, the early space program. While people in this part of the world before World War II were raised amid the politics of the Old South, and likely to be Democrats, military and space program personnel from up north were more likely to be Eisenhower Republicans, and their arrival here, as it did in the heavily military areas in the western Panhandle, broke the stranglehold of the Democratic Party on politics. The second group is the military-industrial-technology workforce that has come since the aerospace industry has matured here. Coming from elsewhere in the country to an area that was mostly undeveloped before the arrival of the space industry, they too, were unencumbered by the allegiances of the Old South. As James Gimpel and Jason Schuknecht put it in their book *Patchwork Nation,* "Military and high tech industries have created a new kind of balkanization, with Central Florida and the Space Coast ... joining Pensacola and the western Panhandle ... as islands of GOP strength." [1]

The district is solidly Republican, having given John McCain and Mitt Romney wins of about 20 percentage points over Barack Obama, and Republican Rick Scott a win in the 2010 governor's race by about the same margin here.

Rep. Ritch Workman, R-Melbourne, the chairman of the Finance and Tax Subcommittee, has been involved in many of the major issues taken up by lawmakers in the last several years, and the sponsor of some of the most controversial.

Workman was first elected to the House in 2008, succeeding Thad Altman of Viera, who had decided not to run for re-election and instead seek election to the Senate. Workman had run once before, in 2003 when Mike Haridopolos left the House to go to the Senate.

---

[1] James G. Gimpel and Jason E. Schuknecht, *Patchwork Nation: Sectionalism and Political Change in American Politics,* (University of Michigan Press, 2004), 107.

That year, Workman lost to Altman in the GOP primary.

Workman has probably gained most attention by pushing changes to the state's pension system, and for an attempt to overhaul the alimony system. He was the sponsor in 2011 of the bill that required state workers to begin contributing to their pension plans, a measure that also made other changes like lengthening time before employees can vest in the plan. In 2013 he sponsored the bill that would put new hires into a defined contribution plan more like a 401 (k) plan, but the bill failed to pass the Senate. Workman is also known for pushing through to passage a massive revamp of the alimony system, ending the concept of permanent alimony and making it harder for people divorced after a short time to collect alimony. That 2013 bill was vetoed by Gov. Rick Scott, however.

He was also the sponsor of a heavily debated 2011 bill that made major changes to the growth management system, a measure aimed at putting more of the decision power on growth at the local level. Some said the measure essentially did away with the state-based system in Florida's 25-year-old growth management law and would have a huge impact over time on how much growth is allowed and what it looks like. Workman has also spent some of his time in the Legislature trying to pass legislation to let local governments post legal notices on their websites, rather than paying to publish the notices in a newspaper. In 2012 the Legislature passed compromise legislation on the subject. Workman also sponsored legislation that was signed into law in 2009 that allows Medigap coverage for younger people with end stage kidney disease. In 2013, Workman was the House sponsor of legislation that prohibits police from using drones for surveillance in most circumstances without a warrant.

Workman's family immigrated to Florida when he was in elementary school because, Workman has said, his father didn't like the socialist policies of the Trudeau government in Canada. Early in his Florida legislative career, Workman was a vocal proponent of legislation similar to Arizona's immigration law, giving police more power to check for papers showing legal residence in the United States. Workman said his family's own hard work to legally become American citizens made him resent people who didn't go through the legal process. Florida never passed such a bill, however.

DISTRICT 52 STATS

Registration (Book closing, 2012)
Republicans 46.8 percent
Democrats 30.3 percent
NPA 19.8 percent

Voting Age Population (2010 Census): 129,159
White (Non-Hispanic) 85.2 percent
Hispanic 6.3 percent
Black 4.5 percent

Median Age: 46.5

Men: 48.7 percent
Women 51.3 percent

2012 PRESIDENT
Mitt Romney 59.3 percent, Barack Obama 39.3

percent (Estimated)*

2012 STATE HOUSE
No race. Rep. Ritch Workman faced no
primary or general election opposition

2010 GOVERNOR
Rick Scott 57.1 percent, Alex Sink 38.6 percent

2008 PRESIDENT
John McCain 58.1 percent, Barack Obama 40.6
percent

HOUSE DISTRICT 53
PALM BAY, SOUTHERN BREVARD

COUNTIES: Brevard

RATING: Swing District

HIGH TECH BOOMTOWN

Palm Bay is one of those cities that started out as a suburb, essentially, and then surpassed its better-known "parent" town in population. With more than 100,000 people, Palm Bay is now much bigger than Melbourne, though probably not as well known. While the town of Palm Bay, then called Tillman, has been around since the 19th Century, the city began its real growth in the early 1960s when General Development Corp. began building the Port Malabar development, riding along in the population echo that trailed the space and high tech boom in Brevard County.

Growth slowed during the recession, but has started again with the recovery. In addition to the national recession, Brevard County was saddled with the difficulty of the shutdown of the Space Shuttle program, which caused contractors to lay off masses of workers. The real median household income for Palm Bay dropped by 15 percent in the late 2000s, from the mid-$50,000s in 2007 to the mid-$40,000s in 2012. The area was one of the places in Florida hit hard by the foreclosure crisis.

House District 53 runs from just south of Melbourne to the Indian River County line, including Palm Bay and Port Malabar. It also includes Barefoot Bay, a manufactured home community of about 10,000 mostly retirees and snowbirds near the Sebastian Inlet.

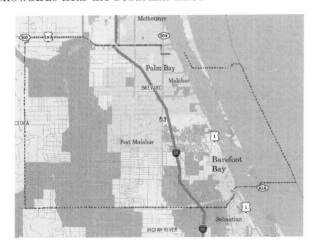

WHO LIVES HERE?

Palm Bay is, like its Brevard County neighbors, home to a large number of high tech professionals, and also has a larger than usual number of people who work in manufacturing, much of it also of the high tech variety. Harris Corp. employs more than 3,000 at its Palm Bay campus, and semiconductor maker Intersil employs several hundred in the city. Nearly a third of the people in the Palm Bay area are in their 40s or 50s. As noted, the district also includes a community of several thousand retirees and snowbirds who live in Barefoot Bay. The district's median age is about 44.

Incomes are generally near or a little above the state median in the eastern parts of the district, and well above the state median west of I-95, with a large Census tract that covers much of the western part of the district having a median household income of about $83,000. The district voting age population is 73 percent white, 13 percent black and 10 percent Hispanic.

POLITICAL ISSUES AND TRENDS

This is one of the most competitive districts in the state in terms of the two parties. Democrats have a slight advantage in registration, but Republicans, including Mitt Romney, Rep. John Tobia, Rick Scott and John McCain, have all won here recently, albeit very narrowly. The district is interesting politically because its competitiveness is unusual given its demographics when compared with trends around the state. That is, it's one of the few districts where a large majority is non-Hispanic, non-Jewish white, and where the median age is over 40 where Democrats get votes. Some of that is likely the influence of some northeastern retirees, added to the 23 percent of the voting age population that is either black or Hispanic.

Tobia, a professor at Valencia College, was first elected to the House in 2008 when former Rep. Mitch Needleman left because of term limits. Before Needleman, this area was represented for a quarter century by Harry Goode.

Tobia survived a very tough Republican primary challenge in 2010 from Indialantic Councilwoman Lori Halbert, amid allegations of dirty campaigning. In the 2010 general election, Tobia defeated Democrat Jodi James, who was hampered by having been a convicted drug trafficker. In his 2012 election, he won re-election by about 5 percentage points over Democrat John Paul Alvarez, one of the closer House elections of the cycle.

Tobia was criticized for having had some of his political science students make calls to voters on behalf of his campaign - or anyone else's - in lieu of a more traditional final exam. He was cleared of wrongdoing for the move by the Ethics Commission, which said he didn't have corrupt intent. Valencia College officials said he used poor judgment, though they didn't punish Tobia either.

Among the high profile issues Tobia has pushed in the House has been a proposal to extend the settlement that the state made with tobacco companies in the 1990s to companies that weren't originally included, a move that has drawn opposition because it would hit Miami-based cigarette maker Dosal. So far, the proposal hasn't passed the Legislature.

Tobia has been something of a contrarian on occasion in the House. When there's a bill that passes the House with one "no" vote, Tobia is more likely than just about anyone else in the chamber to be the holdout.. He was the only House member to vote against legislation aimed at reducing prescription drug abuse by putting new restrictions on clinics, pharmacies, doctors and drug wholesalers. He was also the only House member to vote against the 2013 elections "fix" bill, which reversed some earlier changes that had made it harder to vote, such as reducing early voting times. The new bill allowed supervisors to extend early voting again. He also was one of just five House members to vote against a compensation package for William Dillon, a Brevard County man who spent 27 in years in prison but was later cleared of the crime, and the lone dissenter when the House passed a bill to require smoke alarms have long-lasting lithium batteries. In 2013, Tobia was the only Republican to vote against the budget legislators passed.

Tobia sponsored legislation in 2013 meant to shield applicants for state college president jobs from being found out, with an exemption from the public records law. The bill died in committee. Tobia also sponsored a bill in 2013 that would have deleted a tuition and fee exemption for workforce education and college students who are homeless. That bill also died in committee. In 2010, Tobia also tried to require students on the Bright Futures scholarship to pay back part of their award when they drop a course, and to divide the Bright Futures scholarship program into a tiered system, but those measures also failed.

DISTRICT 53 STATS

Registration (Book closing, 2012)
Democrats 37.8 percent
Republicans 36.8 percent

NPA 22.1 percent

Voting Age Population (2010 Census): 125,864
White (Non-Hispanic) 73.4 percent
Black 12.8 percent
Hispanic 10.1 percent

Median Age: 43.8

Men: 48.3 percent
Women 51.7 percent

2012 PRESIDENT
Mitt Romney 49.8 percent, Barack Obama 48.8
percent (Estimated*)

2012 STATE HOUSE
Rep. John Tobia, R-Melbourne Beach, 52.6
percent, John Paul Alvarez, Democrat, 47.4
percent

2010 GOVERNOR
Rick Scott 50.8 percent, Alex Sink 44.2 percent

2008 PRESIDENT
John McCain 49.5 percent, Barack Obama 49.1
percent

HOUSE DISTRICT 54
INDIAN RIVER, NORTH ST. LUCIE

COUNTIES: Indian River, St. Lucie
RATING: Solid Republican

SIX OLD GROUCHES VOTE GOP

House District 54 starts at the Sebastian River at the northern boundary of Indian River County and includes the city of Sebastian, before continuing down the coast to include all of Vero Beach. Continuing south, the district crosses the line into St. Lucie County and includes the area just north of Fort Pierce. Inland, the district includes huge swaths of protected conservation area and is very sparsely populated. The district also includes Fellsmere, home of the Fellsmere Frog Leg Festival.

WHO LIVES HERE?

Who lives here? Friendly people and six old grouches, according to the sign that welcomes people driving into Sebastian on U.S. 1. There have been a few newspaper stories about the welcome sign, but nobody locally seems to know who the six offending grouches were, or exactly how long the sign has been up. How grouchy they are is hard to answer, but there's no question the district as a whole is home to a lot more than six old people. Tens of thousands have made this their retirement home, and the district is much older than the state as a whole. More than one in three people here is over 60, and the median age in the district is just under 50, compared to the state median of 40.8.

There are, of course, some younger families here as well. Major employers in the district include Piper Aircraft, maker of the Piper Cub, which has its headquarters and manufacturing facility in Vero Beach, and employs several hundred people there - though its payroll has been up and down through the years with layoffs in leaner times that have a big impact locally. In 2011, Piper ended its business jet program and cut about 150 jobs, for example. As with other places that are home to lots of senior citizens, a big part of the workforce is involved in medical and other senior care work.

Vero Beach shrank in the 2000s, with its population declining by about 2,500 people, or 14 percent, between 2000 and 2010, according to Census figures. Big drops in construction employment during the recession were likely mostly to blame, with people leaving to seek work.

District 54 is much whiter than the state as a whole, 77 percent compared to 58 percent for Florida at large. Hispanics, largely of Mexican descent, make up more than 10 percent of the district's population and blacks another 8.5

percent. The Hispanic population in the district is growing, increasing from 6 percent in 2000 to 10.6 percent in 2010.

Overall, the district is moderately affluent, but much of the wealth is on the barrier island off the coast, where median household incomes top $125,000. On the mainland, incomes are generally above the state median, though there's a wide range with some Census tracts having a median household income in the $60,000s, and a couple below $30,000.

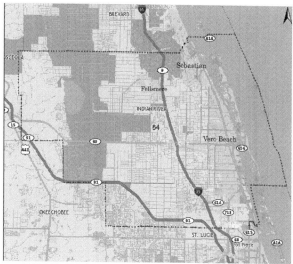

POLITICAL ISSUES AND TRENDS

With such a large number of white, senior citizens, this is Republican territory, without a doubt. GOP candidates up and down the ticket win by nearly 20 percentage points here and Republicans have a 15 point registration advantage. If there's a trend, the area is becoming more Republican, at least in terms of performance. John McCain won by just 12 percentage points here over Barack Obama in 2008, but Rick Scott in the 2010 governor's race and Mitt Romney in the 2012 presidential campaign almost had 20 point margins of victory. Democrats didn't put up a candidate in 2012 to challenge the local Republican state representative, Debbie Mayfield. If the Hispanic population continues to grow as a portion of the whole, the trend could be reversed in the short-term, unless Hispanic voting patterns change.

Mayfield, the owner of a mortgage brokerage firm, was running for the state House District 80 seat in 2008, hoping to succeed her husband, Rep. Stan Mayfield, R-Vero Beach, who was barred by term limits from running that year. In September of 2008, Stan Mayfield died in office from cancer. Debbie Mayfield stayed in the race and won, defeating Neal Abarbanell with more than 60 percent of the vote.

Mayfield has voted consistently with her Republican colleagues, but her signature issue has been a local one, regulation of the utility service in Vero Beach. Mayfield has pushed during her entire term in office to have the local municipal utility regulated by the Florida Public Service Commission, arguing that many of her constituents are customers of the utility, but don't get to vote for Vero Beach officials who oversee it, and that it's unfair for utility customers outside the city to subsidize non-utility city services, which municipal utility revenues sometimes do. Most recently, Mayfield's bill to give the PSC power over some of the municipal utilities' service died in committee in 2013, but she was expected to file a local bill for 2014 requiring PSC approval of municipal utility rates outside of Vero Beach.

Mayfield is an opponent of the "Common Core" education standards and filed legislation for the 2014 session that would prohibit the state from using the national standards. In 2012, Mayfield sponsored a bill that required insurance companies that cover cancer drugs to cover oral medications, not just IV drugs. The measure passed.

DISTRICT 54 STATS
Registration (Book closing, 2012)
Republicans 45.9 percent
Democrats 30.5 percent
NPA 20 percent

Voting Age Population (2010 Census): 126,929
White (Non-Hispanic) 80.9 percent
Hispanic 8.7 percent
Black 8.5 percent

Median Age: 49.2

Men: 48.3 percent
Women 51.7 percent

2012 PRESIDENT
Mitt Romney 66.9 percent, Barack Obama 44.7 percent (Estimated*)

2012 STATE HOUSE
No race. Rep. Debbie Mayfield, R-Vero Beach, faced no primary or general election opposition

2010 GOVERNOR
Rick Scott 57.3 percent, Alex Sink 38.7 percent

2008 PRESIDENT
John McCain 55.3 percent, Barack Obama 43.3 percent

HOUSE DISTRICT 55
RURAL SOUTH CENTRAL FLORIDA

COUNTIES: Highlands, Okeechobee, Glades,
St. Lucie

RATING: Solid Republican

JUST OLD COW HANDS

"Beef, it's what's for dinner," seems to be on
signs everywhere around the town of
Okeechobee and the surrounding county of the
same name. In the local Publix on Valentine's
Day, the front-of-the-store display for guys
who need a last minute gift isn't candy and
flowers. They're selling giant heart-shaped
steaks, because in this part of Florida, well, beef
is what's for dinner. This is cattle country. You
can't miss that. Driving down Highway 441
toward the town of Okeechobee you pass miles
of flat open land with no crops, just cows. You
pass pickup truck after pickup truck, some
pulling cattle trailers, most with drivers wearing

cowboy hats. You pass Okeechobee High School, where the teams are called the "Brahman Bulls." If you're there in March, you can go to the Okeechobee Cattlemens' Rodeo. Okeechobee is the top beef cattle producing county in the state, and the top dairy cattle county. Right behind Okeechobee in beef cattle is neighboring Highlands County, also in HD 55. When people think food production and Florida, undoubtedly citrus and seafood come to mind. But in 2012, fresh and frozen meats were Florida's top agricultural export, valued at more than a half billion dollars, nearly twice the value of Florida seafood exports.

But there is plenty of citrus, here, too. Highlands County is the state's second largest citrus producing county after Polk, and this district is full of orange groves and packing houses.

The town of Okeechobee sits on the north shore of its namesake lake, the largest freshwater lake in the state and the second largest lake entirely within the continental U.S., after Lake Michigan. Fishing on the lake, which is about half the size of Rhode Island, is another economic driver in this area.

District 55 is one of the largest in the state geographically, because this part of Florida is so thinly populated. Besides Okeechobee, there are only four other population centers of any size in the district. At the opposite corner of the district are three of them: Avon Park, best known as home to an Air Force bombing range, Sebring, the Highlands County seat, mostly known as home to the Sebring International Raceway and its 12-hour Grand

Prix, and Lake Placid, the "Caladium Capital of the World" because 98 percent of ornamental Caladium bulbs, also known as elephant ears, come from the town. Southwest of Okeechobee is the tiny town of Moore Haven.

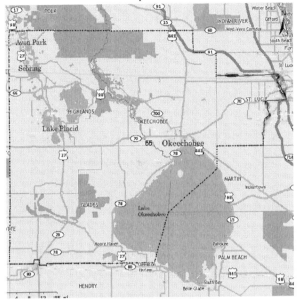

WHO LIVES HERE?

Cattle ranchers. People working in farming, most of them raising either beef or dairy cattle make up more than 15 percent of the workforce in Okeechobee County, likely the largest single profession in the area. Many others work in the citrus industry. About 17 percent of the district's workforce works in various government jobs, also a much higher percentage than in most places, but typical of small, rural towns where there aren't many large private employers. Most other people here work in the schools, in health care, or in retail.

There are also retirees, many living in small retirement neighborhoods, sometimes just a few streets with manufactured homes situated around a lake. The district has a much higher median age than the state and a very high 34 percent of people here are over 60. This is a relatively poor district, with a median household income in the low $30,000s and a median family income in the low $40,000s.

POLITICAL ISSUES AND TRENDS

Rural America votes now for Republicans, generally, and this stretch of rural American landscape is no different. District 55 gave Mitt Romney and John McCain roughly 20 point wins and gave Rick Scott almost the same margin in 2010. The race for the House seat here was closer, with Republican physician Cary Pigman defeating the Democrat, school teacher Crystal Drake, by about 9 points.

Pigman, originally from Ohio, was a doctor in the Navy and Marines, including a deployment to Iraq. After an emergency medicine residency, he moved to Florida and worked for Hardee County Fire and Rescue, and as a volunteer physician. In 2012 when Pigman ran for the newly created House seat, he faced former Rep. Randy Johnson in the GOP primary. The election night count showed Pigman a 26 vote winner, but after a manual recount, his total increased and Pigman was declared the winner by 34 votes.

Pigman was the sponsor in his first session of a bill that requires a certain level of care from physicians if infants are born alive during an attempted abortion, a measure signed into law by Scott. Pigman, now in the Army Reserve, had to Skype in to the governor's signing ceremony from Kuwait, where he deployed after the legislative session. Pigman also successfully sponsored a bill aimed at reducing Medicaid fraud, and a measure expanding a water quality credit trading program. Pigman also carried a measure that would have required screening of newborns for congenital heart disease, but the bill didn't get out of committee.

DISTRICT STATS

Registration (Book closing, 2012)
Republicans 41.7 percent
Democrats 40.3 percent
NPA 14.7 percent

Voting Age Population (2010 Census): 125,035
White (Non-Hispanic) 73.6 percent
Hispanic 16 percent
Black 8.1 percent

Median Age: 47.1

Men: 50.9 percent
Women 49.1 percent

2012 PRESIDENT
Mitt Romney 60.2 percent, Barack Obama 37.8 percent (Estimated)*

2012 STATE HOUSE
Cary Pigman, Republican, 54.7 percent, Crystal Drake, Democrat, 45.3 percent

2010 GOVERNOR
Rick Scott 56.8 percent, Alex Sink 38 percent

2008 PRESIDENT
John McCain 58.7 percent, Barack Obama 39.9 percent

HOUSE DISTRICT 56
CITRUS LAND: BARTOW TO ARCADIA

COUNTIES: Polk, Hardee, DeSoto
RATING: Solid Republican

WHERE YOUR JUICE COMES FROM

Remember the orange juice ads that asked "Where Does Your Juice Come From?" Well the answer, to some degree, is House District 56 in south-central Florida. The district stretches from Bartow in Polk County in the north, through Fort Meade and Wauchula in the middle of the district to Arcadia in the south, and it's dotted with the groves where tens of thousands of boxes of oranges are produced. Polk County is the state's largest citrus producing county, and Hardee County, next door to the south, is the fifth largest. South of Hardee County at the southern end of the district, DeSoto County is the third largest citrus producer. There's also a phosphate industry in this area, and the phosphate and fertilizer company Mosaic is one of the major private employers in Hardee County.

This is also cattle country, where "Florida crackers" used to crack their whips while rounding up the cows, which ranged free across much of South Central Florida until the 1940s. Hardee County remains a rural outpost in a state that has left much of its rural past behind. In part because of that rural isolation, much of this area struggles heavily with unemployment and poverty, with more than one in four people in Hardee and DeSoto counties living below the poverty line. DeSoto County saw 200 jobs vanish in the early 2000s when the G. Pierce Wood mental hospital closed, and now one in three residents of the county who have a job depend on the government for it.

WHO LIVES HERE?

In addition to the farming families who still own groves, and the large number of farm workers who help harvest the fruit, the area supports much of the industry that surrounds citrus production. In addition to the field work, packing houses can be found throughout the area, many owned by the growers. In the small towns that dot this area, they're often vital to the local economy. Peace River Packing Company, for example is the largest private employer in Fort Meade, with about 150 to 200 employees.

While Wal-Mart, which has both a store and a regional distribution center here, and the hospital are the two largest private employers in

DeSoto County, three of the other companies in the top 10 are in farming, two citrus companies and a wholesale orchid nursery.

DeSoto County has a countywide median household income of just $35,683 a year, putting it among the poorest areas of the state. Nearly 27 percent of its residents live below the poverty line. In parts of Arcadia, the median

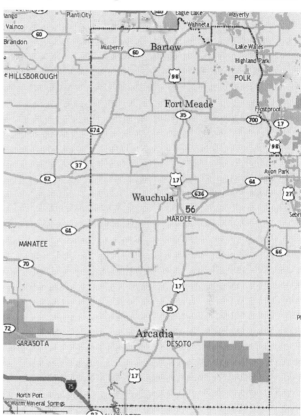

annual household income is in the $20,000s. Just north in Hardee County, the median household income is $36,115, but an even higher percentage of residents, 29.7 percent, live below the poverty line. Most of the southern two-thirds of this district is economically distressed.

Like many places with a farm economy, Hispanics are now irreversibly woven into the fabric of many of these communities. Well over a decade ago, a drive through Arcadia already made it clear that large numbers of Latinos were moving in: "mercados," "lavanderias," shops advertising calling cards, and Mexican restaurants already lined the main road. Now, almost half the population of Hardee County - 43 percent - is Hispanic. And nearly one in three DeSoto County residents now is Hispanic. More than 25 percent of DeSoto's population and 37 percent in Hardee is from Mexico, with most other Hispanics having come from central America.

POLITICAL ISSUES AND TRENDS

Like most rural areas, this part of Florida is solidly Republican in performance, even though registration here still marks it as a remnant of the Old South, with a plurality of registered voters still signing up with the Democratic Party. But Mitt Romney won by about 20 percentage points here, and Rick Scott won by 13. Republican Rep. Ben Albritton, R-Wauchula, faced no opposition in 2012.

But that may not last. As noted, nearly half of Hardee County's residents and a third of DeSoto's are now Hispanic. While many Hispanics here migrate for work, and some aren't eligible to vote because they're in the country illegally, it's likely that as the community matures it will become more politically active. The percentage of Hispanics in this region increased enormously in the early 2000s (it may have decreased some during the recession, but not enough to erase much of the

374

increase). That boom in population at some point is likely to be followed by some degree of political participation as has been the case elsewhere in the state. With the mostly Mexican and central American communities like these, it takes longer than in the Puerto Rican community - because Puerto Ricans are born U.S. citizens. But it wouldn't be surprising to see Democrats make inroads here.

Hispanics may never be a plurality in this district, though. The larger white population in Polk County offsets Hardee and DeSoto counties, which are much smaller, so the district as a whole has a voting age population that's just 23 percent Hispanic. But throughout Florida, as emerging Hispanic populations have matured, they've increasingly registered and, at least in 2012, they voted strongly for Democratic candidates.

Befitting a legislator from this area, Albritton, a citrus grower and a former chairman of the state Citrus Commission, is chairman of the House Agriculture and Natural Resources Subcommittee of the State Affairs Committee. When Rep. Baxter Troutman was prevented by term limits from seeking re-election in 2010, Albritton ran for the then District 66 seat, which included much of the Polk and Hardee parts of the current District 56. He easily won a Republican primary and faced no on-ballot opposition in the general election. Albritton immediately made himself a candidate for a future speakership, but lost out to Rep. Richard Corcoran. In 2012, when running for the new District 56, Albritton faced no primary or general election opposition.

Albritton's first high profile measure would have prohibited the taking of photos on farms without permission, a measure aimed at activists trying to expose how animals are treated on some farms. Albritton said it was a simple matter of private property rights. The proposal failed to become law.

While elected as a farm legislator, Albritton has also made a name as an advocate for foster children. In 2013 he was the House sponsor of a bill that gave foster parents more decision making authority, allowing foster children to take part in more "normal" childhood activities that earlier rules made difficult. The bill passed and was signed into law. Albritton has also sponsored a proposed constitutional amendment seeking to return the Commissioner of Education to an elected Cabinet post, a proposal that failed.

Albritton found controversy accidentally as the sponsor in 2012 of the routine Department of Highway Safety bill, which enacts the agency's wish list, and usually is fairly technical and pro forma. But in 2012 it included a new requirement for an international driver license, a proposal aimed at helping law enforcement officials by requiring drivers to have licenses that were written in English. Almost nobody noticed the proposal until after it became law, and Canadians began hearing that for the first time they'd need a new license to spend the winter in Florida. Many didn't hear about it, and feared they may be arrested. Others said they wouldn't come. It was a public relations nightmare for the tourism industry, and the requirement was quickly repealed in 2013.

DISTRICT 56 STATS

Registration (Book closing, 2012)
Democrats 44.1 percent
Republicans 36.8 percent
NPA, 16.7 percent

Voting Age Population (2010 Census): 115,237
White (Non-Hispanic) 63.6 percent
Hispanic 22.8 percent
Black 11.5 percent

Median Age: 35.9

Men 52.1 percent
Women 47.9 percent

2012 PRESIDENT
Mitt Romney 60 percent, Barack Obama 39.1
percent (Estimated)*

2012 STATE HOUSE
No race. Rep. Ben Albritton, R-Wauchula,
faced no primary or general election opposition

2010 GOVERNOR
Rick Scott 54.4 percent, Alex Sink 41.2 percent

2008 PRESIDENT
John McCain 56.4 percent, Barack Obama 42.3
percent

HOUSE DISTRICT 57
SUN CITY CENTER, SOUTHEAST
HILLSBOROUGH

COUNTIES: Hillsborough
RATING: Solid Republican

TENNIS, GOLF CARTS, AND THE
FORMER WISCONSIN RESIDENTS CLUB

Southeast of Tampa is a community that is perhaps Florida's most enduring stereotype. It's a place where retirees spend their days playing golf and tennis, maybe hitting the early bird special, and one of the big local events is the Golf Cart Parade. This is Sun City Center, a community of about 20,000, where everyone is over 55 and more than 30 percent of the population is over 80. These days, The Villages, near Ocala, has surpassed Sun City Center in size and notoriety, taking over the mantle as Florida's big "city for seniors." But Sun City Center was one of the originals, built by the Del Webb Corporation in 1962. And while filling the stereotype of Florida as a big retirement home, it also lives up to the conventional wisdom about civically involved seniors. People here vote - and they're courted by candidates. Sun City Center leans Republican, but Democratic registration isn't that far behind.

Sun City Center is tucked into the southwest corner of this district, which also includes the Tampa suburbs of Bloomingdale, Fish Hawk, Lithia, and Wimauma.

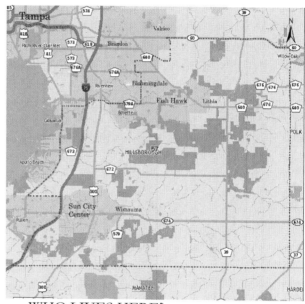

WHO LIVES HERE?

Sun City, in addition to being an over 55 community is nearly an all-white community - 95.8 percent. About 3 percent of its residents are Hispanic and 2 percent black. Sun City residents aren't predominantly from any one part of the country - there's a Wisconsin Club, an Indiana Club, a Tennessee Club, a New England Club and several others for people who want to hang out with pre-retirement neighbors.

The other major area of population in the district is the area on the edge of Brandon, in the district's northwest corner, and including the Boyette neighborhood, Bloomingdale and the Fish Hawk development., one of the wealthiest areas in the region. The median household income there is over $100,000 and median home prices are over $300,000. Fish Hawk is also nearly 90 percent white, and a little over 10 percent Hispanic, mostly Puerto Rican. The district does have a heavily Hispanic area, in the farming community around Wimauma. But the overall numbers are small, and that area's population includes large numbers of migrants, and it's not clear they play a very big role in the electoral politics of the area. Wimauma itself is about 75 percent Hispanic, but the town's population is less than 7,000. Overall, District 57 is 66 percent non-Hispanic white, 20 percent Hispanic and 9 percent black.

POLITICAL ISSUES AND TRENDS

As would be expected with a large population of elderly white people, the district leans comfortably Republican. Mitt Romney defeated Barack Obama by about 15 points here and Rick Scott won by roughly the same amount in the 2010 governor's race. Republican Jake Raburn defeated Democrat Bruce Barnett in the district's House race by 17 points.

Raburn, of Lithia, is the marketing director for his wife's family's farming operation, which produces, packs and ships strawberries and other produce. He was elected in 2012. Raburn was the House sponsor of legislation directing the state to set new water pollution standards for freshwater bodies, needed to comply with an agreement with federal officials. Raburn also carried a bill that would have made school districts encourage non-school uses of school sports facilities, but it died in committee. Raburn filed legislation for 2014 to provide additional tax exemptions for farmers.

DISTRICT 57 STATS

Registration (Book closing, 2012)

Democrats 32.1 percent
Republicans 41.3 percent
NPA 24.9 percent

Voting Age Population (2010 Census): 115,119
White (Non-Hispanic) 70.3 percent
Hispanic 17.1 percent
Black 9 percent

Median Age: 38.5

Men: 48.3 percent
Women 51.7 percent

2012 PRESIDENT
Mitt Romney 56.8 percent, Barack Obama 42.1 percent (Estimated)*

2012 STATE HOUSE
Jake Raburn, Republican, 58.5 percent, Bruce Barnett, Democrat, 41.5 percent

2010 GOVERNOR
Rick Scott 54.5 percent, Alex Sink 41.4 percent

2008 PRESIDENT
John McCain 56.5 percent, Barack Obama 42.5 percent

HOUSE DISTRICT 58
PLANT CITY, NORTHEAST HILLSBOROUGH

COUNTIES: Hillsborough
RATING: Leans Republican

BULLS AND COWS, STRAWBERIES AND CREAM: (OR USF STUDENTS AND RURAL AREAS, STRAWBERRY FARMS AND COFFEE SHOPS)

District 58 includes the northeast corner of Hillsborough County, running from Temple Terrace and the area around the Florida State Fairgrounds, following the Interstate 4 corridor, out to Plant City and the Polk County line. In its northwestern corner, the district bumps up against the University of South Florida, though most of the campus is in neighboring District 63. In the northern part of the district is the semi-rural suburb of Thonotosassa, where 2010 gubernatorial candidate Alex Sink and her now late husband, 2002 gubernatorial candidate Bill

McBride, lived. South of I-4, the district includes part of Seffner and Dover.

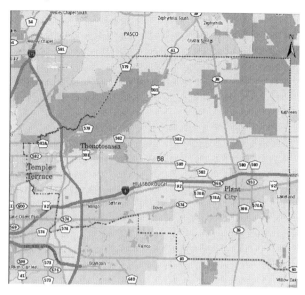

WHO LIVES HERE?

The western border of District 58, N. 50th St., also forms a border of the University of South Florida, and the university influences this area demographically and politically. First, District 58 is relatively young, with a median age a bit under 35, and a large percentage of its population, 8.2 percent, college aged, between 20 and 24. Several students live in the area just east of university, in District 58 between the campus and the Hillsborough River. Temple Terrace is also home to lots of USF faculty, and because of that a relatively high 16 percent of the city's population has at least one graduate or professional degree, while nearly a quarter has at least a bachelor's degree. The presence of a big university in a district, or of lots of university students and faculty, usually pushes a district toward Democratic candidates, though here it doesn't quite balance out the higher population of conservative suburban/rural residents farther out toward Plant City. Florida Attorney General Pam Bondi grew up in Temple Terrace, where her father Joseph Bondi was the mayor.

The district as a whole is just under 60 percent non-Hispanic white, with the voting age population about 64 percent white, 20 percent Hispanic and 12 percent African-American.

The district is fairly diverse economically, but with most of it middle class. Many of the Census tracts in the district have median household incomes in the high $40,000s and $50,000s, just a little above the statewide median. There are some poor neighborhoods, including the northwestern and southeastern sections of Plant City, and an area of farmland and mobile homes between Temple Terrace and Lake Thonotosassa. There are also pockets of affluence, as well, and some of the area near Thonotosassa is starting to draw wealthy people who are buying large tracts of land and building big, expensive homes.

Plant City, despite having the strip malls and big box stores typical of other suburbs, still has a farm town feel, particularly every year when it holds the Strawberry Festival to celebrate the big area crop.

POLITICAL ISSUES AND TRENDS

The mix of young urbanites near the University of South Florida and a large Hispanic population on the one hand, with older suburbanites, exurban dwellers and farm families on the other makes this district nearly competitive, but with a definite Republican lean. Republicans have won by a little over 5 percentage points in most recent up-ballot elections, even including the 2010 governor's race, when Sink, a former resident of the district, couldn't win it, losing to Rick Scott by 7 percentage points. In the state House race, it wasn't particularly competitive - Republican Dan Raulerson, who had been mayor of Plant City, won easily by nearly 15 percentage points.

The district's Hispanic population, including all ages, is 23.5 percent, up from under 15 percent in the 2000 Census, a trend that, if it continues, may boost Democratic votes, and in a relatively close district, swing it.

Raulerson was elected to the House in 2012 running on a promise of shrinking government and reducing regulations. Raulerson said then that he wanted to reduce the amount of money the state takes in, delete un-needed laws from the books and return decision making to local communities. "If you want some guy to go to Tallahassee and ring back a lot of bacon, I'm not your guy," Raulerson said when he entered the race. [1] "Tallahassee can operate with a lot less money." While spelling out his fiscal conservative tendencies, he also warned that he was a social libertarian. "We don't need someone up there trying to regulate morality," Raulerson said. "We have to trust citizens to act sensibly and use their judgment."

Raulerson tried to follow through on his

---

[1] D'Ann White "Plant City Mayor Throws Hat ....," *Bloomingdale-Riverview Patch*, 13 May, 2011.

promise to delete un-needed laws, filing six repealer bills during his first session, but only one of them passed. He also filed legislation to toughen penalties on people who create fake tickets for events like concerts or sporting events, and a bill creating a state poet laureate, both of which failed. He managed to pass a bill cracking down on electricity theft.

DISTRICT 58 STATS

Registration (Book closing, 2012)
Democrats 40.3 percent
Republicans 35 percent
NPA 23.7 percent

Voting Age Population (2010 Census): 118,578
White (Non-Hispanic) 63.8 percent
Hispanic 20 percent
Black 12.1 percent

Median Age: 34.6

Men: 49.5 percent
Women 50.5 percent

2012 PRESIDENT
Mitt Romney 51.9 percent, Barack Obama 46.6 percent (Estimated)*

2012 STATE HOUSE
Dan Raulerson, Republican, 57.3 percent, Jose Vazquez, Democrat, 42.7 percent

2010 GOVERNOR
Rick Scott 51.6 percent, Alex Sink 44.7 percent

2008 PRESIDENT
John McCain 52 percent, Barack Obama 46.8 percent

HOUSE DISTRICT 59
EASTERN HILLSBOROUGH, BRANDON, VALRICO

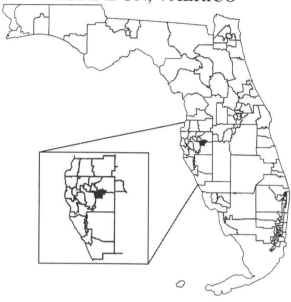

COUNTIES: Hillsborough
RATING: Swing District

FLORIDA'S MOST COMPETITIVE DISTRICT?

It's hard to say what the most competitive House district is – in a high mobility state like Florida they change from year-to-year as people move in and out and political winds shift. One can say that even after the new constitutional restrictions put on legislators in drawing the districts for 2012 and the decade going forward, there are still no more than about 25 truly competitive districts out of the 120 at least for now. About 20 House districts saw a difference of 5 percentage points or less in the presidential race in 2012, and House District 59 in the eastern Tampa suburbs is one of two or three that could certainly lay claim to being the most competitive in the state from a performance perspective. The 2012 presidential race in the district was basically a draw and Republican Ross Spano was elected to the House in 2012, beating Democrat Gail Gottlieb by less than 2 percentage points, making it the rare district outside the old Dixiecrat districts in which the House seat is held by someone from a party not in the majority by registration in the district. In

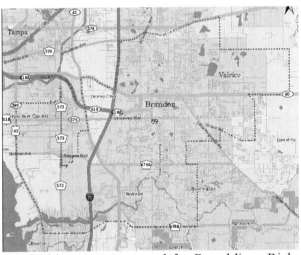

2010, this same area voted for Republican Rick Scott for governor by 2 percentage points over Alex Sink – who lives in the neighboring district to the north - and going back to 2008, Barack Obama beat John McCain 49.9 percent to 49.1 percent.

While Republicans won the House seat and the governor's race in the last two elections, Democrats slightly outnumber registered Republicans 38.1 percent to 35.2 percent, a difference of less than 3,000 voters. NPA voters make up 25.5 percent.

The district takes in most of the suburban Hillsborough County city of Brandon, and parts of neighboring Valrico, Riverview, Palm River-Clair Mel, and Greater Palm River Point all east of Tampa.

WHO LIVES HERE?

In addition to being nearly evenly split in political leanings, the district has a growing Hispanic population, around 20 percent, with 63 percent of the voting age population white and 13 percent black. The roughly 20 percent Latino population is heavily Puerto Rican – in Brandon, for example, nearly 10 percent of residents are of Puerto Rican descent and in Riverview about 8 percent are Puerto Rican. The district is relatively young, with a median age of 35.7, below the state median. The median family income in the area is relatively high, just under $64,000 a year in Brandon, $75,000 a year in Riverview and about $84,000 annually in Valrico. The percentage of people in poverty in the Brandon area is less than half what it is in the county as a whole.

POLITICAL ISSUES AND TRENDS

Hillsborough County has for a while been seen as a swing county, anchoring the political spine of Florida, Interstate 4. And Tampa's eastern suburbs, including House District 59 are the heart of that fence-sitting character. Hillsborough County is a bellwether because ethnically, it's a pretty good microcosm of the country as a whole, although in its relative affluence it doesn't necessarily reflect how things go in the poorest parts of the state or the nation. Eastern Hillsborough also matches up nearly evenly with the state as a whole: registration is close and national elections are tight in both. Campaigns and Elections Magazine called the county as a whole the "most crucial county" to both candidates in the 2012 presidential election, and National Journal called it the "molten core of the political universe." What motivates voters in the suburban area to turn out – which is what is needed to win elections in such a competitive area – is similar to many other Florida suburban areas. Residents in the area are concerned about the economy, education and growth issues. Spano made jobs and economic growth the focus of his 2012 campaign, no surprise with the state coming out of a recession. Still, this general area gave the Legislature one of its most strident social conservatives in recent years, sending Ronda Storms to the state Senate. Yet the pragmatic fiscal conservative Tom Lee, who is a social moderate, also has been elected to the state Senate from this region.

Spano falls in line with his House Republican colleagues in making tax cuts a top priority, having said when he ran that he wanted to do something about the "crippling taxation on businesses and individuals." During his first session he voted for Gov. Rick Scott's priority tax cut, a three year exemption on taxes on new manufacturing equipment, but so did everyone else in the Legislature. The House never took up Scott's other major tax break proposal, a continued increase in the exemption on corporate taxes, which Spano sponsored.

Spano also voted for changes to the pension system to put new state employees in a defined contribution plan and for proposals to put additional accountability measures on state economic development incentives, and consistently voted against incentives for sports teams. Spano voted with most Republicans in reversing an earlier change that had reduced early voting, going along with the 2013 measure that allows local supervisors to increase early voting. He also voted for the Legislature's priority ethics bill, which passed unanimously, and its 2012 campaign finance overhaul, which raised individual contribution limits while doing away with certain types of fundraising committees sometimes used as slush funds. On education issues, Spano joined the Republican majority in supporting legislation to give parents more say in what happens to failing schools, including allowing them to vote to recommend changing it to a charter school, though the bill died in the Senate. In such a competitive district, it's no surprise that a Democrat, Ty Hinnant of Valrico, quickly filed to challenge Spano in 2014.

DISTRICT 59 STATS

Registration (Book closing, 2012)
Democrats 38.1 percent
Republicans 35.2 percent
NPA 25.5 percent

Voting Age Population (2010 Census): 119,584
White (Non-Hispanic) 63.2 percent
Hispanic 18.9 percent
Black 13 percent

Median Age: 35.7

Men: 48.2 percent
Women 51.8 percent

2012 PRESIDENT
Barack Obama 49.4 percent, Mitt Romney 49.2
percent (Estimated*)

2012 STATE HOUSE
Ross Spano, Republican, 50.8 percent, Gail
Gottlieb, Democrat, 49.2 percent

2010 GOVERNOR
Rick Scott 49.1 percent, Alex Sink 47 percent

2008 PRESIDENT
Barack Obama 49.9 percent, John McCain 49.1
percent

HOUSE DISTRICT 60
TAMPA, SOUTH TAMPA, DAVIS ISLANDS

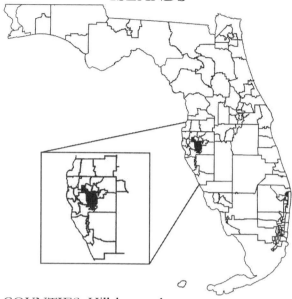

COUNTIES: Hillsborough
RATING: Swing District

TAMPA'S AFFLUENT NEIGHBORHOODS

House District 60 includes the peninsula that juts down into Tampa Bay southwest of downtown Tampa, looking like a foot dangling in the water. It includes some of Tampa's wealthiest areas with beautiful homes in quiet, waterfront neighborhoods. But that peacefulness ends at the bottom of the peninsula, where the roar of jet engines at MacDill Air Force Base shatters the tranquility.

The district also includes the islands that stick down off of downtown Tampa, Davis Islands, which are also among the city's swankier areas. It also runs down the mainland coast of Hillsborough Bay far to the south of downtown, where it includes a town with one of the weirdest histories of any in Florida. Gibsonton gained notoriety as the place where carnival sideshow performers lived in the off-season. It was famously home to "Lobster Boy," and "Percilla the Monkey Girl," among others, and its post office had a special counter for dwarves. The district continues south down the coast to include Apollo Beach.

House District 60 also includes much of downtown Tampa and, across the Hillsborough

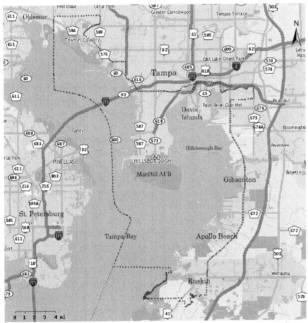

River, the University of Tampa. On the northwest side of the district, a skinny arm runs up the bay shore past the Courtney Campbell Causeway to just south of Oldsmar.

WHO LIVES HERE?

Most of the Census tracts in the district are much more affluent than the Tampa Bay region as a whole and well above the state median in income. The district includes the fashionable Palma Ceia and Hyde Park areas, and the

Culbreath Isles and Beach Park areas where the median household income is nearly $130,000.

More than 10,000 military and 4,000 civilian personnel are assigned to MacDill, and some live near the base, which is one reason more than 15 percent of residents of this area are in their 20s and another 15 percent are in their 30s. It also helps account for the fact that more than 40 percent of the homes in the district are lived in by renters. But the real estate in many parts of South Tampa is too expensive for most military families, many of whom choose to live elsewhere in the Tampa Bay area.

The district is a little over 70 percent white, and 16 percent Hispanic, a mix of people of Cuban, Puerto Rican and Mexican origin. As a whole, the population is a bit over 7 percent black, but the African-American voting age population is a little below 7 percent.

POLITICAL ISSUES AND TRENDS

This has long been a swing district, but with a slight GOP lean. It's hard to say if it simply swung strongly for Mitt Romney in 2012, or whether Romney's 7.5 percentage point win - far more than other recent races - signals a more long-term and bigger Republican leaning trend. John McCain won by fewer than 3 percentage points here and Rick Scott won by just 1.2 percentage points over Alex Sink here. The area's been in Republican hands in the House for several years. Before the current representative, Republican Dana Young, the same general area was represented for 12 of the previous 16 years by Faye Culp, a moderate Republican who retired in 2010.

Young was elected to the House in 2010 after serving on the Hillsborough County Republican Executive Committee. She quickly was pulled into the House leadership circle, being named deputy majority whip in 2011 and then rising to majority whip and deputy majority leader in 2012.

In her first session Young sponsored an interesting bill that brought together dog track owners and opponents of dog racing by seeking to end a requirement that the tracks actually have live racing in order to offer other types of gambling. Tracks want to be free of the racing requirement and offer more lucrative poker rooms, and critics of the industry say it would get dogs out of racing. The bill passed the House but died in messages in 2011, and died in committee in 2012. She also sponsored legislation seeking to allow alternate ballot summaries for proposed constitutional amendments, and a companion bill containing the language passed. Ballot summaries proposed by the Legislature have been rejected on several occasions by the Supreme Court, blocking lawmakers from getting amendments on the ballot.

In 2012, Young passed legislation giving local governments more control over what to do with "re-claimed," water, allowing them to use more of it instead of conserving water. The bill's most controversial provisions were removed, however, before Gov. Rick Scott signed it. She also tried to pass a bill in 2012 creating a series of requirements before a child in the state child welfare system could be given psychotropic medication, but the bill failed to pass.

Young's grandfather, W. Randolph Hodges, served in the Florida Senate from 1953 to 1963 and was Senate president in 1962 and '63. Her uncle, Gene Hodges, served in the Florida House from 1972 to 1988.

DISTRICT 60 STATS
Registration (Book closing, 2012)
Republicans 39.2 percent
Democrats 35.2 percent
NPA 24.4 percent

Voting Age Population (2010 Census): 127,954
White (Non-Hispanic) 72.8 percent
Hispanic 16 percent
Black 6.5 percent

Median Age: 38.1

Men: 49.6 percent
Women 50.4 percent

2012 PRESIDENT
Mitt Romney 53.1 percent, Barack Obama 45.6 percent (Estimated)*

2012 STATE HOUSE
No race. Rep. Dana Young, R-Tampa, faced no primary or general election opposition

2010 GOVERNOR
Rick Scott 49 percent, Alex Sink 47.8 percent

2008 PRESIDENT
John McCain 50.8 percent, Barack Obama 48.2 percent

HOUSE DISTRICT 61
EAST TAMPA, NORTH TAMPA

COUNTIES: Hillsborough
RATING: Solid Democrat

PART OF THE I-4 CORRIDOR NOT UP FOR GRABS

There's no more clichéd conventional wisdom in Florida politics than the notion that the I-4 corridor – the area along Interstate 4 that roughly bisects the state across its middle – is the most important area for statewide candidates. Nearly everything else is solidly blue or red, but this central ribbon is frequently changing, and thought to be up for grabs. But here in the historic Ybor City section of Tampa, built by Cuban, Spanish and Italian immigrants and for decades a center of cigar-making, is the beginning of Interstate 4 – and it couldn't be less "in play" politically. The district near downtown Tampa that includes Ybor, and East Tampa, north through Old Seminole

Heights up to North Tampa, is an enclave of overwhelming Democratic sentiment surrounded by a more modestly Democratic area. Barack Obama got nearly 83 percent of the vote here in 2008 and 2012, and Democratic gubernatorial candidate Alex Sink nearly 80 percent in 2010. The area is almost exactly half African-American, and about 28 percent white and 20 percent Hispanic.

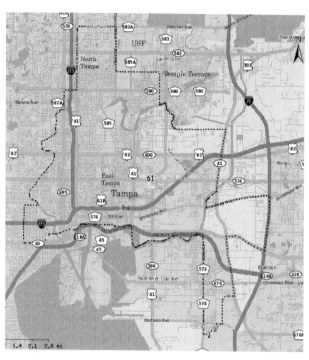

East Tampa was the scene of major rioting in 1987 after a mentally ill black man was choked to death by police around the same time police were cleared of wrongdoing in an arrest in which they bruised the face of baseball star and Tampa native Dwight Gooden. While East Tampa is home mostly to African-Americans, much of the rest of the district is less segregated. North Tampa, for example, is about 38 percent white, 29 percent black, and

29 percent Hispanic.

WHO LIVES HERE?

Household incomes in parts of the district are well below $30,000, and about one in three people is living below the poverty line. But it's diverse – there are pockets of affluence – and neighbors have battled for years against the appearance of urban decay. The Nebraska Ave. corridor paralleling I-275 north of downtown Tampa for years was known as a place frequented by prostitutes and plagued by drug dealers, though local residents have had some victories in a bid to clean up the area. Still, many here cling to only a remote hope of prosperity. More than half the residents of the district live in rented property, rather than a home they own.

While much of the area remains mired in poverty, there are exceptions: the Seminole Heights historic area north of downtown Tampa is revitalizing and a stretch of Florida Ave. south of Hillsborough Ave. just east of the Hillsborough River has drawn some young, more affluent residents. The district has lots of young families – the median age is just 32.7 and 36 percent of households here have at least one child under 18 under the roof (although 16 percent of homes include, in addition to the children, only a female head of household.)

POLITICAL ISSUES AND TRENDS

There's nothing to indicate this district would change in political leaning without major boundary changes. While much of the Democratic strength comes from African-American and Hispanic voters, new white voters moving in, including artists and young professionals, appear to also lean Democrat.

With so many people struggling to get by, the economy and job creation are the biggest issues here. And with a large number living right around the poverty line, social services have also typically been high on the priority list in the district. In Seminole Heights, efforts to revitalize the area, reduce prostitution, drug use and other crimes have long been a major priority. As with many other heavily African-American areas, the voting system and alleged efforts to suppress the black vote are also hot-button issues in the district.

Rep. Betty Reed, D-Tampa, is a retired teacher who was first elected to the Legislature in 2006. She faced no opposition in 2012 and is term-limited, unable to run for re-election in 2014. Four Democrats have filed to try to replace her. Reed has been the ranking member of the House Education Committee and was a long-time community activist before getting elected to the House.

Reed has been an outspoken advocate for the homeless and reducing homelessness during her tenure, pushing affordable housing and grant programs. In 2014, she was sponsoring legislation that would require district school boards to provide classroom teachers with debit cards funded through a state program to pay for school supplies. In 2013, Reed sponsored successful legislation allowing for a driver license applicant to voluntarily donate money for helping the homeless, and was a supporter of the unsuccessful effort to repeal the state's Stand Your Ground self defense law.

During her time in office Reed has also successfully pushed for legislation to prohibit shackling of pregnant prisoners. But generally, as has been the case for most Democrats in the last several years, most legislation she has proposed died without becoming law in the Republican-dominated Legislature.

DISTRICT 61 STATS
Registration (Book closing, 2012)
Democrats 66.2 percent
NPA 21.3 percent
Republicans 11.7 percent

Voting Age Population (2010 Census): 116,073
Black 49 percent
White (Non-Hispanic) 28.3 percent
Hispanic 20.6 percent

Median Age: 32.7

Men: 48.9 percent
Women 51.1 percent

2012 PRESIDENT
Barack Obama 84.5 percent, Mitt Romney, 14.5 percent (Estimated)*

2012 STATE HOUSE
Rep. Betty Reed, D-Tampa, faced no primary or general election opposition

2010 GOVERNOR
Alex Sink 78.3 percent, Rick Scott 18.9 percent

2008 PRESIDENT
Barack Obama 82.6 percent, John McCain, 16.5 percent

HOUSE DISTRICT 62
WEST TAMPA, TOWN 'N'
COUNTRY

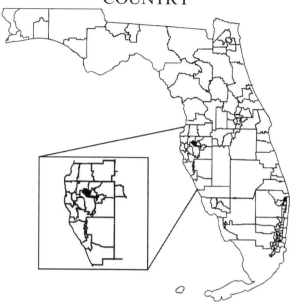

COUNTIES: Hillsborough

RATING: Solid Democrat

TAMPA'S LATIN ROOTS

As the world has taken to seeing Miami as this country's gateway to Latin America, Tampa's Latin beginnings are often forgotten by outsiders. But the link to the city's Cuban and Spanish origins remains in the area where much of the city's industrial growth began, just west of the modern city's downtown, on the other side of the Hillsborough River in West Tampa and Old West Tampa. Here, Cuban men and women once rolled millions of cigars and launched Florida's first Latin American city, while Miami was still a swampy home to a few pioneers. In the late 1800s there had already been some industry, including cigar making, in the Ybor City area of Tampa, but a Scottish immigrant and attorney named Hugh MacFarlane envisioned a larger new manufacturing center near Tampa Bay, and lured Cuban cigar makers to leave Key West and come make their products in the new town of West Tampa.

While peopled largely by Cubans at the outset, West Tampa quickly also became home to large Spanish and Italian communities and some Puerto Rican families, giving the area a mish-mashed, but still Latin feel. Many of the descendants of those initial cigar rollers still live here in the area between downtown Tampa and the airport. House District 62 has the still Spanish-Cuban flavored West Tampa as its southeast quadrant. The district as a whole runs north and west from there, taking in Tampa International Airport and northwest to the suburb of Town 'N' Country and straight north through Northwest Tampa and the area known as Egypt Lake.

WHO LIVES HERE?

As the district runs north, the people are less likely to have Spanish surnames, but because of the heavy concentration of people claiming Latino ancestry in West Tampa, the district is just a bit over 50 percent Hispanic. Many are not recent immigrants, but longtime Tampa Bay families whose ancestors were lured here by the cigar industry. A second wave of Cubans settled in the area in the late 1950s and early 1960s after the Cuban revolution. There are areas, though, where Spanish remains the primary language, due to more recent immigration. Spanish is widely heard in the heart of West Tampa along Armenia Ave., which actually forms part of the eastern border of District 62, separating it from neighboring District 61 to the east. Armenia Ave. is home to a number of Latin businesses like the Cuban West Tampa Sandwich Shop, where President Obama made a surprise lunch stop during his 2012 campaign.

Another major north-south street through

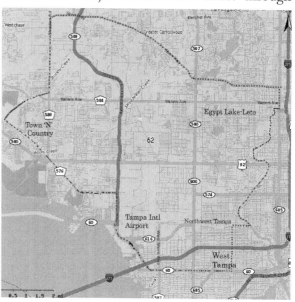

the district has a name more representative of the area's original settlers: Habana Ave. also runs through the heart of West Tampa. Census figures show 21 percent of the people living in the district are of Cuban heritage, while another 14 percent are of Puerto Rican descent. Another 15 percent are "other Hispanic or Latino," including a large number of people whose ancestors came from Spain. The Hispanic community spread out into the new suburb of Town 'N' Country when it grew on former farmland in the 1960s and that area is now about 44 percent Hispanic - about one-third Cuban, one-third Puerto Rican and one-third "other" Hispanic.

The area is mixed economically, but certainly not wealthy, with a median household income of just under $47,000 in Town 'N' Country, and in the low to mid-$30,000s across most of the rest of the district, depending on where you are. The area was hit hard by the late 2000s recession, with the foreclosure rate in Town 'N' Country hitting 8.3 percent in 2009, while it remained below 6 percent in Hillsborough County at large. It's not the poorest area in the region, but income and wealth measurements in the district are slightly lower than the state as a whole. In the poorest part of the district, the area to the southeast of the airport that includes the almost entirely African-American Carver City/Lincoln Gardens neighborhood, and mostly white and Hispanic Oakford Park, about a quarter of families live below the poverty line, compared to just 1 in 10 in the state as a whole.

POLITICAL ISSUES AND TRENDS

The district is solidly Democratic, and has been for decades, and Rep. Janet Cruz cruised to victory in the state House race. Before redistricting, much of the area was in House District 58, which, before Cruz, was represented by Democrat Mike Scionti, and before that, the seat was held by Democrat Bob Henriquez.

Local "neighborhood character" issues – the

sorts of debates around what people want an area to be – come up often in this part of Tampa, with developers talking about the high value of historic areas that are close to downtown work spaces, but longtime local residents worried about being priced out of their homes. Lately, as in many areas, the need for jobs has been a top priority, along with health care and property insurance costs.

Cruz' family roots go back to the cigar factories that brought many Cubans, Spanish and Italians to the area, and to nearby Ybor City. Cruz was elected in a special election in February 2010 to replace Scionti, D-Tampa, who resigned from the seat representing what was then House District 58 to take a job in the Obama administration. Cruz was a Tampa area activist and business owner for years before running for the seat. Cruz voted against the budget in 2011, during the recession, when she said deep cuts to public education would hurt public school students in the district and reduce spending on affordable housing and the Healthy Start program that helps pregnant women.

DISTRICT 62 STATS

Registration (Book closing, 2012)

Democrats 47.4 percent
NPA 27.9 percent
Republicans 23.9 percent

Voting Age Population (2010 Census):
Hispanic 51.9 percent
White (Non-Hispanic) 33.7 percent
Black 10 percent

Median Age: 36.6

Men: 48.6 percent
Women 51.4 percent

2012 PRESIDENT
Barack Obama 64.8 percent, Mitt Romney 34
percent (Estimated)*

2012 STATE HOUSE
Rep. Janet Cruz, D-Tampa, 69.9 percent,
Wesley Warren, Republican, 30.1 percent

2010 GOVERNOR
Alex Sink 56.5 percent, Rick Scott 39.5 percent

2008 PRESIDENT
Barack Obama 61.7 percent, John McCain, 37.2
percent

HOUSE DISTRICT 63
NORTH TAMPA SUBURBS, USF

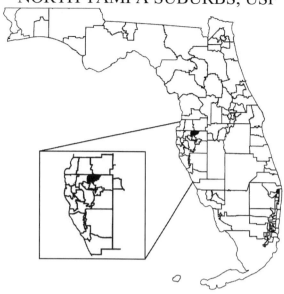

COUNTIES: Hillsborough
RATING: Swing District

SUBURBAN TAMPA SWING DISTRICT

House District 63 starts in Terrace Park on the north side of Tampa and includes the University of South Florida campus and the adjacent University neighborhood. To the west of USF, the district includes the Lake Magdalene area and the eastern part of Carrollwood. The district continues north through leafy suburbs, including Lutz, and ends at the Pasco County line. It also includes New Tampa, one of the fastest growing areas in Hillsborough County. Much of the area was groves just a couple generations ago, but has turned into suburbia with a slightly rural feel, dotted with big parks, several lakes, and a number of golf courses and country clubs.

WHO LIVES HERE?

With a median age of just 33 this is one of the 10 youngest districts in Florida, but while it did vote for Barack Obama, Alex Sink and a Democratic House member (barely), it's a politically diverse swing district where the right Republican could win. Much of the district is family-oriented and suburban, but it is drawn to jut irregularly to the south in one place to include the University of South Florida and the area around it to the north - providing a couple Democratic Party bulwark precincts in a district that otherwise might lean slightly Republican. While many of the university's 47,000-some-odd students likely remain registered to vote (if they are at all) in the precincts where their parents live, many do live close to the school and are registered voters here. The university is at least partly responsible for the district's Democrat lean, and as you get into more upper income and less diverse areas to the north, the votes get more Republican. The registration in the district favors Democrats, though not by much, 39.8 percent to 33.6 percent, a difference of about 6,000 voters out of just under 100,000.

The voting age population is 61.4 percent white, 18 percent Hispanic and 13.1 percent black. Median household incomes range from extremely poor in the University neighborhood just north of USF where students making nothing dramatically lower the median, to over $70,000 a year just to the north in the Tiffany Lake and Hounds Hollow area, and even higher, into the $80,000s in parts of Lutz and neighborhoods along the Pasco line. The northeast corner of the district, including the

Pebble Creek area, is the wealthiest part, with median household incomes in a couple of the Census tracts there topping $100,000.

POLITICAL ISSUES AND TRENDS

In 2012, Barack Obama defeated Mitt Romney by just under 7 percentage points here, and while Obama won a few more of the district's 47 precincts, Romney did very well in many of them, winning 19. Most of the precincts in the district are fairly similar

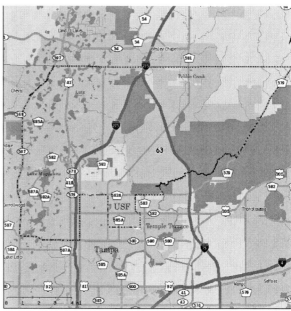

demographically - except for those around USF, and that's where the most obvious demographic-voting correlation is: Obama got 72 percent of the vote in the two precincts around USF. The House race here in 2012 was razor close, with Democratic newcomer Mark Danish pulling off a rare defeat of an incumbent legislator with his win over Republican Shawn Harrison by 728 votes. Harrison quickly filed to run again in the district, hoping to take the seat back from

Danish in 2014. In the 2010 governor's race, Democrat Alex Sink also won narrowly, defeating Republican Rick Scott in this area by just over 4 percentage points.

Danish, of New Tampa, a seventh grade science teacher, won the seat despite being outspent by Harrison. During his first session, Danish claimed some credit for getting increased funding for USF into the budget. He also fought to keep a 3 percent tuition increase out of the budget, but wasn't successful. Danish also was, no surprise, a supporter of a pay raise for teachers that was also pushed by Gov. Rick Scott and ultimately made the final budget. He opposed a bill that would give parents of children in failing schools the right to vote to have the school taken over as a charter school, and supported legislation to boost vocational education at community colleges. As with most Democrats, Danish wasn't successful at passing legislation - all six bills he filed died. One of Danish's priorities was a bill that would have required gas stations with more than two employees on duty to help disabled motorists pump gas if they ask, a measure that was similar to an ordinance already in place in Hillsborough County. Another measure he sponsored would have required school districts to use supplemental instruction money for summer school programs, and another would have created a state list of "chemicals of high concern," requiring companies to disclose when they use them. Danish also tried to pass a "homeowners bill of rights," applying to homeowners' dealings with mortgage lenders and servicers. Danish says he is a supporter of high speed rail, better funding for education, and has promised to fight any effort to cut the budget at USF. He also says he will work against proposed cuts to nursing home funding, and pursue efforts to keep homeowners in homes and pursue unscrupulous banks.

DISTRICT 63 STATS

Registration (Book closing, 2012)

Democrats 39.8 percent
Republicans 33.6 percent
NPA 25.3 percent

Voting Age Population (2010 Census) 124,434
White (Non-Hispanic) 61.4 percent
Hispanic 18 percent
Black 13.1 percent

Median Age: 33

Men: 48.4 percent
Women: 51.6 percent

2012 PRESIDENT
Barack Obama 52.4 percent, Mitt Romney, 46.3 percent (Estimated)*

2012 STATE HOUSE
Mark Danish, Democrat, 50.5 percent, Rep. Shawn Harrison, R-Tampa, 49.5 percent

2010 GOVERNOR
Alex Sink 50.5 percent, Rick Scott 46.2 percent

2008 PRESIDENT
Barack Obama 53.2 percent, John McCain, 45.7 percent

HOUSE DISTRICT 64
NORTH TAMPA BAY SUBURBS

COUNTIES: Pinellas, Hillsborough
RATING: Leans Republican

COMFORTABLE SUBURBIA, LEANS GOP

District 64 includes mostly affluent Tampa suburbs at the top of the bay, including Oldsmar - founded by Ransom Olds, of Oldsmobile fame - and Safety Harbor in Pinellas County and Westchase, Citrus Park, Keystone, and Greater Carrollwood in Hillsborough. Much of this area was ranch or farm land into the 1960s. Westchase wasn't developed until the 1980s and the first houses there weren't sold until 1991.

While the towns are within a short drive of each other, and it's not always clear when you've left one and entered another, Safety Harbor and Oldsmar opposed being lumped in with neighboring Hillsborough towns, arguing they had more in common with Pinellas County neighbors. "It took Pinellas County four long years (1907 to 1911) to secede from Hillsborough County," Safety Harbor Mayor Andy Steingold wrote to Speaker Will Weatherford, opposing the two-county district. The creation of a separate county, he wrote, gave "an accessible government to people naturally divided by a 'small ocean.'"

WHO LIVES HERE

The area is a mix of relatively affluent

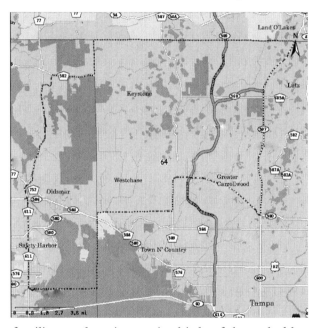

families and retirees. A third of households include children under 18, while another 24 percent of households include someone over 65. The largest age group is people in their 40s, who make up about 17 percent of the population. Most of the district's Census tracts have median incomes over $75,000 and some, in the area between Keystone and Westchase around The Eagles Golf Club having median incomes over $100,000. The voting age population here is 75 percent non-Hispanic white, 14 percent Hispanic and 5 percent black.

POLITICAL ISSUES AND TRENDS

Mitt Romney boosted Republican performance in this area, winning the precincts here by 12 points after Rick Scott won by less than 8 points in 2010 and John McCain beat Obama in 2008 by 8 points. Democrats didn't run a candidate in 2012 against Rep. James Grant, R-Tampa. When the district was drawn, Grant lived in Carrollwood, next door in the new District 63. But Republican Rep. Shawn Harrison also lived there and Grant opted to move to District 64. Harrison ended up losing his re-election bid to Democrat Mark Danish.

Grant, the son of former state Sen. John Grant, is a strong social conservative. He also favors lower taxes, and has advocated replacing property taxes with more reliance on consumption taxes, which he argues would be more fair. Grant started his career working in his father's law firm, and was originally elected in the old District 47 to replace Republican Rep. Kevin Ambler. In the House, Grant has sponsored a high profile claims bill for a man named Eric Brody, who suffered brain injuries in 1998 when his car was hit by a Broward County sheriff's deputy. Brody was eventually awarded $30 million after a long battle in multiple legislative sessions. Grant later chaired the House Select Committee on Claims Bills and tried to figure out a way to get the Legislature out of the claims bill process, arguing it's arbitrary and political. The committee tried to come up with ways to incentivize local governments to buy insurance to pay claims, but in the end, the complicated process remains. Grant has been a supporter of anti-abortion measures, and in 2013 sponsored a bill to make it a separate crime when an unborn child is killed in the commission of a crime, but it didn't get out of committee.

DISTRICT 64 STATS
Registration (Book closing, 2012)
Republicans 41.8 percent
Democrats 31.2 percent
NPA 25 percent

Voting Age Population (2010 Census): 121,282
White (Non-Hispanic) 75.1 percent
Hispanic 14.1 percent
Black 5.1 percent

Median Age: 41.6

Men: 48 percent
Women 52 percent

2012 PRESIDENT
Mitt Romney 55.5 percent, Barack Obama 43.3 percent (Estimated)*

2012 STATE HOUSE
No race. Rep. James Grant, R-Tampa, faced no primary or general election opposition

2010 GOVERNOR
Rick Scott 52 percent, Alex Sink 44.4 percent

2008 PRESIDENT
John McCain, 53.8 percent, Barack Obama 45.2 percent

HOUSE DISTRICT 65
NORTH PINELLAS

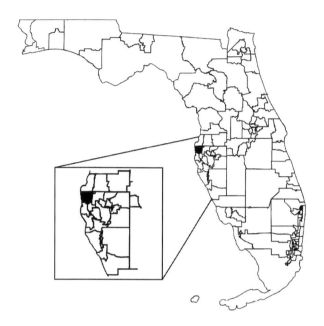

COUNTIES: Pinellas

RATING: Swing District

FROM GREEK FISHING VILLAGE TO ORDINARY SUBURBAN AMERICA

Near the intersection of Dodecanese Blvd. and Athens St., along the road running beside the sponge docks, restaurants like Dimitri's and Hellas, along with the street names, leave little question about who built the town of Tarpon Springs. Many of the last names here still end in S, older residents along the street can be heard speaking Greek, and St. Nicholas Greek Orthodox Church's Epiphany celebration, featuring teen boys diving into a local waterway to try to retrieve a wooden cross, draws Greek-

Americans from all over. Tarpon Springs remains home to the largest percentage of Greek-Americans in the country. The sponge harvesting work that brought the Greeks here is mostly gone, but in typical Florida fashion the city's past and heritage have been turned into a kitschy tourist attraction, keeping the atmosphere alive, anyway. The Greeks arrived, recruited to work as sponge divers, shortly after the industry began. One ad placed in a Greek newspaper seeking divers reportedly resulted in 500 Greek men moving to Tarpon Springs in 1905 and 1906. Divers were recruited mostly from Greece's Dodecanese Islands. But the sponge industry, hit hard by a 1940s red tide bloom and synthetic alternatives, is much smaller than it once was, with tourism replacing it as the town's economic engine.

From Tarpon Springs, House District 65 runs south, straddling U.S. 19 down through Palm Harbor and into Dunedin, both suburbs of St. Pete. The district is entirely within Pinellas County. Aerial photos or maps of the area between St. Petersburg and Tarpon Springs before about 1970 show mostly undeveloped grove land. But most of the growth in Pinellas County – the southern part of the county has long been one of the most densely populated areas in the state – has occurred in planned communities in the northern part of the county over the last 25 years. Palm Harbor is home to the Inverness golf resort, where the Florida delegation stayed during the 2012 Republican convention in Tampa. While the resort is luxurious, many delegates complained about the distance for the home delegation from the convention hall, a banishment resulting from Florida moving its primary earlier.

WHO LIVES HERE?

Everything about House District 65 feels sort of average-ordinary America. There are nice homes near the water, but they're not the multi-million dollar mansions seen in some other districts. The people here are moderately affluent, with median family incomes in the $60,000-$70,000 a year range. U.S. 19 runs up the middle of the district with typical big box stores seen everywhere else. The one exception is in its racial makeup - House District 65 is very white: 89 percent of the voting age population and 87 percent overall.

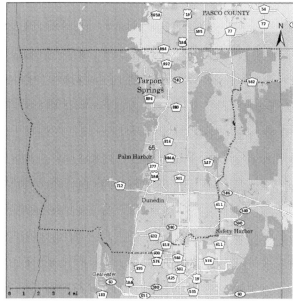

POLITICAL ISSUES AND TRENDS

But in its politics the district is also middle of the road: moderately Republican, but people here will vote for a Democrat. Registration here seems safely in the GOP fold, with Republicans making up 42 percent of voters to just 31 percent for Democrats. But 23 percent have no party affiliation, and appear to be swing voters. While Republican Mitt Romney won here in 2012 by about eight percentage points, 53.2 percent to 45.4 percent, Democrat Carl Zimmermann ousted Republican three-term Rep. Peter Nehr of Tarpon Springs on the same Election Day, also getting 53 percent of the vote. In 2010, Republican Rick Scott won the precincts in now-District 65 in the governor's race, but not by much, defeating Democrat Alex Sink here by less than 5 percentage points, and John McCain only defeated Obama in 2008 by about 3 percentage points.

Zimmermann took advantage of some negative publicity for Nehr, who had owned an internet café just as many state officials were starting to accuse the cafes of simply being illegal gambling parlors. Nehr also filed for personal bankruptcy and sent around shirtless photos of himself that he said demonstrated how he was getting in shape to help his battle with diabetes – but which were seen by some voters as weird vanity shots that called Nehr's thinking into question. Local officials threatened to shut down Nehr's internet café. Zimmermann also credited late advertising that he was able to do after an infusion of cash from the Democratic Party after Nehr's troubles arose. Nehr still outspent Zimmermann $188,000 to $47,000, but the late TV ad and mailings may have helped overcome that. While the district actually got slightly more

Republican in the redistricting, Nehr noted that it included new voters in Dunedin who weren't familiar with him, costing him some of his incumbent's advantage.

Zimmermann, D-Palm Harbor, has taught journalism and media at Countryside High School for nearly 30 years, and before that worked in advertising and owned a used car company. Running in a majority Republican district, Zimmermann hit his GOP opponent on controversies that dogged Nehr, and promised he could work across the aisle, trying to appeal to Republican voters. It apparently worked, with Zimmermann winning relatively easy despite Mitt Romney carrying the district the same day. Zimmermann stuck to popular appeal issues like the high cost of property insurance, a major concern in Pinellas County. During his freshman year in the Legislature, Zimmermann proposed changing requirements for how schools doors lock and for adding bullet proof glass in the wake of the Newtown, Conn., school shooting, but the measure died in committee.

DISTRICT 65 STATS

Registration (Book closing, 2012)

Republicans 41.6 percent
Democrats 30.9 percent
NPA 23.2 percent

Voting Age Population (2010 Census): 130,737

White (Non-Hispanic) 89.3 percent
Hispanic 5.3 percent
Black 2.6 percent

Median Age: 49.2

Men: 47.2 percent
Women 52.8 percent

2012 PRESIDENT
Mitt Romney 53.2 percent, Barack Obama 45.4
percent (Estimated)*

2012 STATE HOUSE
Carl Zimmermann, Democrat, 52.9 percent,
Peter Nehr, Republican (incumbent), 47.1
percent

2010 GOVERNOR
Rick Scott 50.1 percent, Alex Sink 45.5 percent

2008 PRESIDENT
John McCain, 50.8 percent, Barack Obama 47.8
percent

HOUSE DISTRICT 66
PINELLAS: CLEARWATER TO SEMINOLE

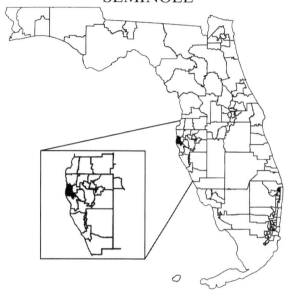

COUNTIES: Pinellas

RATING: Leans Republican

TOPSIDERS, GOLF CLEATS, AND COMFORTABLE ORTHOPEDICS

The Clearwater Regional Chamber of Commerce uses preferred footwear to try to paint a picture of who lives here, calling the area a place of "boat shoes, golf cleats, loafers and high heels." While that's probably accurate to some degree in Clearwater, the local boosters fail to include "comfortable orthopedics," which are probably fairly common in the wider area, a place that's in the oldest quintile of all the House districts, with about a quarter of all residents over 65.

Coastal House District 66 includes the

towns of Clearwater and Clearwater Beach in the north, western parts of Largo, and Seminole and Bay Pines in the south. Along the coast south of Clearwater Beach it includes Belleair and Belleair Beach, Indian Rocks Beach, and Indian Shores. The district includes lots of predominantly residential areas, but also draws lots of tourists, particularly to Clearwater Beach.

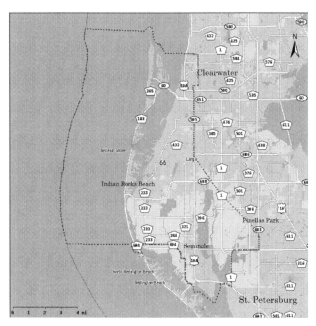

WHO LIVES HERE?

The most common age decade here is actually people in their 50s, who make up 16 percent of the population. The district's median age is lowered by all those young whippersnappers still wearing their boat shoes and high heels and living in Clearwater, where still-working people keep the median age a youthful 44. Among the big employers in the area is technology company Tech Data, which employs 1,700 people on a campus that's on the

Clearwater-Largo line and in late 2013 announced plans to expand. Another big tech company, Honeywell, employs about the same number at its aerospace operation in Clearwater, which is home to hundreds of tech workers employed by those two companies and about a dozen other smaller tech firms. Clearwater has for decades ranked among the state's top cities for manufacturing, much of it high tech.

This is not a wealthy area. People here are squarely in the middle of the state's income spectrum, and Clearwater also has pockets of serious poverty, including a heavily African-American neighborhood just north of downtown Clearwater where the median annual household income is below $20,000 a year. The Census tract that covers much of downtown Clearwater is also laced with poverty, with median annual household incomes in the $20,000s. In most of the districts, residents are in the middle to lower middle part of the income spectrum, with median incomes in the Largo and Seminole parts of the district in the $30,000s and $40,000s. Even along the beach, where the district's relatively affluent residents live, median incomes range from the low $50,000s to just over $70,000 a year - affluent relative to the rest of the district, but modest compared to many other beach communities in the state.

The voting age population in District 66 is about 86 percent non-Hispanic white, 6 percent black and 5 percent Hispanic.

Few places illustrate the competitive, swing district nature of the Tampa Bay area as a whole as this area, where elections at the top of the ticket are won by fewer than 5 percentage points. But recently, they're won by Republicans, barely. John McCain beat Barack Obama in the 2008 presidential race here 49.4 percent to 48.9 percent, which made Mitt Romney's 4.6 percentage point win in 2012 look like a landslide. In 2010, Rick Scott won the district in the governor's race by 3.2 points. And Rep. Larry Ahern, R-St. Petersburg, won in 2012 with 53.1 percent of the vote.

Ahern ousted incumbent Democratic Rep. Janet Long of Seminole in the strong Republican tide of 2010 in the former District 51. Ahern ran on creating jobs, limiting the size and scope of government, helping students overcome "bureaucracy in the education system," reducing abortion, and support of "traditional values," including marriage as only between a man and a woman. He's also a strong gun rights supporter.

In 2013 Ahern sponsored the "offenses against unborn children bill," which would make it a separate offense to cause the death or injury of an unborn child when the mother is injured or killed as a result of a crime. The bill didn't get to the governor, but Ahern has filed it again for the 2014 session. Ahern, who owns a swimming pool remodeling and commercial fountain business, also sponsored legislation that would have changed the eligibility requirements for taking the pool and spa servicing contractor's license exam, but the bill died on the calendar.

DISTRICT 66 STATS

Registration (Book closing, 2012)
Republicans 39.8 percent
Democrats 33.5 percent
NPA 22.3 percent

Voting Age Population (2010 Census): 131,711
White (Non-Hispanic) 86.2 percent
Black 5.7 percent
Hispanic 5.2 percent

Median Age: 49

Men: 47.6 percent
Women 52.4 percent

2012 PRESIDENT
Mitt Romney 51.6 percent, Barack Obama 47
percent (Estimated)*

2012 STATE HOUSE
Rep. Larry Ahern, R-St. Petersburg, 53.1
percent, Mary Louise Ambrose, Democrat, 46.9
percent

2010 GOVERNOR
Rick Scott 49.1 percent, Alex Sink 45.9 percent

2008 PRESIDENT
John McCain, 49.4 percent, Barack Obama 48.9
percent

HOUSE DISTRICT 67
LARGO AND CENTRAL PINELLAS

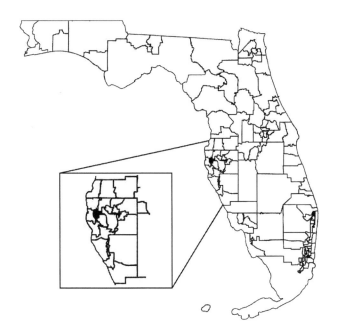

COUNTIES: Pinellas
RATING: Swing District

IT WAS SO MUCH OLDER THEN, IT'S MUCH YOUNGER THAN THAT NOW

House District 67 runs along the bayside of Pinellas County, from Highpoint in the south to Safety Harbor. It also includes the mid-peninsula parts of Largo and Clearwater. Much of this district is typical suburbia in feel, though much of the growth is relatively recent. Largo was mostly a citrus town until the early 1960s. The area was engulfed in the retiree boom that had started in the county in the 1950s, and by the end of the '60s it was full of condos, apartment buildings, mobile home parks, and neighborhoods full of mostly small, affordable single family homes. This is one of the I-4 corridor districts that in the past was typically Republican, but voted for Barack Obama in 2008 and 2012.

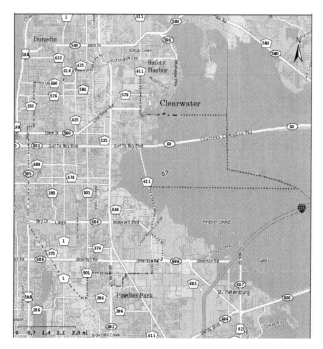

WHO LIVES HERE

A number of demographers and writers have pointed out that the old Pinellas County moniker of "God's Waiting Room," is no longer accurate. The county as a whole has been drawing younger professionals for a couple of decades, shifting much of the area from a place primarily inhabited by retirees to one of young families, though it does still have a significant number of retired people living here. District 67's median age is 44.1, similar to adjacent District 66, younger than about 90 other districts around the state. The county's growth was once fueled by the massive numbers of retirees coming here, but Southeast Florida and even the Tampa Bay suburban counties, like Pasco, have outgrown Pinellas in recent decades. Many of those who retired here starting in the 1950s were factory workers from Ohio, Michigan and Canada, and a pipeline from the upper Midwest and Canada continued for decades.

The Hispanic influx here has lagged a bit behind other places in the region, but the white dominance of the last several decades is fading a bit. In the late 1990s, Largo was 98 percent white, now it is 81 percent white. In House District 67 as a whole, the non-Hispanic white population is 73.7 percent, down considerably from 82.4 percent in 2000. The Hispanic population has nearly doubled: it was 7 percent in 2000, and just under 14 percent in 2010.

For the most part, household incomes here are slightly above the state average, though with a fairly broad range, from the below-the-state-average $30,000s in parts of Largo to well into the $60,000s in the more affluent areas near Safety Harbor.

POLITICAL ISSUES AND TRENDS

Pinellas has long been important to Republicans because more than 5 percent of the state's senior vote is concentrated here, which has historically made the state a strong GOP performer. As noted, the influx of Hispanic voters has played out here as it has in other parts of the state, shifting Pinellas County toward the Democratic Party, though much of that shift has been felt more strongly farther south in the county, including in the city of St.

Petersburg. At the same time that Hispanics have been moving in, the flood of white, Midwestern retirees that has made Pinellas County solidly Republican since about 1950 has slowed considerably, cutting into new GOP registrations.

The combination of a younger population and a more Hispanic one, pushed this area into the Democratic column in the presidential race in 2008 and kept it there in the 2010 governor's race and again in the 2012 presidential. Barack Obama won here in 2012 narrowly, by about 6 percentage points, and it was even closer in the 2010 gubernatorial, with Democrat Alex Sink winning by just 3 points. The district voted closely in the 2012 state House race, too, but swung the other way, going with incumbent Republican Ed Hooper over Democrat Ben Farrell by about 5 points.

Pinellas County has been the state's top county for voting by absentee ballot, with about 250,000 voters returning absentee ballots in the county in the 2012 election - more than 10 percent of the statewide total.

Hooper, a former firefighter from Clearwater, was elected to the House in 2006 and served as deputy majority whip from 2008 to 2010. Hooper has sometimes been an independent-minded lawmaker, breaking with most in his party, for example, in voting against allowing new near-shore oil drilling in 2009, even before the Deepwater Horizon oil spill. As a former firefighter, much of Hooper's focus has been on public safety and fire issues. He pushed, for example, to keep manual fire alarm maintenance required in old buildings, and has been one of the House's most vocal advocates for allowing red light cameras, also putting him at odds with many in his party. He's also sponsored legislation, so far unsuccessfully, that would allow cameras to be placed on school buses to discourage people from ignoring the school bus stop signs.

DISTRICT STATS

Registration (Book closing, 2012)

Democrats 36.2 percent
Republicans 35.3 percent
NPA 24.4 percent

Voting Age Population (2010 Census): 158,424
White (Non-Hispanic) 77.8 percent
Hispanic 11.3 percent
Black 6.9 percent

Median Age: 44.1

Men: 48.8 percent
Women 51.2 percent

2012 PRESIDENT
Barack Obama 51.9 percent, Mitt Romney, 46.5 percent (Estimated)*

2012 STATE HOUSE
Rep. Ed Hooper, R-Clearwater, 52.8 percent, Ben Farrell, Democrat, 47.2 percent

2010 GOVERNOR
Alex Sink 48.8 percent, Rick Scott 45.7 percent

2008 PRESIDENT
Barack Obama 53.1 percent, John McCain, 45.2 percent

HOUSE DISTRICT 68
NORTHERN ST. PETE, PINELLAS PARK

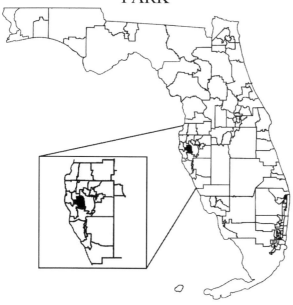

COUNTIES: Pinellas

RATING: Leans Democratic

ONCE 'PENSIONER'S PARADISE',

The 1950 travel film "Let's Look at Florida," had a section on St. Petersburg that opened with a medium shot of rows and rows of older people playing shuffleboard on a sunny day. It then cut to footage of shirt-sleeved elderly men and women who seem to have nothing better to do, so they're sitting on St. Petersburg's famous green benches along a downtown shopping street (though, from the black-and-white film, there was no way to know they're green.) "Here, they settle down happily to a life of leisure, hobbies and gentle sports," the dulcet-toned narrator says. "Florida, they claim, is the next best thing to complete rejuvenation.

Although St. Petersburg is the second largest resort center of the South, it leads the large cities of Florida in percentage of home ownership," the narrator continues. "Many of these homes are enjoyed by retired people who consider St. Petersburg the 'pensioner's paradise.'" [1]

That image of St. Petersburg, like the people in "Let's Look at Florida," now exists only as a black and white memory. St. Petersburg has a charming and increasingly artsy downtown that has revitalized it in the 21st Century, bringing a younger, less stodgy vibe to this classic old "pensioner's paradise."

House District 68 includes much of what the general public thinks of as St. Petersburg, including its downtown landmarks. It includes the visual icon of the city for decades, The Pier, as well as the stately old Vinoy Resort, the Mahaffey Theater, where many political candidates have debated, and Tropicana Field, home of the Tampa Bay Rays. It includes the city's Historic Old Northeast neighborhood, and dozens of older, residential neighborhoods spreading northwest from the city's downtown. There, the district includes the suburb of Pinellas Park. The district doesn't include the heavily African-American southern tip of the city, which is in neighboring District 70.

WHO LIVES HERE

What used to be a city where, for decades, 30 percent of the population was over 65, is

---

[1] "Let's Look at Florida," Film. 1950. (On YouTube: https://www.youtube.com/watch?v=6BO33VEt-gM)

now a place where just 15 percent of the populace falls in that advanced age range. With a median age in the low 40s, this one-time "God's Waiting Room," is that no more, not even in the top quarter when measuring the state's House districts from oldest to youngest. The New York Times noticed the demographic change back in 2008, and referenced those old images of having a restful sit downtown. "Elders idling on park benches have been replaced by artists and young professionals gathering at cafes and restaurants, lulled by the breeze that made St. Pete so popular to begin with," the Times Travel section piece said. [2] While it's not clear if the shuffle boarders found the rejuvenation they were looking for, the rejuvenation of the city itself took off in the early 2000s, with artists, gallery owners and restaurateurs flocking here, followed by a younger set of people moving in.

As with many other gentrifying areas, there's a wide range of income levels here, with many areas having median household incomes around the state median, in the mid-$40,000s, but some areas drawing more affluent residents. The district includes the Venetian Isles area, which is a particularly affluent neighborhood. But just a few blocks to the west is an area that includes a number of mobile homes and has a high number of retirees where the median income is well below the state average.

[2] Paul Reyes, "Revival Beyond the Beach," *The New York Times*, 21, August, 2008.

This area has also seen a significant increase in Hispanic population, but it was so low to begin with that it remains low as a percentage of the overall population. The Latino population in District 68 was 8.1 percent in 2010, up from 4.9 percent a decade earlier. The district's black population is 6.7 percent.

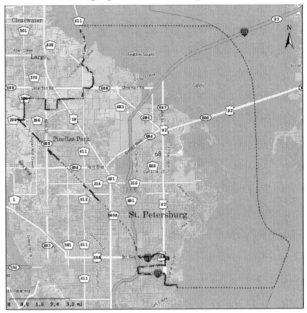

POLITICAL ISSUES AND TRENDS

Pinellas County was the leading edge of the shift from the solid Democratic South to the GOP, starting way back in the late 1940s and early 1950s, long before the Reagan Revolution. Some number of young World War II veterans moved here after the war, bringing Midwestern political values, including Republican tendencies, with them. The post-war period brought prosperity that led a number of middle class people to think about retiring, rather than working until death, and because they had more money, more considered retiring in a place like Florida. These retirees were also the first generation with significant social security and pensions to rely on. The late '40s and early '50s brought a wave of retirees, also mostly moderate, Midwestern farm-state Republicans. These Midwesterners more or less took over a county that had been traditionally Democratic like everywhere else in the South. Pinellas voted for Republican Tom Dewey for president in 1948, and in 1954 made William Cramer the first Republican to go to Congress from the old Confederate states since reconstruction. Cramer's aide, C.W. "Bill" Young, would succeed him and stay in the seat until his death in 2013. [3] A moderate-tinged Republicanism dominated suburban Pinellas County politics for years and the county continued to elect middle-of-the-road Republicans, including state legislators like Dennis Jones, Don Sullivan and Jack Latvala, toward the end of the 20th Century and into the 21st.

But while the GOP continues to have success in Pinellas County, the city of St. Petersburg, as it got younger over the decades, became a place that elected Democrats. Former Rep. Rick Kriseman, a liberal Democrat, was elected mayor of St. Petersburg in 2013. For much of the first decade of the 2000s, a major part of St. Petersburg was represented in the House by another liberal Democrat, Rep. Charlie Justice, who later won a Senate seat. The city isn't walled off to Republicans, part of the area was previously represented in the House by Republican Jeff Brandes, who then got elected to the Senate, and, before Kriseman,

---

[3] Fiedler, 745.

the two most recent St. Pete mayors, Rick Baker and Bill Foster, were Republican. "Voters here tend to vote for the candidate and not the party," Dennis Jones said of the area in 2012. [4]

But District 68 has been a reliably Democratic district by 10 percentage points for the most recent half decade. Barack Obama beat John McCain by 10 points in 2008, and Democrat Alex Sink beat Republican Rick Scott by 9 points in the district in the 2008 governor's race. In 2012, Obama defeated Mitt Romney by just under 10 points, and Democrat Dwight Dudley defeated former House member, Republican Frank Farkas, by about 7 points.

Dudley started out in politics as an aide in the Legislature right out of Florida State University's law school, before returning home to St. Pete to work in the public defender's office. After eight years doing that, he started a private law practice. Dudley won the District 68 seat in 2012, defeating Farkas for what was an open seat, with Brandes, the incumbent representing much of the area before redistricting, having decided to run for the Senate. During his campaign and first legislative session, Dudley was highly critical of a law that allowed power companies to charge customers for building nuclear power plants before they are online, arguing for its repeal. The law was changed in 2013, to set new benchmarks for collecting pre-construction fees, but didn't fully repeal the law, or offer refunds to customers who were charged under it. For 2014, Dudley

---

[4] Michael Peltier, "House District 68, Farkas v. Dudley in St. Pete District," *The News Service of Florida.*

filed a proposed constitutional amendment seeking to prevent power companies from charging for plants before they're in operation. Dudley was a vocal critic of utility regulation in general, and filed a bill in 2013 that would have made the Public Service Commission an elected body once again. The bill failed.

DISTRICT 68 STATS

Registration (Book closing, 2012)
Democrats 37.7 percent
Republicans 34.7 percent
NPA 23.5 percent

Voting Age Population (2010 Census): 158,551
White (Non-Hispanic) 81.4 percent
Hispanic 7.1 percent
Black 5.6 percent

Median Age: 42.3

Men: 48.7 percent
Women 51.3 percent

2012 PRESIDENT
Barack Obama 53.8 percent, Mitt Romney, 44.4 percent (Estimated)*

2012 STATE HOUSE
Dwight Dudley, Democrat, 50.9 percent, Frank Farkas, Republican, 44.2 percent, Matthew Weidner, NPA, 4.8 percent

2010 GOVERNOR
Alex Sink 52.2 percent, Rick Scott 42.9 percent

2008 PRESIDENT
Barack Obama 54.2 percent, John McCain, 44.2 percent

HOUSE DISTRICT 69
REDINGTON SHORES TO ST. PETE BEACH

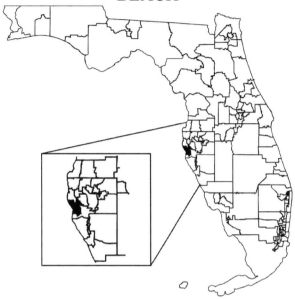

COUNTIES: Pinellas

RATING: Swing District

PARTY LOYALTY SPLIT IN ST. PETE'S BEACH TOWNS

The beachfront high rise has become an icon of modern Florida and that's one of the dominant features of coastal Pinellas County. High rise condos compete for space with smaller family homes on the stretch of barrier island off the Pinellas coast. District 69 includes the western and northwest neighborhoods of St. Petersburg, and the towns along the beach from Redington Shores in the north down through Madeira Beach, Treasure Island, St. Pete Beach, Pass A Grille and Tierra Verde. Mainland towns include Gulfport, Pasadena and South Pasadena.

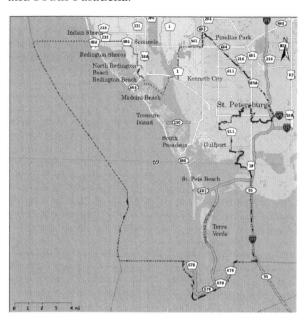

The northern part of the district around the Redington Beach and Treasure Island areas are mostly a quiet, affluent residential area of homes and condos, though there are also some resort hotels. The beach here is lined with high rises, but on the bay side of the island there are fingers of land sticking into the bay that are covered with single family homes. Treasure Island is similarly residential. The historic one-block wide, 31-block long Pass-A-Grille Beach, has kept the high rises out, and has cultivated something of a bohemian Key West-type atmosphere, welcoming artists and small businesses. A travel article in the early 2000s said the neighborhood (it's technically part of St. Pete Beach) once held a group hug for a resident who was sick and 40 people showed up. The area is also home, however, to the hulking Don Cesar resort, a massive fortress-like pink resort right on the beach. Gulfport, on the mainland, was once a fishing village, but is also now known as an artists' haven, or, in one real estate ad, a "bohemian hideaway." and a "haven for art and music." Madeira Beach, and much of St. Pete Beach are mostly vacation spots, full of resort hotels, restaurants and tourist businesses like parasailing and jet ski concessions. Another mainland town in the district is the small, generally non-descript suburb of Kenneth City, possibly most notable as the town where a new police chief in 1988 prohibited his officers from going to Dunkin' Donuts, where they'd been spending too much time.

WHO LIVES HERE?

The district as a whole is mostly white, 82.5 percent, and it is an older district, with nearly half of residents here over 50. People in their 50s make up the biggest group, at just over 16 percent.

The district is remarkably diverse, economically. There are a few areas that could be considered fairly poor, including parts of Gulfport and South Pasadena. Even the areas along the beach, where many residents have a coveted view of the Gulf of Mexico or Boca Ciega Bay, there are neighborhoods were the median household incomes are relatively modest, right around the state norm, though the high number of retirees on the barrier island of the district definitely keeps the median income low. The most affluent part of the district is at its southern-most tip on the islands that make up Tierra Verde, where the median household income is over $90,000.

District 69, which was carved out of three previous districts, is similar to neighboring District 68, politically, a swing district that has leaned Democratic recently, but has similar numbers of conservatives, moderates and liberals. Before redistricting, parts of the district were most recently represented by a Republican, either Larry Ahern or Jim Frishe, and parts by liberal Democrat Rick Kriseman, now mayor of St. Petersburg. Registration is nearly even, and voters here may be ticket splitters - it is one of a few districts where Barack Obama won the presidential count, but a Republican House candidate beat a Democrat. Kathleen Peters won the seat in 2012, getting 52.3 percent to 47.7 percent for Democrat Josh Shulman. Obama, meanwhile, won with 51.1 percent. Obama also won here in 2008, with 51.4 percent that time. In between, in 2010, Democrat Alex Sink beat Rick Scott by about 5 points in the governor's race.

Peters had owned a convenience store and was mayor of the tiny town of South Pasadena when she narrowly defeated Shulman in the race for the seat in 2012, overcoming a push from the Democratic Party to win this Democratic-leaning district. She came into the Legislature saying her focus would be on improving education in the state, and got onto the Education Committee in her first session. She supports the state's new merit pay system for teachers, but said early on she didn't have any big picture education-related proposals to advance. Much of the legislation she sponsored in her first session was fairly technical, though she did try to pass legislation to allow veterans of the armed forces to be automatically considered Florida residents for the purposes of tuition if they come to Florida and attend a college or university. The bill died in committee.

DISTRICT 69 STATS

Registration (Book closing, 2012)

Democrats 36.2 percent
Republicans 35.3 percent
NPA 24.4 percent

Voting Age Population (2010 Census): 158,424
White (Non-Hispanic) 77.8 percent
Hispanic 11.3 percent
Black 6.9 percent

Median Age: 44.1

Men: 48.8 percent
Women 51.2 percent

2012 PRESIDENT
Barack Obama 51.9 percent, Mitt Romney, 46.5 percent (Estimated)*

2012 STATE HOUSE
Rep. Ed Hooper, R-Clearwater, 52.8 percent, Ben Farrell, Democrat, 47.2 percent

2010 GOVERNOR
Alex Sink 48.8 percent, Rick Scott 45.7 percent

2008 PRESIDENT
Barack Obama 53.1 percent, John McCain, 45.2 percent

HOUSE DISTRICT 70
SOUTH ST. PETE, BRADENTON,
NORTH SARASOTA

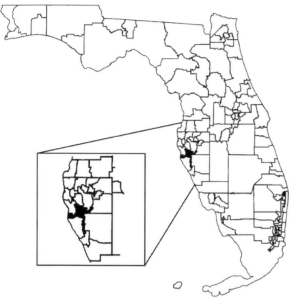

COUNTIES: Pinellas, Hillsborough, Manatee, Sarasota

RATING: Super Democrat

BLACK ACCESS DISTRICT FOR ST. PETE, BRADENTON, SARASOTA

House District 70 is one of those classically contorted districts drawn to unite far-flung communities to create a minority access district, one where the large number of members of a particular minority is likely to result in a member of that community being elected. District 70 is a black minority access district that includes south St. Petersburg, and then jumps across Tampa Bay to Hillsborough County, where it includes eastern parts of Ruskin. The district then becomes a narrow strip running south into Manatee County

446

picking up the Memphis community and part of Palmetto, before crossing the Manatee River and widening a bit to include black neighborhoods in Bradenton. There, it includes Bradenton's massive Tropicana juice plant, just south of the Manatee River, the Bradenton area's second-largest employer after the school system, Here, more than 300 semis arrive daily and more than 600,000 bottles are filled with OJ, and then leave by rail for the rest of the country. The district, still relatively narrow, continues south through the Tallevast area and crossing into Sarasota County to include much of Sarasota's black community of Newtown.

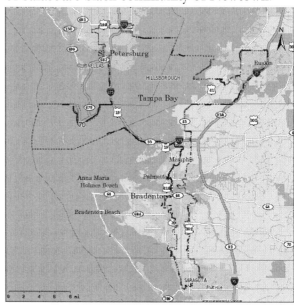

WHO LIVES HERE?

Blacks don't have a full majority, just a plurality, making up 47 percent of the population and 44 percent of the voting age population. Whites, meanwhile, make up 38.5 percent of the voting age population and Hispanics about 15 percent. The district is relatively young - with a median age of 35.9 - and the largest age group by decade is teenagers. Those between the ages of 10 and 19 make up 15 percent of the population, so clearly this is a district of young families.

While there are some very low income areas, the district also includes several middle class Census tracts. In St. Petersburg, there are poor areas with median incomes in the $20,000s, but also some with median incomes in the $50,000s. The areas on the other side of the bay are generally more likely to be poor, with median incomes mostly in the $20,000s in the Bradenton area, and the $30,000s in Sarasota. One exception is the Tallevast area near the Sarasota-Bradenton airport, where incomes are middle class, with the median in the $50,000s.

POLITICAL ISSUES AND TRENDS

Barack Obama had no trouble winning here, beating Mitt Romney by nearly 50 percentage points in 2012 and John McCain by nearly 60 points in 2008. The enthusiasm for Obama dampened a bit. He got 73 percent of the vote here in 2012 and about 79 percent in 2008. Democrat Alex Sink won the governor's race here in 2010 by just under 50 percentage points. Rep. Darryl Rouson, D-St. Petersburg, had no opposition in 2012.

Rouson, thought by many to be one of the better floor speakers in the House, also has one of the most unusual backgrounds for a successful politician. He's a lawyer, with unquestionable influence in his community. But for about 20 years he was also a crack cocaine addict. It was an addiction that started when he was a law student at the University of Florida and one that cost him his first wife. His second wife died of cancer, and Rouson reportedly spent much of a life insurance payout on drugs.[1]

But somehow, he managed to avoid being caught. He was never prosecuted for any drug crimes, which might have derailed his law career. He went into rehab in the late 1990s to keep family members from taking away his son. He's been clean since, and has made fighting the drug epidemic, particularly in the black community (Rouson is African-American) one of his main missions. He became known in St. Petersburg for taking on shops selling drug paraphernalia, raising his profile as a community activist. He also became head of the local NAACP, all while working as a criminal defense attorney - who often represented drug criminals. Rouson had a middle class upbringing, the son of a college administrator and a high school teacher in St. Petersburg. But the drug addiction led to other challenges. In addition to divorce, there was a period of homelessness and a bankruptcy. Rouson has said those difficulties have made him empathetic, a good quality when legislating.

Rouson was criticized when he ran for the Legislature in 2008 as a Democrat, because he had previously been a Republican. He was elected anyway to replace his longtime friend Frank Peterman, who had been appointed head

---

[1] Christina Silva, "Rouson's Party Switching Concerns Some Democratic Leaders, *The St. Petersburg Times,* 8 March, 2008.

of the Department of Juvenile Justice.

Rouson in 2010 successfully passed a measure aimed at reducing the sale of drug paraphernalia by regulating shops selling bongs and pipes. In 2013 he went further, sponsoring legislation to ban their sale outright. The measure passed and was signed by Gov. Rick Scott. Rouson was the only Democrat to support a measure that would have allowed drug testing of some state employees, saying nobody should be afraid of testing for drugs in the workplace. But he has also argued for fairness in drug testing efforts. For example, when Republicans pushed to drug test welfare recipients, Rouson suggested maybe lawmakers should be tested, and their pensions taken away if they fail. Rouson also breaks with much of his Democratic caucus on abortion, sometimes voting for bills that put restrictions on abortion. Shortly after the 2012 election led to long lines at voting sites, Rouson was the first House member to file a bill to expand early voting.

In early 2013, Rouson was narrowly elected as the minority leader-in waiting for 2014, defeating Rep. Mia Jones by one vote. But after the 2013 session he came under fire from some members of his caucus who said Rouson was alienating some key Democratic constituencies, particularly the state's teachers union, and the association that represents plaintiffs' attorneys. Rouson further angered other Democratic leaders by setting up a fundraising committee for House Democrats without coordinating with the state party organization. In September, 2013 Democrats in the House voted 24-17 to replace Rouson as their next floor leader, and shortly after elected Rep. Mark Pafford to replace him. Rouson also made news politically in 2010 when he backed independent Charlie Crist, long a Rouson ally, in his bid for U.S. Senate, rather than his own party's Kendrick Meek. Both ended up losing to Republican Marco Rubio.

DISTRICT 70 STATS

Registration (Book closing, 2012)
Democrats, 63 percent
NPA 18.6 percent
Republicans, 16.3 percent

Voting Age Population (2010 Census): 114,432
Black 44.3 percent
White (Non-Hispanic) 38.5 percent
Hispanic 15.3 percent

Median Age: 35.9

Men: 48.1 percent
Women 51.9 percent

2012 PRESIDENT
Barack Obama 73.1 percent, Mitt Romney, 25.9 percent (Estimated)*

2012 STATE HOUSE
No race. Rep. Darryl Rouson, D-St. Petersburg, faced no primary or general election opposition

2010 GOVERNOR
Alex Sink 73 percent, Rick Scott 23.6 percent

2008 PRESIDENT
Barack Obama 78.7 percent, John McCain, 20.3 percent

HOUSE DISTRICT 71
BRADENTON, COASTAL SARASOTA

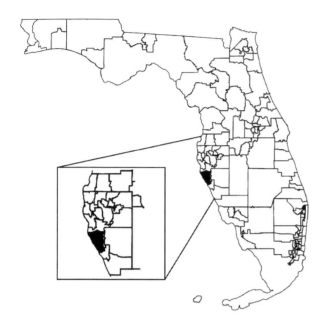

COUNTIES: Manatee, Sarasota
RATING: Leans Republican

RETIRED FOLKS ON THE GULF COAST, LIKE IT USED TO BE

Bradenton and Palmetto came of age as produce markets. They were ports on the Manatee River where citrus and fruit and vegetables were boxed up and shipped around the world, and for a long time they were mainly that. But after World War II, as air conditioning, ease of travel, Social Security and marketing by developers joined to create a boom in retirees moving to Florida, it was only a matter of time before they settled in Manatee

452

County, sandwiched between two other established retirement havens, St. Petersburg and Sarasota.

With wealthier retirees preferring established "society" retirement locations farther south in Sarasota, or on the east coast in Palm Beach County, and growth in St. Petersburg escalating prices there, most of those moving to Manatee County were squarely middle class, many of them blue collar workers from the Midwest. By the time they started coming in large numbers in the 1950s, Bradenton had already become home to several mobile home communities - which suited retirees on modest incomes and made the town even more of a popular retirement destination. In fact, Bradenton may have been home to the first Florida mobile home park. The local Kiwanis Club had opened Bradenton Park in 1936, and it had nearly 2,000 lots by 1954. [1] Another park in Bradenton, Trailer Estates, opened in 1955 to be marketed to snowbirds, It pioneered the idea of allowing buyers to purchase not only a trailer, but the lot that it sat on, using affordable "land ownership" as a new selling point with middle income retirees.[2] The Bradenton area, before too long, was primarily known as a retirement town. By the 2000s, the Bradenton-Sarasota-Venice metropolitan area had the largest percentage of senior citizens of any metro region in the

---

[1] G.C. Hoyt, "The Life of the Retired in a Trailer Park," *American Journal of Sociology*, January, 1954.

[2] Allan Feldt et al., "Retirement Subdivisions, Trailer Estates, Manatee County, Florida," *Journal of Housing for the Elderly*, Winter, 1983.

nation, with nearly 27 percent of residents over age 65, more than double the national percentage.

It used to be even higher - but the percentage of seniors in the area declined 6 percent in the 1990s and another 6 percent in the 2000s as Manatee County officials worked hard to lure businesses and manufacturers to Bradenton, and were largely successful. That brought jobs, and, in turn, younger people. The county suffered a business blow in 2004 when orange juice maker Tropicana moved its headquarters out of downtown Bradenton to Chicago when it was acquired by PepsiCo. But Tropicana still has its main plant in Bradenton, a sprawling facility with a distinctive smell that most people in Bradenton know. The plant is next door in District 70, but with more than 1,600 workers is the area's second largest employer after the school system. The retailer Beall's has its headquarters in Bradenton, employing more than 1,500.

On the mainland, the district includes most of Bradenton west of Tamiami Trail, and in places, a little to the east of it. It includes much of Palmetto, all of South Bradenton, and a narrow strip of land between the coast and U.S. 41 south to Sarasota, where it broadens and includes most of that city's downtown. Offshore, it includes the vacation and condo communities of Anna Maria, Holmes Beach and Bradenton Beach on Anna Maria Island. It also includes Longboat Key, Lido Key and the fashionable St. Armand's Circle area, Bird Key and the very northern tip of Siesta Key.

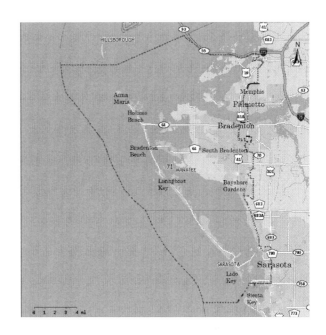

WHO LIVES HERE

While younger people are moving in, this remains one of the oldest districts, just one of 10 where half the population is over 50. The largest group of people here by age decade is those in their 60s, who make up more than 15 percent of the population. The district voting age population is nearly 85 percent white, 9.5 percent Hispanic and just 4 percent African-American.

The district retains a middle class feel on the mainland, and while the coastal barrier islands have affluent enclaves, for sure, they have an old Florida feel, and lots of homes for "normal people," rather than the super rich who live on some other islands around the state. Anna Maria Island has mobile home communities across the street from the beach, where middle class retirees carefully tend small plots and can walk to Rotten Ralph's for a fish sandwich overlooking the bay. Dockside restaurants, trailer parks, small motels, and bungalow houses give the island that "old Florida" look and feel, as does the lack of big box stores and strip malls. In fact, the median household income in Holmes Beach and Bradenton Beach, on Anna Maria Island, suppressed by a large retiree population, is a very low $34,000, much less than the state median. At the top of the island in the town of Anna Maria, the median household income is above the state average, but at $57,000, those who live there aren't the state's wealthiest either.

Farther south, there are some high rise condos, and St. Armand's Circle near Sarasota is trendy and much more upscale, with half million and million dollar family homes. On Longboat Key, median household incomes are much higher, over $100,000.

The mainland part of the district in the north, including Palmetto and Bradenton is diverse, economically, with some relatively poor neighborhoods in Palmetto and South Bradenton, and middle income neighborhoods through most of the city of Bradenton.

Downtown Sarasota is also commercially upscale, home to the Ritz-Carlton, the Sarasota Opera House, and a marina where you'll find some pretty pricy yachts. But people actually live in downtown Sarasota, as well, including in the Laurel Park neighborhood, an area of historic homes, condos and apartment buildings. The people there are also about average in terms of income, with a median household income in the high $40,000s, nearly right at the state median. The district continues east for a few blocks into a slightly poorer area where the median household income is in the low $30,000s.

POLITICAL ISSUES AND TRENDS

The district leans Republican and the GOP has a 43 percent to 33 percent advantage in registration over Democrats, with no party voters making up another 21 percent. Because so many precincts in Manatee County are split among House districts it is difficult to pinpoint the exact margin of victory, but Mitt Romney won here in 2012, as did John McCain in 2008, when he beat Barack Obama by 3.5 percentage points. Rick Scott improved on McCain's showing, winning in the 2010 governor's race here over Democrat Alex Sink by 8.5 points. Rep. Jim Boyd, R-Bradenton, beat Democrat Adam Tebrugge in the 2012 House race here by 11 points.

Boyd was elected to the House in 2010 and, having made his living in insurance, quickly got heavily involved in that issue. In 2011, his first session, he was sponsor of a bill aimed at shrinking state-run Citizens Property Insurance by raising its rates and phasing in rules meant to force some of its customers back into private insurance. A compromise bill that finally passed and focused heavily on sinkhole claims wasn't Boyd's original bill, but had his imprint nonetheless.

But the next year, 2012, Boyd was the House's central figure on insurance issues, sponsoring a high profile overhaul of the personal injury protection auto insurance system that eventually became law, and continuing to push legislation on Citizens. The PIP bill was probably Gov. Rick Scott's biggest priority of the 2012 legislative session, so Boyd was under a microscope. The measure nearly died amid wrangling between groups of health care providers, but passed just before lawmakers adjourned. The bill put restrictions on PIP coverage and people injured in accidents in a bid to lower car insurance premiums. That same session, Boyd sponsored legislation to allow unregulated "surplus lines" insurers to take policies out of Citizens. But that bill died without a final vote after the House, over Boyd's objection, made the measure one where customers would have to approve the take-over.

In 2013 Boyd shifted focus, but remained in a high profile position, as he chaired the House Ethics and Elections Subcommittee that would deal with voting problems that emerged in the 2012 election. The panel worked through proposals to move the state back toward more early voting after it had been reduced earlier. The bill that passed the subcommittee also sought to limit the length of ballots. Also in his capacity as chairman of the subcommittee, Boyd was the sponsor of a major ethics bill that year that was a priority of legislative leaders. Both measures became law. In 2014, Boyd was made chairman of the House State Affairs Committee.

Boyd started his political career on the city council in Palmetto and later was the city's mayor for four years. Boyd's grandfather, Hugh Boyd, served a term in the state House in the 1940s, and his uncle, Wilbur Boyd, was in the

House and Senate from 1958-1972.

DISTRICT 71 STATS

Registration (Book closing, 2012)
Republicans 42.8 percent
Democrats 33 percent
NPA 21.1 percent

Voting Age Population (2010 Census): 132,794
White (Non-Hispanic) 84.5 percent
Hispanic 9.5 percent
Black 4 percent

Median Age: 51.3

Men: 47.7 percent
Women 52.3 percent

2012 PRESIDENT
Unable to determine based on large number of
precincts split between multiple House districts

2012 STATE HOUSE
Rep. Jim Boyd, R-Bradenton, 55.9 percent,
Adam Tebrugge, Democrat, 44.1 percent

2010 GOVERNOR
Rick Scott 52.1 percent, Alex Sink 43.5 percent

2008 PRESIDENT
John McCain 51.2 percent, Barack Obama 47.7
percent

HOUSE DISTRICT 72
SARASOTA, SIESTA KEY

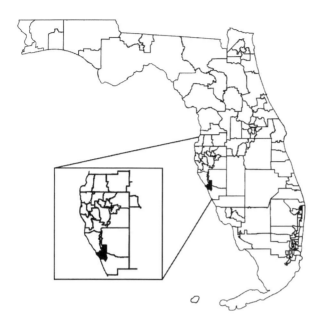

COUNTIES: Sarasota

RATING: Swing District

ONCE A POLO AD, NOW MORE DIVERSE

For many, the image of Sarasota is sailboats on the bay, museums, the arts, and other images that evoke the lifestyles of the wealthy. Or, as Tom Fiedler put it in the 2000 Almanac of Florida Politics, this community is "polo by pony, Polo by Ralph Lauren."

But that's not the full picture, at least anymore. While it is true that there are some wealthy areas around Sarasota, particularly on the barrier islands across the bay, overall much of Sarasota is slightly above average in terms of income, but not spectacularly rich as is the perception. There are plenty of golf holes, and some very nice yachts tied up here, but many of the mainland neighborhoods in District 72, which covers much of Sarasota, have median household incomes in the $40,000 - $60,000 range. It's true that in a place like Sarasota, with large numbers of well-off retirees, that median income isn't the best measure of wealth. Many people here have smaller ongoing incomes in their retirement, but have nice homes and boats - but the really high incomes are mostly on the islands like Siesta Key, and north of here in the barrier islands that are part of District 71, like Longboat Key and St. Armands Key. The wealthy class is still here - but in terms of numbers, it's been overshadowed by the recent growth in middle class people, many of them the people who work for the wealthy, from bankers, stock brokers and yacht captains, to waiters, teachers and cops.

In the 20th Century, we've come to know pretty well the Florida resort town born and marketed as a golf destination. Whether it's Ponte Vedra, Palm Beach or Doral, luring people to the state with a promise of a beautiful Back 9 out their back door is pretty ordinary. But rarely does anyone think of Old Florida - pre World War II - in that way. But Sarasota started it all. Scotsman John Gillespie built a two-hole golf course here to remind him of home, and his company marketed Sarasota heavily to buyers back in Great Britain in the 1880s and 1890s. Later, Gillespie's son would build Florida's first 18-hole golf course, and by the Roaring '20s, Sarasota was a playground for the rich, for sailing and golfing and just lounging around. [1]

The circus came later. Among the rich who spent time in Sarasota were the Ringling Brothers, who made the area the winter home of their circus. The Ringlings also left a legacy of amenities here, like the local art museum.

The district includes Sarasota generally between U.S. 41, and Interstate 75, including the Kensington Park area, Fruitville, and Sarasota Springs. In the south, it includes South Sarasota, Siesta Key, Gulf Gate Estates, Vamo, and Osprey.

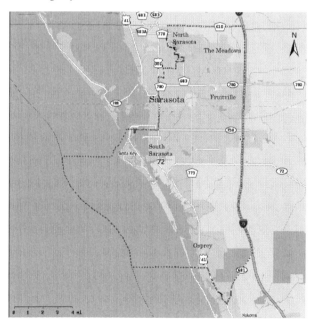

WHO LIVES HERE?

Apart from slightly above average incomes, the district stands out as home to a large number of retirees and people at the upper end of their working years. The largest groups by

---

[1] Fiedler, 801.

age decade are people in their 50s, who make up 15 percent of the population, and people in their 60s, who make up about 14 percent. Another 21 percent of the population is over 70.

The district is mostly white, at about 84 percent overall, and 86 percent of the voting age population. Hispanics make up about 11 percent of the population and black residents make up 3 percent.

POLITICAL ISSUES AND TRENDS

Sarasota's main House seat has swung back and forth between Democrats and Republicans since the early 1990s, and it remains a swing district, though Republicans have won here at the top of the ticket most recently. Mitt Romney won the presidential race here in 2012, though only by about 3 percentage points. While Rep. Ray Pilon, defeated Democrat Liz Alpert by about 8 points in 2012, he is toward the moderate part of the Republican spectrum. And while Rick Scott won here in 2010, he won by less than a percentage point. And in 2008, Democrat Barack Obama won the precincts here in the presidential race by 3 points. The area was represented through the 1990s by Democrat Shirley Brown, but when she left the House in 2000, Republican Donna Clarke won here. Then, in 2006, Keith Fitzgerald won the seat back for Democrats and held it until Pilon narrowly defeated him in the Republican tide of 2010.

Pilon, a former police officer, served previously on the Sarasota County Commission. When he was elected, he was community and government affairs director for the Peace River-Manasota Regional Water Supply Authority. He has focused in the House on areas he knows best, law enforcement issues and water policy, and often takes on low profile and technical issues that keep him below the radar. He was in the spotlight in 2012, however, as the House sponsor of a bill to ban texting while driving, a measure ultimately signed into law by Gov. Rick Scott. Pilon has also been a backer of measures aimed at reducing the prison population, in part by trying to be smart, rather than just tough, on crime. Pilon has sponsored legislation, for example, seeking to have local agencies issue citations to juveniles for certain offenses, rather than locking them up. In 2013, Pilon was the House sponsor of a measure aimed at setting out new juvenile sentencing laws to comply with U.S. Supreme Court opinions on how kids must be treated, but so far the bill has failed to pass.

Pilon does vote with his party on most issues, but not always. He broke with this GOP colleagues, for example, on a proposed ban on abortions based on gender or race, saying it unfairly burdened doctors to determine someone's motive for seeking an abortion. He's also been a critic of "Common Core" standards for schools, putting him at odds with some other Republicans.

DISTRICT 72 STATS

Registration (Book closing, 2012)
Republicans 44.5 percent
Democrats 32.8 percent
NPA 19.4 percent

Voting Age Population (2010 Census): 134,094

White (Non-Hispanic) 86.4 percent
Hispanic 8.9 percent
Black 2.5 percent

Median Age: 50.4

Men: 47.6 percent

Women 52.4 percent

2012 PRESIDENT
Mitt Romney 51.1 percent, Barack Obama 47.7 percent (Estimated*)

2012 STATE HOUSE
Rep. Ray Pilon, R-Sarasota, 53.9 percent, Liz Alpert, Democrat, 46.1 percent

2010 GOVERNOR
Rick Scott 48.6 percent, Alex Sink 47.7 percent

2008 PRESIDENT
Barack Obama 50.9 percent, John McCain, 47.9 percent

HOUSE DISTRICT 73
INLAND MANATEE, NORTHEAST SARASOTA

COUNTIES: Manatee, Sarasota
RATING: Solid Republican

AFFLUENT FAMILIES AND FARMS; SOLIDLY REPUBLICAN

As Manatee and Sarasota counties have grown, more and more new construction has been out in the formerly rural eastern areas, east of Interstate 75. Many of these are upscale planned communities, with Spanish tile roof homes and enclosed swimming pools, manicured lawns and parks, golf courses and new charter schools. These are homes to affluent families, places like Lakewood Ranch, carved out of timber land in the 1990s, or the gated River Wilderness golf and boating community, and other places with exclusive sounding names like Heritage Oaks, and The

Enclave at the Villages of Pinetree. Almost all of these communities, most of which are right along the east side of I-75 are new, having been built in the 1990s and 2000s.

There are also plenty of retirees out here - with people in their 60s, the largest single

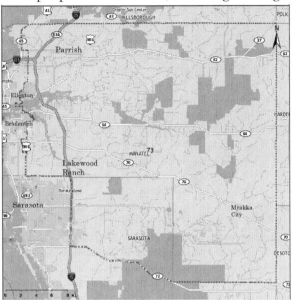

decade age group, making up more than 15 percent of the population. The area is dotted with country clubs, and many of the housing developments surround the clubs and their golf courses. Most of the population in the district lives in this corridor, running from east of Bradenton out to Parrish in the north, down to the area east of Sarasota in the south.

Life in these beautiful new homes up against the fairways contrasts sharply with life for farm workers who are their often unseen neighbors in the vast agricultural area farther east in District 72. Eastern Manatee County has lots of undeveloped farm land, where mostly migrants pick fruit and vegetables and live in much more modest accommodations. Many aren't part of the official demographic picture, particularly for voting, because they're guest workers from other countries or, in some cases, in the country illegally. These communities struggle with the social ills that come with poverty, compounded by the difficulties of life in a foreign country with a different language, and a problem that is growing in the shadows of the immigrant communities, human trafficking.

In addition to the eastern reaches of Bradenton, the district also includes Parrish, Ellenton, Lake Sarasota, Lakewood Ranch, Myakka City, and part of Fruitville.

WHO LIVES HERE?

The western part of this district, closest to Bradenton and Sarasota, is extremely affluent. Several Census tracts between I-75 and Lake Manatee have median household incomes over $100,000 a year, and almost all of the Census tracts in the western part of the district have median household incomes over $70,000, well above the state median. Farther east, they drop a bit as you get into the more rural part of the district, but even there, the medians are above the state average, generally in the $50,000s and $60,000s.

While the median age here is 46.5, people in their 60s make up the largest group, at 15.4 percent of the population. There are plenty of kids, too, though. More than a quarter of the people in the district are under the age of 25.

The district is mostly white, 83.5 percent, with just under 9 percent Hispanic. Another 4.4 percent are black.

POLITICAL ISSUES AND TRENDS

The district is strongly Republican, with top-of-the-ticket GOP candidates, including Mitt Romney, Rick Scott and John McCain, winning here by about 20 points. Rep. Greg Steube, R-Sarasota, didn't have a Democratic opponent in 2012 and easily defeated a no-party candidate. For nearly a decade before Steube was elected, much of this area was represented by Ron Reagan.

The local issues in this area have revolved heavily around growth, as they have in so many other Florida areas on the boundary between the rural and the urban. With more and more development east of Interstate 75, locals have wrestled with how to keep the area's rural and agricultural character in the face of encroaching development.

Iraq War veteran Steube is a native of the district, and the son of Manatee County Sheriff Brad Steube. After graduating from the University of Florida, Steube served as a U.S. Army lawyer, and then was elected to the House in 2010 in the old District 67. In his first bid for re-election, he ran in the newly drawn 73rd, which includes much of the same area. Steube has generally voted with his Republican colleagues on major issues. His most noticed bill was a measure that would have allowed school principals to designate a district employee to carry a gun in each school in a bid to bolster security. The 2013 bill didn't pass. Another high profile bill by Steube during the 2012 legislative session would have shortened the time banks have to pursue a homeowner for unpaid mortgage debt, a complicated measure aimed at reducing the backlog of foreclosure cases. The bill died in committee. Steube successfully sponsored legislation that is intended to make it harder for divorced parents to use false sexual abuse allegations to restrict the other parent's visitation.

DISTRICT 73 STATS

Registration (Book closing, 2012)
Republicans 49 percent
Democrats 27 percent
NPA 20.9 percent

Voting Age Population (2010 Census): 126,220
White (Non-Hispanic) 86.3 percent
Hispanic 7.2 percent
Black 3.5 percent

Median Age: 46.5

Men: 48.6 percent
Women 51.4 percent

2012 PRESIDENT
Mitt Romney 59.4 percent, Barack Obama 39.6 percent (Estimated*)

2012 STATE HOUSE
Rep. Greg Steube, R-Sarasota, 73.6 percent, Bob "Doc" McCann, NPA, 26.4 percent

2010 GOVERNOR
Rick Scott 57.7 percent, Alex Sink 38.7 percent

2008 PRESIDENT
John McCain 58.2 percent, Barack Obama 40.8 percent

HOUSE DISTRICT 74
VENICE AND NORTH PORT

COUNTIES: Sarasota
RATING: Solid Republican

THE WHITEST PLACE IN FLORIDA

House District 74 takes in the area along the Gulf south of Sarasota, through the coastal towns of Venice and Englewood full of Midwestern retirees, and just inland the younger, more working-class town of North Port.

Venice was started in the early 20th Century as a retirement town for railroad engineers, and for years was the winter home of the Ringling Brothers Circus. North Port is adjacent to Port Charlotte (which is in neighboring House

District 75 to the South.) When North Port was created in the 1950s, it was originally North Port Charlotte, but residents voted to drop the Charlotte in the 1970s. North Port is where the largest number of people in the district live, with a population of nearly 60,000, about three times the number who live in Venice. North Port has grown quickly and massively – it's now actually larger than the city of Sarasota, the county seat. In the 2000 census, just 22,000 people lived here, a third of those here now. And the growth since the 1990 census is even more astounding – at that time the city had just about 12,000 people. House District 74 is entirely within Sarasota County.

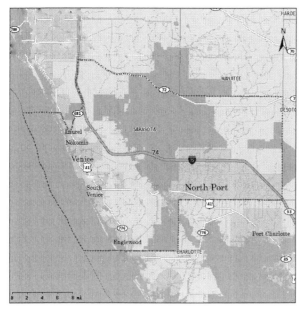

WHO LIVES HERE?

Retired white people, mostly. This area makes up the whitest House district in the state. The district's voting age residents are 92 percent white, 3.9 percent Hispanic and just 2.4 percent black. It's also a fairly old district, with a median age (55.9) 15 years older than the state median, driven up by the 67.6 year median age in Venice, one of the oldest population centers in the state, and the 63.6 year median age in Englewood. That is balanced out by the median age in North Port, which is just under 41, lower than the state as a whole. A large number of residents of Venice are snowbirds, and the town is much emptier in summer. Traditionally, southwest Florida, including southern Sarasota County, has been a retirement destination mostly for Midwesterners, with Ohio and Michigan in particular, being major places of origin for many of those living here. For years, they simply followed Interstate 75 to vacation spots on the west coast and when it came time to retire they went to the area they already knew.

POLITICAL ISSUES AND TRENDS

The district is about 44 percent Republican and 29 percent Democratic by representation, with another 24 percent having no party affiliation. North Port – in part because so many here are relative newcomers – and also because it is a city of younger, working people, is often seen as less politically active and engaged than its elderly neighbors. It's also the part of the district where its few Democratic votes come from – Venice and Englewood and most of the rest of South Sarasota County are solidly Republican. President Obama got more votes in a couple of North Port precincts in 2012, but Romney easily won the overwhelming majority of precincts in the district and the best Obama did in any one precinct was a narrow 5 percentage point win in

North Port's Precinct 339, an area straddling U.S. 41 just north of the Charlotte County line.

For much of the district, typical issues for elderly retirees are front and center here, from health care and the general cost of living to the federal issues of social security and Medicare solvency. Sarasota's per capita property taxes are higher than the state average and its per capita schools taxes are among the highest in the state. Red tide algae blooms, which have hit southwest Florida several times in recent years, are a concern, partly because of locals' desire to enjoy the beaches and partly because of fears for vacation rental bookings.

House District 74 is represented by Rep. Doug Holder, R-Venice. A businessman who moved to Florida in 1997, Holder was first elected to the House in 2006 and re-elected subsequently. He's a member of the business-oriented wing of the GOP. Holder was mentioned as a possible replacement for Lt. Gov. Jennifer Carroll when she resigned amid a gambling scandal, but he has mostly worked quietly in the Legislature. He sponsored legislation in 2013 aimed at pushing some policyholders out of Citizens Property Insurance, and joined his Venice colleague, Sen. Nancy Detert, in sponsoring the 2013 bill that bans texting while driving in some circumstances. Holder has filed paperwork to be able to raise money to run for the overlapping Senate District 28 in 2018.

DISTRICT STATS

Registration (Book closing, 2012)
Republicans 43.7 percent

Democrats 28.9 percent
NPA 24.4 percent

Voting Age Population (2010 Census): 133,818
White (Non-Hispanic) 92 percent
Hispanic 3.9 percent
Black 2.4 percent

Median Age: 55.9

Men 47.7 percent
Women 52.3 percent

VOTING PERFORMANCE

2012 PRESIDENT
Mitt Romney 56.9 percent, Barack Obama 43.1
percent (Estimated*)

2012 STATE HOUSE
No Race. Rep. Doug Holder, R-Venice, faced
no opposition.

2010 GOVERNOR
Rick Scott 52.2 percent, Alex Sink 42.7 percent

2008 PRESIDENT
John McCain 52.6 percent, Barack Obama 46.2
percent

HOUSE DISTRICT 75
CHARLOTTE COUNTY

COUNTIES: Charlotte

RATING: Solid Republican

MIDWESTERN RETIREES, RELIABLY REPUBLICAN

House District 75 is exactly contiguous with Charlotte County – the only district with borders the same as one full county and that county only. It's solidly Republican, giving Mitt Romney 56.6 percent of the vote in 2012 to 42.4 percent for President Obama – even though registered Republicans make up only 43.4 percent of the electorate. It's the sixth oldest district in the state with a median age of 55.8 and is heavily populated by blue collar retirees from the Midwest. The district includes the cities of Punta Gorda and Port Charlotte and the developments of Englewood East and Rotonda West on the peninsula that sticks down into Charlotte Harbor. It also includes

Little Gasparilla Island and part of Manasota Key. The area was the downfall of Ponce de Leon, who was shot by a native's arrow while exploring the harbor, and returned to Cuba where he died from his wound. The towns in this district were hit hard by Hurricane Charley, which made landfall near Port Charlotte in August 2004, with 150 mile an hour winds.

WHO LIVES HERE?

The character of Charlotte County may be

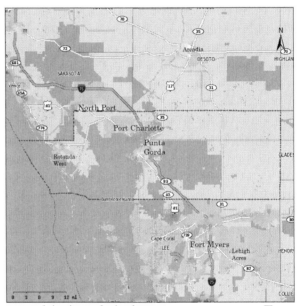

rooted in its relatively recent emergence. Even as late as the 1950s, the county was mostly pasture land owned by cattle ranchers, an area that before air conditioning was just too far south for large residential development. It's still fairly rural today east of Interstate 75, but at the time, there was no urban development around the mouths of the Myakka and Peace Rivers, which form the natural harbor. But in the 1950s, with southern Florida opening up in the post war period, brothers Elliott, Robert and

Frank Mackle formed the General Development Corporation, bought up cheap farmland, subdivided it, and sold "mail order" lots through ads in weekly magazines promising "The Florida Dream." Their marketing was aimed principally at blue collar northerners, particularly from the Midwest. The lots were cheap even then, going for a $10 down payment and $10 a month, and deals were first done by people mailing in coupons. GDC also hired brokers in Midwestern cities and Canada, and bussed and flew people down to Florida to get them to buy houses. It was affordable to the working class, and as Tom Fiedler noted in the 2000 Almanac of Florida Politics, "sophisticated people didn't buy mail-order land."

While the wealthy flocked to other Florida get-aways, like Palm Beach on the other coast, Sarasota to the north and Naples to the south, "Charlotte got the retired shop foremen, the school teachers, the NCOs, the mid-level civil servants, many on fixed pensions," Fiedler wrote. [1] There continued to be a strong Midwest pipeline – I-75 connects Michigan and Ohio with southwest Florida, while the east coast of Florida is more conveniently connected to the northeast via I-95. As Jewish northeasterners retired to Boca Raton, Catholics and Methodists from the middle of the country came to Port Charlotte.

While many of the initial retirees were blue collar workers, some of them union members, today, the registration is solid Republican, with

[1] Fiedler, 236.

478

the GOP claiming about 43 percent of voters to just 31 percent who are Democrats. The other 22 percent or so are in neither party.

The district is overwhelmingly white, 88.2 percent among the voting age population, with blacks and Hispanics about 5 percent each. The district is also home to a large number of snowbirds who can't vote, those from Canada, who winter in southwest Florida, but return north in the summer.

POLITICAL ISSUES AND TRENDS

Charlotte County is solidly Republican and trending more so, having given both Mitt Romney and Rick Scott 14 percentage point wins after John McCain won by just a little over 7 percentage points in 2008. Democrats didn't bother to put up a candidate for the state House in the district in 2012.

Some of these former blue collar workers were Democrats in their younger days. But like other aging, white "factory retirees" who once made up the conservative part of the Midwestern and Rust Belt Democratic Party, many of them have abandoned the party and now vote mostly for Republicans. [2] Some became Reagan Republicans decades ago. But while wary of high taxes, many do believe that government has a role to play - and they could turn if someone seriously threatens their

---

[2] For more on shifts in working class voting patterns, see: Richard Florida, "What is it, Exactly, That Makes Big Cities Vote Democratic?" *The Atlantic* (Online, 19 February, 2013.)
http://www.theatlanticcities.com/politics/2013/02/what-makes-some-cities-vote-democratic/4598/

entitlements.

Charlotte County is also largely devoid of the groups that have driven Democratic success in recent elections. With Hispanics and African-Americans each making up just 5 percent of the voting age population, and no sizable community of young people, some of the Democratic Party's best hopes are absent. There's also little in the way of a knowledge economy, which correlates with Democratic voting - no high tech or creative-class community to draw liberal-leaning voters.

Rep. Ken Roberson, R-Punta Gorda, is this area's representative, and in many ways, he is indeed representative of its population. Like nearly a quarter of residents here, he's over 70, and he's a conservative, pro-business, white Republican. Like nearly everyone else, he's from somewhere other than Charlotte County originally, though Roberson is unusual here in that he's a Florida native, having been born in Bradenton. A funeral director by profession, Roberson is chairman of the Health Quality Subcommittee. He was elected in 2008 to the old District 71, defeating Democrat Betty Gissendanner 54 percent to 46 percent. Roberson won re-election easily in 2010 and in 2012 Democrats didn't bother to put up a challenger.

In 2010 Roberson shepherded to passage a bill that requires more training for 911 dispatchers, a measure inspired by the death of a North Port woman due to a botched 911 call. Roberson also has passed legislation that allowed for certain Lottery tickets to be sold from automated vending machines, among other measures. In 2012, Roberson was the co-sponsor of a large economic development bill that included the August sales tax holiday. Roberson was unsuccessful in a 2011 effort to get the state prison system to speed up deportation of inmates who are in the country illegally.

DISTRICT 75 STATS

Registration (Book closing, 2012)
Republicans 43.4 percent
Democrats 30.8 percent
NPA 21.7 percent

Voting Age Population (2010 Census) 137,100
White (Non-Hispanic) 88.2 percent
Black 5.1 percent
Hispanic 4.7 percent

Median Age: 55.8

Men, 48.6 percent
Women, 51.4 percent

VOTING PERFORMANCE

2012 President
Mitt Romney 56.6 percent, Barack Obama 42.4 percent

2012 State House
Rep. Ken Roberson, R-Punta Gorda, faced no primary or general election opposition.

2010 Governor
Rick Scott 54 percent, Alex Sink 40 percent

2008 President
John McCain, 52.9 percent, Barack Obama 45.6 percent

HOUSE DISTRICT 76
FORT MYERS BEACHES, ESTERO AND BONITA

COUNTIES: Lee

RATING: Solid Republican

RETIREES, COUNTRY CLUB REPUBLICANS

House District 76 includes Estero and Bonita Springs, the suburbs that basically link Fort Myers to Naples, making it one big suburban area along the southwest Florida coast. The district, which is overwhelmingly Republican, also includes the beach towns on the barrier islands off Fort Myers, including the golf-cart town of Boca Grande – one of the richest places in Florida – and Pine Island, Sanibel and Fort Myers Beach. Many of these beach communities are home to seasonal residents, filled with retirees and vacation renters.

Boca Grande once was home to year round working class residents who worked at a port on the island through which phosphate was shipped. They shared the island with wealthy winter residents. The port's now closed, and Boca Grande is an upscale vacation and retirement beach town, where many of the residents drive around on golf carts rather than in cars. Former President George H.W. Bush and his family vacationed here for several years and the classic old Gasparilla Inn, where gentlemen are still required to wear jackets to dinner during much of the year, was the vacation destination for J.P. Morgan, the duPonts, Cabots and Firestones. The 33921 zip code of Boca Grande is one of the wealthiest in Florida, with a median per family income around $100,000 and average home values around $1 million. Pine Island, the biggest island on Florida's Gulf Coast, includes the village of Matlacha, the marina and country-club town of Pineland, St. James City, and Bokeelia. Waterfront homes here start at a half million dollars.

The district also includes the southwest corner of Fort Myers, including the Iona area, Punta Rassa, and part of the Harlem Heights neighborhood, a relatively low-income area that is home mostly to Latinos and African-Americans.

First populated by a utopian religious community known as the Koreshan Unity, and a few fishing families, Estero became, and remained for many years, a citrus community. But now it has grown into a typical American suburb of wide roads and big box chain stores.

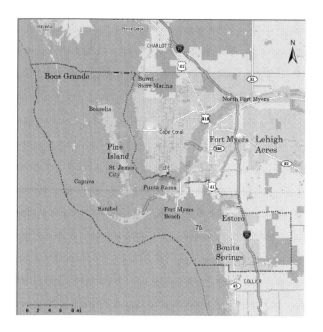

Strip malls line U.S. 41 seemingly forever heading south out of Fort Myers down through Estero and Bonita Springs, seamlessly becoming the Naples area. The housing developments off 41 have always been full of retirees, and the population here drops in the summer, the roads filling up with northerners in the winter. There seems to be a golf course down just about every side road. Gated, master-planned condo communities also stretch for miles. It's not all golf, tennis and swimming, and there are some mobile home communities and middle class neighborhoods, but the area's vibe of a nice suburban, coastal area for retirees isn't in danger. Estero is about to get an influx of young professionals, though. The Hertz Corp. announced in May 2013 that it would be moving its corporate headquarters to the southern Lee County town and expects to have 700 employees there, many of them moving from New Jersey.

The population centers of the district for now are Bonita Springs, which has more than 40,000 residents, and the northern part of the district that is in the city of Fort Myers, which includes about the same. Estero is home to about 20,000, and an area next to Estero known as San Carlos Park, includes another 15,000 or so residents.

WHO LIVES HERE?

What jumps out demographically about House District 76 is the median age of 56.3, well over the state median age of 40.7 years. This is retirement country, and many of the retirees live part of the year up north.

Republicans outnumber Democrats here 2-1, but like in many other places in Florida, the GOP here has lost registration - not to the Democratic Party but to the no-party camp. In 2012, HD 76 was 49.2 percent Republican 24.3 percent Democrat and 23.5 percent NPA. Whoever coined the term "country club Republicans," might have had this area in mind. It's well-to-do, laid-back and generally fairly moderate. Sanibel Island was the home of longtime Congressman Porter Goss, the former CIA chief who settled down on the beach island and then got involved in politics. Goss's moderate stances – he was a member of the Main Street Republican moderate caucus – reflected those of the middle-of-the-road, well-off Republicans in this area.

In most of the district, at least one in three people has a Bachelor's Degree and in some areas the educational attainment is higher. In Estero, about 40 percent have at least a

Bachelor's and nearly one in five has an advanced degree. While not in the district, Florida Gulf Coast University is just outside it, across I-75 from San Carlos Park.

POLITICAL ISSUES AND TRENDS

While there may be some moderates here, make no mistake about how much this is GOP country. In 2012, Mitt Romney won 37 of 38 precincts in the district, most of them overwhelmingly, and just barely lost the other. Overall, Romney got about 65 percent of the vote in the district to 35 percent for Obama.

The rapid and massive growth of this area, which has ballooned in population in the last couple of decades, permeates many of the political issues locally, from economics to battles over efforts to open new health care facilities and whether certain areas should remain in unincorporated Lee County or become part of a city. Preserving the natural beauty of places like Sanibel, Captiva and Estero Bay has long been an interest here, making Republicans a bit green. It's hardly anti-growth, though, with many here trying to find a balance between population and infrastructure growth and preservation. Generally, voters here like staunch fiscal conservatives who are pro-business and moderate-to-conservative on social issues. A candidate from the corporate world like Mitt Romney or Rick Scott is the kind of candidate who can do well in the district, although it would be hard for any serious Republican to lose in this region.

The district is represented by Rep. Ray Rodrigues, R-Estero, who was elected after winning a three-way GOP primary in 2012 and, making the point about how solid a Republican district this is, faced no general election opposition. In the primary, Rodrigues got 50 percent of the vote, well ahead of former Rep. Michael Grant, who actually lived in neighboring Charlotte County but planned to move. Grant got 28 percent of the vote and a third GOP candidate, Chauncey Solinger, got 22 percent. Rodrigues moved to Estero after college in Georgia, and works as the budget manager for the College of Arts and Sciences at Florida Gulf Coast University. He's a former county Republican vice chairman. During his first term in the Legislature, Rodrigues carried a bill being pushed by veteran Sen. Joe Negron that guarantees the right of the public to speak at local government meetings, a measure that passed and was signed into law. Rodrigues has also pushed for the development of alternative and renewable energy business in Southwest Florida.

DISTRICT 76 STATS

Registration (Book closing, 2012)
Republicans 49.2 percent
Democrats 24.3 percent
NPA 23.5 percent

Voting Age Population (2010 Census): 133,427
White (Non-Hispanic) 87 percent
Hispanic 10.1 percent
Black 1.3 percent

Median Age: 56.3

Men 49.2 percent

Women 50.8 percent

VOTING PERFORMANCE

2012 PRESIDENT
Mitt Romney 64.4 percent, Barack Obama 35.6
percent (Estimated*)

2012 STATE HOUSE: Republican primary:
Ray Rodrigues 50 percent, Michael Grant 27.9
percent, Chauncey Solinger 22.2 percent.
Rodrigues faced no general election opposition.

2010 GOVERNOR
Rick Scott 62.7 percent, Alex Sink 34.1 percent

2008 PRESIDENT
John McCain 58.9 percent, Barack Obama 40.2
percent

HOUSE DISTRICT 77
CAPE CORAL

COUNTIES: Lee

RATING: Solid Republican

A LAND SCAM THAT WORKED, SORT OF

House District 77 is roughly contiguous with the city of Cape Coral, which sits on the north bank of the Caloosahatchee River across from Fort Myers. Cape Coral was another of South Florida's many designed, planned communities that grew more than most had imagined it would. Founded in the late 1950s, the city now is home to more than 150,000 people. While it started as a Gulf-front "suburb" it has since not just outgrown its older neighbor, but is more than twice as large as better-known Fort Myers.

The growth stopped in the late 2000s - as the real estate bubble burst and, like other areas of Southwest Florida, Cape Coral found itself at the epicenter of a foreclosure crisis. In 2010, a real estate agent drew plenty of national press for running "foreclosure tours," putting tourists and homebuyers in a van to show them neighborhoods full of empty homes and possible deals. "Yes, it has come to this in Cape Coral, a reluctant symbol for the excesses of the great American real estate bubble: foreclosed homes served up as tourist attraction," Peter S. Goodman wrote in The New York Times in 2010. "[1]

Back at the beginning this was one of the "fly and buy" communities, where the developers would fly prospects down to show them the area and hope to get them to buy property before leaving. Cape Coral's developers had their own private aircraft to fly customers over the area, and some deals were even signed before they landed. With what some said were sketchy high pressure tactics, the developers, Baltimore brothers Leonard and Jack Rosen, convinced the first buyers to purchase homes in a "town" that didn't yet exist, but with a promise that it would soon be a "water wonderland." Tom Fiedler, writing about Lee County in the 2000 Almanac of Florida Politics, quoted a resident who called Cape Coral "a land scam that actually succeeded." [2] It's unlikely many of those first fly-over buyers could have imagined, however,

---

[1] Peter S. Goodman, "Real Estate in Cape Coral is Far From a Recovery," *The New York Times*, 2 January, 2010.

[2] Fiedler, 534.

that the scrubby point sticking out into the Gulf would come to be what it is now - the largest city between Tampa and Miami. [3]

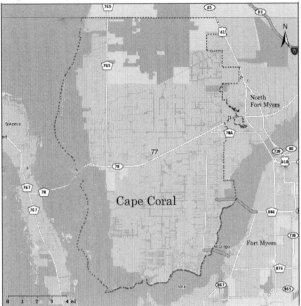

It's also hard to imagine that it essentially happened twice. After Cape Coral seemed to have filled up, the speculation boom of the early 2000s filled it up some more, precipitating the 2008 crash. Goodman called it "The Story, the fable that waterfront living beyond winter's reach exerts such a powerful pull that it justifies almost any price for housing." That fable, he wrote, "propelled the orgy of borrowing, investing and flipping that dominated life here and in other places where January doesn't include a snow blower." He noted that the median home price was down to around $90,000 in Cape Coral in 2009. It had been

[3] For more on sketchy early development, and particularly its impact on the environment, see Cynthia Barnett, *Mirage, Florida and the Vanishing Water of the Eastern U.S.* (University of Michigan Press, 2008.)

$278,000 in 2005.

WHO LIVES HERE

The housing crash and resulting foreclosure crisis hit most of Southwest Florida hard. While it wasn't as big an exodus as was seen across the river in Lehigh Acres, Cape Coral did see lots of people leave at the height of the recession. Others were forced to move when they lost their homes. Local officials said the number of cars on the road during the deepest part of the recession in 2009 was reduced to what it had been a decade earlier, before a huge period of growth. [4] Since then, there have been signs of recovery. Single family home permits in Cape Coral rebounded in early 2013 to pre-recession levels. Traffic returned to the roads, too.

Which people left and which people remained is hard to determine. The median incomes in the area, according to estimates from the 2012 American Community Survey, are mostly solidly middle class, in the $40,000s and $50,000s. Neighborhoods right on the Gulf are more affluent, but even there, median household incomes are only mostly in the $70,000s. The only Census tract in the district with a median household income above $80,000 is a small development known as Burnt Store Marina in the farthest northwest corner of the district.

The district is 74 percent white, 19 percent Hispanic and 4 percent black. The population is right around the state median in age, with a

---

[4] Chad Gillis, "Lee County Recovery Brings Traffic," *Fort Myers News-Press*, 14 March, 2013.

median here of about 43, despite the fact that it continues to be heavily marketed to retirees.

POLITICAL ISSUES AND TRENDS

Cape Coral and Lee County in general have been solidly Republican for nearly a generation, and Cape Coral in particular has been one of the most reliably Republican performing cities in the state. But it's not one of the most overwhelmingly Republican districts - that is, Republicans almost always win here, but not by particularly large margins. Mitt Romney won the presidential race in these precincts by about 16 percentage points in 2012. There were more than 20 Florida House districts where Romney's margin was wider, and it's nowhere near the kind of Republican dominance seen in places like Santa Rosa County in the Panhandle, where Romney won by more than 50 points, or several districts in north Florida where he bested Barack Obama by more than 40 points. Likewise, Republican Rick Scott won easily here, beating Alex Sink in the 2010 governor's race by more than 20 points. But there were several House districts where Scott's margin of victory was more than 30 points. And John McCain only got 54 percent of the vote here. Also, Cape Coral voters in 2013 elected a Democrat, Marni Sawicki, as mayor. So the area is conservative, but it's not one of the most conservative places in the state.

And it may be getting less Republican (the election of Sawicki may point some to that conclusion). One of the biggest changes in Cape Coral's demographics over the previous decade may have been overshadowed by the economic upheaval, but the Hispanic population in the area doubled. A Latino community that was 9 percent of the population here in 2000 was 19 percent of the population in 2010. It's likely that some of the Hispanics responsible for that growth are not eligible voters, with some of the increase attributable to migratory construction workers and new arrivals not yet eligible to vote. But many Hispanics are eligible voters and have shown a propensity to vote for Democrats in the last couple of elections.

District 77 is represented by Dane Eagle, who before he was elected, was known to many around the Capitol as a former aide to Gov. Charlie Crist. He was Crist's deputy chief of staff, and later a spokesman for and then finance director of Crist's U.S. Senate campaign. Eagle's father, Greg Eagle, was a major real estate broker in Cape Coral and a supporter and friend of Crist, which is how Dane Eagle got into politics. The younger Eagle also works for his family's real estate business. In his first session Eagle passed legislation that would set up a regulatory structure for the future storage of natural gas underground and a bill prohibiting protests within a certain distance of a funeral. He also passed legislation that requires judges, to hold sex offenders without bail.

DISTRICT 77 STATS

Registration (Book closing, 2012)
Republicans 42.6 percent
Democrats 28.3 percent
NPA 25.9 percent

Voting Age Population (2010 Census): 117,930

White (Non-Hispanic) 77.2 percent
Hispanic 17 percent
Black 3.4 percent

Median Age: 42.9

Men 48.9 percent
Women 51.1 percent

2012 PRESIDENT
Mitt Romney 57.2 percent, Barack Obama 41.3 percent

2012 STATE HOUSE
Dane Eagle, Republican, 62.4 percent, Arvella M. Clare, Democrat, 37.6 percent

2010 GOVERNOR
Rick Scott 58.7 percent, Alex Sink 37.1 percent

2008 PRESIDENT
John McCain 54 percent, Barack Obama 44.9 percent

HOUSE DISTRICT 78
FORT MYERS

COUNTIES: Lee
RATING: Solid Republican

DEMOCRATS AREN'T USUALLY EMBRACED

In early February of 2009, Fort Myers was the perfect backdrop for the newly elected president, Barack Obama, to try to drum up support for passage of a stimulus package to try to jumpstart an economy that had recently crashed. In one sense it was hostile territory for the president - this is unquestionably Republican turf, but Fort Myers and the area around it were among the worst-hit areas in the country in the recession. This was the place, the White House believed, that most needed the stimulus. Southwest Florida had boomed because of growth, and construction underpinned the area's economy. That construction was gone, nearly overnight. Two days earlier the New York Times had splashed the Fort Myers suburb of Lehigh Acres (next door in House District 79) onto its pages as the poster child for the nation's foreclosure crisis. "Desperation has moved into this once-middle-class exurb of Fort Myers, where hammers used to pound," that story began.[1]

There weren't many Republicans there to welcome Obama. A couple of them did show up though, and one of them enthusiastically greeted Obama. "Mr. President! Welcome to Fort Myers," that Republican, Gov. Charlie Crist, said. And then, Crist hugged Obama. "I didn't know it yet. But that high-spirited day in Fort Myers ... ended my viable life as a Republican politician," Crist wrote in his 2014 book. [2]

The incident that would help doom Crist as a Republican is as good a metaphor as any for the general political outlook in Fort Myers - Democrats are welcome to come around, but people here don't fully embrace them.

The district includes the city of Fort Myers, and some of the area right around it including the Whiskey Creek and Cypress Lake areas and the corridor along McGregor Blvd. to the

---

[1] Damien Cave, "In Florida, Despair and Foreclosures," *The New York Times*, 7 February, 2009.

[2] Charlie Crist and Ellis Henican, The Party's Over: How the Extreme Right Hijacked the GOP and I Became a Democrat, (Dutton, 2014)

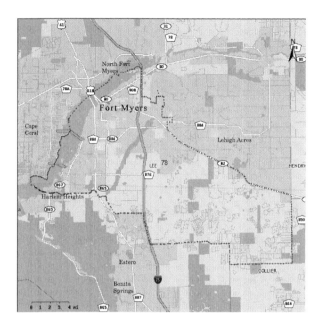

southwest of the city. It also includes the Southwest Florida International Airport and a large area southeast of the city and the airport, going far enough south to include, at its far southern end, Florida Gulf Coast University.

WHO LIVES HERE

While almost all of Lee County's black population is in the city of Fort Myers, and the district has a growing Hispanic community, the district remains more than 60 percent non-Hispanic white, and it's voting age population is almost 70 percent white. But growth in the Latino population is a notable demographic feature here - Hispanics went from about 12 percent of the population in 2000 to about 18 percent in 2010, a 50 percent increase. If that were to continue, by 2020 the Latino population would be nearly 30 percent. The black population makes up about 16 percent of the district's overall population, but just 13 percent of the voting age population.

The district struggles with poverty in its urban core. The heavily black area around central downtown Fort Myers is extremely poor, with most of the Census tracts near downtown having a very low median income in the $20,000s. One Census tract near downtown, including the neighborhoods of Velasco Village, Sable Palm, and Renaissance Preserve, has a median income below $20,000, putting it among the poorest areas in the state. Incomes increase, however, as you move away from the city center, rising quickly into the $60,000s, and $70,000s in Reflection Isles, and over $100,000 farther out.

POLITICAL ISSUES AND TRENDS

The Republican lean of this district and of surrounding Lee County in general has been exaggerated a bit in a lot of the political conventional wisdom. Yes, Republicans win here, and usually comfortably. Reportedly the fiscal conservatism goes way back - there's a story that when local resident Thomas Edison (yes, that Edison) offered to install his new electric lights for free, the city turned him down, not wanting to pay for light poles and wires. But Democrats get votes here, too. Obama got 46.5 percent of the vote in 2008 in this district, and about 44 percent in 2012. And, of course, for years, the whole area was a Democratic stronghold, though of the Old South conservative kind. But as recently as the 1990s, Fort Myers residents sent Democrat Keith Arnold to Tallahassee as their representative for eight terms, even after the GOP had gained a majority. It's worth noting the demographics - while the combination of blacks and Hispanics doesn't create a bloc big enough to overcome white, mostly GOP voters, if the Hispanic population continues to grow as it has, that would eventually happen.

House District 78 is represented by Rep. Heather Fitzenhagen, a Republican from Fort Myers. Fitzenhagen's most high profile work in the House so far has been in support of a bill called "Rebecca's Law," which would create the felony crime of aggravated bullying. The bill is named after a girl who committed suicide after being bullied online. In 2013, Fitzenhagen was a backer of successful legislation to change the makeup of the Lee County Tourist Development Council, and also worked to help her community entice Hertz to move its corporate headquarters to Estero. Fitzenhagen has also expressed concerns about releases of water from Lake Okeechobee into the Caloosahatchee River. Before election to the House, Fitzenhagen, a lawyer, started a mediation and arbitration company and was the marketing director at a law firm.

DISTRICT 78 STATS

Registration (Book closing, 2012)
Republicans 43.1 percent
Democrats 32.4 percent
NPA 21.5 percent

Voting Age Population (2010 Census): 123,892
White (Non-Hispanic) 68.8 percent
Hispanic 15 percent
Black 13.3 percent

Median Age: 41.8

Men 49 percent
Women 51 percent

2012 PRESIDENT
Mitt Romney 54.5 percent, Barack Obama 44.2
percent

2012 STATE HOUSE
Heather Fitzenhagen, Republican, 67.3 percent,
Kerry Babb, Independent, 32.7

2010 GOVERNOR
Rick Scott 56.6 percent, Alex Sink 39.9 percent

2008 PRESIDENT
John McCain 52.6 percent, Barack Obama 46.5
percent

HOUSE DISTRICT 79
NORTH FORT MYERS, LEHIGH ACRES

COUNTIES: Lee

RATING: Solid Republican

DREAMS FOR SALE: THE EPICENTER OF THE FORECLOSURE CRISIS

When the New York Times went looking in 2009 for a place to illustrate the nation's housing crash and foreclosure crisis, it landed in Lehigh Acres. The sprawling community east of Fort Myers had been a boom town. The lots were laid out in the 1950s, but they were sold dirt cheap, $10 down and $10 a month, with the idea that by the time buyers were ready to retire, they'd have enough to build a home.

Infrastructure wasn't built early on - developers thought it would be a while before anyone actually moved here. And they were right. But in the 2000s, when Southwest Florida went into a real estate frenzy, fueled by a strong economy, and speculation, suddenly developers were coming from all over looking to build new houses. Lehigh Acres was an easy place for a boom - the land was cleared and the lots were already there - there was even a street grid. All that was needed, it seemed, were homes. And they were quickly built. As all of Southwest Florida boomed, the growth intensified as people moved here to take advantage of that boom. That is, as more people wanted to move here, more people moved here to build those houses.

Financing was easy, banks were practically giving away home loans. As the boom continued, Lehigh Acres became home to many of the construction workers and tradesmen who were building the houses, and the people who worked in the suddenly cropping up appliance and furniture stores, selling stuff to fill those new homes. The peak year was 2005 - and the number of houses in Lehigh Acres nearly doubled in less than two years.

And then it crashed. In the exuberance, too many homes had been built. Some were faulty. Some people couldn't actually afford what they'd bought. It was a little like a Ponzi scheme too - the reason people were moving here was to build homes for people moving here. As long as homes were being bought and built, there was work. But much of the boom had been driven by amateur speculators.

"People who wouldn't normally have any experience in real estate investing were speculating on the fact that all they had to do was buy something, hold it for a brief period of time, and suddenly they would receive windfall profit," former state Rep. Gary Aubuchon, a real estate executive, says in "Dreams for Sale," a film about the crash. Eventually, panic set in. Home values plummeted, businesses closed.

Lee County lost a higher percentage of jobs from June 2007 to June 2008 than any other county in the nation, according to federal statistics. Unemployment jumped from a little over 3 percent in early 2007, to nearly 10 percent by late 2008. "By last spring, life as they knew it had come to an end," wrote Damien Cave in The New York Times. "In Lehigh Acres, homes are selling at 80 percent off their peak prices. Only two years after there were more jobs than people to work them, fast-food restaurants are laying people off or closing. Crime is up, school enrollment is down, and one in four residents received food stamps in December, nearly a fourfold increase since 2006." [1]

The situation was made worse by the fact that a number of homes in Southwest Florida had been built using faulty Chinese drywall that

[1] Damien Cave, "In Florida, Despair and Foreclosures," *The New York Times*, 7 February, 2009. For a film on Lehigh Acres and the experience of the real estate bust, see "Dreams For Sale: Lehigh Acres and the Florida Foreclosure ..." (Viewable online at https://www.youtube.com/watch?v=OcrKdWcxS8c)

emitted sulfur and made people sick. Some homeowners learned that they would have to rip out drywall and maybe wiring that had been damaged by it; in some cases the repairs would cost nearly what the houses were now worth in the market downturn. Many just up and left. People who worked in business tied to real estate and construction lost their jobs and stopped making mortgage payments. Many walked away from their homes, and in 2009 Travel and Leisure Magazine put Lehigh Acres on a list of "World's Eeriest Abandoned Places."

To focus on the devastation wrought here by the recession and housing crash may seem to ignore what else there may be to characterize this area - but it's hard to overstate how much of an impact the crisis had on shaping what this part of the state looks like. Huge areas had few people. Then one day, they had way too many. Then, another day, the houses were empty. Joseph Whalen, the president of the Lehigh Acres Chamber of Commerce, tried to capture the essence of the community in that New York Times article - but had a hard time without invoking the crash. "'That's one of the things we struggle with: What is our identity?' said Joseph Whalen ...We don't want to be the bedroom community of southwest Florida; we don't want to be the foreclosure capital.'" Alas, that's what this area was. But there are starting to be signs of recovery - local officials noted in 2013 that traffic counts - the number of cars on the roads - were up, meaning people must be coming back. Real estate web sites still show a lot of bargains, but people are starting to buy.

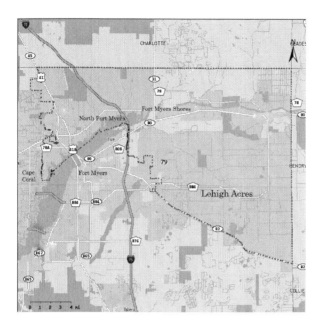

WHO LIVES HERE?

It's hard to gauge the politico-demographic makeup of an area in such flux, and for that matter, hard to discern exact political implications of the recession in a community where so many people fled, or were forced to leave. As Jenna Buzzacco-Foerster put it in 2012, "In this sprawling community of senior citizens and the chronic unemployed, yard signs for Barack Obama and Mitt Romney aren't as common as for-sale signs." [2]

So who lives here? Who knows? "Recent" government numbers don't capture much of what's happened. Information from the 2010 Census was collected at the height of the exodus here. The Legislature's data, used in

---

[2] Jenna Buzzacco-Foerster, "Swing State: Foreclosure and Medicare issues make Lehigh Acres vote key," *Naples Daily News*, 8 October, 2012.

redistricting, was based on 2010 Census information. It showed a district population of about 154,000 people, but whether that's the case now isn't clear.

According to that data, the district is about 63 percent white, 23 percent Hispanic and 12 percent black. The median age is about average, right around 42, slightly over the state median of about 41. It's possible the median age has gotten a bit higher as thousands of younger workers have moved out of town. The Hispanic number has likely shifted as well - important in any political calculation. Many Latinos, particularly Mexicans and Central Americans, were drawn to areas with lots of construction to work on new homes. With that industry having mostly left, many Hispanic people likely did as well. But as the homebuilding returns, it's likely that so too, will the Hispanic population.

Incomes are also difficult to pinpoint because of the massive change in the economy here in the last half decade. Any data more than about a year old is suspect because of changes in the employment market.

POLITICAL ISSUES AND TRENDS

The devastation of the recession touched everything here, including, likely, the political calculations of many voters. Candidates certainly came here, using the problems of the community as a backdrop to their talk of changing things. President Obama was in Fort Myers in 2009 to try to sell the stimulus. Later, Republican candidate Mitt Romney stood in front of a foreclosed home in Lehigh Acres for a speech about creating jobs.

Taking a long term look, most of the people here have been fairly conservative. For many of them, low taxes had been a lure to move to Florida in the first place (though many also came for jobs during the construction boom.) In 2008, just as the bust was starting, voters beat back a proposal to incorporate Lehigh Acres, partly out of a fear that it would mean higher taxes.

Many moved here from the Midwest, and a number of them from small towns, bringing conservative social values with them. Some political observers have said they expect a drop-off in political participation here. That's partly because the community is smaller, but also because of a disillusionment that often sets in after economic disaster. There's little question, though, that Republicans will continue to have a solid grip here in the immediate future. Romney won in this district by about 7 percentage points in 2012, after Republican Rick Scott, promising to put Florida back to work at the depths of the recession, won in this unemployment-stricken area by nearly 20 points in 2010. Back before anyone realized what was happening, at the very beginning of the recession at the end of 2008, Democrats did better, with Barack Obama getting nearly 47 percent of the vote to just 52 percent for John McCain.

The district's House member certainly knows what it's been like for the people here. Rep. Matt Caldwell is a rarity among legislators - he has the same economic standing as his constituents. Caldwell, ironically a real estate appraiser, bought his Lehigh Acres home for $144,000 at the top of the boom, and watched as its value shrank to about $25,000. In a Legislature full of millionaires, Caldwell had to publicly file a financial disclosure showing a negative net worth at one time. "I tell people I'm nothing special, I've experienced the same types of challenges that many other people have gone through," Caldwell told The News Service of Florida. [3]

If he were a professional athlete, sportswriters would have called 2013 a "breakout season" for Caldwell. After a quiet first term, and then re-election in 2012, Caldwell was out front and successful in coming up with solutions on some major problems that lawmakers had wrestled with for some time. He was the sponsor along with Sen. Wilton Simpson, R-Trilby, of vital legislation that sets out a payment plan for Everglades restoration for years to come, avoiding what was expected to be a rough fight between several stakeholders. The very same week it passed the Everglades bill, the House passed a compromise bill, sponsored by Caldwell, to allow optometrists to prescribe certain oral medications - ending a years-long fight over the issue. Caldwell also has one of the major chairmanships, heading the Agriculture and Natural Resources Subcommittee of the State Affairs Committee.

---

[3] Lilly Rockwell and Michael Peltier, "Florida Legislature Home to Dozens of Millionaires," *News Service of Florida*, 12 July, 2011.

DISTRICT 79 STATS

Registration (Book closing, 2012)
Republicans 39.1 percent
Democrats 34.5 percent
NPA 22.8 percent

Voting Age Population (2010 Census): 117,930
White (Non-Hispanic) 69 percent
Hispanic 19.5 percent
Black 9.5 percent

Median Age: 41.9

Men 49.1 percent
Women 50.9 percent

2012 PRESIDENT
Mitt Romney 52.8 percent, Barack Obama 45.5
percent (Estimated)

2012 STATE HOUSE
Republican primary: Rep. Matt Caldwell, R-
Lehigh Acres, 85.7 percent, Jon Larsen
Shudlick 14.3 percent. Caldwell faced no
general election opposition.

2010 GOVERNOR
Rick Scott 56.2 percent; Alex Sink 39 percent.

2008 PRESIDENT
John McCain 52.1 percent; Barack Obama 46.8
percent

HOUSE DISTRICT 80
INLAND COLLIER, HENDRY
COUNTIES

COUNTIES: Hendry, Collier
RATING: Solid Republican

ORANGES, TOMATOES AND SUGAR CANE

The mostly rural area to the inland east of Fort Myers and Naples at the edge of the Everglades takes in huge expanses of swamp and scrub land stretching for miles between human inhabitants in order to pick up the needed 150,000-plus people to make a up a House district. The district takes in all of Hendry County and roughly the northeast quadrant of Collier County, ranging from just east of suburban Fort Myers all the way to Lake Okeechobee in the center of the state and then south through parts of the Corkscrew Swamp right up to the outer edges of tony Naples,

511

taking in a few golf course communities and country clubs on the edge of that town.

The fly-over of the district as a whole may leave one with pictures of tin roofs, swamps and long rows of sugar cane and tomatoes, but the overview of the areas where the votes are is more Spanish tile roofs, swimming pools and long par fours dog-legging right. While geographically this is mostly farm country and swampland, the bulk of the voters are clustered in the nice subdivisions along I-75 running up the east side of Naples.

Still, much of the district's land is agricultural. Hendry County is home to more than 10 million citrus trees – the most in the state and almost one tree for every two Floridians. And, according to state figures, 8 out of every 10 jobs in the county, about 15,000, is related to agriculture. Jobs, however, are scarce in Hendry County, which has often had the state's highest unemployment rate over the last several years. There isn't much work here that's not seasonal. The district is also one of the most Hispanic in the state outside of Miami-Dade County – 33 percent for all residents and about 30 percent of the voting age population - and it's mostly Mexican, with more than 1 in 5 voting age residents in the district of Mexican origin.

The population centers are in three of the four corners of the district, and in the middle, the farm worker town of Immokalee. In the northwest corner of the district is tiny LaBelle, which hugs the Caloosahatchee River and hosts the annual Swamp Cabbage Festival in February. It's a typical rural Florida town -

quaint, old downtown and the Log Cabin Barbecue restaurant, with a parking lot full of pickup trucks, across the street from City Hall - except that more than a third of the people here are recent Mexican or Central American immigrants. In the northeast corner of the district is the place that calls itself America's sweetest town," the sugar company town of Clewiston, bisected by "Sugarland Highway," and home to the U.S. Sugar Corp. The company says its Clewiston plant is the largest sugar refining and manufacturing facility in the world, grinding nearly 40,000 tons of cane a day during the October to March harvesting season. It employs 1,700 people at the plant in Clewiston, about one in four people who live in the town. In 2008 Gov. Charlie Crist proposed to have the state buy U.S. Sugar's land in the area as part of a massive effort to restore the Everglades. Initially it would have meant the end of the plant in Clewiston, but after the state's finances took a hit in the recession and heavy opposition from locals, the plan was scaled back to one in which the state bought just 27,000 acres from the company for the environmental project.

In the southwestern corner of the district are most of the votes, in the wealthy subdivisions in suburban Naples, many of them on golf courses and some gated. Upper middle class Orangetree, and Valencia Lakes, and Twin Eagles with its million dollar homes are among the neighborhoods in the area. The median household income in this part of the district is over $60,000, well above the state median of $44,299. In the 34119 zip code, with its upscale

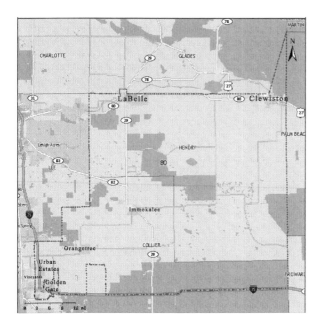

planned communities like The Vineyards and Island Walk, the median household income jumps to just under $75,000, and unemployment is almost non-existent.

In the west-central part of the district is Immokalee, its largest town with about 24,000 residents, more than 18,000 of them, or 75 percent, Hispanic. The town, known as the "tomato capital of the world," could almost be in southern Mexico or Guatemala. Businesses along the two main roads in the city include the Tienda de Guatemala, the Tienda el Quetzal and the Azteca Super Centro, a food store that's part of a local chain with a couple other area locations. The local party supply store is called Mimi's Piñatas. The Collier County part of the district, including the Naples and Immokalee areas, has about four times the voting population as the Hendry County part. In the 2012 HD 80 election about 43,000 votes were cast in Collier County and just about 9,200 in Hendry County.

WHO LIVES HERE?

It's tempting to focus on the striking characteristic of the area, its large Hispanic population. But it's important to remember that two out of three voters aren't Hispanic. The largest precincts in terms of votes cast are in Collier County, and the one with the biggest vote total in 2012, Collier Precinct 303 near Island Walk, went for Mitt Romney for president by an almost 3-1 margin. The next largest vote totals were Collier Precincts 551 near The Vineyards and 590 near Twin Eagles, which Romney won by 2-1 margins. These precincts just along I-75 on the outskirts of Naples are overwhelmingly white and Republican. Precinct 303, for example, has 2,992 registered Republicans to just 1,008 Democrats. The two Immokalee precincts gave President Obama about 70 percent of their votes, but with just over 3,000 ballots cast, those two precincts together don't equal just the largest single Naples area voting precinct.

But the huge Central American and Mexican presence here does stand out. While some are relatively new immigrants, some are descendants of migrant farm workers who have been here for a couple of generations. In fact, some of their grandparents could be seen in Edward R. Murrow's "Harvest of Shame" documentary in 1960, which showed the substandard conditions many people around Immokalee worked in at the time – although back then, many of the workers were African-American. Immokalee remains one of the world's leading tomato producing centers –

515

Lipman Produce, North America's largest field tomato grower, is based here. And while conditions have improved some for field workers and they regularly demand (and sometimes get) higher pay from the big fast food and grocery chains that buy their tomatoes, life in the area is still a hard one on the fringes of the American dream. A drive through Immokalee shows it better than the statistics: many streets right off Highway 29 are lined with tiny tin-roof, un-air conditioned shacks or trailers where farm workers live. The statistics illustrate the poverty too – the median household income is around $22,000 but many families make less than $10,000 a year. The Collier County School District says more than 90 percent of children in Immokalee are "economically needy." The Census Bureau estimates about 44 percent are below the poverty line – compared to 15 percent of Florida residents overall.

Today, about 65 percent of the farm workers are from Mexico, though there are also large numbers of Guatemalans, and other Central Americans and Haitians. Clewiston is also about half Hispanic, with Latinos having migrated to the area to work in sugar fields for decades. While Mexicans are the largest group of those Hispanics in the Clewiston area, about 12 percent are of Cuban descent as well. Eighty percent of Immokalee residents speak a language at home other than English. But many of the workers aren't rooted here, and it's clear lots don't register and vote, or aren't eligible. Large numbers of those tomato pickers around Immokalee are migrants, spending part of the year in Georgia, New York or Michigan harvesting there. For years, U.S. Sugar imported labor from the Caribbean, guest-workers from Jamaica or Dominica who toiled long hours cutting cane for low wages. And even some of the skilled workers who do much of the contract labor – such as working on the plant's boilers - are temporary residents who come in from out of town after the harvest for the maintenance season.

With Hispanics of Mexican descent trending Democratic in recent years, the registration in District 80 suggests many of the Latinos in this area aren't registered to vote, in part because so many of them, as migrants, aren't full time residents of the state (an undetermined number are likely in the country illegally, as well, and thus ineligible to vote). Republicans hold a 45 to 32 percent advantage in the district, with another 20 percent registered with no party affiliation. Overall, among the voting age population, whites are still the majority, at about 59 percent. Both Hendry and Collier counties were covered by Section 5 of the Voting Rights Act, two of the five Florida counties that needed federal preclearance for any voting changes. The requirement, which was thrown out by the U.S. Supreme Court in 2013, was in place because in 1972 less than half of the voting age residents in the counties were registered to vote and the non-English speaking population was above five percent while voting materials were only produced in English.

In Hendry County, fewer than 10 percent of people over 25 have a Bachelor's Degree or higher. More than 35 percent didn't graduate from high school, and more than 20 percent left school before high school. In the part of the district around Immokalee, educational attainment is even lower. Census figures show 44 percent of Immokalee residents with less than a 9th grade education and 68 percent with no high school diploma. The part of the district that is on the outskirts of Naples is considerably better educated with as much as a quarter of those in some neighborhoods having a college degree and 10 to 20 percent having a graduate or professional degree.

POLITICAL ISSUES AND TRENDS

Most of the voters in the Naples area would mirror those in other well-off South Florida suburbs, with concerns about taxes and job growth, quality education and the affordability of property insurance. Close proximity to some of the state's most unique natural areas in the Everglades and along the less-developed far southwest Florida Gulf coast and Lake Okeechobee make people here more attune to some environmental concerns. The future availability of fresh water is a concern for many officials in the area, even if the average homeowner doesn't think much about it.

For the farm workers, the ongoing struggle over wages is the consuming issue. The Coalition for Immokalee Workers has pushed growers to pay more, with a strategy that's mostly based on pressuring the customers – chain restaurants like McDonalds and Taco Bell, and the big grocery chains like Wal-Mart. It has won wage concessions and improvements in working conditions. The immigration issue is nuanced differently in areas that depend on farming. Because growers depend so heavily on immigrant labor, the mostly white business owners are wary of the anti-immigrant sentiments of many conservatives. Efforts to require employers to do more to check the immigration status of workers don't tend to play well in areas like Hendry County or rural Collier, and for that matter most other talk of additional rules and regulations on food producers is winced at here too.

But clearly, the biggest issue in this area of late has been jobs – or lack of them. Every month when state officials release unemployment figures Hendry County is in the top 3 for joblessness. Efforts to attract employers have struggled with the area's relative geographic isolation and the impression that much of the local workforce is unskilled.

Rep. Matt Hudson, R-Naples, represents District 80, having been first elected in 2007, and re-elected subsequently. Before redistricting and being elected to HD 80 in 2012, he represented HD 101, which stretched all the way across the state into the Broward County suburbs. Hudson, a real estate broker, lives in the Golden Gates area of Naples. Hudson has been chairman of the House committee that writes the health care part of the budget, and is particularly interested and involved in health care issues in the House. He led an effort to overhaul the Department of Health, and headed the special House committee that looked at the state response to the federal health care law, which Hudson opposes.

DISTRICT 80 STATS

Registration (Book closing, 2012)
Republicans 45.2 percent
Democrats 32.4 percent
NPA 20.3 percent

Voting Age Population (2010 Census): 116,289
White (Non-Hispanic) 56.4 percent
Hispanic 33.2 percent
Black 8.3 percent

Median Age: 37.8

Men 51.1 percent
Women 48.9 percent

2012 PRESIDENT
Mitt Romney 60.8 percent; Barack Obama 39.2
percent (Estimated*)

2012 STATE HOUSE
Matt Hudson, R-Naples, 66 percent; Pam
Brown, NPA, 34 percent.

2010 GOVERNOR
Rick Scott 62 percent; Alex Sink 35 percent.

2008 PRESIDENT
John McCain 58 percent; Barack Obama 41
percent

HOUSE DISTRICT 81
"MUCK CITY": LAKE 'O' SOUTH SHORE; WESTERN BOCA

COUNTIES: Palm Beach
RATING: Solid Democrat

ON ONE SIDE OF CANE FIELDS, GRINDING POVERTY, ON THE OTHER, BLINDING WEALTH

Before the Baltimore Ravens and San Francisco 49ers played in the Super Bowl in early 2013, national media took notice of the fact that five of the players on the field were from two tiny towns on the edge of the Everglades, Belle Glade and Pahokee. The area with the two towns, a place known as Muck City, has produced two of the best high school football teams in the country, and numerous NFL players, even though the population of the two sugar cane towns is miniscule. "In Muck

City, the well-worn line that 'football is like religion' doesn't even begin to convey its importance," Bryan Mealer wrote in The New York Times. "Football is salvation itself, a fleeting window of escape from a place where prison or early death are real and likely outcomes." The two schools have produced more than 60 NFL players. That's the good news. That Times piece, and others about this area remarkable for its football hope amidst general hopelessness, also relayed the bleakness that is life for many in Pahokee and Belle Glade.

There's a Palm Beach Sheriff's estimate that half the men between 18 and 25 in the area had been convicted of a crime. It noted that the region was once known for having a very high AIDS rate and that shootings were "inescapable." It mentioned that unemployment in early 2013 might have been as high as 40 percent in the area. "The town's migrant quarter resembles something on the outskirts of Port-au-Prince, Haiti, or Kampala in Uganda," wrote Mealer, who wrote a book on the area called *Muck City: Winning and Losing in Football's Forgotten Town.* [1] Besides football, the area south of the lake is known for that "muck" - when Pahokee and Belle Glade play each other it's known as the "Muck Bowl." That mucky soil is what grows the sugar cane here, and before that vegetables, and what brought workers out here

---

[1] Bryan Mealer, "The Way Out," *The New York Times*, 2 February, 2013. See also, Mealer, Muck City, Winning and Losing in Football's Forgotten Town (Three Rivers Press, 2012.)

to the northern edge of the Everglades, on the southern rim of Lake Okeechobee. And it's known for a third thing, that grinding poverty.

This isn't the whole district though. Across the cane fields, over on the western rim of the West Palm Beach suburbs, is a far different world from the poverty and hopelessness of Muck City. These mostly white, affluent areas in the western reaches of Boca Raton and a small strip of nice neighborhoods squeezed between Boynton Beach and the Loxahatchee National Wildlife Refuge are home to entrepreneurs, corporate executives, and equity fund managers along with some neighborhoods of mostly Jewish retirees.

The 2012 presidential campaign came to this district and when it did, the district was unwittingly encapsulated. Republican candidate Mitt Romney was at the opulent home of Marc Leder, a place with a columned portico out front that Bloomberg called "The Boca Raton home private equity built." While there, Romney made a remark that may have helped him lose the election.[2] Ironically, in summing up two Americans that he saw, he painted a picture of District 81, in which he was standing that night. He said there were 47 percent of people who would vote for President Barack Obama "no matter what." These were poor people Romney was talking about, like those living across the district in Muck City. Romney also said that those people were "dependent upon government" and "believe they are victims, who believe the government has a responsibility to care for them..." He also said they didn't pay income taxes. Whether so many people in the country actually believe they're victims and entitled to government help became a nationally debated point during the campaign, and continues to be so, and certainly plenty of poor people on the south side of Lake Okeechobee don't feel that way. But there's no question that they represent one side of a society, while people who own the homes like the one in which Romney was speaking on the other side of District 81 are a different side of society. And they live in this district, not exactly together, but separated by just a short drive across the expanse of sugar cane.

WHO LIVES HERE?

The neighborhoods on the east side of the farming areas are unquestionably, though not uniformly well off. One of the largest Census

---

[2] Mark Silva, "The Boca Raton Home Private Equity Built," *Bloomberg*, 19, September, 2012.

tracts in this part of the district, a long, skinny area west of the Turnpike that's full of neighborhoods winding around golf courses, has a median household income just over $120,000. Several of the tracts here have median incomes over $70,000. In one of those neighborhoods, near an area known as Whisper Walk, lives Leder, who also has a home in the Hamptons and on the island of St. Barts. That eastern part of the district also includes, however, the Hamptons at Boca Raton, a large retirement area where the median age - the median - is over 70 and where people may have accumulated wealth, but are living on low retirement incomes that put the median household income here around $30,000. More than a quarter of the development's 12,000 residents are Jewish, as are many of the other retirees in this area.

The region across the sugar cane fields is undeniably impoverished. "While the soil surrounding Pahokee is rich, the people who live there are poor," is how USA Today put it in another story revolving around football, but describing that area, in 2009. [3] Mechanization of the sugar industry is widely blamed for miring this area in poverty. Two generations ago, African-Americans came to this area to work the muck growing mostly vegetables. They were poor, but they worked, and they got by. As sugar came to dominate the region, more came to cut cane, along with imported workers

---

[3] Jim Halley, "In struggling farm town, Pahokee football team prospers," USA Today, 11 November, 2009.

from the Caribbean, and then Hispanic migrants. But the sugar industry was mechanizing, and using fewer and fewer workers. The Glades area, which in addition to Belle Glade and Pahokee includes the small city of South Bay, is isolated, 40 miles of cane fields from the more populated part of Palm Beach County. The county's economic development agency in 2009 noted that the lack of opportunities in the area is dire. "The Glades is a community with no visible means of support, a situation that is creating angry and disenfranchised adults with few options to a stable and productive life."

Most of the Census tracts along the south rim of Lake Okeechobee have median household incomes in the $20,000s - and as that is the median, half the households are bringing in less, some much less. In parts of the region, the median household incomes dip below $20,000. And though it may not seem so based on reading newspaper stories about the towns, most here aren't rescued by football. "For the other 96 percent left in the shadow of football - and especially teenage girls who accounted for 31 percent of all pregnancies in the Glades - getting a college scholarship was a hard-fought slog up a mountain, one whose peak was reached by only the most focused and diligent students," Mealer wrote in the book, *Muck City*.[4]

POLITICAL ISSUES AND TRENDS

While it will remain open to debate whether

---

[4] Mealer, 8.

and how much the people here resemble Romney's view of 47 percent of America, there's no question that lots of people here wouldn't vote for him - and they didn't. While there are pockets of extreme wealth, and some people like Marc Leder, who travel in Romney-like social and economic circles, the vast majority here vote for Democrats. The voting performance is a result of the combination of the heavily black areas, along with some Hispanics, in the Muck City area near the lake, and a large concentration of elderly northeastern retirees, many of them Jewish, out at the western edge of Boca Raton. Obama defeated Romney in the precincts in District 81 by 21 percentage points, and beat John McCain in these same neighborhoods by almost 30 points. In between, Democrat Alex Sink won by 25 percentage points here in the 2010 governor's race. Democrat Kevin Rader easily won the House seat in 2012, with 64 percent of the vote.

Rader, an insurance agent, served in the House from 2008 to 2010, but left the House and ran for a state Senate seat when Sen. Dave Aronberg resigned to run for attorney general in 2010. Rader lost that race to Lizbeth Benacquisto, but quickly began eyeing a return to the Legislature. He started a run for another Senate seat, but then decided to challenge sitting Democratic Rep. Steve Perman of Boca Raton in the newly drawn House District 81 in 2012. Rader defeated Perman in the primary with about 57 percent of the vote and went on to defeat Republican James Ryan O'Hara in the strongly Democratic district in November.

With so much of the district including the sugar cane growing region between Boca and Lake Okeechobee, Rader was appointed to the Agriculture and Natural Resources Committee and is its ranking Democratic member.

In 2013 Rader sponsored a proposed constitutional amendment that would have set minimum salaries for teachers in Florida, requiring them to be equal to the national average by 2015. The bill died in committee. Also that year, Rader was the sponsor in the House of a bill that would have restored a ban on loud car stereos after an earlier law was thrown out in the courts. The bill failed in the Senate, and so never got a vote in the House. Another bill Rader filed, which also failed, would have let school districts levy higher property taxes for school operations for one year if school boards voted by a super majority to do so. School districts have complained that state cuts have cut into their funding and they can't raise more money to replace it. Rader also unsuccessfully sought to create minimum staffing levels for registered nurses in hospitals, but the bill died in committee.

DISTRICT 81 STATS

Registration (Book closing, 2012)
Democrats 48.3 percent
Republicans 25.5 percent
NPA 23.4 percent

Voting Age Population (2010 Census): 119,431
White (Non-Hispanic) 62.8 percent
Hispanic 16.7 percent
Black 16.4 percent

Median Age: 42.6

Men: 49 percent
Women 51 percent

2012 PRESIDENT
Barack Obama 60.2 percent, Mitt Romney, 38.9
percent (Estimated)*

2012 STATE HOUSE
Kevin Rader, Democrat, 64.4 percent, James
Ryan O'Hara, Republican, 35.6 percent

2010 GOVERNOR
Alex Sink 61.3 percent, Rick Scott 36.3 percent

2008 PRESIDENT
Barack Obama 63.4 percent, John McCain 36
percent

HOUSE DISTRICT 82
NORTHERN PALM BEACHES; THE
RESEARCH COAST

COUNTIES: Palm Beach

RATING: Solid Republican

LIVING THE GOOD LIFE AND
LOOKING FOR LONG LIFE

House District 82 includes the northern Palm Beach area some would consider the southern part of the Treasure Coast, so named because of Spanish treasure that washed ashore in the area in the 1960s from a 1715 wreck near the Sebastian Inlet. The district includes southern Martin County, from the St. Lucie inlet south of Stuart down the coast to include Jupiter in Palm Beach County. From the coast, the broad district stretches inland to include huge swaths of farm land, running from Port Salerno and Palm City near the coast in the northeast corner of the district to the shore of Lake Okeechobee. The district includes Hobe

Sound and Jupiter Island, home to wealthy coastal residents.

It was in one of those homes, one belonging to golfer Greg Norman, where then-President Bill Clinton slipped on the steps in 1997 and injured his knee. Norman originally designed the local Medalist Golf Club in Hobe Sound, but later split with the club when it was redesigned. Norman also later put his 8-acre estate on Jupiter Island up for sale for $65 million, so that will drive up any "average home value" data for the area. But even correcting for the Shark's mansion, it's still pretty high. Homes on the golf course start at $1 million. Another affluent area in the district is Palm City, which sits along the St. Lucie River on the district's northern border. Here, homes are sold along the fairways and canals of "golf and yacht" clubs and the median family income is a high $92,000 a year. Inland, the district is completely different - though hardly anyone lives there.

Much of the district's land is agricultural, and Indiantown is the only populated place of any size west of I-95. As the name implies, it has a Native American past, having started as a Seminole tribe trading post, but white settlers began moving there to work farm fields starting in the late 1800s. Indiantown is now home to just about 6,000 mostly Hispanic people, nearly a quarter of whom work in farming. Almost a third of families in the town live below the poverty line. Another large employer in Indiantown is Florida Power & Light. Its gas and oil burning plant there is the nation's largest fossil fuel burning power plant, and the company recently added a large solar power plant at the facility.

JUPITER: THE RESEARCH COAST

In the early 2000s, after Florida took a hit from a massive drop in tourism following the Sept. 11, 2001 terrorist attacks - when many Americans didn't want to fly - state officials, and in particular Gov. Jeb Bush, started thinking about ways to diversify the economy. Florida has never been able to attract much manufacturing, in part because of its location, down at the bottom of the country, far from many markets. The high paying alternative that state leaders began to think about was cutting edge research, especially in biosciences, attractive in a state where a large elderly population, like one of the state's earliest Europeans, Ponce de Leon, has for a couple of generations sought the fountain of youth. Bush worked secretly to lure the Scripps Research Institute to Florida, hoping the private research facility would anchor a cluster of labs. Scripps landed in Jupiter, partly because of the work of local officials in Palm Beach County. And with help from boosters for the area in Tallahassee, including Lt. Gov. Frank Brogan, a former Martin County school superintendent, and Sen. Ken Pruitt, R-Port St. Lucie, there soon came to be a small cluster of life sciences research facilities along the Treasure Coast. Scripps was followed by a Florida outpost of the German Max Planck Society, also in Jupiter. Among others, the Torey Pines Institute for Molecular Studies and the Mann Research Center, came to Port St. Lucie, just north of District 82.

WHO LIVES HERE?

While the farming community of Indiantown has a median family income below $50,000 - about $10,000 a year below the state median - the town and the vast expanse of farmland around it only account for a tiny portion of the district's population. Most of the population lives along the coast amid manicured lawns and golf courses and brings home an income that's well above the state

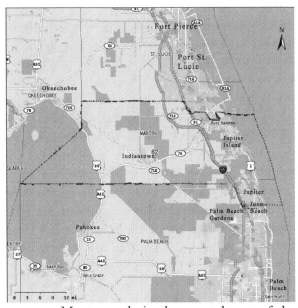

average. Most people in the coastal part of the district are professionals, working in education or health care, or in retail. The district's total population is 80 percent non-Hispanic white, about 4 percent black and about 14 percent Hispanic. The Latino population grew as a percentage during the last decade - it was a little below 10 percent of the population of this area in 2000. Because of the research cluster, the district includes a number of scientists from all over the world, though many of them also live south of the district in other parts of Palm Beach County outside of Jupiter. The median household income in Jupiter is well over the state median, and it's a more highly educated town than most in Florida, with nearly half of residents having at least a Bachelor's Degree.

POLITICAL ISSUES AND TRENDS

Martin County has remained lightly populated and unhurried because people here want it that way. Many political issues in the county, especially along wealthy but subdued Jupiter Island, return to the county's low-growth ethic. The buildings have height restrictions - and most of the real estate brochures play that as a big bonus. There are no high rises along the beach here to block the view or the sea breeze. There's also a related strong environmental ethic that prevents growth from making Martin County look more like Palm Beach County to its south. Of course, the wealthy can afford low-growth policies, and there have been critics of the mindset who would like to see the county court more growth, but there's has been for decades a minority voice here.

With wealth typically comes Republican voters. The 46.7 percent of voters registered in the GOP make District 82 the 13th most Republican of the 120 House districts, and the only southeast Florida district where Republicans make up more than 45 percent of the electorate. Another 27.9 percent are registered Democrats and 20 percent have no party. And as in other wealthy districts, Mitt Romney did better here than previous Republican candidates. Romney won the district with about 60 percent of the vote in 2012 over President Obama, after John McCain was only able to get 55 percent in 2008 and Rick Scott the same in 2010. Democrats know they face little hope of winning here. The district's Republican House member was elected as a newcomer in 2012 with no opposition in the general election.

MaryLynn Magar of Tequesta was a political insider, having already been a Martin County GOP State Committeewoman, when she ran as a legislative race newcomer for the open District 82 seat in 2012. Magar, the vice president and general manager of a health care imaging company, had to survive a crowded primary that included former House member Carl Domino. Magar won with 42 percent of the vote, with Domino coming in second with 31 percent. She faced no opposition on the general election ballot.

Magar ran on opposing all tax and fee increases. "I am a limited government, fiscal conservative, and I do not believe that bigger or more intrusive government will ever be a solution for our economic woes," Magar wrote on her campaign materials. Magar also said she wouldn't support any spending increases "no matter how noble the cause." Magar did vote, however, for the 2013-2014 budget bill, though it was larger than the previous year's budget and contained spending increases. Magar also opposes the acceptance of federal money for transportation projects when state matches are required. In 2013 Magar was the initial sponsor of Gov. Rick Scott's legislation streamlining and expanding the sales tax break on manufacturing equipment. The Legislature eventually passed a broader bill that included Magar's among others. She's also been one of the most vocal advocates for improving water quality in the St. Lucie estuary, which touches her district. Magar generally voted with her Republican colleagues during her first session, and she also passed a bill giving businesses alternative ways to collect on bad checks.

DISTRICT 82 STATS
Registration (Book closing, 2012)
Republicans 46.7 percent
Democrats 27.9 percent
NPA 20 percent

Voting Age Population (2010 Census): 127,339
White (Non-Hispanic) 82.6 percent
Hispanic 11.5 percent
Black 4 percent

Median Age: 47.4

Men: 50.1 percent
Women 49.9 percent

2012 PRESIDENT
Mitt Romney 60.5 percent, Barack Obama 38.3 percent (Estimated)*

2012 STATE HOUSE
MaryLynn Magar, Republican, faced only write-in opposition

2010 GOVERNOR
Rick Scott 55.7 percent, Alex Sink 41.2 percent

2008 PRESIDENT
John McCain 55.2 percent, Barack Obama 43.9 percent

HOUSE DISTRICT 83
PORT ST. LUCIE, STUART

COUNTIES: St. Lucie, Martin
RATING: Swing District

AFTER HEAVY GROWTH, SWING AREA

Port St. Lucie, a generally upper middle class town with lots of retirees, the coastal suburban town of Jensen Beach and Stuart, which calls itself the "Sailfish Capital of the World," are the main population centers of House District 83, which is half in coastal Martin County and half in inland south-central St. Lucie County. The district also includes the southern end of the barrier Hutchinson Island.

Port St. Lucie, like other late 20th Century Florida "pop up cities," like Cape Coral, Spring Hill, or Lehigh Acres seemed to emerge from nothingness almost overnight. Despite what the name implies its center is well inland, up the St. Lucie River from where it dumps into St. Lucie Bay. As recently as the 1950s, this area had just a few businesses to serve the area's citrus farms and fishing camps, but little development. But (and this is a familiar story in Florida history) in the late 1950s, the General Development Corp. bought some land on the north bank of the river, and built a bridge across it. By 1961, there were about 250 homes there - still very small, and about that time, the Legislature passed a bill by Rep. Rupert Smith creating the city of Port St. Lucie. In 1988, Port St. Lucie hit 42,000 residents, passing Fort Pierce to become St. Lucie County's largest town. By 2010, Port St. Lucie's population was approaching 165,000, about 60 percent of the county's population.

But when the housing market collapsed in the late 2000s, the area, like most other boom towns, was hit hard by the foreclosure crisis. National Public Radio called it a "suburban dream gone bad," in a 2009 story. [1] As in other hard-hit towns, the recovery has started, but the housing market isn't fully back.

Stuart was a tiny railroad depot town in the midst of a pineapple farming region, but in the 1920s and '30s was gaining fame as a great place for a fishing trip. Around the same time, the residents of the area were growing weary of paying Palm Beach County taxes, most of which seemed to benefit people in the more populated part of the county farther south, around the town of Palm Beach. A delegation went to Tallahassee in 1925 to try to get lawmakers to create a new county, with

---

[1] Greg Allen, "Hard-Hit Boomtown Considers Emergency Measures," National Public Radio, 18, February, 2009.

proposed county names including Inlet County and Golden Gate County. The effort was bogged down and appeared unlikely to pass. That's when someone suggested calling the new county "Martin County" after the sitting governor, John Wellborn Martin, who quickly went to bat for the idea. The bill carving Martin County out of St. Lucie and Palm Beach counties passed the Senate in May of 1925 and was happily signed by Martin two days later. [2]

The district also includes Jensen Beach, across Hoggs Cove from Stuart and the southern end of Hutchinson Island. In the far western part of the district, west of Interstate 95, are the edges of the vast Indian River citrus belt which runs parallel to the coast from Palm Beach County well to the north, into Brevard County.

WHO LIVES HERE?

For years, St. Lucie was primarily an agricultural county, annually one of the state's largest citrus producing counties, and as Phil Long wrote in the 2000 Almanac of Florida politics, "the kind of place where people were more comfortable in buckskin and saddles than in Bermuda shorts and golf carts." But by the time that almanac was written in 2000, it had changed dramatically, thanks largely to the growth of Port St. Lucie. After the typical late-mid 20th Century boom, Port St. Lucie filled up with retiring "Main Street" Republicans from the north. A little over a decade ago, that was still mostly who lived here. "Port St. Lucie's

---

[2] Sandra Henderson Thurlow, *Stuart on the St. Lucie, A Pictorial History*, (Sewall's Point Co., 2001)

residents are mostly the retired middle-class clerks or small business owners who vote Republican, but hardly consider themselves in tune with the party's Wall Street Wing," wrote Long, a longtime Miami Herald Treasure Coast-based reporter. Many of the retirees moving in then - and continuing today - were from the New York City area and Long Island, and from New Jersey. St. Lucie County had become, Long wrote in 2000, "dominated by middle-class retired Republicans in fast-growing Port

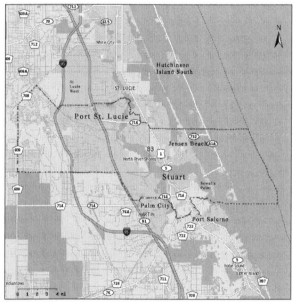

St. Lucie, a town that didn't even exist three decades ago." [3] For three years in the mid-2000s, St. Lucie County was among the fastest growing counties in the nation, and while the growth slowed in the recession of the late 2000s, the area today is unrecognizable from just a couple of decades ago.

Lately the growth in Port St. Lucie has

[3] Phil Long, in Fiedler and deHaven Smith, 835.

included lots of people moving to the community from other parts of Florida, rather than just from the northeast. In part, that's because this area is starting to look and feel a bit urban, but without many of the urban headaches of South Florida or central Florida, and is cheaper than many of the larger urban areas.

The area has also diversified quite a bit from the place that was once mainly home to retirees and young people just starting out looking for a cheap house before moving. For years, Port St. Lucie was known as home to "the newlywed and the nearly dead."

The district remains nearly 70 percent white, but the Hispanic population has boomed in the 2000s, going from 5.5 percent in 2000 to about 15 percent in 2010. Black residents make up another 13 percent of the district.

The median household incomes in Stuart vary considerably, from the poor $20,000s and $30,000s on the south bank of the river near the city's downtown to much more affluent Census tracts on the peninsula called Sewall's Point, and on Hutchinson Island. In Jensen Beach, median household incomes are around or just slightly below the state median. In Port St. Lucie, median household incomes are generally above average and the area west of the city's downtown (but south of St. Lucie West) is particularly affluent, with a median household income just under $80,000.

Like with other places hit hard in the foreclosure crisis, like towns near Fort Myers on the west coast, it's hard to say exactly who still lives here and who doesn't. The housing bust sent many elsewhere, and it's not clear if they'll all come back.

POLITICAL ISSUES AND TRENDS

St. Lucie County had been trending toward Democrats after years of being a GOP stronghold, likely at least in part because of the influx of Hispanic voters. Before 2010, statewide Democratic candidates had carried the county in four of the last five elections. But then in 2010, Republican Gayle Harrell won in what was then state House District 81, defeating Democrat Adam Fetterman, who had won the seat just two years earlier. And while Democrat Barack Obama won the now-District 83's precincts in 2008, Republican Rick Scott won here in the 2010 governor's race, though only by 2.5 percentage points, and Mitt Romney narrowly won here in 2012. So Republicans are seeing a mini-bounce back here, though it's not exactly clear yet what's driving it.

Republicans had held the House seat covering most of this area since its creation in the early 1970s, and Fetterman's win in 2008 was a major coup for the Democrats. Harrell had held the seat earlier, but was term limited and couldn't run in 2008, leading to an open seat situation that gave Fetterman and the Democrats that opportunity. Harrell had run for a seat in Congress, but after losing that race, decided to run against Fetterman in 2010, and unseated him, getting 56 percent of the vote to 44 percent for Fetterman.

Harrell had lost to fellow Republican Tim

Mahoney in that 2008 congressional run, and was out of political office before winning the state House seat back in 2010. She faced no Democratic opposition in 2012.

Harrell has been active on health care issues in the Legislature, which makes sense because she has worked as a health technology consultant and her husband is a retired doctor. Most notably, she has worked with Democrats to try to make it easier for children to be enrolled in KidCare, the state subsidized health insurance program, most recently pushing for presumptive eligibility for children under a certain age.

In 2008, Harrell took the lead on the conservative side on immigration, filing legislation, ultimately unsuccessful, that would have required police to report suspected illegal immigrants to federal officials, and providing for penalties for failing to do so. She also has been vocal on her strong support of offshore oil drilling. When many backed away from support of new offshore drilling after the Deepwater Horizon spill, Harrell didn't and called in 2011 for there to be new oil drilling nationwide. When campaigning and asked about drilling, she responded that drilling needed to be made safer, and that the country shouldn't "move backward" by halting American offshore energy production.

DISTRICT 83 STATS

Registration (Book closing, 2012)
Republicans 39.2 percent
Democrats 35.8 percent
NPA 20.8 percent

Voting Age Population (2010 Census): 121,688
White (Non-Hispanic) 73.6 percent
Hispanic 12.8 percent
Black 11 percent

Median Age: 43.1

Men: 48.7 percent
Women 51.3 percent

2012 PRESIDENT
Mitt Romney 52 percent, Barack Obama 48
percent (Estimated)*

2012 STATE HOUSE
Rep. Gayle Harrell, R-Stuart, faced only write-
in opposition

2010 GOVERNOR
Rick Scott 49.3 percent, Alex Sink 46.8 percent

2008 PRESIDENT
Barack Obama 51.2 percent, John McCain 47.8
percent

HOUSE DISTRICT 84
FORT PIERCE, ST. LUCIE WEST

COUNTIES: St. Lucie

RATING: Leans Democrat

AN OLD WORKING CITY, AND A NEW SUBURBAN BOOMTOWN

While many places in Florida started as towns for not working - places for people to retire and live a life of leisure, Fort Pierce started as a working town, and remained one. In the 19th Century it was a fishing and fish canning town - at some point it was actually known as "Cantown" - and some of the early settlers here worked harvesting pineapples. Henry Flagler's railroad came through in the 1890s, and the company put its maintenance yards at Fort Pierce, mainly because it was about halfway between St. Augustine and Key

West, and that brought more working people here. With the railroad in town, the city also became home to citrus packing houses, and the place where inland cattle ranchers would drive their cows to send them on the rails to market. Much of the work here for years was low wage work, in canneries, or packing houses, or out in the rail yards or pineapple farms under the hot sun - the kinds of jobs most people don't do by choice. As recently as 1990, the low wage and blue collar scene here led a newspaper article to call Fort Pierce the "Toledo of the region."[1]

Working class people remain here, the descendants of the early Florida cracker ranchers, and farm, railroad and cannery workers, many of them African-American. In fact, Fort Pierce is distinguished in part by its large black population - over 40 percent in the city itself, a large percentage for cities of its size (a little over 40,000 people). Whites make up just about 35 percent of the population in Fort Pierce and Hispanics 20 percent. But over the years has city has also been plagued with poverty, and sometimes higher crime than is usually found in towns of its size.

The district also includes the large St. Lucie West development in the southwestern corner of the district, where much of the county's growth went in the 1990s and early 2000s. This new extension of the Port St. Lucie community was built around golf course communities and upscale homes, and is also where much of the wealth in District 84 is. It's typical upper middle

[1] Henry Leifermann, "Indian River Country, a Rich Coastal Gumbo," *The Orlando Sentinel*, 8 July, 1990.

class suburbia - row after row of similar looking, but nice, homes on non-descript streets that seem to stretch for miles.

WHO LIVES HERE?

While the large African-American population is one of the defining demographic characteristics of Fort Pierce, the black population in the broader District 84 is diluted by heavily white areas to the south and southwest in the district, including St. Lucie West.

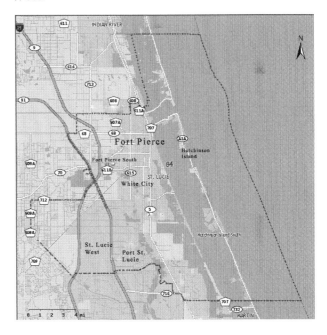

The district's total population is just under 60 percent white, just over 21 percent black, and over 13 percent Hispanic. While the Latino population here is relatively small, it's grown from 9 percent in 2000.

In the early 1980s, after some Haitians were brought to the Fort Pierce area to pick fruit, more followed, and soon, the city and the surrounding area had a pretty large Haitian population that kept growing. By mid-1982 there were about 4,000 Haitians living in cramped quarters in what was essentially a ghetto in Fort Pierce, at the time a city of only about 30,000 people, leading local officials to try to publicly discuss possible plans to "get rid of" them by shipping them out of state. The city held a meeting to openly discuss the "Haitian problem," and plans to try to induce them to move out of town. "I don't like this open-door policy," city commissioner Havert Fenn said at the time. "They should be restricted just like any other nationality." [2] The Haitian population in Fort Pierce itself is no longer that large, with the most recent American Community Survey showing about 1,700 Haitian-born people living in the town, though that number doesn't count Haitian-Americans born in the United States. Now, the Haitian population is overshadowed by the larger Mexican population, which is about twice as large. There are still more Haitians, however, living in surrounding St. Lucie County. Both the Haitians and the Mexicans in this area tend to work in the citrus industry, either in the groves or in the packing houses.

Fort Pierce has struggled mightily, economically. It's much poorer than the state as a whole, and at one point in 2012 the unemployment rate in the city was astonishingly high, just under 20 percent, the highest in the state. More than 1 in 4 people in the city were living below the poverty line. While the city has

---

[2] Dave Gourevitch, "Fort Pierce May Move Haitians," *The Palm Beach Post*, 1 July, 1982.

long been home more to working people than retirees, those retirees who did come to the area often won battles over the character of the region - fighting to keep out new heavy industry that would have provided jobs, but spoiled the scenery of the shoreline of the Indian River. The development of Port St. Lucie and St. Lucie West didn't help Fort Pierce, either. The wealthiest of Fort Pierce's residents often left for the neighboring city to the south.

St. Lucie West, on the other hand, is relatively affluent, with median household incomes ranging from around the state median in the high $40,000s, to well above it in the high $70,000s.

POLITICAL ISSUES AND TRENDS

This part of St. Lucie County is Democratic territory, though Republican voters in St. Lucie West and other southern parts of the district turn out well and keep it close. The numbers spiked for Democrats here when Barack Obama ran in 2008, with more than twice the voters in heavily black north Fort Pierce turning out than had in 2004, giving Obama a 55-43 win over John McCain in the precincts now in District 83. Four years later, the enthusiasm seems to have waned a bit, though Obama beat Mitt Romney by about 7 points in the district. In between, there were, perhaps, signs of the dwindling enthusiasm among Democratic voters. While Democrat Alex Sink won these precincts in the governor's race, she got just 50 percent of the vote, to 45.5 for Rick Scott.

Democratic Rep. Larry Lee, a political newcomer, also narrowly won here, beating Republican Michelle Miller by less than 5 percentage points in 2012. Lee, who is African-American, and a Fort Pierce native, energized the black community, but was weaker in heavily white precincts. Lee, an insurance agent, gained some degree of local attention with his radio show, "Pay It Forward Friday." Lee had decided in 2005 that there wasn't enough "good news" in the news and so he bought a local radio station and gave himself his own show on Fridays, where he focused on good news. He also started a local foundation to help underprivileged kids and assist seniors with prescription drug costs. In 2012 Lee ran in the Democratic primary against former Rep. Adam Fetterman and Fort Pierce teacher Kevin Stinnette, winning with 53 percent of the vote.

So far in the House, Lee has been a vocal supporter of cleaning up Lake Okeechobee and the Indian River lagoon, and, as an insurance agent, outspoken on the need to bring private home insurers back into the Florida market. He sponsored only three bills in his first session, one of which became law. That bill allowed insurers to put certain information online rather than mailing it out to customers in some circumstances. Two other bills by Lee were unsuccessful. One would have prohibited utilities from turning off senior citizens' gas or electric service for non-payment during periods of extreme temperatures. Another would have created a pilot literacy project in St. Lucie County.

DISTRICT 84 STATS

Registration (Book closing, 2012)
Democrats 43.8 percent
Republicans 31.9 percent
NPA 20.6 percent

Voting Age Population (2010 Census): 124,070
White (Non-Hispanic) 65.6 percent
Black 18.5 percent
Hispanic 13.6 percent

Median Age: 44.5

Men: 48.8 percent
Women 51.2 percent

2012 PRESIDENT
Barack Obama 53.2 percent, Mitt Romney 45.9
percent (Estimated)*

2012 STATE HOUSE
Larry Lee, Democrat, 52.2 percent, Michelle
Miller, Republican, 47.8 percent

2010 GOVERNOR
Alex Sink 50 percent, Rick Scott 45.5 percent

2008 PRESIDENT
Barack Obama 55.4 percent, John McCain 43.3
percent

HOUSE DISTRICT 85
NORTH PALM BEACH AND PB
GARDENS

COUNTIES: Palm Beach
RATING: Swing District

SWING DISTRICT, BUT TRENDING REPUBLICAN

With major streets in House District 85 called PGA Blvd. and Jack Nicklaus Dr., it should not be difficult to guess something about the area. The roads are well-named for this area, which is home to the Professional Golfers Association headquarters, and the PGA National Golf Club, which has hosted the Ryder Cup, the PGA Championship, and for many years was home of the Senior PGA Championship. In fact, PGA National Resort and Spa is the third largest employer in Palm Beach Gardens, the main city at the center of

House District 85. In addition to the places where the pros play, lush, gated golf course communities like Ibis Golf and Country Club and Frenchman's Creek dot the district. House District 85 includes the north and northwest suburbs of West Palm Beach north of Riviera Beach (which is set off in majority black House District 88). District 85 runs from North Palm Beach to Juno Beach on the coast, and inland it includes Palm Beach Gardens and western parts of the city of West Palm Beach (including Ibis) and areas west of Jupiter that have several equestrian training facilities. Juno Beach is the home to the headquarters of Florida Power & Light. This is a swing district that voted for President Obama in 2008, but Mitt Romney in 2012.

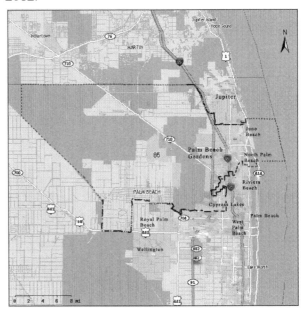

WHO LIVES HERE?

Well, Jack Nicklaus for one. The golfing legend lives in North Palm Beach and designed its public golf course. With all the golf, horse show jumping, beaches, gated communities, and at least one millionaire golf pro, you could probably guess the district is affluent, and you'd be right. Just under 20 percent of families in Palm Beach Gardens make more than $200,000 a year and the median family income in the town is about $93,000. Nicklaus isn't the only millionaire. Elin Nordegren, the former wife of golfer Tiger Woods, recently built a $20 million mansion in North Palm Beach, and while they may not be tabloid fodder a number of other very wealthy people share the stretch of beach nearby.

POLITICAL ISSUES AND TRENDS

This district is hard to figure politically – it is sometimes comfortably Republican, for example giving state Rep. Pat Rooney a 15 percentage point win in 2012, but also has voted for Democrats, including Barack Obama in 2008. In 2010, Democrat Alex Sink beat Rick Scott in the governor's race by 0.1 percentage points in the precincts that now make up the district, the closest the vote was anywhere in the state in that race. And while Obama defeated John McCain by about 4 percentage points, in 2012 he lost to Mitt Romney by about 5 points in these precincts, indicating, along with Rooney's easy win, that perhaps the district is trending Republican slightly. (With a high number of equestrian enthusiasts, some might also guess that Romney, whose wife Ann competes in dressage, seemed like someone with whom people here could identify.) Registration is very close as well: 37 percent Republican and 35 percent Democrat, with 23.5 percent neither. Before Rooney, much of the area was represented by Republican Carl Domino.

Rooney, was elected to the House in 2010, originally in District 83, easily defeating Democrat Mark Marciano with 63 percent of the vote, filling a seat left vacant by the departure of Domino, who was term-limited. Rooney, a grandson of Pittsburgh Steelers founder Art Rooney, is one of several politicians in his family. Younger brother Tom Rooney represents south-central Florida in Congress, and another younger brother, Brian, lost a race for a congressional seat in Michigan in 2010 and now has an appointed state government job in that state. Starting in the early 1980s, their father, Patrick Rooney, Sr., ran the Palm Beach Kennel Club that was owned by Art Rooney. Pat Rooney, Jr., got a law degree at Villanova and an M.B.A. from Lehigh before moving to Palm Beach County and taking over the running of the dog track from his father and is now its president. He also helped run sports-themed restaurants his family opened in the area. Before he was elected to the House he had served on a local sports commission, and the local water management district governing board and was active in various business and charity organizations.

In the House, Rooney has been a reliable Republican vote, earning a 100 percent rating from the Florida Chamber and the National Federation of Independent Business and supporting bills to cut taxes, limit appeals in death penalty cases, allowing parents to recommend turning failing schools into privately run charter schools, and drug testing for welfare recipients. The Palm Beach Post in endorsing Rooney for re-election in 2012, though, wrote that Rooney was willing to seek consensus on issues and wasn't an ideologue. Rooney isn't among the most outspoken members of the Legislature, preferring to work quietly, mostly behind the scenes. Rooney has probably gotten the most attention for sponsoring legislation, first filed in 2011, to prohibit protests at funerals of military personnel or emergency workers, children or elected officials. The measure died in committee in 2011, and after Rooney filed it again in 2012, the bill died in messages between the chambers. Rooney finally passed the bill, aimed at the protests of military funerals by the Westboro Baptist Church, in 2013 after changing it to make it apply to all funerals to alleviate constitutional concerns. Gov. Rick Scott signed the bill into law. In 2012 Rooney won re-election in the newly drawn district, defeating Democrat David Lutrin with 58 percent of the vote.

DISTRICT 85 STATS

Registration (Book closing, 2012)
Republicans 37.1 percent
Democrats 35 percent
NPA 23.5 percent

Voting Age Population (2010 Census): 126,885
White (Non-Hispanic) 78.5 percent
Black 10.4 percent
Hispanic 7.4 percent

Median Age: 45

Men: 48.7 percent
Women 51.3 percent

2012 PRESIDENT
Mitt Romney 52.4 percent, Barack Obama 47.6
percent (Estimated)*

2012 STATE HOUSE
Republican Pat Rooney 57.6 percent, Democrat
David Lutrin 42.41 percent

2010 GOVERNOR
Alex Sink 48.8 percent, Rick Scott 48.7 percent

2008 PRESIDENT
Barack Obama 51.5 percent, John McCain, 47.7
percent

HOUSE DISTRICT 86
WESTERN PB COUNTY: ROYAL PALM BEACH, WELLINGTON

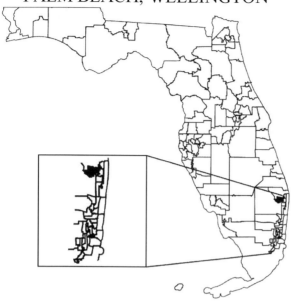

COUNTIES: Palm Beach

RATING: Solid Democrat

THE POLO CLUB, BUT ALSO, CENTURY VILLAGE

House District 86, in inland central Palm Beach County, is a mostly affluent suburban district where the day's difficult decision is often whether to use a long iron or a driver off the tee on the par 4 fifth. The landmarks in the western part of the district include The Breakers Rees Jones Course, the Palm Beach Polo and Country Club, and several others. The view of the district from an airplane almost looks like one giant 198-hole course, with the only interruptions being U.S. 441 and the Florida Turnpike. The western part of the district, out past the Turnpike, includes Wellington, Royal Palm Beach, Olympia and

Golden Lakes.

The district is divided, however, with the northeastern corner, east of the Turnpike, being much less affluent. Here, you'll find Century Village of West Palm Beach, the original Century Village, just off the Turnpike north of Okeechobee Rd., which has for decades been home mostly to Democratic leaning retirees of modest means from the northeast. Century Village may not have the clout it once did on the campaign circuit, but it's still important, as evidenced by the fact that President Obama stopped here during his 2012 re-election campaign. You'll also find the Plantation Mobile Home Park, with more than 1,200 residents, large enough to make it a Census-designated place, among a number of mobile home parks in this area.

WHO LIVES HERE

The district is divided by income, with

several Census tracts in the western part of the district having median household incomes over $75,000, while most of the eastern part of the district is less affluent, with median household incomes generally in the $40,000s.

The area is also divided ethnically, and is one of the most diverse districts in the state. About 55 percent of the total population is non-Hispanic white, including a heavy Jewish population. Blacks make up about 20 percent of the district's population, mostly living in the northeast corner of the district in places like the Stacey Street, Lake Belvedere Estates and Schall Circle neighborhoods, among others. Hispanic residents make up another 20 percent of the population.

The district does have a significant number of retirees - more than 1 in 5 residents of the area is over 60. But mostly, it is a place of younger people still in the workforce: the biggest decade age group here is people in their 40s, who make up more than 15 percent of the population. About one out of every three households has a child under 18 under the roof, and nearly the same number has an adult over 65. The overall median age is 40.

POLITICAL ISSUES AND TRENDS

Like Broward County, its neighbor to the south, Palm Beach County was once solidly Republican. Richard Nixon, Ronald Reagan, and George H.W. Bush were all winners in this county. Eventually, the huge numbers of Jewish retirees and the growing black and immigrant populations passed the number of older conservative, wealthy white voters who once dominated the county. The switch started in the 1980s, and Bill Clinton won the county in 1992 and 1996.

Now Palm Beach County is a Democratic bulwark and House District 86 is one of the strong Democratic areas in the county. That strength comes in part from 40 percent of the residents being either black or Hispanic, and a portion of the white voters being elderly Jewish retirees. Barack Obama won here by very comfortable margins of about 20 points in 2008 and 2012, as did gubernatorial candidate Alex Sink in 2010. The area's House member, Rep. Mark Pafford, won by about the same amount in 2012 and is one of the most consistently liberal members of the House.

Pafford is slated to become the leader of the House Democrats staring in November 2014, assuming he keeps his seat in the election. First elected to the House in 2008 and the caucus' policy chairman since 2012, he was elected to be the caucus' leader in September 2013 after Rep. Darryl Rouson lost that job in a no-confidence vote. Pafford has been one of the more engaged and vocal members of the Democratic caucus, and widely seen as having a strong grasp of policy issues.

He started his political career as an aide to Congressman Lawrence J. Smith and then worked for state Rep. Lois Frankel. Pafford worked for about a decade as executive director of the Alzheimer's Association in Palm Beach County, and now is a consultant for non-profits.

Pafford has been in line with other House

Democrats on most issues, opposing, for example, the bill that ended teacher tenure and replaced it with a merit pay system, and the statewide shift to managed care in Medicaid. He also was in favor of accepting federal money to expand Medicaid to add new enrollees as part of the federal health care law and has been an abortion rights supporter. Pafford has carried some of the more liberal proposals in the House, including a bill to create a needle exchange program in Miami-Dade County, a bill seeking to require background checks for buyers of guns at gun shows, and a measure to provide domestic partnership protections to let non-married people get their partners on their work health care plans. None of those measures have passed.

DISTRICT 86 STATS

Registration (Book closing, 2012)
Democrats 43.6 percent
Republicans 28.7 percent
NPA 24.3 percent

Voting Age Population (2010 Census): 119,913
White (Non-Hispanic) 59.4 percent
Hispanic 19.1 percent
Black 17.1 percent

Median Age: 40

Men: 47.9 percent
Women 52.1 percent

2012 PRESIDENT
Barack Obama 58.7 percent, Mitt Romney, 40.3 percent (Estimated)*

2012 STATE HOUSE

Rep. Mark Pafford, D-West Palm Beach, 60.4 percent, Tami L. Donnally, Republican, 39.6 percent

2010 GOVERNOR
Alex Sink 58.5 percent, Rick Scott 39 percent

2008 PRESIDENT
Barack Obama 60.8 percent, John McCain, 38.5 percent

HOUSE DISTRICT 87
WEST PALM TO LAKE WORTH

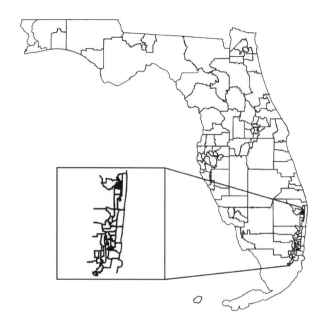

COUNTIES: Palm Beach
RATING: Solid Democrat

DIVERSIFYING DISTRICT; SOLIDLY DEMOCRATIC

House District 87 starts to the south and west of downtown West Palm Beach, following Australian Ave. southward past the Westgate neighborhood and Palm Beach International Airport, which is in the district, along South Congress Ave., down to Lake Worth at the southern end of the district. The district also includes the Royal Palm Estates area west of the airport, the Trump International Golf Club and in the southwest of the district, the Greenacres area and the Lake Worth Corridor.

WHO LIVES HERE?

The thing that immediately jumps out when making a demographic look at House District 87 is that it has gotten much less white in the past 10 years. In the 2000 Census, the area that makes up this House district was 51 percent non-Hispanic white. In the 2010 Census, it was 29.5 percent non-Hispanic white. The black population in this area has increased as a percentage, but the big difference has been the influx of Hispanics, with the Latino percentage going from 34 percent in 2000 to 52 percent in 2010, a nearly 20 point increase. The district now has the largest Hispanic population of any in Palm Beach County, though a large percentage of them aren't registered to vote. The county as a whole has seen a huge increase in Hispanic population, growing by 78 percent between 2000 and 2010. And this central part of the county is where most of that growth has concentrated. The West Palm area has seen a large number of Hispanics of Cuban descent migrate to the area from Miami-Dade. It's also seen growth in the population of people of Puerto Rican heritage, Mexicans and in the percentage of "other Hispanics," such as central and South Americans. The city of Lake Worth is now 40 percent Hispanic and 20 percent black, and Greenacres 38 percent Hispanic and 17 percent black. Both of those areas were places where most of the residents were lower to middle income whites just a decade ago. Things nobody heard or saw in Palm Beach County in the 1990s - radio stations in Spanish, stores advertising sales on Quinceañera clothes, Cuban restaurants - are now commonplace.

The growth in the black population - boosted in part by significant growth in the number of people moving here from the Caribbean - has been notable as well over the last two decades, but has been overshadowed by the larger growth in the Hispanic community. In fact, to those not there in those neighborhoods, Haitian immigration to Palm Beach County is one of the least noticed demographic trends in the county. Of the nearly one in four residents of Palm Beach County born outside the United States, the largest group, more than 50,000, was born in Haiti. [1] They're less concentrated in one area than other Haitian communities - like Little Haiti in Miami - but they were a significant contributor to black population growth in

---

[1] David Fleshler, Georgia East and Dana Williams, "Palm Beach County's Foreign-Born Population Grows," *Sun-Sentinel*, 10 May, 2012.

several districts in Palm Beach County, including HD 87.

Here's an odd side note that probably has little bearing on politics, but is interesting: Lake Worth also has one of the largest populations by percentage of people of Finnish heritage in the United States, the descendants of a community that developed in the 1920s and flourished after World War II. In the early 1990s, the Sun-Sentinel reported that 10,000 Finns lived in Lake Worth and thousands more visited every year. The community, however, since has spread out and declined. [2]

House District 87 is one of the youngest in the state, one of just seven districts with a median age under 33, and well below the statewide average age. Oddly in South Florida, a region known for having so many retirees, this district hardly has any. Less than 10 percent of the district's population is over 65.

For the most part, this area in central Palm Beach County is about average in terms of wealth and income, though there are some pockets of affluence. Most of the Census tracts in the district have median household incomes in the $30,000s and $40,000s, just a little below the statewide median. In the southeast of the district, there are some areas of poverty, in the area between Palm Springs and Lake Worth where median incomes dip into the $20,000s. By contrast, the Lake Clarke Shores neighborhood, the wealthiest part of the

---

[2] Josh Hafenbrack, "Finnish Society Fading Away," Sun-Sentinel. 14 June, 2005.

district, has a median household income over $70,000.

POLITICAL ISSUES AND TRENDS

Democrats make up just under half of registered voters in this district, outnumbering no party voters 47.4 percent to 26.8 percent. Republicans aren't totally irrelevant here, but at just 23 percent of registered voters, they certainly don't have a huge impact on the area's electoral politics.

The influx of Hispanic voters, in particular, but also the increased voting clout of black voters compared to whites, has pushed this district even more solidly into the Democratic column. While Barack Obama won this district by about 30 percentage points in 2008, by 2012 he had gained votes, and defeated Mitt Romney by more than 37 percentage points in the district. Alex Sink was a comparably weak Democratic candidate in this area, and beat Rick Scott by only 22 points in the district in the 2010 governor's race. It's probable that the anomaly was Obama, not Sink - that Obama's numbers are inflated in the district by virtue of his strength among black and Hispanic voters, and that white Democrats could expect to get margins similar to Sink's.

Dave Kerner, a civil litigation lawyer, former special prosecutor and former police officer, had never run for office before when he sought the newly drawn House District 87 seat in 2012. In the Democratic primary, Kerner faced Mike Rios of West Palm Beach. Rios implied that he had the upper hand because of his Puerto Rican heritage. "I encourage him to run in my district," Rios told The Palm Beach Post. "And I say it's my district because there are 80,000 Hispanics in the district.... Latinos really don't have a representative they can talk to." Kerner said he would work hard for Hispanics too and made extra efforts to campaign in the Latino community. Rios was probably hurt by his past, having been fired from the Palm Beach County sheriff's office twice. Kerner won the primary easily and faced no opposition in November.

Kerner came into office wanting to improve spending on education and put money into repair and protection of the Everglades. He was also in favor of having the state collect tax on internet sales and against having local police check immigration status. He also was against linking teacher pay to student test scores.

During his first session of 2013 Kerner passed a bill aimed at cracking down on shady massage establishments used as fronts for sex trafficking. Kerner also sponsored a bill requiring labeling of beef containing "pink slime," but the measure died in committee.

DISTRICT 87 STATS

Registration (Book closing, 2012)
Democrats 47.4 percent
NPA 26.8 percent
Republicans 22.9 percent

Voting Age Population (2010 Census): 115,237
Hispanic 50 percent
White (Non-Hispanic)33.3 percent
Black 14.1 percent

Median Age: 32.5

Men: 51.6 percent
Women 48.4 percent

2012 PRESIDENT
Barack Obama 68.8 percent, Mitt Romney, 31 percent (Estimated)*

2012 STATE HOUSE
Democratic Primary: Dave Kerner, of Lake Worth, 68.1 percent, Mike Rios, West Palm Beach, 31.9 percent. Kerner faced no opposition in general election.

2010 GOVERNOR
Alex Sink 59.4 percent, Rick Scott 37 percent

2008 PRESIDENT
Barack Obama 64.9 percent, John McCain 34.2 percent

HOUSE DISTRICT 88
WEST PALM, RIVIERA BEACH

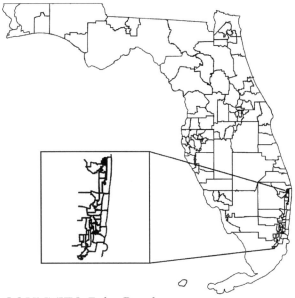

COUNTIES: Palm Beach
RATING: Super Democratic

PALM BEACH'S AFRICAN-AMERICAN DISTRICT

While Henry Flagler got lots of places named for him and is credited in history with opening up Florida by extending a railroad down the peninsula, he of course, did not actually build the railroad.

Flagler's money paid for it - but thousands of men, mostly African-Americans - built that railroad, putting in long hours of backbreaking work under an unforgiving sun in the dismal, creature-infested swamps of a mostly uninhabited land. Those who survived (and many didn't) often stayed in Florida for more opportunity to work for a growing number of rich white folks, both residents and vacationers, who needed gardeners, bellhops and cooks to make this new life of leisure in the subtropics possible. Palm Beach County was no exception - the black community here traces its roots to that railroad.

In the early 1890s the firm of McDonald and McGuire recruited 1,000 black laborers to extend the East Coast Railway into the Palm Beach area, a railroad that was being built mainly to take wealthy Americans to a resort hotel Flagler was building on Palm Beach Island. In addition to the guests at the Royal Poinciana Hotel, Flagler's new community attracted millionaires who came for the whole winter, and often built their own mansions rather than staying in the hotel. The mansions were big enough to need staff, and many black men earned a good living as butlers, wheelchair pushers, chauffeurs, cooks and even caddies on the new golf courses. In the hotels, the bellhops were all black men. These men's wives often worked as domestic servants to the millionaires, cooking for them, washing their sheets and clothes and attending to children or visiting grandchildren. Many at first lived in an area called The Styx right on the western shore of Lake Worth, but that was valuable land and in 1912 an area in what is now northern West Palm Beach was developed specifically for this growing African-American community of professional servants. As people who worked among the high society crowd, and in many cases were paid a decent wage compared to many black laborers, particularly poor farmers, these early Palm Beach County African-Americans were moving in to what was marketed as a "high class colored subdivision" full of single family homes with fruit trees in the yards. The area was called Pleasant City.

By most accounts, this community was treated well by local whites, at least by the standards of the time. Many basically worked half a year for these early snowbirds and while they took care of empty homes for half the year, they were paid the same year round. And a black professional class grew around this community (by necessity because in this segregated era, many white businesses wouldn't serve black residents.) There was a funeral home, a school, neighborhood stores, and several churches. It wasn't all great - the Ku Klux Klan operated in the area, and opportunities were limited. But a prosperous black middle class developed, and many of the descendants of these pioneers remain in the same areas of Palm Beach County today. [1]

Through the years, the black population spread out from Pleasant City, through Riviera Beach and West Palm, and down into part of Lake Worth. More recently, numbers of black residents have moved into Boynton Beach, Royal Palm Beach and Greenacres.

House District 88 was created as a majority-minority district in Palm Beach County. To get to just over 50 percent black residents, it stretches oddly from Lake Park in the north,

[1] For a detailed account of the early days of black life in Palm Beach County, including pictures of many of the area's first African-American families, see Everee Jimerson Clarke, *Pleasant City, West Palm Beach*, (Arcadia Publishing, 2005).

through Riviera Beach (which is 66 percent African-American), and then through Mangonia Park and parts of West Palm Beach. In West Palm, it includes the area around Lake Mangonia, and the historic black area of Pleasant City. South of there, the district narrows to a tiny strip that in some places is only a couple blocks wide, which runs south to Lake Worth, where it widens back out. It then runs down through part of Lantana and the heavily black part of Boynton Beach known as

the Heart of Boynton neighborhood. Another narrow strip then connects Boynton Beach to Delray Beach.

WHO LIVES HERE?

Much of this area now struggles with poverty. After desegregation, many middle class and professional African-Americans moved out of historically black areas, and in some cases those older communities fell on hard times. In an effort to help poor residents that ended up simply creating ghettoes, the federal government during the Depression built one of Florida's first public housing complexes right near those Florida East Coast railroad tracks that brought African-Americans here in the first place. That early public housing complex, Dunbar Village, which was built solely for African-Americans during a segregated era, was particularly dismal because it was built to resemble army barracks, rather than regular homes. The complex, between Lake Mangonia and the Lake Worth Lagoon, is now a bleak, high crime area where well over half the residents are below the poverty line, and about 1 in 5 has a high school diploma. There are some areas that are better off, including the Lake Park area near the top of the district and some parts of West Palm near Clear Lake, but overall, most of District 88 is poor. Median incomes in nearly all the Census tracts in Riviera Beach are below $30,000 a year.

Palm Beach County's black population increased during the last decade, though part of that increase has been driven by new immigration from the Caribbean. Haitians have increasingly settled in areas in and around District 88. One town in particular has become Palm Beach County's "Little Haiti." In Lake Park, a town at the northern end of the district, 50 percent of the 2,300 residents were born in Haiti. Before current Rep. Bobby Powell was elected to represent the district it was represented for three years by Haitian-born Rep. Mack Bernard.

POLITICAL ISSUES AND TRENDS

While half the residents of the district are

black, it shouldn't be overlooked that just under 15 percent of the district is Hispanic. With both of those demographic groups tending to vote for Democrats - and a combined 65 percent of the district falling into one of those groups, it should be no surprise that this is one of the most dominant Super-Democratic districts. Democrat Barack Obama got 80 percent of the vote here in 2012, as did Alex Sink in the 2010 governor's race. In 2008, Obama got 82 percent of the vote.

Palm Beach County has had a heavily black district that has been strongly Democratic going back a few decades. Through the 1990s, most of this area was represented by Rep. Addie Greene, who had also been the first black mayor of Mangonia Park, before going on to a long tenure on the Palm Beach County Commission. Greene was followed in the seat in the 2000s by Democrats Hank Harper, Priscilla Taylor, and Bernard, who left in 2012 to make an unsuccessful run for state Senate.

Powell was Bernard's aide in the House, and when Bernard left the seat to run for the Senate, was one of four Democrats who filed to run for the seat. Powell defeated the other three, Charles Bantel, Nikasha Wells, and Haitian-American activist Evelyn Garcia. Powell, a native of Riviera Beach, had worked as a city planner for the city of West Palm Beach before going to work in Tallahassee for Bernard.

During his first session in 2013, Powell gained attention for filing a bill that would let local governments ban concealed weapons at certain public events, like sports events or concerts. The bill died in committee. Powell also filed legislation seeking to make it more difficult to prosecute children for crimes as adults, which also failed to become law.

DISTRICT 88 STATS

Registration (Book closing, 2012)
Democrats 63.4 percent
NPA 19.8 percent
Republicans 14.3 percent

Voting Age Population (2010 Census): 119,233
Black 50.8 percent
White (Non-Hispanic) 32.2 percent
Hispanic 14.3 percent

Median Age: 35.2

Men: 49.1 percent
Women 50.9 percent

2012 PRESIDENT
Barack Obama 79.9 percent, Mitt Romney, 16.7 percent (Estimated)*

2012 STATE HOUSE
Democratic Primary: Bobby Powell, 51.2 percent; Evelyn Garcia, 24 percent; Nikasha Wells, 16.8 percent; Charles Bantel, 8.1 percent. Powell faced no general election opposition

2010 GOVERNOR
Alex Sink 79.1 percent, Rick Scott 18.9 percent

2008 PRESIDENT
Barack Obama 82.4 percent, John McCain 17.1 percent

HOUSE DISTRICT 89
PALM BEACH AND BOCA

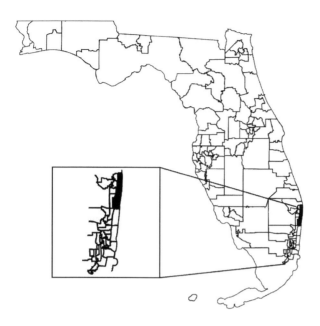

COUNTY: Palm Beach
RATING: Swing District

SOCIETY GET-AWAY, RETIREMENT HAVEN AND IBM-ERS

To say the island of Palm Beach is wealthy is a gross understatement. The iconic barrier island's 33480 zip code is the second wealthiest in the state based on income tax filings, with a 2008 average per person filing income of just under $350,000. The median family income in the zip code is over $140,000. The district also includes Singer Island, the very edge of the city of Lake Worth along the coast, Lantana, parts of Delray Beach, and in the southern part of the district much of Boca Raton. It would also be fair to say this is a swing district – with a pretty small difference in the number of Democrats and Republicans, though Palm

Beach County as a whole has seen Democrats do progressively worse on several levels in recent elections for reasons operatives are still debating. The district is 37 percent Republican by registration and 35.2 percent Democrat, with another 29 percent with no party or in minor parties. While the district sent a Republican to the House in Rep. Bill Hager, it narrowly voted for President Obama 52-47 percent in 2008, but flipped in 2012, giving Mitt Romney 52 percent and Obama 48 percent, and went for Republican Rick Scott by 50-48 percent in 2010.

PALM BEACH

The 13-mile long barrier island of Palm Beach for years was known as winter home to old money, the heirs of northeastern industrial and merchandising fortunes. The Kennedy estate, where America's "royal political family" frolicked until selling it in the 1990s and where

President Kennedy had his winter White House, was originally built for the Wannamakers of Philadelphia, who owned department stores. Many of the names of the people who still attend the society balls on Palm Beach are familiar because of the products their families made, or the empires of industry and commerce they built. Merriweather Post, Pulitzer, Kraft, Cabot, are all names of families with homes here. During the coverage of the early 1990s rape trial of William Kennedy Smith one writer described the bar where the evening in question started (it's no longer open) as a "chichi nightspot where trust-fund idlers, obscure blue bloods, bejeweled society matrons and erstwhile celebs … go for gossip and $12 cheeseburgers." [1]

Palm Beach has changed in the last couple of decades – with new money (gasp) moving in and shaking things up a bit. Now, hedge fund managers, software moguls, real estate developers, and other first generation rich are buying up many of the old family mansions, changing the formerly more Brahmin atmosphere a bit, and in some cases injecting some new money: the area is likely wealthier now than a few decades ago, even after the recession.

There have been culture clashes – Donald Trump bought the Merriweather Post family's Mar A Lago and turned part of it into a country club that welcomes anybody willing to pay – and one new millionaire got in trouble for

[1] Michelle Green, "Boy's Night Out in Palm Beach," *People Magazine*, 22 April, 1991.

buying an old mansion and tearing it down. But the place is still full of money, wherever it came from – and is a frequent call for the political fundraisers. A separate island in the district is Singer Island, (founded by the Singer sewing machine family), and on that island the town of Palm Beach Shores, where the wealthy financier John D. MacArthur (of the foundation bearing his name) for many years lived in an apartment above the Colonnades Beach Hotel and conducted his business from a table in the coffee shop.

BOCA RATON

While Henry Flagler brought the railroad to South Florida that would encourage early 20th Century growth, two other men were instrumental in the development of this area. Addison Mizner, an architect, had dreams of a planned Mediterranean style city and developed several homes in the area in the 1920s that lured people to live here, leading him to be known as the man behind the development of Boca Raton, although he went bankrupt doing so. Mizner also developed many of the mansions along Palm Beach, including the Kennedy estate. Later, aluminum magnate Arthur Vinings Davis started the development company Arvida, which picked up where Mizner left off, building miles and miles of sprawling, planned, sometimes gated subdivisions that marked the continuing growth of Boca Raton and southern Palm Beach County. Boca Raton's population grew by more than eight fold in the 1960s, and nearly doubled again in the 1970s. Many of the people moving to Boca in the 1950s and 1960s were moving into Arvida homes as Davis bought up thousands of acres of farm land at the western edge of the city and built homes and streets. One of Arvida's early communities, Royal Palm Beach Yacht and Country Club, was one of the first gated communities in the United States.

The other major factor in the growth of Boca Raton was the arrival of IBM in 1967, which bought 550 acres from Arvida for a campus on which it would build a new-fangled computer that might one day be used by ordinary people. The Boca campus of IBM would be the birthplace of the IBM PC and the OS/2 Warp operating system. IBM moved its manufacturing work out of Boca Raton in the mid-1990s, though a small research development arm remained. Florida Atlantic University also arrived in the 1960s, spurring more growth. The university was built mostly on the grounds of an old World War II army air base that had earlier brought some of the first transplants to the area.

WHO LIVES HERE?

As noted, Palm Beach is home to the rich, both the old money trust fund type and newer tycoons. For many years, the Kennedys were unusual on the island, which was a bastion of board-room and charity ball Republicanism. And while it's still the case that lots of big money GOP donors (think Trump) live or spend time on the island, the new money crowd also has brought in some Democratic supporters. Boca Raton is also full of well-educated, mostly affluent residents, in part because of the IBMers, and in part because homes here have always been on the expensive side. The median family income of $97,000 a year in Boca is well above the norm in the state.

The district is also heavily Jewish, although likely not as much as neighboring House District 91. Exact statistics on where Jewish people live are hard to come by, but the academic tracking of "Jewish Population in the United States," shows that about 34,000 people say they are Jewish and living in central Boca Raton and about 9,000 in eastern Boca Raton, most of whom would live in the district. Another 45,000 live in Boynton Beach, some of whom would live in the district and some of whom would live in HD 91 and HD 88. While it's difficult to say exactly how many are in each district precisely, Palm Beach County has just under 210,000 permanent Jewish residents – one of the highest concentrations in the United States, and many of them vote in House District 89. And Temple Beth El, in District 89 in downtown Boca Raton, is one of the largest Reform Jewish synagogues in the United States.

POLITICAL ISSUES AND TRENDS

Palm Beach County appears to be trending Republican, slightly, which is unusual in a county where the non-Hispanic white share of the population is shrinking. Barack Obama did worse in the county as a whole in 2012 (58.5 percent) than he did in 2008 (61.5 percent) or than John Kerry in 2004 (60.7 percent) and in House District 89, Obama lost in 2012 to Mitt Romney after beating John McCain in the same precincts in 2008. In fact, Palm Beach County was the only large urban county where Kerry did better in 2004 than Obama did in 2012. Statewide candidates Alex Sink and Bill Nelson also lost traction in 2012 from earlier governor and U..S. Senate race results in the county.

Local political operatives say there's been some "leakage" of Jewish voters from their traditional Democratic home to the Republican Party that appears to have started soon after Sept. 11, 2001 through years when some voters came to see Republicans as tougher on Islamic terrorism. It likely continued into the Obama years, when the GOP specifically targeted Jewish voters, attempting to portray Obama as not friendly enough to Israel. Some of the shift has been seen in neighboring House District 91 to the west, but that district is so strongly Democratic, it hasn't mattered – and exit polls show Jewish voters still overwhelmingly voted for Obama over Mitt Romney. But in HD 89, a swing district, a small shift in party loyalty among white voters, particularly Jewish voters that appears to have occurred, could help other Republicans if the party identification switch carries down ballot. It also could be one of the big factors leading to an increase in no-party registration here. The non-Hispanic white population – typically the stronghold of the Republican Party – has shrunk by 10 percent in Palm Beach County as a whole, which should cancel out any increases in Republican voting by Jewish voters, but it doesn't appear to have fully done so. Before the current House member, Rep. Bill Hager, the area was represented by Republican Adam Hasner.

Hager is a lawyer and insurance arbitrator and also was a founder of a local technology incubator company. Before he moved to Florida, he worked as an assistant Iowa attorney general and served as insurance commissioner in Iowa. He also was on the school board in West Des Moines, Iowa. Before he was elected to the House in 2010, Hager served three terms on the Boca Raton city council and served as the town's deputy mayor. In 2010 when Republican Adam Hasner was term-limited, Hager ran for then-District 87 and defeated Democrat Hava "Hava for the House" Holzhauer with 63 percent of the vote. In 2012, Hager moved to Delray Beach and ran for the new District 89, at first facing Democrat Pamela Goodman. But she withdrew because her husband had health problems. Local Democratic officials chose Tom Gustafson, who served in the House from 1976 to 1990, including a stint as House speaker in 1989 and '90, to replace Goodman on the ballot. Hager won 52.7 percent to 47.3 percent.

During his first session in 2011 Hager proposed a constitutional amendment seeking to make it easier to throw appeals court judges and Supreme Court justices off the bench in merit retention elections. The proposed amendment would have required judges to be approved on the merit retention ballot by a 60 percent threshold instead of a simple majority, but the proposal didn't pass. In 2012, Hager sponsored unsuccessful legislation to change coverage levels and limits in the Hurricane Catastrophe Fund, but was successful in pushing for "Caylee's Law." Although the bill that passed wasn't Hager's original version of the bill, he was a co-sponsor of the final bill, which was passed in the wake of the case of Casey Anthony, who was acquitted of murdering her child Caylee, but convicted of providing law enforcement false information in the case, which at the time was a misdemeanor. The bill made it a felony to lie to police about a missing person's investigation. In 2013, Hager sponsored a bill that would have insulated nursing homes from damages in certain lawsuits, but the bill died in committee.

Hager has also taken a particular interest in insurance legislation throughout his tenure in the House, though many of the insurance bills Hager has sponsored have been fairly technical. In general, Hager has voted in line with his Republican colleagues in the Legislature. He's generally in favor of looser gun restrictions, lower taxes, and making it harder for plaintiffs to win lawsuits. He has also been the co-sponsor of a number of safety bills, including measures to require older children to be in car booster seats, and banning texting while driving.

DISTRICT 89 STATS

Registration (Book closing, 2012)
Republicans 37 percent
Democrats 35.2 percent
NPA 24.5 percent

Voting Age Population (2010 Census): 133,938
White (Non-Hispanic) 80.4 percent
Hispanic 9.5 percent
Black 7.3 percent

Median Age: 49.8

Men: 48.4 percent
Women 51.6 percent

2012 PRESIDENT
Mitt Romney 52.2 percent, Barack Obama 47.8 percent (Estimated)*

2012 STATE HOUSE
Republican Bill Hager 52.7 percent, Democrat Tom Gustafson 47.3 percent

2010 GOVERNOR
Rick Scott 49.8 percent, Alex Sink 47.7 percent

2008 PRESIDENT
Barack Obama 52 percent, John McCain, 47.3 percent

HOUSE DISTRICT 90
WEST-CENTRAL PALM BEACH COUNTY

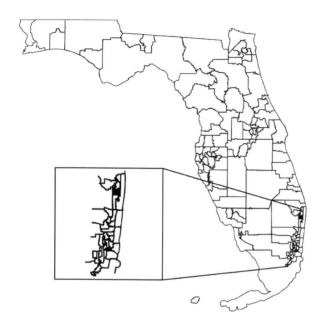

COUNTIES: Palm Beach

RATING: Solid Democrat

IF YOU'RE JEWISH, YOUR GRANDMOTHER PROBABLY LIVES AROUND HERE

House District 90 is the inland part of middle-Palm Beach County. It runs west of Interstate 95 from Lake Worth Rd. in the north to Boynton Beach Blvd. in the south. In the far northwest of the district, it includes the western parts of Greenacres. The district is entirely inland, with no part touching the ocean. Maybe this suburban area should somehow be described in the number of golf strokes it takes to go from one corner of the district to the other, a sort of area par measurement. From Atlantis Golf Club in the northeast corner to Palm Beach National in the northwest, from The Links at Boynton Beach and Aberdeen Golf and Country Club in the southwest to Cypress Creek in the southeast to Winston Trails in the middle, District 90 may have more golf holes than some small states.

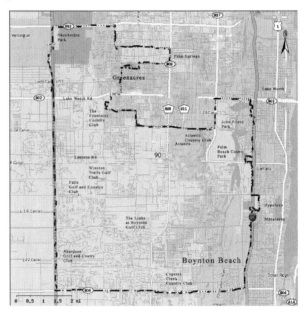

WHO LIVES HERE?

In the 1990s and early 2000s, the Jewish population of Boynton Beach exploded, with Jewish retirees and empty nesters either leaving or not going to some other formerly heavily Jewish areas in Broward and Palm Beach counties that were changing demographically. Boca Raton, long a destination for migrating New York Jews, was getting more and more expensive. That, in part, led Jewish people from the northeast and from South Florida to start retiring instead to Boynton Beach. In the 1980s, there were fewer than 10,000 Jews in this part of Palm Beach County south of West Palm Beach. By the late 1990s, there were nearly 40,000 and by the mid-2000s there were almost 60,000 Jews in Boynton Beach, more than the entire city of St. Louis, Mo., according to the Jewish Demography Project at the University of Miami. [1] By the mid-2000s, more than 40 percent of people in Jewish households in western Palm Beach County lived in Boynton Beach. These were not young Jewish families - fewer than 3 percent of the Jewish households in Boynton Beach had children under 17 back when the last study of Jewish population was done. In fact, it was a rather old group, with a median age of 72. Nearly 40 percent of these Jewish residents in Boynton were 75 or older. As the Jewish Daily Forward put it in 2012 in an article for its Jewish readers around the country: "If your grandmother doesn't live within a half an hour of the Boynton Beach (Jewish Community Center), her sister probably does." [2]

It's not as affluent as other communities like Boca Raton, but more affluent than places like the original Century Village, where retirees of

---

[1].Jewish Federation of Palm Beach County and Ira Sheskin, "Jewish Community Study," (2005, Online: http://www.jewishdatabank.org/Studies/downloadFile.cfm?FileID=2291) . See also: Stewart Ain, "The Boynton Boom," *New York Jewish Week*, 16 December, 2008

[2] Josh Nathan-Kazis, "Election Holds Little Hope for Florida Jews," *The Jewish Daily Forward*, 19 October, 2012.

modest means settled. "This is a blue jeans kind of place," Rabbi Anthony Fratello of Temple Shaarei Shalom near Boynton Beach said in that same Forward story. "It's a solid middle-class area. Yes, you've got doctors and lawyers. But we have an awful lot of teachers."

Obviously such a huge Jewish community has a major impact on voting here, with the vast majority by far voting for Democrats. But Jewish residents make up a little less than half of the population in the district as a whole. But two other groups that vote primarily Democrat, Hispanics and blacks, make up about half the remaining residents. And in 2010, in Boynton Beach, Jose Rodriguez, a Cuban native who grew up in Lake Worth, became perhaps the first Hispanic mayor of a large Palm Beach County municipality. That leaves a little over 25 percent of the district that is non-Jewish, non-Hispanic white.

POLITICAL ISSUES AND TRENDS

The demographic breakdown of this district almost ensures Democratic wins. Republicans do well in Florida with non-Jewish, non-Hispanic, white voters over 40, and the super wealthy, and those are relatively small groups here. There are some affluent households in this district. The huge number of retirees drags down the median household incomes, yet they're still above the state median generally, running mostly in the $50,000s and $60,000s a year. That means there are some households with high incomes counterbalancing the retirees. But there clearly aren't enough Republicans to seriously challenge Democratic candidates here.

Registered Democrats outnumber registered Republicans by about 20,000 and Barack Obama won here by about 26 points in 2012 and nearly 30 points in 2008. Democratic gubernatorial candidate Alex Sink and state Democratic Rep. Lori Berman also won easily in this district.

Berman, a lawyer from Lantana, was elected to the House in 2010 and was Democratic deputy whip starting in 2012. Berman has been a vocal supporter of bans on texting while driving, and she managed to pass a bill in her first session that would have required traffic school courses to include information about the dangers of using cell phones while driving, but the bill was vetoed by Gov. Rick Scott.

Berman is unquestionably a liberal. Among the bills she's sponsored was a measure to give companies tax credits for hiring the homeless, and another banning ammunition clips that can hold dozens of rounds. That bill also banned the carrying of guns, and certain other weapons on school property. Both those bills died in committee in 2011. In 2012, the Legislature also rejected Berman's effort to prohibit licensed gun owners from carrying guns into government buildings or child care facilities, and a 2013 effort to require universal background checks for non-dealer gun sales. While she has generally failed to pass major legislation, most of her bills are substantive, and she has taken the lead on major liberal issues, like guns, while knowing the bills weren't likely to pass. She also tried to pass legislation prohibiting discrimination against pregnant women, and a bill seeking to ban performance enhancing drugs.

Berman has also sponsored bipartisan legislation seeking to boost penalties in public corruption cases, and a bill seeking to require vehicles owned by child care facilities to have alarms to remind drivers to check for children before getting out. Both those measures also failed.

DISTRICT 90 STATS

Registration (Book closing, 2012)
Democrats 46.7 percent
Republicans, 25.8 percent
NPA 23.7 percent

Voting Age Population (2010 Census): 115,237
White (Non-Hispanic) 67 percent
Hispanic 16.8 percent
Black 12.6 percent

Median Age: 44

Men: 46.9 percent
Women: 53.1 percent

2012 PRESIDENT
Barack Obama 62.3 percent, Mitt Romney 36 percent (Estimated)*

2012 STATE HOUSE
Rep. Lori Berman, D-Lantana, 67.7 percent, Sean Michael Kasper, Republican, 32.3 percent

2010 GOVERNOR
Alex Sink 62.3 percent, Rick Scott 35.1 percent

2008 PRESIDENT
Barack Obama 64.2 percent, John McCain 35.1 percent

HOUSE DISTRICT 91
WESTERN BOCA RATON TO BOYNTON BEACH

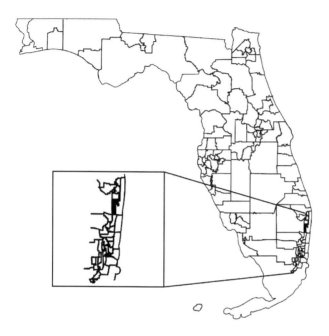

COUNTIES: Palm Beach
RATING: Solid Democrat

FLORIDA'S OLDEST AND MOST JEWISH DISTRICT; LAND OF LEISURE

Leisureville only makes up the very northeast corner of House District 91, but its name could fit for this whole area, which has tons of retirees, many with some means, living between and around a huge number of golf holes and tennis courts. There's plenty of leisure in Leisureville and this broader "leisure district," where more than half of the residents are of retirement age. The district runs through the western side of Boca Raton (west of Military Trail and I-95 in the southern part of the district) and jutting east into Boynton Beach in the northern part.

This is the Florida House district with the oldest median age, at 62.8. In addition to Leisureville, the district includes the Boca Del Mar and Boca Pointe planned communities in the south, the retirement community the Villages of Oriole in the middle of the district, and the gated "active adult" community of Mizner Falls in the northwest corner, among others, while the northeast corner is in the city of Boynton Beach.

This is also likely the most heavily Jewish district in the state, though exact statistics aren't kept on the religion of voters, and parts of Miami Beach are also very heavily Jewish. An academic attempt at keeping track of the number of Jews in America's communities, however, lists southern Palm Beach County as the most Jewish place in the United States. In the late 2000s, Boca Raton Mayor Steve

Abrams said that the areas of western Boca Raton and the nearby unincorporated Palm Beach County areas were 80 percent Jewish. [1] The Kings Point retirement community in western Delray, which is in this district, has nearly 15,000 residents, more than 90 percent of whom are thought to be Jewish. "You look at the registered Democrats in Kings Point - 90 percent are retirees, 90 percent are from the Northeast, 90 percent are products of FDR politics," Delray Beach political activist Andre Fladell told the Sun-Sentinel in a 2008 story about the persistence of the condo communities' political clout.[2]

It's not all retirees here – half the district is under age 62. As the population of Boca Raton grew – increasing by 600 percent in the 1950s and another 325 percent in the 1960s – its western fringes began to absorb much of the growth, particularly in the 1970s. The Arvida development company, owned by aluminum company magnate Arthur Vinings Davis, had bought up thousands of acres of mostly farm land on the western edge of Boca Raton and continued building planned subdivisions – and that would become the norm for southern Palm Beach County as other developers got in on the action. IBM's arrival in Boca Raton in the late 1960s (see House District 89) would mean more growth and more homebuilding. Boca

[1] Larry Luxner, "The Jewish Traveler," *Hadassah Magazine*, February, 2007.

[2] Josh Hafenbrack, Michael Turnbell, Ryan McNeill, "Condo Villages' Retirees Retain Democratic Clout," *South Florida Sun-Sentinel*, 10 February, 2008.

Del Mar, planned in the early 1970s on about 2,300 acres is now one of the biggest, home to about 25,000 people who live in large homes with manicured lawns and sometimes a pool, all near one of two golf courses.

WHO LIVES HERE?

In short, retirees, liberals and Jewish people just about sum up this district.

RETIREES

In Florida's oldest House district, half of the people here are older than 62. In the zip code that includes Boca Del Mar, the largest age cohort is people over 85, who make up 7.6 percent of the population, and nearly one in three people in Boca Del Mar is over 65. Some parts of the district, like Leisureville at the north end, are 55-and-up only, as far as owning a home.

LIBERALS

These retirees are mostly liberal, many from the northeast, originally. While about 50 percent are registered Democrats, compared to 25 percent who are Republicans, many of the no-party voters (about another 22 percent) evidently will vote for a Democrat, having given President Obama one of his largest margins of victory in 2012. Obama garnered about 72 percent of the vote here compared to about 28 percent for Mitt Romney.

JEWS

The main reason Democrats do so well here is quickly evident when looking at JewishDataBank's "Jewish Population in the United States." Southern Palm Beach County –

much of it in House District 91 – is the most Jewish place in America, when looking at large geographic areas (there are some neighborhoods in the New York City area where everyone is Jewish, but the numbers are smaller). According to JewishDataBank, about half of the households in southern Palm Beach County have at least one Jewish person in them and about 40 percent of people here say they are Jewish. [3] In addition to House District 91's representative, Irv Slosberg, who is Jewish, the two members of Congress whose districts overlap HD 91, Ted Deutsch and Lois Frankel are as well. While Republicans have tried to make inroads in the Jewish community – trying to portray President Obama's foreign policy as not friendly enough to Israel – exit polling shows most Jewish voters still overwhelmingly preferred him in the last election.

The area is also far above average in affluence, although there's some diversity in means, as well. In the extreme southwest of the district, in the Boca Pointe development, the median family income is over $100,000. In Boca Del Mar, which takes up much of the southern end of the district, the median income is lower, but at roughly $70,000, still far above the state norm. Homes and condos in the southern end of the district run to the high end, with a number in gated developments and

---

[3] Jewish Databank. *Jewish Population in the United States*. (Online) http://www.jewishdatabank.org/Studies/downloadFile.cfm?FileID=2917

several on golf courses and man-made lakes. In the northern end of the district, however, in places like Leisureville, the homes are more basic and affordable for retirees of more modest means. They're still close to golf courses, and on canals, but many are smaller, and older. Median household and family incomes here are still above $50,000, however, so these people are by no means poor.

POLITICAL ISSUES AND TRENDS

With the distinctive feature of the district being its advanced average age, the district is a super performer in terms of voting. These retiree-heavy communities are the reason for the stereotype of the politically engaged senior citizen, frequently accounting for larger percentages of votes cast than they do of the electorate. That makes this area a frequent stop for statewide and national candidates, particularly Democrats trying to boost their turnout. Back in 2000, Tom Fiedler cited the Villages of Oriole in his Almanac of Florida Politics, saying it and other communities like it, with retired frequent voters "are political engines not to be ignored by any politician."

Growth, sometimes seemingly uncontrolled, has been probably the dominant political issue in southern Palm Beach County for decades. In the early 1970s residents voted to have the city of Boca Raton stop growing, as those who'd already gotten in tried to close the doors behind them to preserve the area's character. The referendum capped the number of residents in the city at 40,000 – at the time it was around 30,000. Arvida was one of two landowners that sued the city over the new cap, foreseeing an end to building homes in the area. The trial court struck down the growth cap saying there was no reason to limit growth, and a series of appeals courts agreed, all the way up the U.S. Supreme Court. The city is now pretty much built out, leaving much of the debate over growth for those who live farther out, near the Florida Turnpike and farther west. In addition to constant talk about how much growth should be allowed, the typical issues of concern to seniors (many of them federal issues like social security and other entitlements) are big here, along with issues of health care funding and insurance costs. With the large number of Jewish residents, candidates for federal office in this area would do well to be as pro-Israel as possible.

Rep. Irv Slosberg ran for the Legislature for one tragic reason, and one reason only. His daughter Dori was killed in a car crash. She wasn't wearing a seat belt. Slosberg ran for office to try to make the roads safer for kids. Though he was largely unknown in political circles, the pugnacious Chicago native, a relatively wealthy businessman in Boca Raton, won, unseating Democratic Rep. Curt Levine in a nasty primary in which Levine accused Slosberg of buying votes and compared him to Yugoslav war criminal Slobodan Milosevic. Slosberg won the primary by fewer than 50 votes, leading to a Palm Beach County recount in October of 2000 - a trial run for a more widely-watched recount in the county later that fall. Slosberg faced no general election opposition in the heavily Democratic district.

The biggest knock - though not the only -

on Slosberg during his first six years in the House was that he was too focused on one issue, and seemed to have little interest or deep understanding of any others. Given his past, one might forgive Slosberg for that single-mindedness. He spent most of his first three terms - before leaving and then returning to the House - trying to make the state's seat belt statute a "primary enforcement law," allowing police to pull over drivers if they see them not buckled up. The law for years was only allowed to be secondarily enforced, meaning police could only ticket drivers if they had already stopped them for something else. Slosberg made primary enforcement and other driving safety efforts his nearly exclusive mission from 2000 to 2006. He was only partly successful, leaving the House to make a failed state Senate bid without having passed a full primary enforcement law. (He did manage to pass a bill allowing primary enforcement for drivers under 18.) But in 2009, after Slosberg had returned to South Florida, lawmakers who continued his quest succeeded, and Slosberg watched from the galleries as the chambers passed the bill, which bears his daughter's name. Gov. Charlie Crist signed it into law later that year.

Slosberg was also criticized for being about as subtle as a boulder in his effort to shame fellow lawmakers into passing traffic safety laws. He angered leaders by saying that in failing to pass certain legislation, they had "blood on their hands." He made long, sometimes snarky speeches in committee and on the floor, that often were as much about the majority party leaders he felt were blocking his progress as about the safety legislation itself. Rather than winning friends and influencing people, Slosberg was often seen as creating enemies that kept him from influencing change. He also was quirky - and sometimes dismissed by observers, including the press, as a goofy showman, trying to use gimmicks to advance his policy ideas, and generating eye rolls with his unconventional floor speeches.

For a time, as Slosberg came to realize that like many of his fellow Democrats, he would have trouble advancing legislation, he complained that he wasn't being allowed to represent his constituents and began rising on the floor to demand that the House leadership "let Irv serve." When Democratic Sen. Ron Klein ran for Congress in 2006, Slosberg decided to run for Klein's Senate seat rather than seek a fourth term struggling to be heard in the House. But Slosberg lost in the Democratic primary to Ted Deutch. The House seat Slosberg vacated was won by Kelly Skidmore, and when she opted to run for the Senate in 2010 rather than seek re-election, Slosberg ran for his old seat and won, defeating Sheldon "Klassy" Klasfeld in the primary and Alison Rampersad in the general election. Since returning, Slosberg has picked up where he left off on traffic safety issues, becoming a vocal advocate in the Legislature for bans on texting while driving, a measure that passed in 2013. He also pushed the House to pass legislation giving the state some enforcement ability for federal rules barring truckers and school bus drivers from talking on cell phones while driving. Slosberg has also sponsored legislation (so far unsuccessfully) seeking to allow companies to put advertising on school busses as a means of raising more money for schools, and pushed to allow the state to sell corporate naming rights to certain state property, like the Turnpike, rest areas, or public school cafeterias.

DISTRICT 91 STATS

Registration (Book closing, 2012)

Democrats 48.5 percent
Republicans 25.7 percent
NPA 22.1 percent

Voting Age Population (2010 Census): 138,975
White (Non-Hispanic) 86.1 percent
Hispanic 7.2 percent
Black 3.5 percent

Median Age: 62.8

Men: 45 percent
Women 55 percent

2012 PRESIDENT
Barack Obama 72.3 percent, Mitt Romney 27.7 percent (Estimated)*

2012 STATE HOUSE
Rep. Irv Slosberg, D-Boca Raton, faced no opposition in the primary or general election

2010 GOVERNOR
Alex Sink 63.7 percent, Rick Scott 33.8 percent

2008 PRESIDENT
Barack Obama 64.7 percent, John McCain, 34.7 percent

HOUSE DISTRICT 92
NORTH BROWARD

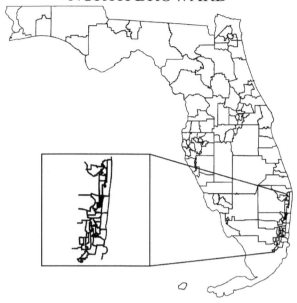

COUNTIES: Broward
RATING: Super Democrat

SOUTH FLORIDA DIVERSITY ON DISPLAY - JEWISH CONDO COMMANDOS, AFRICAN-AMERICANS, YOUNG PROFESSIONALS, BRAZILIANS

When President Bill Clinton was facing impeachment and was looking for support from Democrats in Congress, he told then-U.S. Rep. Robert Wexler that he should gauge what to do by talking to "Trinchi." Wexler would later recall that Clinton didn't know Wexler's name - "but he knew Trinchi." [1] He was referring to the late Amadeo "Trinchi"

---

[1] Musgrave, Jane. "Broward's Amadeo 'Trinchi' Trinchitella Recalled Fondly for Political Clout," *The Palm Beach Post*, 9 February, 2005.

Trinchitella, a Yonkers, N.Y.-born nightclub owner who retired to Deerfield Beach and would come to lead a Broward County Democratic constituency that may have rivaled the old time New York and Chicago machines in terms of delivering votes, if not methods.

It wasn't so much Trinchi's support that Clinton was counting on - but the huge number of people Trinchi could mobilize. They're the so-called "condo commandos." The retired northeastern Democrats, many - perhaps most - of them Jewish, in northern Broward and Palm Beach counties, vote so reliably and live here in such large numbers that every politician who wants to win here has spent lots of time talking to Trinchi and the residents of the four Century Village retirement communities. While there is much more to northern Broward County, Deerfield Beach and House District 92, the sprawling Century Village community along Hillsboro Blvd. and S. Military Trail in Deerfield is the area's political heart. Or at least it was, for decades. As Broward County has grown and diversified beyond New York retirees, the influence of places like Century Village in Deerfield Beach and sister developments in Pembroke Pines and in Palm Beach County, are declining. Trinchitella died a few years ago, and many of the condo commandos are dying too, though they still remain in fairly large numbers and continue to command attention.

But young and middle-aged professionals, many of them fleeing crowded Miami, have also moved in to the area in large numbers. And the younger retirees moving into these and similar communities now are no longer so likely to be former union workers from New York and other liberal cities, nor are they as likely to be Jewish as they used to be. Still, they remain a dominant political feature in this inland, north Broward Democratic stronghold of a district.

The district, which runs west of Dixie Highway from the Palm Beach County line in the north, to a few blocks south of Commercial Blvd. in the south, also takes in heavily African-

American areas and blacks make up 1 in 3 voting age people in the district. The Florida Turnpike makes most of the district's western border, though in some places it stops short of the Turnpike and in some it goes a bit farther west. The area in many ways is typical of any other urban-suburban fringe region in Florida. Major strip mall-lined thoroughfares run through the district, including Commercial Blvd., which is one of the Fort Lauderdale area's main east-west roads. Just off Commercial, and many other major roads, are relatively quiet neighborhoods of middle-class homes.

WHO LIVES HERE?

For decades, Broward was mostly known as New York's retirement haven, particularly for Jewish New Yorkers. In the 2000 Almanac of Florida Politics, veteran Florida political journalist Steve Bousquet called the county "virtually a sixth borough of New York."[2] But even back in 2000, Bousquet noted that those Franklin Roosevelt voters who forced Fort Lauderdale to grow ever westward to the Everglades were dying off. As large numbers of the "condo commandos" have died, the people replacing them in Broward are less politically active and aren't as easy to organize and campaign amongst as the remaining elderly condo residents.

Fort Lauderdale basically got its start in the 20th Century and as recently as the 1950s was pretty much just a little beach town. But as the community has matured, more people are actually from here, and they're overshadowing the transplants from New York who once were the dominant demographic. One way in which you can track the difference is by looking at where Broward commissioners were born. When the 2000 almanac was published, four of the county's seven commissioners were born in the New York City area, one in Buffalo, New York, one in California and one in Indiana.

---

[2] Steve Bousquet in Fiedler et al., 201.

None were born in Broward County. That's much different now, with three of the now-nine commissioners lifelong residents of the county, another from Miami, and another who was born in Jamaica, reflecting an influx of Caribbean residents to Broward County in the last 20 years or so. Only one of the current commissioners was born in New York City. That's not to say there isn't still a sizeable population of Jewish New York natives. The north-central Broward area, including Palm Aire and Century Village in HD 92, has thousands of them, though many now live farther west, in towns like Plantation, and Sunrise.

Broward County has seen growth in its black population in the last decade, with some of it being driven by immigration from the Caribbean. While a lot of that Caribbean influx is more evident farther west, in places like Lauderhill, there are members of the Caribbean Diaspora adding to the black population of HD 92. Pompano Beach has seen an influx of Haitians, who now make up 6 percent of that town's population. A few thousand Haitians also live in Deerfield Beach. A large number of non-Caribbean African-Americans live in neighborhoods in the northwest of Pompano Beach in an area straddling I-95, between Dixie Highway and the Turnpike, north of Atlantic Blvd. Much of the area of inland Pompano Beach has fallen on hard times, with a large number of people living below the poverty line and some notably high crime areas in the western parts of that city. The district is represented by Rep. Gwyn Clarke-Reed, who is

African-American, and one of the few black lawmakers whose district is majority white.

The area overall is one of the most diverse, ethnically, in the state. In addition to being 33 percent black and having a large Jewish population, the district is about 18 percent Hispanic. Large numbers of Puerto Ricans and Colombians live in Deerfield Beach and Pompano Beach, while there's also a sizeable Dominican population in Deerfield Beach and Pompano has significant populations of Mexican-Americans, Cuban-Americans, and has seen a recent influx of Venezuelans. Also, Deerfield Beach is among the communities in South Florida to which Brazilians have flocked - and they account for about 4 percent of that city's population. Most of these Hispanic communities overwhelmingly voted Democratic in the last election.

Median family incomes are a little below average in most of the district; around $50,000 a year in Deerfield Beach and Pompano Beach. In the northern part of the district, including Century Village and the western part of Deerfield Beach, the median income goes up to around $60,000 a year, a little above the statewide median. As mentioned, the exception is in parts of Pompano Beach west of Dixie Highway that had already become poor and were hit particularly hard during the recession.

POLITICAL ISSUES AND TRENDS

While this is a Super Democratic district that shows no immediate sign of drastic change, it is worth pointing out that the stranglehold the Democratic party once had on retiree votes in the area may be lessening. While it's been better documented in other South Florida areas like Pembroke Pines, there are indications that the "condo commando" vote, as noted earlier, isn't as strong as it used to be and that there are actually some Republican votes now coming out of some of those precincts. Still, as recent elections show, this is far from being a competitive area. President Obama got about 74 percent of the vote here in 2012 and Republicans didn't have a candidate to challenge Clarke-Reed in 2012.

As one might expect in an area with so many retirees, federal issues of concern here have long focused on the entitlement programs for seniors like Medicare and social security, but candidates here should probably be strongly pro-Israel as well. Organized labor, which many people here credit with their being able to retire and move to the area, is also well-respected in Broward County, even if younger people here aren't typically unionized.

Clarke-Reed, one of the few African-American legislators to represent a majority white area, was elected to the House in 2008, and most recently in 2012 faced no opposition to her re-election. Clarke-Reed succeeded former Rep. Jack Seiler of Fort Lauderdale when he was forced to step down because of term limits. Before her election to the House, she was a 12-year veteran of the Deerfield Beach city commission. Her legislative agenda has generally reflected the concerns of her constituents, at least to the degree possible in a district where the people, while mostly Democrats, are a broad mix, socioeconomically, culturally and ethnically. During her first term, Clarke-Reed could take credit for a new law that required a national background check for people who want to change their name for some reason other than adoption or marriage, an effort to reduce identity theft that wasn't controversial. She also passed a bill that required state analysts to study the outreach efforts of Florida's KidCare subsidized health insurance program for poor children. For years, advocates have said that Florida doesn't do enough to make sure that poor families who are eligible learn about KidCare and enroll their children.

But along with her classmates, Clarke-Reed came into the Legislature at a tough time, just as the economy was tanking and lawmakers for the first time in years were looking at shrinking a budget instead of growing one. She and others were sent to Tallahassee by voters who may have expected some return - but had to come back for several years and apologize that there wasn't much they could do to bring home state help to the district, because there just wasn't any money. It was particularly tough for Clarke-Reed, who had hoped to help boost affordable housing, and push for more education spending. She also was vocal in her first term about trying to make sure the 2010 Census didn't undercount poor minorities, another issue tied to helping the local community bring in needed outside money. Clarke-Reed was born in South Florida, but moved to New York and later was a teacher in New York City public schools. During that time, she also served on the local school board in New York, but in the mid-1980s returned to Florida. She was elected to the Deerfield Beach commission in 1993.

DISTRICT 92 STATS

Registration (Book closing, 2012)
Democrats, 58.1 percent
NPA, 22.1 percent
Republicans, 18.2 percent

Voting Age Population (2010 Census): 122,959
White (Non-Hispanic) 45.8 percent
Black 33.1 percent
Hispanic 17.8 percent

Median Age: 39

Men: 49.8 percent
Women 50.2 percent

2012 PRESIDENT
Barack Obama 73.8 percent, Mitt Romney 25.6 percent (Estimated)*

2012 STATE HOUSE
No race. Rep Gwyndolen "Gwyn" Clarke-Reed faced no primary or general election opposition

2010 GOVERNOR
Alex Sink 68.9 percent, Rick Scott 28.6 percent

2008 PRESIDENT
Barack Obama 73.3 percent, John McCain, 26.1 percent

HOUSE DISTRICT 93
COASTAL NORTH BROWARD

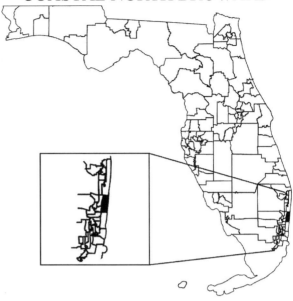

COUNTIES: Broward

RATING: Swing District

WHERE THE BOYS ARE, AND WHERE THE REPUBLICANS ARE

House District 93 is a narrow strip running down the Broward coast from the Palm Beach County line to Port Everglades. The district only goes a few miles inland, with Dixie Highway serving as the western border most of the way, except south of Sunrise Blvd., where the border becomes U.S. 1. This is a generally wealthy area, where the condos have ocean views and many of the houses have docks - and yachts. At the southern end of the district is the area most people envision when they think of Fort Lauderdale - there are the cruise ships at Port Everglades, the beach along Fort Lauderdale Beach Blvd., the Elbo Room bar,

and the shopping and restaurant-lined Las Olas
Blvd. From the heavily commercial southern
area, the district becomes more residential
going north, with the middle part of the district
a condo canyon of mid-rise and high rise
residential buildings lining the coast. Inland, the
area remains heavily commercial, with big box
stores and chain restaurants and hotels lining
Fort Lauderdale's main north-south road
Federal Highway, and the major cross streets.

The district continues through the eastern
part of Oakland Park and up to Pompano
Beach and, at the northern end of the district,
Lighthouse Point and Hillsboro Beach, with
nice single-family homes right near the water
and Deerfield Beach at the very top of the
district. District 93 is the Fort Lauderdale that
the city boosters want to project - beautiful
homes along canals, high end retailers and good
looking people walking and rollerblading along
the beachfront.

WHO LIVES HERE?

Along the water in Fort Lauderdale are some of the most expensive homes in the area, most on canals, and many of them with yachts tied up at the backyard dock. In fact, Fort Lauderdale is probably home to more yacht brokers, yacht clubs, yacht charters and other companies with the word yacht in them than just about anywhere else in the country. The median family income in the 33301 zip code, which includes the islands that make up the East Fort Lauderdale, Las Olas Isles, Nurmi Isles and Seven Isles neighborhoods in the southern part of the district, is $116,000, one of the highest in the state. In much of the district, the median income is lower - but still high compared to the state as a whole. Median family incomes generally are above $60,000, although in the northern part of the district in Deerfield Beach, family incomes drop into the high $40-thousands. Besides the islands at the southern end of the district, incomes are highest in the small north Broward coastal communities like Lauderdale-by-the-Sea ($97,431 median family income), Hillsboro Beach ($100,833 median family income) and Lighthouse Point ($98,357 median family income).

The district is a mix of relatively highly paid corporate professionals and wealthy retirees - the median age here is just under 50, nearly a decade higher than the state as a whole, but not the retiree-dominated kind of place that you find on the southwest Florida coast. These aren't old-money country club conservatives, generally - many of the people here are investment bankers, real estate brokers, doctors and lawyers - in short, they're the longtime backbone of the corporate wing of the GOP. Most are staunch economic conservatives, but generally moderate on social issues, and economic concerns typically drive the political discourse. The Democrats are a mix of mostly young, progressive, often-transplanted, professionals, professional-class retirees from the northeast, and a small, but growing number of non-Cuban Hispanics, including significant numbers of Brazilians living in Deerfield Beach and Pompano Beach. There are also more than 10,000 Jewish residents in eastern Broward County, many of whom vote Democratic. The district is 81 percent white, 11 percent Hispanic and 5 percent black.

POLITICAL ISSUES AND TRENDS

A 1960 movie, and the Connie Francis song that went along with it, may have put Fort Lauderdale beach in the minds of a generation as the place "Where the Boys Are." Politically, though, the coastal part of Broward County is where the Republicans are. That's relative, of course. Broward County is the state's most reliable big county for Democrats, and one of the bluest counties in the entire nation. But Republicans do get elected here, and when they do, it's in this area near the water where they get the votes. But even including the relatively wealthy, professional, enclave along the beach, the district includes large numbers of Democratic leaning voters, too, making it a classic swing district. Republicans outnumber Democrats in the district by a tiny percentage - less than 1,000 voters - and in 2012 Mitt

Romney won the district's precincts by about 4 percentage points. Voters here also elected Republican George Moraitis to the House, chose Republican Rick Scott by about 3 percentage points over Alex Sink in 2010, and this is the area that used to help send Republicans Connie Mack to Tallahassee and Clay Shaw to Washington. Locally, much of the district is represented by Chip LaMarca, the only Republican on the Broward County Commission.

But it's not a GOP lock by any means - Democrat Ron Klein ousted Shaw in the Democratic wave year of 2006, and Barack Obama won this district's precincts narrowly in 2008 over John McCain. Part of this area makes up state Senate District 34, in which Democrat Maria Sachs defeated Republican Ellyn Bogdanoff in 2012. This is a district where the no party vote clearly matters - and a quarter of registered voters in the district aren't in one of the two major parties.

The trend lines are hard to read. Obama did better in this area in 2008 than he did in 2012, which could be related to a comfort that many affluent voters had with Mitt Romney they may not have had with John McCain. Also not clear is the effect of growing Latino in-migration to Broward County, and the degree to which is affecting this district, which is now just over 11 percent Hispanic. Broward County's Hispanic population was the fastest growing in the state in 2012. The Sachs-Bogdanoff race was very close, as have been most contested elections in this area, though Moraitis won by about 10 percentage points in 2012. Depending on who moves in and out of this district over the next decade, it is likely to remain a swing district that will be hard to call on demographics alone.

Moraitis, elected in 2010 and re-elected in 2012, is a graduate of the U.S. Naval Academy and served seven years on active duty as a submarine officer. A major focus for Moraitis in the House has been local economic issues, including securing money for beach re-nourishment and for upgrades to Port Everglades, both intended to help the local economy and create jobs. Not surprising for a representative of a district with so many condo residents, Moraitis also has worked on condo legislation, and passed a bill to clarify tenant and owner responsibilities for association and maintenance fees, for example. He supported, along with his Republican colleagues, merit pay for teachers, drug testing for welfare recipients, tax credits for private school tuition scholarships, and has been largely in line with his GOP colleagues on most tax and spending issues. He supported Gov. Rick Scott's decision to kill a proposed high speed rail program, agreeing with the governor that it wouldn't be financially supported by riders. Moraitis is on record as opposing new oil drilling in Florida near-shore waters, saying any potential damage to tourism and property values from a spill would outweigh any financial benefits.

DISTRICT 93 STATS

Registration (Book closing, 2012)
Republicans 36.9 percent
Democrats 36.2 percent
NPA 24.6 percent

Voting Age Population (2010 Census): 136,996
White (Non-Hispanic) 80.8 percent
Hispanic 11.2 percent
Black 5 percent

Median Age: 48.9

Men: 51.6 percent
Women 48.4 percent

2012 PRESIDENT
Mitt Romney 51.5 percent, Barack Obama 47.6
percent (Estimated)*

2012 STATE HOUSE
Rep. George Moraitis, R-Fort Lauderdale, 55.1
percent, Gerri Ann Capotosto, Democrat, 44.9
percent

2010 GOVERNOR
Rick Scott 50.5 percent, Alex Sink 47.1 percent

2008 PRESIDENT
Barack Obama 49.9 percent, John McCain, 49.3
percent

HOUSE DISTRICT 94
WESTERN FORT LAUDERDALE

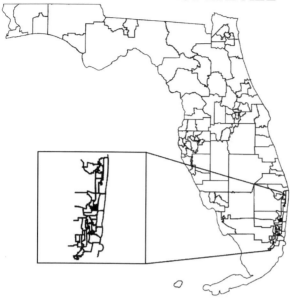

COUNTY: Broward

RATING: Super Democrat

BROWARD'S AFRICAN-AMERICANS

House District 94 is a majority African-American district taking in neighborhoods west of downtown Fort Lauderdale, stretching west to include part of Plantation and Lauderhill. The district juts north into Oakland Park, and includes Wilton Manors, which has one of the largest gay populations in the country.

WHO LIVES HERE?

When Major William Lauderdale arrived along the New River to lead an effort to protect settlers from Seminole Indians, he encountered black people living in the area, mainly escaped slaves who lived among the Native Americans - and fought with the Seminoles against the white man's army. From those beginnings, the area around what would become Fort Lauderdale has nearly always had a population of black people, which over the years was bolstered by in-migration from the Caribbean. Bahamians, Jamaicans, Haitians, and other Caribbean blacks have through the last century moved in significant numbers to South Florida, many settling in Fort Lauderdale. Large numbers are clustered in neighborhoods north and west of downtown near the New River.

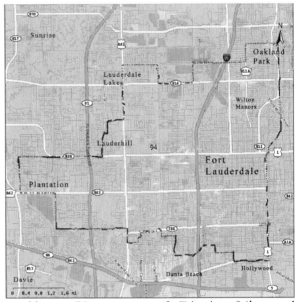

About 58 percent of District 94's total population is black. Lauderhill, which is split between Districts 94 and 95, is an increasingly diverse city - once nearly all white and mostly Jewish, but now a top destination for Caribbean immigrants, as well as South Asians, Arabs and Latinos. Lauderhill is about 60 percent black, and that group is split roughly evenly between U.S.-born African-Americans and immigrants from the Caribbean, most of whom started coming in the 1980s. Nearly 12,000 residents of Lauderhill were born in Jamaica, according to the American Community Survey. Lately, Lauderhill has also attracted several hundred Romanian residents.

The 2010 Census made the first attempt at counting gay couples living together in the United States, and found Wilton Manors, in the northeast corner of District 94, had the largest per capita population of gay people in Florida. Nearly 800 same-sex couples live in the tiny town adjacent to Fort Lauderdale, giving Wilton Manors 125 same-sex couples per 1,000 households, more than double the rate of the No. 2 city on the list, neighboring Oakland Park, part of which is also in District 94. [1]

POLITICAL ISSUES AND TRENDS

It's a bit of an understatement to classify this as a Democratic stronghold. Take the Dorsey Riverbend neighborhood in northwest Fort Lauderdale, a heavily African-American community squeezed in between the city's downtown and Interstate 95. To say Barack Obama did well here in 2012 wouldn't quite paint the picture the way the vote totals for the neighborhood polling station at the L.A. Lee Branch YMCA do. There, Obama got 1,037 votes, and Mitt Romney got 7. And there were several other precincts in this district where Obama similarly crushed Romney - in fact he shut him out in one precinct. A little farther west out Broward Blvd., in the Melrose Park

---

[1] Williams Inst., University of California Law School. *Analysis of Same-Sex Couples by Census Tract.* (Online, 2011) http://williamsinstitute.law.ucla.edu

neighborhood, voters gave Obama 25 votes and Romney none. Just a few blocks north, at Parkway Middle School in Lauderhill, the tally was 726 for Obama, 4 for Romney. You get the picture, but there were precincts all over this district with similarly lopsided margins for Obama in 2012. Obama ended up winning the district as a whole 83.1 percent to 16.3 percent, an identical margin to 2008 in these same neighborhoods. Democrat Alex Sink got about 81 percent of the vote in 2010, and while Republicans did have a candidate, Scott Herman, in the 2012 House race, he was trounced by Democrat Perry Thurston, who got over 84 percent of the vote. It's safe to say that, barring major demographic shifts or wholesale change in voting patterns, Republicans have no chance of winning up-ballot races in this district in the near future.

Thurston, D-Plantation, is the current House minority leader, having been elected by his Democratic colleagues to lead the party's caucus in the House from 2012 to 2014, when he will be prevented by term limits from seeking another term and is running for attorney general of Florida. Before he was elected to the House, Thurston, a lawyer, worked for the Broward Public Defender's Office and then went into private practice as a defense attorney. He had an earlier career in banking. Thurston first ran for the House in 1998 when Rep. Mandy Dawson quit the House to run for the Senate, but Thurston lost a Democratic Party primary run-off to Chris Smith. But in 2006 when Smith was term-limited, Thurston ran again and won the primary and general election easily.

As the House Democratic leader, Thurston has pushed for the state to expand Medicaid to cover more people to help meet the goals of the Affordable Care Act, and while Gov. Rick Scott agreed with the Democrats' position on that particular issue, House Republicans opposed expansion of the program, fearing its possible eventual costs. During the 2013 session, as Thurston and other Democrats sought to have expansion of Medicaid considered by the full House, he and his colleagues engaged in maneuvers to slow the House down, including forcing bills to be read in their entirety, aimed at preventing other Republican priorities from coming up for a vote in the final days of the session. "It's unfortunate that we have had to take such unusual action today, but my Democratic colleagues and I believe that a drastic situation requires drastic tactics," Thurston said at the time. Eventually, Democrats capitulated and the House quit for the year without voting to take federal dollars to expand Medicaid.

Thurston has also led the caucus to advocate for a repeal of or changes to the Stand Your Ground law, which was questioned in the wake of the Trayvon Martin case in which an unarmed teen was shot to death by a neighborhood watch volunteer who claimed self defense. Thurston has also pushed for the state to boost taxpayer funding for colleges and universities, rather than relying on tuition increases, and has been a vocal proponent of making it easier for former felons to have their civil rights restored. Thurston has also made affordable housing a top personal issue, pushing for incentives for local governments to provide housing for poor people. He's also been on the side of keeping property insurance rates low artificially, rather than allowing rates for Citizens Property Insurance to go up and has been in favor of higher spending on K-12 education and mass transit.

DISTRICT 94 STATS
Registration (Book closing, 2012)
Democrats 67.8 percent
NPA 18.1 percent
Republicans 13 percent

Voting Age Population (2010 Census): 121,003
Black 53.5 percent
White (Non-Hispanic) 32 percent
Hispanic 12.1 percent

Median Age: 36.9
Men: 51.7 percent
Women 48.3 percent

2012 PRESIDENT
Barack Obama 83.1 percent, Mitt Romney 16.3 percent (Estimated)*

2012 STATE HOUSE
Rep. Perry Thurston, D-Fort Lauderdale, 84.2 percent, Scott Herman, Republican, 15.8 percent

2010 GOVERNOR
Alex Sink 80.7 percent, Rick Scott 17.7 percent

2008 PRESIDENT
Barack Obama 83.1 percent, John McCain 16.3 percent

HOUSE DISTRICT 95
CENTRAL BROWARD

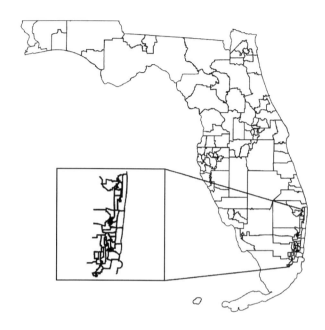

COUNTY: Broward

RATING: Super Democrat

DEMOCRATIC STRONGHOLD, CARIBBEAN FLAVOR

Northwest of Fort Lauderdale in the working class suburbs of central Broward County is one of Florida's most reliably Democratic districts, House District 95, where President Obama got more than 80 percent of the vote, and Republicans didn't bother to try to find a House candidate the last time the seat was up. Broward County as a whole is the center of the Democratic universe in Florida, with twice as many Democrats as Republicans, and this district in the middle of the county, with more than half of its voters African-American or blacks from the Caribbean, is among the most Democratic in the county. Only Leon County, which includes Tallahassee, tops Broward County in the percentage of Democrats, among counties with more than 100,000 voters.

Once a popular retirement area for Jewish New Yorkers who have mostly moved farther west in the county, the district now has one of the largest populations of Caribbean-Americans in the state, with particularly large numbers of Jamaicans, Haitians and Trinidadians. The demographics and political calculations in District 95 are similar to neighboring District 94.

Fort Lauderdale area residents would call this "out west" – well west of Interstate 95 and straddling the Florida Turnpike, but not as far west as the booming suburbs on the edge of the Everglades like Weston. The compact, densely-populated district is north of Sunrise Blvd. and west of U.S. 441, running along

Oakland Park Blvd. and Commercial Blvd. and taking in at least part of the cities of Sunrise, Lauderhill, Lauderdale Lakes, and North Lauderdale. The district is sort of split in two geographically, with a big green area created by Woodlands Country Club and Inverrary Country Club plopped down in the middle.

WHO LIVES HERE?

Large numbers of Caribbean-Americans have made this area their home. In Lauderdale Lakes, more than 36 percent of the population is West Indian-born and in North Lauderdale, Haitians make up nearly 20 percent of the population with Jamaicans comprising more than 10 percent. The district's House member, Rep. Hazelle Rogers, D-Lauderdale Lakes, was born in Jamaica, as was Lauderdale Lakes Mayor Barrington Russell, Sr.

It wasn't always a majority black area – in fact, in 1970 the city of Lauderhill had one black resident. And the area around Inverrary County Club was essentially closed to black people. One academic said of Lauderhill that now, however, it's "like being in Kingston (Jamaica), but more upscale." [1] The Woodlands Country Club in Tamarac and the community built around it is a middle class community of families and retirees. While once more exclusive, it's now economically and ethnically

---

[1] Elliott, Andrea. "South Florida's Caribbean Population ..." *The Miami Herald* 6 Aug., 2001. For more on the demographic shift in Lauderhill, see Collie, Tim, "Lauderhill symbolic of changing demographics in South Florida," *Sun-Sentinel,* 16, December, 2007.

diverse. The Woodlands community was the setting for a strange lawsuit in the 1980s - it used to be an adults only community, but one couple unexpectedly had a child and faced eviction, but fought it through the courts.[2] Now the community is full of children.

While the two country clubs take up a big chunk of the area, overall, this is no country club district. The people who live here are mostly working class – the median household incomes in Lauderdale Lakes and Lauderhill are about $35,000, a little higher in North Lauderdale at about $42,500. The recession hit hard here, with construction jobs disappearing, tough in a place with a number of people previously employed in the trades. Unemployment in Lauderhill shot up to over 14 percent and was nearly 16 percent in Lauderdale Lakes right around the time the 2010 Census was being taken.

POLITICAL ISSUES AND TRENDS

This is a Democratic super district where Republicans appear to have little shot of winning barring something very unusual. The GOP didn't have a House candidate in the 2012 election. Campaigns in this district in recent years have focused on the broader economy because of the impact of the recession here, and job creation and government services for the working poor remain major issues of concern in the district. Rogers ran promising to find ways to blunt the impact of budget cuts on

[2] Demarest, Lynn. "Couple: Area Prefers Monkeys Over Children," *The Miami Herald,* 18 May, 1984.

needed government services, and she was a co-sponsor of legislation aimed at making the children of parents who are in the country illegally eligible for in-state tuition.

Rogers, who, like many of her constituents, was born in Jamaica, was a long-time Lauderdale Lakes commissioner elected to the state House in 2008. Rogers, real estate consultant,, came under criticism in 2013 along with several other House members for owning a house outside the district in addition to listing an "official" residence in the district.

DISTRICT 95 STATS

Registration (Book closing, 2012)
Democrats 67.7 percent
NPA 20.4 percent
Republicans 10.9 percent

Voting Age Population (2010 Census): 116,852
Black 56.2 percent
White (Non-Hispanic) 23.1 percent
Hispanic 16.9 percent

Median Age: 36.2

Men: 46.2 percent
Women 53.8 percent

2012 PRESIDENT
Barack Obama 86.1 percent, Mitt Romney, 13.4 percent (Estimated)*

2012 STATE HOUSE
No race. Rep. Hazelle P. Rogers, D-Lauderdale Lakes, faced no primary or general election opposition.

2010 GOVERNOR
Alex Sink 82.1 percent, Rick Scott 16.2 percent

2008 PRESIDENT
Barack Obama 84.1 percent, John McCain, 15.4 percent

HOUSE DISTRICT 96
PARKLAND, MARGATE,
COCONUT CREEK

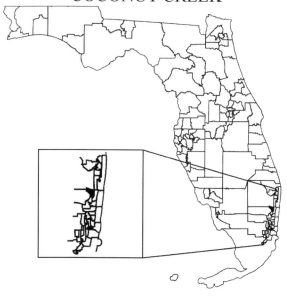

COUNTY: Broward

RATING: Strong Democrat

A 'ROUTINE STRETCH OF SUBURBIA,' BUT A FAIRLY DIVERSE ONE

The fast-growing northern Broward County bedroom communities near the Palm Beach County line make up House District 96. Towns in the district include Parkland in the northwest of the district, Margate and the planned community of Coconut Creek, the self-proclaimed Butterfly Capital of the World. The district runs from the county line in the north to just south of Atlantic Blvd. in the south, and is west of the Florida Turnpike. This area is the epitome of middle class suburbia - author Robert Lang wrote in "Edgeless Cities, Exploring the Elusive Metropolis," that the Margate and Coconut Creek area is a "routine stretch of suburbia," full of office parks and strip malls, in essence "what metropolitan America is really all about."[1]

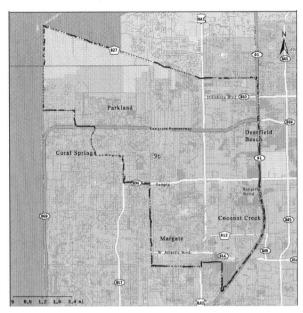

But it's far from the mostly-white, think-alike culture that the word suburbia might have implied a generation ago. In fact, it's a diverse area, economically, and ethnically. Politically, it's a strong Democratic performing area, mostly reflecting the influence of elderly Jewish retirees, immigrants, African-Americans and working class residents, but also including some progressive upper middle class white voters in the professional class who have moved in to the area in the last couple of decades. Still, half of voters here are either Republicans or no party voters.

Parkland is affluent, with a median family income just over $125,000 a year, and it does

---

[1] Robert Lang, Edgeless Cities, Exploring the Elusive Metropolis. (2003), 52.

have a sense of escape from the urban environment - having resisted commercial development for many years. While there are some businesses in the town now, for a long time Parkland prided itself as a quiet community of homes and little commercial development far away from the busier streets of the city. Much of the western half of the district is a string of golf courses, broken up from each other by subdivisions of typical suburban homes and man-made lakes and what elsewhere would be called strip malls, but here are usually called "The Shoppes" of somewhere. South of the Sawgrass Expressway are the more densely populated and busier communities of Margate and Coral Springs. Coconut Creek - which gets its butterfly nickname from an attraction and research facility called Butterfly World - has gentrified and grown with new housing developments in the last decade, and now has more of its own identity, rather than continuing to be what some Broward residents used to call the area: "near Margate and Coral Springs." It's a mixed income community - there are mobile home parks that are home to retirees and working class people, as well as more expensive subdivisions of middle class homes. Middle class professionals have moved into the city, considering it a slightly more affordable alternative to similar suburbs farther west, like Coral Springs.

WHO LIVES HERE?

Margate is particularly diverse, with a large population of immigrants from the Caribbean and South America. According to the Census Bureau's most recent American Community

Survey, there were nearly 2,000 Jamaicans, just under 2,000 Haitians and 1,500 Colombians living in Margate in 2009. There are also a few hundred Mexicans, Central Americans, Venezuelans, Vietnamese and Filipinos in the city, in addition to a few hundred Canadian snowbirds. More than a quarter of Margate's residents are black, and another 22 percent are Hispanic. These are working people - the median family income in Margate is over $50,000, a little above the state median, though about 13 percent of the city's residents live at or below the poverty line. The city blends into upper middle class Coral Springs to the west in House District 97, and poorer, working class North Lauderdale across Atlantic Blvd. to the south in House District 95. Coconut Creek is much whiter than Margate - about 75 percent - but is also about 20 percent Hispanic. Overall, the district is 60 percent white, about 20 percent Hispanic and 15 percent black. There are also large numbers of Jewish residents in the district, likely more than 30,000 based on multi-community estimates of the American Jewish Yearbook.

POLITICAL ISSUES AND TRENDS

Just under 50 percent of voters here are registered Democrats, while Republicans and no party voters are nearly even at about 25 percent each. Democrats have enough of a cushion and enough support from NPA voters to make this district safe for the party. President Obama got a little more than 60 percent of the vote here in 2012 and 2008 and Democrat Alex Sink got just under 60 percent in the 2010 governor's race. The area's House member, progressive Democrat Jim Waldman, faced no opposition in 2012.

Waldman, long a fixture of Coconut Creek politics as a former commissioner and mayor of the city, has been one of the most steadily progressive members of the Legislature in his three and a half terms. Waldman has sometimes been a voice in the wilderness, a staunch liberal in an overwhelmingly Republican chamber, and while in line with his Democratic colleagues on most major issues, is sometimes on his own or with a small group of like-minded liberals on some votes.

He isn't afraid to vote to allow tax increases, or for new spending, and probably most notably has been a major proponent of higher taxes on cigarettes, most recently proposing in 2011 to boost taxes by $1 a pack, but using the revenue to allow for a roll back of recently passed fee increases on motorists. He also sponsored the original 2009 cigarette tax hike of $1 a pack, which Republicans went along with in the midst of the recession-driven revenue shortfall, though it was labeled a "surcharge." Waldman also sponsored, for example, a bill in 2013 that would have allowed county voters to levy special new property taxes to pay for upgrades to public school security, a measure that came in the wake of the Newtown, Conn. school shooting. The measure failed.

On most of the Democrats' signature issues, Waldman has been a consistent party line vote. He has been a vocal advocate for accepting federal money for expanding Medicaid to cover more Florida residents under the Affordable

Care Act, and has typically favored gun control measures, or at least local control on the issue. In 2013 Waldman filed a bill for the 2014 session to give local communities the ability to more strictly regulate guns than the state does. Notably, in 2013 Waldman was against one of the most high profile bills passed by the Legislature, a ban on so-called internet cafes, which backers of the legislation said were just fronts for illegal online gambling. Waldman said the cafes were legitimate businesses that provided needed jobs. His was the lone vote against the ban in committee. Waldman leaves the House in 2014 because of term limits - and is running for the state Senate. Broward County Mayor Kristin Jacobs and former Rep. Steve Perman, both Democrats, are running for the District 96 seat.

DISTRICT 96 STATS

Registration (Book closing, 2012)
Democrats 46.8 percent
Republicans,25.8 percent
NPA 25.7 percent

Voting Age Population (2010 Census): 118,602
White (Non-Hispanic) 60 percent
Hispanic 19 percent
Black 15 percent

Median Age: 40.2

Men: 47.4 percent
Women 52.6 percent

Vote for president
Barack Obama 61 percent, Mitt Romney, 38.3 percent (Estimated)*

2012 STATE HOUSE
No race. Rep. Jim Waldman, D-Coconut Creek, faced no primary or general election opposition.

2010 GOVERNOR
Alex Sink 59 percent, Rick Scott 38.5 percent

2008 PRESIDENT
Barack Obama 62.2 percent, John McCain, 37.1 percent

HOUSE DISTRICT 97
NW BROWARD: CORAL SPRINGS, TAMARAC, SUNRISE

COUNTIES: Broward
RATING: Strong Democrat

SUBURBAN DEMOCRATIC STRONGHOLD

As America's post-war economy boomed, air conditioning became commonplace, and more and more people moved to South Florida looking for a new start, new housing developments pushed farther and farther into the interior. The more people came, the more developers bought old farm fields and swamp land, filled it in and built whole new planned cities from scratch. The towns of western Broward County mostly emerged from those fields and swamps around the same time, during the Kennedy administration. Most were aimed at people who wanted to live the good life - they had names like Sunrise Golf Village, evoking an image of how people would live in this new southern frontier. One place reclaimed from bean fields, cow pasture and the Everglades in the early 1960s was Coral Springs. Initially, it was planned as a retirement city, but young executives kept showing up asking to buy houses in the new manicured town. In 1965, more than 10,000 people showed up for a "Land Rush Sale," during which Johnny Carson made an appearance and potential homebuyers were fed three tons of barbecue and two miles of hot dogs. They bought 1,100 lots for $5 million.[1] Perhaps it should have been called "Corporate Springs," as the area quickly filled up with "suits," and it seemed this is where all the executives in Broward County were moving. Most of western Broward grew - just as the rest of the nation's suburbs - to resemble everywhere else, with the defining element being that there weren't really any truly defining local elements.

Coral Springs sought, however, to be a little different, enacting famously strict zoning laws that kept it from being exactly the same. In fact, the first Trivial Pursuit game had a question about Coral Springs' tough building requirements: "What U.S. city would not let McDonalds put up the Golden Arches?" Despite the tough sign ordinance, McDonalds opened its restaurant in 1975 without the arches, so in the end, Coral Springs was more like other suburbs than not, it just looked a little

[1] Book of Coral Springs Trivia (Online) www.coralsprings.org/publications/TownTriviaBook2005.pdf

different. The city's sign restrictions also prevented K-Mart from having its giant K. [2]

Meanwhile, just east of Coral Springs, Wisconsin developer Ken Behring was building another new suburb, envisioned as an "active retirement community" centered around a golf course. Behring owned a chain of carwashes in Wisconsin called "Car-a-mat." When he built his new town in Florida, he reversed the spelling and called it Tamarac. While Coral Springs quickly became home to younger families, Tamarac's cheaper and smaller homes made it more attractive to the retirees to whom it was marketed, and for years, that's mainly who moved there. Behring also developed a country club community called the Woodlands, which is a bit southeast of the main part of Tamarac and in today's House District 95. And about the same time, developer Norman Johnson was creating Sunrise, which was marketed as a remote, almost rural, "golf village." While Johnny Carson was hawking homes in Tamarac, Johnson's gimmick was to build an upside down house, which drew attention and media interest in the new town.

Most of western Broward is known mostly as a place where people live. Sunrise, however, has emerged in most South Florida residents' minds not as a place from which people come

---

[2] See: Kathy Bushouse, "In Springs, it is Signs of the Times," *Sun-Sentinel,* 18 July 1998, and Rochelle Broder-Singer, "Corporate Culture," *South Florida CEO*, November 2003.

to the city to do things, but as a place to which people go to do things - mainly work, shop and watch hockey. At the western edge of Sunrise, just inside District 97 is the BB&T Center, home to the NHL's Florida Panthers, and across the street the enormous Sawgrass Mills Outlet Mall, the largest outlet mall in the country. Those two attractions have put Sunrise on the map as more than a housing subdivision - and routinely draw not just Floridians but people from all over to Sunrise. Wealthy South Americans, from Colombia and Venezuela especially, make special trips to Florida just to go shopping at Sawgrass Mills. The area has also attracted corporate headquarters or regional offices for a number of health care, technology and insurance companies.

WHO LIVES HERE?

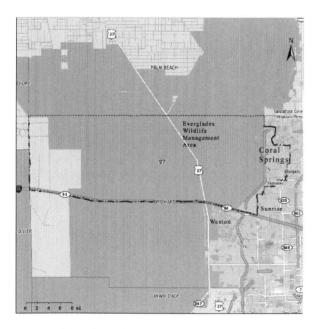

Coral Springs has remained a place where white collar corporate employees live - and where local government works to keep property values high. It is relatively affluent, with a median family income just under $80,000, more than a third higher than the state median. Tamarac remains home to large numbers of retirees, with a third of the population there over 60. And while families live in Tamarac too, it's cheaper than Coral Springs, and much less affluent, with a median family income lowered by the high percentage of retirees to just over $50,000, which is below the state median. Sunrise is in between the two economically, with a median family income around $60,000, just a bit over the state median. The district as a whole is home mostly to white collar workers, though Tamarac has some blue collar families in addition to the large number of retirees. Just over half the voting age residents of District 97 are non-Hispanic white, and just under 16 percent are black. Nearly a quarter of the district's residents are Hispanic, with significant numbers coming from all over Latin America, but the largest groups being Colombians and Puerto Ricans.

POLITICAL ISSUES AND TRENDS

Like most of Broward, this has long been Democratic country, going back to when New York retirees, many of them Jewish, dominated Broward County. In that era, the Tamarac Democratic Club was akin to the old northern machines, holding rallies, driving Democrats to the polls, grooming candidates. Longtime Broward County political reporter Buddy Nevins wrote that it was the Tamarac Democratic club that once "fueled Broward's nationally fabled Democratic steamroller." But as the demographics here changed, the club declined in the 2000s, and eventually had its charter pulled by the state party. Nevins described what the old Tamarac club had become as the end neared, after giving a speech to the group in 2009: "In the audience were two people with walkers. One guy breathing from an oxygen tank. Another guy being guided by his Caribbean caretaker," Nevins wrote. [3] The original Broward Democratic machine, created by New Deal Roosevelt backers and packed at its zenith by the Kennedy generation, is dying. But here, like elsewhere in South Florida, it's being replaced by young Latinos who have voted for the party nearly as reliably. Exit polling showed non-Cuban Democrats like the Puerto Ricans and South Americans who are increasingly moving to Broward's western suburbs voted overwhelmingly for Barack Obama in 2012. Democrats generally are 30 points better than Republicans in a given election in this district, with Obama winning by about that much in 2008 and 2012, and Democrat Alex Sink by the same amount in the 2010 governor's race. The district's House member, Democrat Jared Moskowitz won in 2012 by nearly 40 points.

Moskowitz first turned heads in Tallahassee when he was still a candidate for the House,

---

[3] Buddy Nevins, "Tamarac Democratic Club Killed by State Party," BrowardBeat.com, 20 May 2010. http://www.browardbeat.com/tamarac-democratic-club-killed-by-state-party/; For Tamarac history see: http://thewoodlandstamarac.com/briefhistory/

raising amounts of campaign money that put him among the top fundraisers, in a league with powerful Republican incumbents. At the time, Moskowitz was just 30 years old and a city commissioner in the small town of Parkland. At times during that 2011-2012 campaign, Moskowitz was the top fundraiser among all Democratic House candidates. It didn't come as a surprise to South Florida political watchers - Moskowitz is the son of prominent Democratic fundraiser Michael Moskowitz, who once hosted a fundraiser at his home that was attended by Bill Clinton and was once seen as a possible state party chairman. So it may have been expected that the younger Moskowitz become a young political star. He had been elected to the Parkland commission at age 25 and had already served six years on the commission when he was elected to the House in 2012 to replace Democrat Ari Porth. Previously, Moskowitz had been a White House intern, earned a law degree, clerked for a circuit judge, and worked on Connecticut Sen. Joe Lieberman's campaign. Somewhere in there, Moskowitz also found time to climb Mount Kilimanjaro.

In his first session, Moskowitz said his signature legislation was a measure to strengthen penalties for people who abuse animals, a bill which passed and was signed into law. He also passed a measure in 2013 requiring the governor to adopt flag etiquette rules but another bill he sponsored in his first session that would have required officials to give copies of inspection reports on child care facilities to parents failed to pass. Moskowitz was also primary sponsor of legislation aimed at forcing the collection of tax on internet sales, with an offsetting reduction in the communication services tax, but that bill died in committee. Moskowitz started out his second year in the House calling for the Legislature to remove the state's ban on gay marriage.

Like several of his colleagues, Moskowitz came under scrutiny in 2013 for where he lives. Moskowitz has an apartment in Coral Springs, inside his district, fulfilling the requirement of state law. But he still owns a home in Parkland, where his wife had to maintain a residence because she is a state committeewoman for that area, leading critics to question whether Moskowitz was actually living in the Coral Springs apartment.

DISTRICT 97 STATS

Registration (Book closing, 2012)
Democrats 49.7 percent
NPA 25.6 percent
Republicans 23.1 percent

Voting Age Population (2010 Census): 119,122
White (Non-Hispanic) 54.2 percent
Hispanic 24.3 percent
Black 15.9 percent

Median Age: 39.3

Men: 46.9 percent
Women 53.1 percent

2012 PRESIDENT
Barack Obama 65.7 percent, Mitt Romney, 33.6 percent (Estimated)*

2012 STATE HOUSE
Jared Moskowitz, Democrat, 68.8 percent,
James Gleason, Republican, 31.2 percent

2010 GOVERNOR
Alex Sink 63.4 percent, Rick Scott 34.3 percent

2008 PRESIDENT
Barack Obama 66.1 percent, John McCain, 33.2
percent

HOUSE DISTRICT 98
WEST BROWARD

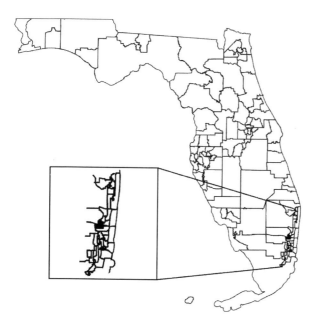

COUNTIES: Broward
RATING: Strong Democrat

IN BROWARD 3.0, WESTERN SUBURBS REMAIN COMFORTABLY DEMOCRATIC

The seemingly endless similar swaths of semitropical suburbia that make up western Broward County include House District 98, which runs from just north of Oakland Park Blvd. in Sunrise southward along N. Nob Hill Rd., across Sunrise Blvd., and I-595 down to Griffin Rd. in Davie. In the southeast the district runs along University Dr. and takes in the campus of Nova Southeastern University. In the southwest, the district runs west to roughly where the city of Weston begins. Davie, though largely suburban now, for many years was semi-rural and is home to a rodeo grounds. It still has a few ranches, and you may see some horses, but the "old west" theme of the building facades in the town's center were a gimmick - a zoning requirement put in place in the 1980s to help give the area an identity separate from the surrounding look-alike suburbs.[1] The district also includes part of the city of Plantation.

WHO LIVES HERE?

Like most of western Broward, House District 98, is relatively affluent, professional and a mix of families with children and retirees. The median family income in Davie is a high $74,000 a year, while in Sunrise it is about $60,000, both higher than the state median family income of $57,600. In terms of age, the district is mixed - and with a median age just under 40, this is the median of the House

[1] Daniel P. Ray, "Davie's Western Theme Lassos Criticism," *Sun-Sentinel*, 17 September 1989.

districts in terms of age, with half of them lower and half of them higher. About 1 in 5 residents here is over 60. About one in three households has children under 18. The area includes some of the youngest precincts in Broward, areas in Sunrise where fewer than 20 percent of voters are over 60, and some precincts in Plantation that are among the oldest, with more than half of voters over 60. Also, some of the most highly educated precincts in Broward County are in a cluster in Sunrise just north of I-595, where more than half of voters have at least a Bachelor's Degree.

The district is about 56 percent non-Hispanic white, and about 25 percent Hispanic. Another 13 percent of residents are black. While Cuban-Americans do make up the largest single group of Latinos in Davie, they're outnumbered in the district by non-Cuban Hispanics with fairly recent arrivals from South America and large numbers of Puerto Ricans also living in the area. Sunrise is home to nearly 5,000 Colombians and about the same number of Puerto Ricans, while another 3,500 Colombians and 6,100 Puerto Ricans live in Davie - and it's an important distinction politically because both groups voted overwhelmingly for Democrats in the last election. Sunrise and Davie are also each home to about 2,000 Peruvians and 1,500 Venezuelans.

Western Broward County remains one of the most Jewish places in the country (though not as heavily Jewish as southern Palm Beach County.) Some 70,000 Jewish people live in west-central and southwest Broward, with likely more than 25,000 of them in House District 98, more than 15 percent of the area's population.

POLITICAL ISSUES AND TRENDS

This is Broward 3.0. For a good part of its history, Broward County was Republican country, made up of the rural white people who founded the place and lived here long before it was urban. Though there was an African-American community here from the beginning, it was small and, frankly, largely politically disenfranchised. The few people who moved to the area before World War II, and the thousands who moved there immediately after, were mostly young, white pioneers and war veterans starting families. Many of them came because they· had trained at South Florida military bases during the war, and liked the idea of warm winters. Through the continued growth of the 1960s, most here voted GOP - particularly as the Democratic Party came to be seen as more liberal during that decade. In 1960 Richard Nixon beat John F. Kennedy in Broward by 20,000 votes. Barry Goldwater won with 55 percent of the vote in 1964. Nixon crushed Hubert Humphrey in 1968 in Broward County. Republicans dominated locally, too. The county's state legislative delegation in the 1970s included George Williamson, a lawyer and developer originally from Tennessee, Van Poole, and Jim Scott, all Republicans. J.W. "Bill" Stevens of Parkland, known as "Mr. Republican," as a Broward County commissioner for most of the 1960s and '70s, was later elected to the Senate, beating Williamson in a GOP primary.

But starting in the 1960s and picking up steam in the 1970s, retirees from the northeast, particularly New York, and many of them Jewish and liberal, began making Broward County their home. Soon, they outnumbered the original mostly conservative people who had moved here to work right after the war. The shift to a Democratic stronghold, driven by the condo-dwelling retirees, was on. That was Broward 2.0. For decades, it was home to those old New Deal Democrats, many of them former union members, and by the 1990s, that was Broward, politically - retired and liberal. In a couple of decades, those retired newcomers had transformed the area into what political journalist Steve Bousquet would call "virtually a sixth borough of New York." [2] And its center, politically, had shifted west to places like this district, once fringe towns like Plantation and Davie and others in neighboring districts like Tamarac and Coral Springs. By 2000, Broward was the most reliable Democratic county in the South, and the party held every seat on the county commission and 16 of its 18 legislative seats. Republicans started calling it "the People's Republic of Broward." But those old Jewish liberals are dying.

Broward 3.0 is still dominated by Democrats - only they're increasingly young, progressive professionals moving to the area to follow companies that have expanded here, and large numbers of non-Cuban Hispanics. Another longtime Broward County political observer, journalist Buddy Nevins, said he has noticed

---

[2] Fiedler and de Haven-Smith, Pg. 201.

the change at the local Publix. "Over the past few years, I noticed many younger Hispanics in the aisles and more shelves filled with foods that appeal to Hispanics," Nevins said. "There has also been an influx of Caribbean black families and exotic foods from the islands are stocked as well. Where you once heard Yiddish and Italian, you are more likely to hear Spanish, English with a Jamaican lilt, and Creole." Many are coming to the area from South America - there may be 8,000 to 10,000 Colombians in this part of west Broward. Those moving in are voting for Democrats in similar numbers to their mostly New York Jewish predecessors. The district, like the neighboring ones in west Broward, remains a safe one for the party. The district's House member, Katie Edwards, won easily in 2012, defeating Republican Cara Pavalock 67 percent to 33 percent and Barack Obama beat Mitt Romney in the district's precincts in the 2012 presidential race 60 percent to 39 percent.

Edwards grew up in Plantation surrounded by the politics of west Broward as the daughter of Plantation Commissioner Bruce "Dead Bug" Edwards. (His name came from the family pest control business - Bruce's mother Joan and father Robert founded the company, called Dead Bug Edwards in Plantation in 1959. By the time Bruce was running for office in the 1990s, most people in Broward knew the name.) Katie Edwards, though, didn't go into the family business, but went to work for the Dade County Farm Bureau and served as its executive director starting when she was just 22. In that job, she got deeply involved in statewide public policy, came to be well-known at the Capitol, and an expert on agriculture policy and small business. Before winning the District 98 seat in 2012, Edwards had lived in southern Miami-Dade for her farm bureau job, and in 2010 she was recruited by Democrats to run for a South Dade seat in the Legislature in an area that was nearly even in partisan make-up and appeared to be trending slightly Democratic. She lost, though, to Republican Frank Artiles. Edwards then moved back to her hometown in Broward to run for an open seat after re-districting and the departure of Democratic Rep. Martin Kiar. Touting her Farm Bureau experience in public policy work, she defeated attorney Louis Reinstein in the Democratic primary and then defeated Pavalock in the general election.

Edwards is a centrist, and takes pragmatic stances on a number of issues, sometimes putting her at odds with her Democratic colleagues, particularly those from liberal Broward County. Her background as an advocate for farmers makes her a farm-friendly candidate in an otherwise urban region. And she stands out from her South Florida Democratic colleagues on one major issue - guns. She got an A rating from the NRA, and was a prime co-sponsor of a bill seeking to clarify that if someone brandishes a gun or fires a warning shot when they're being threatened, they could use the Stand Your Ground self defense law to avoid prosecution for assault or wanton endangerment, just as someone who actually shoots someone may use the law to avoid charges. The measure was expected to draw almost as much attention as a bill Edwards filed during her first session that would have legalized the possession of medical marijuana, a bill that died in committee. Edwards has advocated extensively for loosening some drug sentencing laws, saying the state can't afford to continue to imprison minor drug offenders. She filed a bill for the 2013 session that would increase the amount of prescription painkillers that someone would have to be carrying to be convicted of trafficking. Another measure from Edwards' first session would have allowed the sale of 64-ounce growlers of beer, a measure pushed by craft brewers and brewpubs. She also filed a bill for the 2013 session that was co-sponsored with several Republicans that would prohibit certain people on probation from viewing or possessing pornography, regardless of the relevance to their crime.

DISTRICT 98 STATS

Registration (Book closing, 2012)
Democrats 47.7 percent
Republicans 26.4 percent
NPA 24.2 percent

Voting Age Population (2010 Census): 121,430
White (Non-Hispanic) 58.8 percent
Hispanic 23.7 percent
Black 12 percent

Median Age: 39.6

Men: 47.2 percent
Women 52.8 percent

2012 PRESIDENT

Barack Obama 60.3 percent, Mitt Romney, 39 percent (Estimated)*

2012 STATE HOUSE
Katie Edwards, Democrat, 67.1 percent, Cara Christine Pavalock, Republican, 32.9 percent

2010 GOVERNOR
Alex Sink 60.8 percent, Rick Scott 36.9 percent

2008 PRESIDENT
Barack Obama 62.3 percent, John McCain, 37 percent

HOUSE DISTRICT 99
SOUTH BROWARD

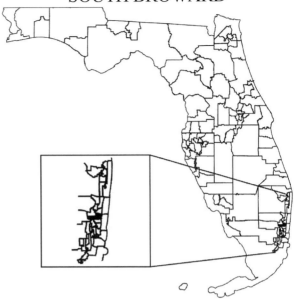

COUNTIES: Broward
RATING: Solid Democrat

DIVERSE, DEMOCRATIC DISTRICT

House District 99 takes in neighborhoods southwest of downtown Fort Lauderdale, part of the city of Davie, and the wealthy bedroom community of Cooper City, south of Griffin Road. It stretches west to Interstate 75, including part of Southwest Ranches. In the east, the district includes the part of Dania Beach west of U.S. 1, just south of the Fort Lauderdale-Hollywood International Airport, which is also entirely within the district. The district also dips just south of Sheridan St. into the city of Hollywood, including the majority black neighborhood of Liberia. It also includes the Seminole Hard Rock Hotel and Casino right off the Florida Turnpike. The district touches more interstate highway than perhaps any other in South Florida. The Turnpike, I-595 and I-95 all run through the district, while I-75 serves as its western border.

WHO LIVES HERE?

The area south and west of downtown Fort Lauderdale that makes up District 99 is, socioeconomically and ethnically, incredibly diverse. The overall population is 52 percent non-Hispanic white, 30 percent Latino and 13 percent black, and the area also has a high concentration of South Asians - mostly from India. Cooper City, for example, is about 6 percent Asian, one of the highest percentages of any Florida community. About half of those Asians are of Indian descent, though in addition to the sub-continent, many came here from elsewhere in the Indian Diaspora, such as Trinidad or Guyana. In light of that, the district has a cricket ground, in Cooper City. The South Florida Hindu Temple is also in the district, in western Cooper City near Southwest Ranches.

But the region's diversity is on full display in the neighborhood - around the corner are a Jewish Temple, a Pentecostal church, a Catholic church and high school and a Methodist Church. Turn another corner and you'll pass an Islamic academy and an Armenian Apostolic Church. Cooper City and Davie are also home to thousands of Jewish residents.

There's a broad economic diversity as well. Cooper City is among the wealthiest towns in Broward County, with a median family income over $100,000 a year. Davie is also relatively well off, with a median family income over $70,000, more than $10,000 above the state median. The district also includes Lauderdale Isles, a wealthy enclave of high-end homes near the New River and along canals leading to the river. That neighborhood is home to upper middle class families and some retirees. But Broadview Park and Chula Vista are working-class neighborhoods that include lots of apartments and some mobile homes, and the Liberia neighborhood in Hollywood, which is about 90 percent African-American, is one of that city's poorer areas and has long been plagued by crime and drug problems.

The district also is diverse in terms of age - Cooper City is one of the youngest parts of Broward County, with an average age just over 30, while farther west in Southwest Ranches the median age is more than a decade older, just under 44 years old. On the eastern edge of the district in Dania Beach the median age is also over 40. The median age in the district as a whole is 39.1.

While it is full of residential neighborhoods,

the district also includes major business-lined thoroughfares like Griffin Rd., Stirling Rd. and Sheridan St., all going east-west, and U.S. 441/SR 7, South University Dr., and Flamingo Rd., running north-south.

POLITICAL ISSUES AND TRENDS

The area is solidly Democratic, giving Barack Obama 61 percent of the vote in 2012 and 2008, with Democratic gubernatorial candidate Alex Sink getting 60 percent in 2010. Rep. Elaine Schwartz won with more than 65 percent of the vote in 2012. Registered Democrats make up just under half the registered voters, at 49.1 percent, with the other half split nearly evenly between Republicans and no party voters. While exact figures are hard to calculate, well over 10 percent of the voters here are likely Jewish, and another 12 percent African-American, providing a near automatic voting bloc of more than 20 percent of the district for Democrats. With Latino voters going heavily for Democrats in recent elections, the district appears a solid lock for the Democratic Party for the foreseeable future.

Schwartz was an accomplished lawyer, having worked at the Federal Reserve Bank of New York, and then as an assistant city attorney for the city of Hollywood, before getting elected to the House in 2006. She was named Democratic whip that same year. But as a strongly liberal member of an overwhelmingly Republican House, she has mostly had to be content with trying to influence policy around the edges, and with her votes, rather than by pushing legislation to passage, which she has largely been unable to do. Schwartz has been a vocal advocate for abortion rights, and for expansion of the KidCare subsidized health insurance program, and for accepting federal money to expand the state Medicaid program to pick up new recipients who need coverage under the federal health care law. She has also been a critic of plans to shift the state Medicaid program to a managed care delivery system.

Schwartz has also repeatedly opposed a measure that could invalidate some decisions or rulings that are based on some sort of foreign legal system. She has been a proponent of some forms of gambling, and was one of just seven House members in 2013 to oppose the bill shutting down the Internet cafe industry, saying that the businesses offered an enjoyable activity that should be regulated and taxed. In 2013 Schwartz sponsored legislation that would have allowed counties to create special taxing districts to pay for services for the elderly, a bill that died in committee. She also was a co-sponsor of unsuccessful legislation to allow local governments to ban guns at certain events at government buildings or venues, and an unsuccessful bipartisan bill to reduce drug trafficking sentences. In fact, with the exception of ceremonial resolutions, every bill Schwartz sponsored or co-sponsored in 2013 failed to pass, and none of the substantive bills of which she was the primary sponsor passed in 2010, 2011 or 2012. In 2009, however, legislation Schwartz sponsored that removed the term "shylock and shylocking," offensive references to Jewish people, from the usury statutes, did become law. A long-term care insurance consumer protection bill that Schwartz sponsored became law in 2008. But overall, her legislative career has been marked by sponsoring legislation that couldn't pass in a Republican-controlled Legislature.

DISTRICT 99 STATS

Registration (Book closing, 2012)
Democrats 49.1 percent
Republicans 25.3 percent
NPA 24.1 percent

Voting Age Population (2010 Census): 119,857
White (Non-Hispanic) 54.3 percent
Hispanic 29.1 percent
Black 11.8 percent

Median Age: 39.1

Men: 49.1 percent
Women 50.9 percent

2012 PRESIDENT
Barack Obama 61.1 percent, Mitt Romney, 38.1 percent (Estimated)*

2012 STATE HOUSE
Rep. Elaine Schwartz, D-Hollywood, 65.5 percent, Elizabeth Anne "Libby" Eddy, Republican, 34.5 percent

2010 GOVERNOR
Alex Sink 60.3 percent, Rick Scott 37.3 percent

2008 PRESIDENT
Barack Obama 61.8 percent, John McCain, 37.4 percent

HOUSE DISTRICT 100
COASTAL SOUTH BROWARD, NORTH MIAMI-DADE

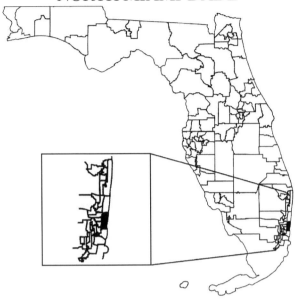

COUNTIES: Broward, Miami-Dade
RATING: Solid Democrat

OY VEY, MON DIEU. AND AY, DIOS MIO! EVERYBODY IS FROM SOMEWHERE ELSE

The accents of House District 100 are those of Brooklyn Jewish neighborhoods and French-speaking Quebec, with a little bit of Latin American Spanglish thrown in. Everyone here, it seems, is from somewhere else, whether they're just here for the winter, or retired to live on the beach until their last day.

The district starts in the north at Port Everglades in Fort Lauderdale, where cruise ships leave for the Caribbean, and includes the French Canadian snowbird haven of Hollywood Beach, where the signs advertising efficiency apartments often say "on parle francais," and the cars have license plates promising "Je me souviens." It also includes the condo canyon of Hallandale Beach, with its water tower painted to look like a beach ball - and Gulfstream Park Racing and Casino. South of the county line in Miami-Dade is Aventura - known to most people in South Florida as miles of tangled traffic on U.S. 1 trying to get into strip malls full of high end stores, chain eateries or the Aventura Mall. It is also home to the Turnberry Resort, with its golf course tucked in amid the condos and boutiques. The district also includes the tiny exclusive enclave of Golden Beach, and then to the south more high

rise condos in Sunny Isles Beach.

At the southern end of the district are Bal Harbour, Bay Harbor Islands, and the town of Surfside, communities where the accent is decidedly New Yorker and where on certain days the sidewalks are full of traditionally dressed Jewish families heading to services. Bay

Harbor Islands includes one island of mostly low-rise and mid-rise condo and apartment buildings, many of them home to retirees, but some also home to young families, and one island of upper middle class single family homes. Surfside, while lined with high rises on the beach, also hides side-street residential neighborhoods full of young families, about half of them immigrant families, who live in relatively modest homes, but just a couple blocks from the ocean.

The Turnberry Resort played a sordid role in political history - it was there presidential candidate Gary Hart spent time on the yacht Monkey Business with a woman who wasn't his wife. That indiscretion, along with a report by The Miami Herald that the woman, Donna Rice, also spent the night at Hart's Washington townhouse, lead to his withdrawal from the 1988 campaign. Shortly after Hart dropped out in 1987 the New York Times described the Aventura setting, which also gives a sense of what Turnberry was like then. "The boat was moored at the yacht club that was part of South Florida's Turnberry Isle Country Club, a glamorous, fast-paced resort where attractive men and women, some famous from the worlds of rock music and movies, relaxed in a sun-washed enclave of exclusivity and wealth. Hollywood's James Caan and Don Johnson of the "Miami Vice" television drama were guests at the resort. John McEnroe owns a condominium there and, until he sold it recently, so did Jimmy Connors." [1]

---

[1] E.J. Dionne et al, "Courting Danger, the Fall of Gary

WHO LIVES HERE?

While there's no way to measure it definitively, it would be a safe bet that House District 100 would be near the top of a list of districts with the most people who are from somewhere else, along with the area around the retirement community of The Villages in north-central Florida and the Florida Keys. First, District 100 is home to a huge number of retirees - they live in the high rise condos of Bal Harbour, Sunny Isles Beach, Aventura and Hallandale Beach, and on Bay Harbor Islands. Many are seasonal residents, but a number of others are here to stay, a Florida stereotype, leaving their ocean view condos to play a little golf, meet at the club for drinks, or walk along the beach. There's a good chance they're Jewish - in some parts of the district it's almost a certainty - and if they're full time residents they vote often. There's also a chance they don't vote, because they're citizens of Canada, or they vote in New York, New Jersey, or Massachusetts. A large number of eastern Europeans, many of them Jewish, including Russians and Romanians in particular, have also moved to the area, mostly settling in Aventura.

A third of the district's voting age population is Hispanic - and it is mostly non-Cuban Latinos, and includes a large number of new immigrants who have arrived in the last decade. In particular, Jews from Latin America, have made Aventura home - thousands of Venezuelan Jews fleeing the Chavez regime

---

Hart," *The New York Times*, 9 May 1987.

have settled there. [2] In addition to Jewish Latinos, Aventura is also home to a burgeoning population of Brazilians and increasingly large numbers of Colombians and non-Jewish Venezuelans. Surfside, with a laid-back small beach town feel despite sitting on the northern end of the island that includes glitzy Miami Beach, is also a mini-global village, with about 45 percent of its residents having been born in another country. Among those are significant numbers (percentage-wise at least, since the town is home to fewer than 6,000 people) of residents born in Cuba, India, Argentina, Colombia, Canada, Germany and Venezuela. Given the mix of origins in the district, the list of candidates running for the seat in 2014 - when Rep. Joe Gibbons, D-Hallandale Beach, will be prevented by term limits from running again - isn't a surprise. One candidate is the son of a Peruvian immigrant father and a Jewish mother, there are several other Jewish candidates, including one who previously was responsible for Jewish and Hispanic outreach in U.S. Rep. Kendrick Meek's office, and a Libertarian who grew up in Brooklyn. And Gibbons is African-American.

House District 100 is above average in wealth, though median income figures aren't the best way to measure it because of the large percentage of retirees. Median family incomes are below the state average in Hallandale Beach, Dania Beach, and Sunny Isles Beach but well above the state average in Aventura, Surfside

[2] The Associated Press, "Venezuelan Jews: New Year, New Home," 6 September 2013.

and Bay Harbor Islands. Bal Harbour, where beachside condos are or have been owned by celebrities like Bob and Elizabeth Dole and the late David Brinkley, has a median family income over $100,000, but the median household income - which would factor in non-family households like elderly retirees living alone - drops to about $66,000. Still, overall this is a pretty well-off district.

POLITICAL ISSUES AND TRENDS

With the coalescence of a large number of Jewish voters, retirees from the northeast, and immigrants from Latin America, it's not a surprise that this is a solidly Democratic district that has typically given top-of-the-ticket Democrats 18-20 percentage point wins. Barack Obama dropped off a bit in 2012, winning the area's precincts by just 16 points after Alex Sink won by nearly 20 in 2010 and Obama beat John McCain by about 20 in 2008. Republicans didn't field a candidate for the House District 100 seat in 2012.

Gibbons was first elected to the House in 2006 and is term-limited from running again in 2014. He served as the leader of House Democrats from 2010 to 2012 and was chairman of the Black Caucus in 2008. Before his election to the House, Gibbons was on the Hallandale city commission from 2003 to 2006. As might be expected of a Democrat in a Republican-dominated House, Gibbons has passed very little legislation during his seven legislative sessions. In fact, every single substantive bill Gibbons filed in 2008, 2009 and 2012 failed. Gibbons did eventually see, after trying for three years, his proposal to require screening of youth sports coaches against sexual offender registries pass in 2010. And in 2007, Gibbons worked to get legislation passed to increase penalties for leaving children unattended in cars. Gibbons has been a major proponent of additional early voting hours, seeing mixed success - his early efforts at expanding early voting failed, but eventually he saw Republicans agree to allow the addition of early voting times in 2013. Gibbons has generally been a friend to the gaming industry - not a surprise with Gulfstream Racing and Casino and the Mardi Gras Casino and Hollywood Greyhound track in his district. Gibbons' 2007 and 2008 effort to pass legislation to authorize high stakes poker and dominoes tournaments at certain pari-mutuels failed. For 2014, Gibbons filed legislation that would require state analysts to do racial and ethnic impact statements describing anticipated effects of proposed legislation on minorities as analysts do now for the effect of a proposed bill on local governments, or on the budget.

DISTRICT 100 STATS

Registration (Book closing, 2012)
Democrats 46 percent
NPA 28 percent
Republicans 23.8 percent

Voting Age Population (2010 Census): 131,857
White (Non-Hispanic) 58.1 percent
Hispanic 34 percent
Black 5.3 percent

Median Age: 45.7

Men: 47.9 percent
Women 52.1 percent

2012 PRESIDENT
Barack Obama 57.5 percent, Mitt Romney, 41.8 percent (Estimated)*

2012 STATE HOUSE
Democratic Primary: Rep. Joe Gibbons, D-Hallandale Beach, 55.3 percent, Sheldon Lisbon 44.7 percent. Gibbons faced no general election opposition.

2010 GOVERNOR
Alex Sink 58 percent, Rick Scott 39.5 percent

2008 PRESIDENT
Barack Obama 60 percent, John McCain, 39.2 percent

HOUSE DISTRICT 101
SOUTH BROWARD: HOLLYWOOD
TO MIRAMAR

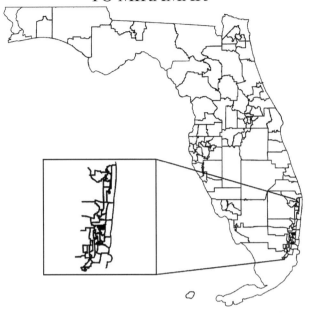

COUNTIES: Broward

RATING: Solid Democrat

DIVERSE MAJORITY-MINORITY
DISTRICT, DEMOCRATIC LOCK

House District 101 includes the mostly African-American eastern part of Miramar and, just to the east, the small towns of West Park and Pembroke Park, both also majority black. In the north, the district includes the parts of the city of Hollywood west of Dixie Highway, including the majority black Washington Park and the Highland Gardens neighborhood, a low-income and high crime neighborhood that the South Florida Sun Sentinel politely called "rough-around-the-edges," in a 2012 story.[1] It also takes in the eastern end of Pembroke Pines. West Park is a relatively new city, having been created only in 2004. The Broward College South Campus is on the western edge of the district. The district is also home to large numbers of Hispanic and Caribbean immigrants.

WHO LIVES HERE?

HD 101, while designed to be a minority access district with black voters making up the largest group, is actually one of the most ethnically balanced in the state. Its voting age population is just over a third African-American, about one third Hispanic and just under a third non-Hispanic white - making this one of the very few areas where all three major

---

[1] Tonya Alanez, "Hollywood's First Eco-Friendly Park..." *Sun-Sentinel*, 11 July 2012

ethnic groups in the state have about equal voting power.

But this is also a district in flux - one where large numbers of immigrants from Latin America and the Caribbean have moved in recent decades. A non-descript little restaurant on Pines Blvd. in Pembroke Pines might best illustrate the demographic change in this part of Broward County. It used to be called the Pembroke Diner, and it was a place (mostly) older white people went for an old fashioned roast beef sandwich or some ham steak with apple sauce. "Sipping some of the world's best iced tea from plastic cups with straws, the Budget Diner and guest watched their neighbors, some clad in three-piece suits, others in shorts, down breakfasts of fried eggs with bacon and ham and pancakes," the South Florida Sun-Sentinel's "Budget Diner" reviewer wrote back in the restaurant's heyday in 1985. But by the late 2000s, those neighbors who liked ham and pancakes had mostly died or moved on. The place finally closed in 2009. And in 2011, the same newspaper had a note about a new restaurant that was taking over the building. Pinolandia serves Nicaraguan carne asada and gallo pinto. The new restaurant reflects a 65 percent jump in the Hispanic population of Pembroke Pines in the 2000s, much of it in this eastern part of the city. The old one served a population that isn't as prominent in this part of Broward anymore. Black Caribbean immigrants have moved here, too, particularly from Jamaica, and the city of Miramar now counts 15 percent of its residents as being of Jamaican ancestry.

The district is mostly working class, and largely working age, with a median age of just 36.8, though there are retirees scattered in a few mobile home parks and senior living communities.

POLITICAL ISSUES AND TRENDS

With the African-American population of this area having increased in the last decade, this district as drawn became a majority-minority district, though blacks just barely beat out Hispanics for largest ethnic group in these precincts. No matter from a partisan perspective, really, because the Hispanic vote went largely for Democrats in the last election, and while a large number of the Latinos in District 101 are Cuban-Americans, many of whom moved north from Miami, exit polling in 2012 showed that even Cubans are starting to consider Democratic candidates, particularly in cases where the voter is young. There's also a significant portion of Latinos here who are from Central and South America, and they, too, were likely to vote Democrat. The preference isn't close - Democrats win here by more than 50 percentage points typically, and Barack Obama, perhaps not surprisingly in a district with so many African-Americans, did extremely well, closing in on a 60 point margin. Republicans didn't field a candidate for the state House seat here.

Shevrin Jones had one of the easiest paths to the state House - he signed up for it and went to Tallahassee. Jones was the only person who filed qualifying paperwork to run for the new House District 101 in South Broward, though initially Pembroke Park Mayor Ashira

Mohammed was also campaigning for the seat. Jones, a research specialist for the Broward Sheriff's Office, is a 2006 graduate of Florida A&M University in biochemistry and molecular biology. While state representative is his first elected office, Jones ran and lost for the Broward County commission in 2010 and is familiar with politics because his father, Eric Jones, is the mayor of West Park. Shevrin Jones previously taught chemistry in Broward public schools. His most high profile legislation likely won't pass - he's sponsoring a bill to delay implementation of the evaluation procedures for the new public school performance pay law. Another controversial measure Jones filed for 2014 would make certain minimum mandatory drug sentencing laws apply only on second or subsequent convictions. He also is sponsoring legislation to require background screening of youth sports coaches. As a freshman Democrat, Jones did manage to pass one bill in 2013, a measure providing for the regulation of "biosimilar biological products" that are substituted for other drugs or vaccines.

DISTRICT 101 STATS

Registration (Book closing, 2012)
Democrats 61 percent
NPA 22 percent
Republicans 15.7 percent

Voting Age Population (2010 Census): 117,747
Black 33.8 percent
Hispanic 33.7 percent
White (Non-Hispanic) 29 percent

Median Age: 36.8

Men: 48.1 percent
Women 51.9 percent

2012 PRESIDENT
Barack Obama 79 percent, Mitt Romney, 20.4
percent (Estimated)*

2012 STATE HOUSE
No race. Shevrin Jones was the only candidate
to qualify in the race, and faced no primary or
general election opposition

2010 GOVERNOR
Alex Sink 74.8 percent, Rick Scott 23.1 percent

2008 PRESIDENT
Barack Obama 76.7 percent, John McCain, 22.7
percent

HOUSE DISTRICT 102
PEMBROKE PINES, MIRAMAR, MIAMI GARDENS

COUNTIES: Broward, Miami-Dade
RATING: Super Democrat

MIDDLE CLASS AFRICAN-AMERICANS, CARIBBEAN-AMERICANS AND HISPANICS

House District 102 is a majority-minority district that straddles the central-west Broward-Miami-Dade County line, taking in parts of Pembroke Pines and Miramar in Broward County and part of Miami Gardens in Miami-Dade County. The district is more than half African-American, and about 37 percent Hispanic, and though not wealthy, it is economically mixed, and in most places home to middle-class working people.

677

WHO LIVES HERE: MIAMI GARDENS

The black people of the Miami area for a long time didn't determine where they wanted to live as much as they had it determined for them. In the city's early days Jim Crow laws herded African-Americans into Overtown, though it was called Colored Town then. Starting in the 1930s, with concern about the unsightly ghetto Overtown was becoming, and fears that Miami's downtown couldn't grow, a new "colored city" was envisioned in what is now Liberty City. Then, in the 1960s, when Interstate 95 came to downtown Miami, it ripped through Overtown, erasing whole neighborhoods from the map. One interchange claimed the housing of 10,000 African-American people. Many poor Overtown residents moved to Liberty City. Some with higher incomes, the black community's business owners, moved from Overtown to unincorporated northwest Miami-Dade County, an area without a large established white community to prevent black people from owning homes. Also moving in: middle class blacks from Liberty City who were displaced by new poor African-Americans forced out of Overtown.

The area where these refugees from Miami-proper moved grew into its own sprawling, urban-suburban community that would, much later, become Miami Gardens, the largest city in Florida that is majority African-American. The city, now about 107,000 people and 78 percent black, incorporated in 2003 - and to the surprise of many observers who believed it was too poor of an area to effectively provide city services - voted in higher property tax rates. That allowed for the creation of a large police force (though that force has recently come under scrutiny for overzealousness, and even racial profiling), trash pickup and other services. The city also took in the area that includes what is now Sun Life Stadium, home of the Miami Dolphins, putting the new town on the national sports map. While there's still plenty of poverty and crime in the area, many residents of Miami Gardens have a certain pride in having created this city where they live, rather than having had it created for them like the places their ancestors lived. Most of the power structure is black, and though Hispanics are increasingly moving here, the area continues to be primarily seen as a haven for the Miami area's working class African-Americans.

MIRAMAR AND PEMBROKE PINES

Just north of the county line in Broward is Miramar, a city that's split into three districts with its eastern and western ends in other districts. It was one of the fastest growing cities in the state in the last couple of decades, growing to over 120,000 people in the most recent Census. But if asked to describe Miramar, the first thing many people might mention is that it has become one of Broward County's "Caribbean cities," along with Lauderhill and Lauderdale Lakes. Jamaicans, in particular, have moved into Miramar's central and eastern areas, and now make up 15 percent of the city's population. In 2003, three Jamaican-Americans were elected to the city's commission, making it the nation's first majority Jamaican-American city legislative body. The city now looks extremely different than it did a few decades ago, when it was Broward County's Italian-American enclave, and that 2003 city commission election really made it clear. In addition to the Jamaican candidates, there were two Haitian-American candidates and two Hispanic candidates. Overall, black residents make up 45 percent of Miramar's population. Hispanics make up 37 percent, and whites 11 percent, but many of the city's Hispanic and white residents are clustered in the city's west end, in House District 103. Asians make up another 5 percent of the population here.

Pembroke Pines is also split into multiple districts, but the southern and eastern parts of the city are in House District 102. The city started in the mid-1950s when Flamingo Development bought the land from one of several dairy farms in western Broward, and was small and quiet for years, but boomed in population in the 1990s after Hurricane Andrew. Thousands of people who moved out of southern Miami-Dade County after the storm fled to Pembroke Pines, which was among the fastest growing cities in the nation in that decade and now numbers more than 150,000 people. Many of those moving in were Hispanic - the percentage of Latinos in the city tripled in the 1990s and then doubled again in the 2000s, now accounting for 41 percent of the city's population.

POLITICAL ISSUES AND TRENDS

Miami Gardens was at the heart of the surge in new black voters that helped propel Barack Obama into the White House in 2008, as the Huffington Post noted during that year's early voting period, writing about a voting line at the city's North Dade Regional Library "that begins at the library doors, folds in two, covers the parking lot, stretches out the sidewalk, then snakes around a very large block." [1] District 102 as a whole is reliably and actively Democrat territory, where Obama got nearly 85 percent of the vote in 2012, slightly more than the 83 percent he got in 2008 in these precincts. Democrat Alex Sink got 83 percent of the governor's race vote here in 2010 and Republicans, not surprisingly, didn't bother with this district in the most recent legislative

---

[1] John Hood. "Mass. Gov. Deval Patrick Hits Miami to Help ..." *Huffington Post* 1 November, 2008.

elections.

Democrat Rep. Sharon Pritchett is a former Miami Gardens councilwoman and retired as chief investigator for the Miami-Dade County Public Defender's Office. Before her 2012 election, she narrowly lost a bid for a House seat in a special election in 2011. She lost that race to now-Rep. Barbara Watson in the primary to replace Oscar Braynon, who had been elected to the Senate. In 2012, Pritchett defeated another former council member, Melvin Lewis Bratton, in the Democratic primary but faced no on-ballot opposition in the general election.

In her first session, Pritchett filed legislation arising from her work experience, pushing a bill to allow for minors to have records expunged after completing a diversion program. While her measure died in committee, another bill that did pass contained some of its provisions. She supported her party, voting for legislation to expand early voting, backing efforts to allow children of illegal immigrants to get in-state tuition, to prohibit workplace discrimination based on sexual orientation, and to allow the creation of legal domestic partnerships for unmarried adults. She joined her Democratic colleagues in opposition to a bill changing standards for acceptance of expert witness testimony in lawsuits, and in opposing a bill giving parents more say in letting charter school companies take over public schools. She also opposed the bill seeking to speed up death penalty appeals, and against various efforts to make it harder to sue. Her most notable vote may have been against closing down so-called

"Internet cafes," when she was just one of seven House members to vote no on one of the signature bills of the 2013 session.

DISTRICT 102 STATS

Registration (Book closing, 2012
Democrats 66.1 percent
NPA 20.3 percent
Republicans 12.7 percent

Voting Age Population (2010 Census): 116,881
Black 48.8 percent
Hispanic 38 percent
White (Non-Hispanic) 10.4 percent

Median Age: 34.2

Men: 46.6 percent
Women: 53.4 percent

2012 PRESIDENT
Barack Obama 84.5 percent, Mitt Romney, 15.1 percent (Estimated)*

2012 STATE HOUSE
Democratic Primary: Sharon Pritchett, D-Miami Gardens, 58.2 percent, Melvin Bratton, 41.8 percent. Pritchett faced only write-in opposition in the general election.

2010 GOVERNOR
Alex Sink 83.1 percent, Rick Scott 15.6 percent

2008 PRESIDENT
Barack Obama 83.4 percent, John McCain, 16.2 percent

HOUSE DISTRICT 103
WESTERN MIRAMAR, HIALEAH GARDENS, MEDLEY

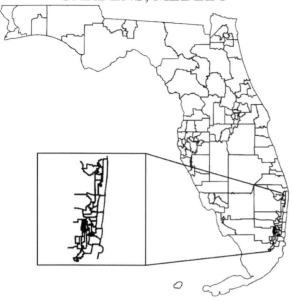

COUNTIES: Broward, Miami-Dade

RATING: Leans Democrat

THE LATINO SURPRISE PRECINCTS

In 2012, the basketball team from Hialeah Gardens High School did something that wouldn't turn a lot of heads in Miami-Dade County, but was a little different for people watching the state tournament. The Gladiators put an all Hispanic team on the court, with players born in Cuba, the Dominican Republic and Venezuela. And then they won the 8A state championship, the first predominantly Hispanic team to do so. During their championship run that took them to places in central Florida less accustomed to such diversity, they endured chants of "U-S-A," and other taunting from fans. [1] The clash of cultures may be a harbinger of what's to come in Florida as the rest of the state slowly starts to look the way Miami long has - multi-colored and multi-cultural. In the suburbs west of Miami, including the economically diverse, but mostly Hispanic House District 103, which runs from northwest of the Miami airport into southwest Broward County, the Latin look of the Hialeah Gardens Gladiators isn't unusual, though it would be wrong to suggest there aren't still cultural tensions here.

District 103 includes some of Miami-Dade's more industrial areas, including Medley, a dense, but tiny city that's primarily home to businesses and industrial companies. Medley is one of the places where the Miami area's blue collars actually work, at concrete and cement companies, lots of construction supply firms, distributorships, and near the airport, cargo companies and importers and exporters. Next door, Hialeah Gardens is similarly home to many of the companies that make, store, or deliver the products that Miamians use. For example, Blue Bell, an ice cream company, recently opened a distributorship in the town from which it delivers all its ice cream to groceries all over South Florida.

But the district also includes more traditional suburbs that serve primarily as a place where people live, like Miami Lakes,

---

[1] Walter Villa, "Hialeah Gardens players say taunts provided motivation," *The Miami Herald*, 29, January, 2013.

developed out of the dairy farm owned by former U.S. Sen. Bob Graham's family, and now a comfortable, leafy, affluent suburb that is 80 percent Hispanic.

House District 103 includes western Miramar, west of Flamingo Road, and western Miami Lakes. Going toward the south the district crosses U.S. 27 and that's where you find Medley and Hialeah Gardens. In the far southwestern corner of the district, it dips

slightly into Doral.

WHO LIVES HERE?

Like most of Miami's western suburban districts, House District 103 is mostly Hispanic, around 80 percent. Most of the Hispanics living in this area are Cuban-Americans, though there is a significant population of Venezuelans, near Doral. A quarter of the households in the district include someone over age 65, so there is a sizable population of elderly Cuban-

Americans, some of them first generation exile. But mostly, this is an area of younger families; one in three households in the district has children under 18 at home. In Miami Lakes, the population is 60 percent Cuban-American, with smaller populations of Colombians and Dominicans. Similarly, Hialeah Gardens is 66 percent Cuban-American, but also is home to a few thousand Nicaraguan-Americans.

Miami Lakes is relatively affluent, with a median household income well above the state average. Most of the Miami Lakes Census tracts in District 103 have median household incomes above $70,000 and some are in the $90,000s. Miramar is similar, economically. The part of Miramar that is in District 103, south of Pembroke Rd. and west of Flamingo Rd., has a median income of about $86,000. Farther south, the district is more working class, but, for the most part, not poor. The Hialeah Gardens neighborhoods in the district mostly have median incomes in the high $40,000s, right around the state median. There is an area in the southeastern corner of the district, including parts of Hialeah Gardens and into Medley, where median household incomes drop into the $30,000s and lower, well below the state average. The southwestern corner of the district, however, which includes part of Doral, is affluent.

POLITICAL ISSUES AND TRENDS

This is one of that handful of Miami districts that were part of Barack Obama's "Latino surprise," in 2012, districts thought to be at least slightly Republican, as they were in 2008, but which voted for Obama. Anyone who was paying close attention to the demographics may have guessed (and many did) that these districts might flip from GOP supporters to backers of Obama, at least, if not other Democrats, but many people were stunned. Neighborhoods don't often change dramatically in their political leanings, and often when they do it's either a watershed political year (think 2008 or the post-Watergate years of 1974 and '76), or it's the culmination of a long, gradual shift. Arguably, the latter was true in Miami-Dade County, a shift in Hispanic voting patterns, particularly among Cuban-Americans, has been quietly going on for several years. But hardly anyone other than local residents is likely to have truly realized the degree to which the non-Cuban Hispanic population has grown in some parts of Florida, and that its members have been here long enough to register to vote, and the degree to which they would turn out for Obama.

Obama won by just over 10 percentage points, in district 103, where voters gave Republican Rick Scott a 5 point win just two years earlier, and voted for John McCain over Obama (though by less than a percentage point) in 2008. As was the case in many other predominantly Hispanic South Florida districts that have traditionally voted Republican, Democrats didn't run a candidate here. The party isn't particularly well situated to run local candidates in these districts - there aren't many experienced Democratic politicians, and much of the ground level political organization that got Obama votes here was parachuted in by the Obama campaign and the national and state parties. So Rep. Manny Diaz, a Republican in a district won at the top of the ticket by a Democrat, faced no opposition.

Diaz, a school assistant principal from Hialeah, is the vice chairman of the K-12 Subcommittee of the House Education Committee, and has focused his legislative attention mainly on education. He's sponsored legislation seeking to create pilot projects for single-gender public schools and legislation seeking to require schools to teach financial literacy, and about the Sept. 11 terrorist attacks. He's also filed legislation to add a list of crimes, from human trafficking to treason to the offenses that would disqualify someone from being certified as a teacher. In 2013, Diaz successfully pushed legislation to encourage schools to offer more online, or virtual courses. Before becoming an administrator at Hialeah-Miami Lakes Senior High, Diaz taught at the school, and earlier was a teacher and coach at Miami Springs Senior High. While Diaz didn't have a Democratic opponent in 2012, he defeated two other Republicans, including former Rep. Renier Diaz de la Portilla, in the GOP primary.

DISTRICT 103 STATS

Registration (Book closing, 2012),
Democrats 35.1 percent
Republicans 33.9 percent
NPA 29.5 percent

Voting Age Population (2010 Census): 116,173
Hispanic 82.1 percent
Black 7.9 percent
White (Non-Hispanic) 6.6 percent

Median Age: 36.8

Men: 47.7 percent
Women 52.3 percent

2012 PRESIDENT
Barack Obama 55.7 percent, Mitt Romney, 43.9
percent (Estimated)*

2012 STATE HOUSE
Republican Primary: Manny Diaz, Jr., 55.2
percent, Renier Diaz de la Portilla, 39.3 percent,
Alfredo Naredo-Acosta, 5.5 percent. Diaz faced
only write-in opposition

2010 GOVERNOR
Rick Scott 51.7 percent, Alex Sink 46.5 percent

2008 PRESIDENT
John McCain 50.2 percent, Barack Obama 49.4
percent

COUNTIES: Broward
RATING: Solid Democrat

DIVERSE, AFFLUENT DISTRICT VOTES FOR DEMOCRATS

When U.S. News & World Report went looking in 2008 for great places to retire based on their political leanings, it suggested Democrats should choose Pembroke Pines. It wasn't a particularly deeply studied piece - basically the magazine looked at its "Best Places to Retire," and searched for places that lean strongly toward one party. But the piece gives a pretty good summation of the political demography of the western parts of Pembroke Pines - many people you meet are likely to be retired and they're likely to vote for Democrats. One thing the article didn't mention is that there's also a good chance they're Hispanic. Latinos make up 41.4 percent of the population in Pembroke Pines - and they make up the largest percentage of the voting age population of this district as a whole at 43.2 percent.

The district straddles Pines Blvd. from Flamingo Road west and turns north into the affluent planned community of Weston.

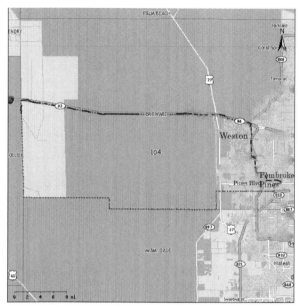

Weston is a new city, established only in 1996, but taking advantage of ongoing movement to western Broward that made it immediately relatively large, and it's now home to 65,000 people. The Everglades form the western edges of both Pembroke Pines and Weston, and District 104 continues far to the west into the uninhabited Everglades Wildlife Management Area. Out at the west end of the district, is the town of Southwest Ranches, which was the center of the region's biggest recent controversy. The town includes land owned by Corrections Corporation of America on which the U.S. Immigration and Customs Enforcement agency wanted to open a 1,500 bed immigration detention center. While officials in Southwest Ranches wanted the site because of the revenue it would provide, the larger nearby city of Pembroke Pines didn't, and voted not to provide water and sewer service to the site. Many area residents were opposed to the plan, which was scrapped in 2012, though officials say it could re-emerge.

WHO LIVES HERE?

One of the predominant demographic features here is the large number of Hispanics, a reminder that South Florida's affluent population isn't just white European-Americans. Hispanics slightly outnumber non-Hispanic whites among the voting age population, 43.2 percent to 40.8 percent, with non-Hispanic blacks making up just under 10 percent. Latinos live throughout the district - about 45 percent of the residents of Weston are Hispanic, and about 40 percent of the population in Pembroke Pines and one-third of the population of Southwest Ranches is Latino.

This is a district with both a Whole Foods (I-75 and Pines Blvd.) and a Cracker Barrel (I-75 and Sheridan). But the area is overall well above the average in terms of wealth and most of the district's residents are more Whole Foods people than Cracker Barrel people. The median family income in Weston is high, more than $103,000, which is nearly double the statewide median. A 2006 entry in Money Magazine's profiles of "Top-earning towns," said this about Weston: "Cultural diversity, masterful landscaping and sunny skies make this resort-like community a paradise for its ritzy residents. Incorporated in 1996, the designer town is ultra chic with Royal Palms lining the streets and luxuriant foliage surrounding its signs." Southwest Ranches has an even higher median family income of about $113,000, and though not as high as in Weston and Southwest Ranches, the median household and family incomes in Pembroke Pines are also above the average for the state as a whole.

The part of Pembroke Pines in House District 104, as U.S. News & World Report's suggestion implied, has lots of retirees. But the district's overall median age is right about 40, which is the statewide median as well. It's kept low because of large numbers of young families, especially in Weston, but also in parts of Pembroke Pines.

POLITICAL ISSUES AND TRENDS

The image conjured by the magazine's retirement suggestion is most apt in the southeast corner of District 104, where the stereotypical retired, condo-dwelling former northeasterner lives, and likely belongs to a Democratic club centered around a retirement community, like Century Village-Pembroke Pines. That development sprawls around a golf club and a seemingly endless supply of doctor's offices in an area of Pembroke Pines that sort of bleeds into Miramar, which is in the next district to the southeast. While the rest of the district is more family-oriented than retirement community, this is overall a moderately strong Democratic district, where Barack Obama won by 17 percentage points in 2012 and Democrat Alex Sink beat Rick Scott by nearly 20 points in the 2010 governor's race. It's not the super-Democrat sort of place that many South Florida districts have become. A Republican did get nearly 40 percent of the vote in the last state House race here, and nearly 30 percent of voters are registered Republicans, much higher than a number of Broward districts where GOP registration percentages are in the low to mid-20 percent range.

Insurance broker Richard Stark of Weston was elected to the House in 2012, defeating Republican Doug Andrew Gordon Harrison by about 20 percentage points. While all of the bills that Stark filed in his first session in 2013 failed, he took on several substantive issues. Most notably, he carried a bill that would have repealed the law limiting what doctors can say to patients about guns in the home. He also sponsored a broad elections bill generally aimed at making it easier to vote, including increasing days and hours for early voting, and allowing people to vote in their new precinct if they've moved to another county. Both those bills died in committee. Stark also pushed legislation to expand protections already in the law for insurance customers barring companies from using genetic information against them, which also died in committee. And he sponsored legislation providing requirements for accessibility for the disabled at gas stations, another measure that failed to get to the floor. For 2014, Stark has filed legislation to double the fine for texting while driving in a school zone. Stark also has proposed a bill for 2014 that would repeal a state statute that says that if unmarried men and women "lewdly and lasciviously associate and cohabit together," they're committing a second degree misdemeanor. One reason that generally unenforced law may be a problem is that other parts of the statute, for example, determining whether a grandparent may have visitation rights, depend on someone not having been guilty of lewd and lascivious cohabitation.

DISTRICT 104 STATS

Registration (Book closing, 2012)
Democrats 42.7 percent
Republicans 29.1 percent
NPA 26.7 percent

Voting Age Population (2010 Census): 113,419
Hispanic 43.2 percent
White (Non-Hispanic) 40.8 percent
Black 9.9 percent

Median Age: 40.1

Men: 47.3 percent
Women 52.7 percent

2012 PRESIDENT
Barack Obama 58.2 percent, Mitt Romney, 41.2 percent (Estimated)*

2012 STATE HOUSE
Rick Stark, Democrat, 60.9 percent, Doug Andrew Gordon Harrison, Republican, 39.1 percent

2010 GOVERNOR
Alex Sink 58.8 percent, Rick Scott 19.5 percent

2008 PRESIDENT
Barack Obama 58.1 percent, John McCain, 41.3 percent

HOUSE DISTRICT 105
THE EVERGLADES DISTRICT: RURAL COLLIER AND MIAMI-DADE

COUNTIES: Collier, Miami-Dade, Broward

RATING: Swing District

IN STEAMY EVERGLADES HEAT, A HOTLY CONTESTED DISTRICT

House District 105, stretching from the outer edges of Naples on the west coast across the Everglades to Miami-Dade and Broward counties, is one of a small handful of swing districts where voters chose Barack Obama in 2012 after voting for Rick Scott in 2010 or John McCain in 2008. It's also one of the most hotly contested swing districts, a place where Obama defeated Mitt Romney by a very close margin, after Republicans carried the district by a little bit larger margin for the four previous years. More than half the district's population (58 percent) is in Miami-Dade County, with most of that in Sweetwater and the western part of Doral. Another 32 percent is in Collier County, mostly in heavily Hispanic Golden Gate, and the Naples Manor area. And 11 percent is in Broward County, in western Miramar.

District 105 is majority Hispanic (69 percent of the voting age population), including heavily Cuban-American areas in Miami-Dade and Broward, but also many non-Cuban Hispanics, giving the district its Democratic lean.

Sweetwater in Miami-Dade County is 96 percent Hispanic, and home to the largest concentration of Nicaraguan-Americans in the United States, leading some to call it Little Managua. Sweetwater is still nearly half Cuban-American though, and while there is a documented shift in Cuban-American voting patterns toward Democrats, a large number still vote Republican, balancing out the large numbers of non-Cuban Hispanics. In addition to the 50 percent of the city's population that is Cuban-American and 25 percent that is Nicaraguan, about 5 percent is Colombian.[1]

Sweetwater didn't start out as home to Cubans and Nicaraguans, but as a haven for retired midget Russian circus performers, who bought an old orange grove to create a retirement town. Its first mayor was the troupe's manager and promoter, Joe Sanderlin

---

[1] For more on the Nicaraguan community in Sweetwater and Miami, see Alejandro Portes and Alex Stepick, *City on the Edge: The Transformation of Miami,* (University of California Press, 1993), Chapter 7, "The Nicaraguan Exodus," Pg. 150.

and according to the town's website, it used to be known as "the midget community." [2]

The Miami-Dade part of this district also includes the western reaches of Doral, sometimes called "Doralzuela" because it has the largest expatriate Venezuelan community in the United States, between 10 and 20 percent of the city's population. (See House District 116, which includes most of Doral). In Broward, the district includes far western Miramar, an area that's about 52 percent white and 47 percent Hispanic. The Latino population in this corner of Broward County is about 40 percent Cuban-American, about 15 percent Colombian, and includes smaller, but still large, populations of Puerto Ricans, Ecuadorians, Venezuelans and Peruvians.

Across the state in Collier County, out on the eastern edge of Naples, the district takes in most of the Golden Gate area, which is more than 60 percent Hispanic, with Mexicans the majority. The area also includes large Guatemalan and Honduran populations.

The district is mixed economically, but for the most part, middle-income. Some parts are struggling. In areas of Sweetwater east of the Turnpike, median household incomes are in the $30,000s. In the Census tracts west of the Turnpike, median incomes more than double. In western Miramar, the residents are quite affluent, with median incomes over $90,000.

---

[2] Sweetwater History. City of Sweetwater Website.

In Collier, Golden Gate is right around the state median in terms of income. Most people in that area are working class, helping fuel the tourism industry in southwest Florida, owning the restaurants, manicuring the lawns. But they're not poor, with median incomes in the area generally in the $40,000s and high $30,000s. The Collier part of the district also includes relatively affluent homes in neighborhoods in the Rural Estates area and the middle-income Naples Manor

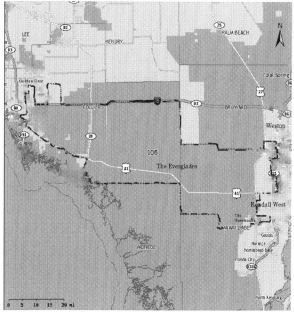

neighborhood.

POLITICAL ISSUES AND TRENDS

The neighborhoods in the Miami-Dade part of House District 105 were a major part of President Obama's Hispanic Coup in Florida in 2012. These precincts, as noted, gave Republican Rick Scott a 10 percentage point win in 2010, and went for GOP presidential candidate John McCain over Obama by about four points in 2008. But through a combination of demographic changes (more non-Cuban Hispanics moving in), political shifts (more Cuban-Americans willing to vote for a Democrat) and a ground game that targeted Hispanic votes and boosted turnout, Obama was able to pick up large numbers of votes in these areas in 2012. Obama's margin of victory in Miami-Dade County as a whole was almost 50 percent higher than in 2008, and he got nearly 70,000 more votes in the county than he did four years earlier. Places like Sweetwater were a major part of that. Exit polling data from the Bendixen firm showed that non-Cuban Hispanics overwhelmingly voted for Obama in 2012, and the Venezuelan-Americans in Doral, the Nicaraguan-Americans in Sweetwater, the Mexican-Americans in Golden Gate, and Colombian-Americans in Miramar were part of putting this district in the Democrats' column at the presidential level in 2012.

With younger Cuban-American voters the ones who are more likely to vote for Democrats, the district likely will continue to shift toward voting for Democrats at the top of the ticket. With non-Cuban Hispanic communities not having a well-developed or organized political presence in some of these areas, developing local candidates may take longer. The Democrats didn't run a candidate in this district in 2012, which they may regret considering they would end up winning it at the presidential level.

Miami Republican Rep. Carlos Trujillo first elected in 2010 and re-elected in 2012, is probably best known in the House as the sponsor of legislation that would give parents of students in underperforming schools the ability to vote in favor of having a charter school company take over the school. The bills is part of a national "parent empowerment" movement that has bipartisan support and is sometimes called the "parent trigger" bill because parents could trigger major changes in school management. The bill, which has failed twice in the Senate, has been highly controversial in Florida, where opponents have said it is being pushed to benefit for-profit charter school companies.

Trujillo also drew attention for carrying a bill that would allow children of illegal immigrants to get in-state college tuition, even if they too are undocumented, if they graduate from a Florida high school. The bill died in committee. Despite those two educational efforts, Trujillo, an former assistant prosecutor in Miami, doesn't pigeonhole into one policy area. He's chairman of the Economic Development and Tourism Subcommittee, and mostly serves on economic and finance committees and health care committees. He has been heavily involved in substantive health care legislation, including pushing in 2012 to open up the process for deciding when hospitals can open trauma centers - sponsoring an amendment to remove state regulation. And he has been one of the lawmakers seeking to repeal the law allowing the use of red light cameras, co-sponsoring unsuccessful repeal legislation with Rep. Daphne Campbell. Trujillo was also notable in 2013 for being one of three Miami-area House Republicans who opposed a bill that could have allowed public money to help the Miami Dolphins upgrade their stadium. That has reportedly made Trujillo, Jose Felix Diaz and Michael Bileca, targets of the team's owner Stephen Ross.

DISTRICT 105 STATS

Registration (Book closing, 2012)
Republicans 34.3 percent
Democrats 32.8 percent
NPA 31.3 percent

Voting Age Population (2010 Census) 117,197
Hispanic 69 percent
White (Non-Hispanic) 18.6 percent
Black 9.6 percent

Median Age: 35.3

Men: 50.8 percent
Women: 49.2 percent

2012 PRESIDENT
Barack Obama 50.1 percent, Mitt Romney, 49.8 percent (Estimated)*

2012 STATE HOUSE
Republican Primary: Rep. Carlos Trujillo, R-Miami, 55.8 percent, Paul Crespo, 44.2 percent. Trujillo faced only write-in general election opposition.

2010 GOVERNOR
Rick Scott 54.1 percent, Alex Sink 43.6 percent

2008 PRESIDENT
John McCain 51.8 percent, Barack Obama 47.6 percent

HOUSE DISTRICT 106
NAPLES, MARCO ISLAND

COUNTIES: Collier
RATING: Super Republican

RICK SCOTT'S NEIGHBORS: THE SUPER REPUBLICAN AND THE SUPER RICH

If when you're in Naples you head toward the Gulf, and go south on Gulf Shores Blvd., past the Naples Pier, down to where Gulf Shores ends, the peninsula that separates Naples Bay from the Gulf splits into several fingers of land to form a neighborhood called Port Royal. The road that runs down the peninsula along the coast is Gordon Drive. About halfway down the peninsula, in a subdivision called Gulf View Estates, you'll pass a beautiful home set far back off the road that backs up to the Gulf and is valued at more than $10 million. That's Gov. Rick Scott's house. The point of bringing it up here is that it's not unusual at all in his Port Royal neighborhood along the Naples coast. In fact, two of Scott's neighbors sold waterfront mansions on Gordon Drive for $40 million each in 2012. The Census Tract for Port Royal has a median annual income of $238,281, which puts it among the highest in the state. This is a place where Sotheby's handles quiet, private real estate deals, and buyers and sellers of properties often are listed as someone's trust fund. And like Scott, many of the people here are self-made millionaires, people who got rich not by inheritance, but by building or running companies, and most of them vote Republican.

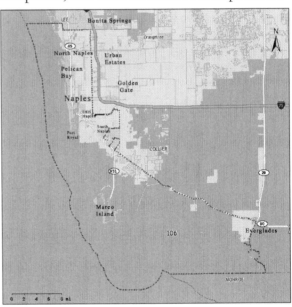

The district that includes this super wealthy coastal enclave is House District 106, which, in addition to being one of the richest districts, is also one of the strongest Republican performing districts in the state. The district is mostly coastal, running inland only a few miles, stopping short of Interstate 75. It starts at

North Naples and includes Naples, more middle class (and more Hispanic) East Naples, and continues south of the city to include Marco Island, another affluent area, though nowhere near as rich as Port Royal.

The district is also older than most, with a median age of 58.

WHO LIVES HERE?

In addition to Rick Scott, lots of more or less similar people live along the coast in Naples. In addition to being Republican voters, they're Republican donors. In some cases they're super donors. One of Scott's neighbors in the 34102 zip code in Naples is William Bindley of Bindley Capital Partners and a former owner of the Indiana Pacers in the NBA. He gave $25,000 to the Mitt Romney campaign. Just north of Scott's neighborhood, in the Pelican Bay area, lives Domino's Pizza and Ave Maria University founder Tom Monaghan, who contributed to Romney and his presidential rival Rick Santorum. Another neighbor is Arthur Allen, Jr., who founded software maker Allen Systems, and who was a major donor to Romney and several other Republicans. Another house in the neighborhood belongs to Ken and Grace Evenstad. She was a nurse and he was a drug store pharmacist but eventually he bought a drug factory and turned it into a $250 million business. They live part time in Naples, and Grace gave $30,000 to the Republican National Committee and $250,000 to American Crossroads in 2012. Many of the people who live here live in the same social and socio-economic world as Scott, and private equity firm executive Romney.

While relatively affluent overall, not everyone in House District 106 is rich, though most who live right along the coast are. Median incomes in the Census tracts that run along Naples' Gulf coast have median household incomes typically over $90,000. As you go inland, there are Census tracts in the district where the median income drops off considerably, but they remain mostly above the state average. There are pockets where incomes are low - in East Naples there are low income families living in an area where the median household income is just about $30,000 a year, well below the statewide median. In much of East Naples, the incomes are right around the statewide average, with about half of households earning less than the mid-$40,000s.

The other distinguishing demographic feature about House District 106 is its relatively high age. With half its residents over age 58, this is the third oldest district in the state. More than 40 percent of the population here is over age 65. That age distribution also contributed to the district's Republican tendency if the overall Florida age-voting overlay is an indicator. Districts with median ages above 37 tended to vote Republican while districts with median ages under 37 tended to vote Democratic in 2012.

Across Naples Bay from Port Royal, near U.S. 41 and Bayshore Dr., there's a neighborhood that contrasts sharply with its neighbor on the coast. In this area, Collier County Census Tract 107.02, just under half the population was foreign-born, mostly from

Mexico. They live in an average area economically - the Census tract's median household income is just a tiny bit below the statewide median. While Naples is a playground for the rich and famous, somebody has to work in the service industry. Many who run the restaurants, park the cars, fix the boats, and landscape the resort hotels live in these neighborhoods, just a short drive from the mansions and hotels. Many others live farther east, in an area called Golden Gate, particularly in two Census tracts of Golden Gate, which are in House District 105. There are also small communities of people from Belize and El Salvador living in the East Naples area, which is the only significant non-white part of House District 106. The district is 82 percent non-Hispanic white overall, 12.5 percent Hispanic and 3.6 percent black.

POLITICAL ISSUES AND TRENDS

The Republican domination in the area is almost total. There were no elected Democrats in office in Collier County in 2012. Romney got more than 66 percent of the vote in the district, as did hometown candidate Rick Scott in the 2010 governor's race. John McCain beat Obama by just under 30 percentage points as well, and the district's GOP state representative, Kathleen Passidomo, got 79 percent of the vote against a Libertarian candidate. It's not just establishment Republicans from the wealthy corporate wing of the party that this area likes. Before Michele Bachmann was a presidential candidate, her congressional campaign's top zip code for fundraising outside of her own state of

Minnesota was the 34102 zip code in Naples.

Passidomo, a prominent Naples real estate attorney, was elected to the old District 76 in 2010, succeeding Tom Grady, who decided not to seek re-election. Initially, Passidomo faced opposition from Grady's wife Ann, but when Ann Grady dropped out, Passidomo was the only one seeking the seat and was elected automatically. Passidomo came into office touting her practical experience in navigating the foreclosure crisis and said she had ideas on clearing some of the backlog of cases in the courts. And during her time in the House that has probably been where Passidomo has most distinguished herself. In 2013 she passed legislation aimed at speeding up foreclosures with changes in rules for lenders, homeowners and the way courts handle the cases. She worked for two years on the bill, and addressed some of the early concerns that her measure favored lenders over homeowners, but still faced some criticism on that point when the final bill passed. Consumer advocates had asked Scott to veto the bill, a plea he rejected. In 2012, after Naples was moved into the new House District 106, Passidomo easily won the Republican primary and defeated Libertarian candidate Peter Richter in the general election.

DISTRICT 106 STATS

Registration (Book closing, 2012)
Republicans 55.7 percent
Democrats 21.6 percent
NPA 20.1 percent

Voting Age Population (2010 Census): 135,129
White (Non-Hispanic) 85.5 percent

Hispanic 10.2 percent
Black 2.8 percent

Median Age: 58

Men: 48 percent
Women 52 percent

2012 PRESIDENT
Mitt Romney 66.3 percent, Barack Obama 32.3
percent (Estimated)*

2012 STATE HOUSE
Rep. Kathleen Passidomo, R-Naples, 78.9
percent, Peter Richter, Libertarian, 21.1 percent

2010 GOVERNOR
Rick Scott 66.6 percent, Alex Sink 30.8 percent

2008 PRESIDENT
John McCain 63.4 percent, Barack Obama 35.8
percent

HOUSE DISTRICT 107
NORTH MIAMI BEACH, GOLDEN GLADES, NORLAND

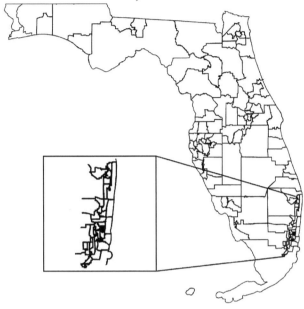

COUNTIES: Miami-Dade

RATING: Super Democrat

LIFE AND POLITICS, KREYOL-STYLE

It's often said that Miami is the only truly bilingual city in the United States, and it is true that in many parts of the city, Spanish is by far the predominant language. But in the northeast corner of Miami-Dade County, the part of the Miami metro area that makes up House District 107, a third language is at least as common and probably more often heard than either Spanish or English. Haitian Creole is the dominant sound in this area, which includes Golden Glades, the most Haitian community in the

United States by percentage, where nearly 10,000 residents - 60 percent of the population - are Haitian-born, and that doesn't count those who are the American-born children of Haitian immigrants. The district also includes North Miami Beach (which is inland and not on the beach), which has about 6,500 Haitian-born residents, and part of North Miami, which includes another 18,000 or so Haitian-born immigrants, plus thousands of second generation Haitian-Americans.

The district also includes the mostly African-American neighborhoods of Andover and Norland, which also has a significant population of immigrants from the English-speaking Caribbean, including Jamaica. In the northeastern corner, the district includes the affluent neighborhood of Ojus, which some consider part of Aventura.

WHO LIVES HERE?

Immigrants. And it's not just the Haitians. District 107 has a significant foreign-born population, more than 1 in 3 people in most parts of this area were born outside the United States. In addition to the huge percentage of Haitian-born residents, the district includes large numbers of Jamaicans, mostly in Norland and Ives Estates; Cubans, Colombians and Peruvians in the North Miami Beach area; and there are hundreds of South Americans in Ives Estates, including about 500 Colombian-born residents. The main Census tract in Ojus has a large percentages of people born in Peru, Cuba and Israel.

Haitian-Americans have followed some of

the same pattern as other immigrant groups in the United States, settling first in a poor area of the urban core where all of their neighbors are from the same place and they can get by speaking only their language. That's Little Haiti in neighboring House District 108, in the city of Miami itself. But, just as Cubans did when many left Little Havana for most of the rest of the Miami area, those Haitians who have been prosperous are starting to move out of the original area, and settling in other parts of the region. So far, however, most Haitians have only moved a short distance north, and almost entirely to the three "Haitian towns" of northern Miami-Dade County, North Miami, North Miami Beach and Golden Glades. Some stopped in between, and have settled in El Portal, and a few have moved out to areas farther west such as Miramar in Broward County, where they're in the minority. [1]

Between the Haitian community in those three towns, and the largely African-American population in Norland and Andover, more than half the population of House District 107 is black. There are pockets of white and Hispanic residents, however. More than 35 percent of the residents of North Miami Beach and about 27 percent of those in North Miami are Hispanic. Ojus is also mostly white.

The district has a wide range of incomes,

---

[1] See: The Brookings Institution, "The Haitian Community in Miami-Dade," (2005, Online: http://www.brookings.edu/~/media/research/files/report s/2005/9/miami%20dade%20sohmer/20050901_haiti.p df)

with some areas quite affluent, most of the area right around the state average, and a ring of relatively poor neighborhoods. Most of the district is like Norland - a middle class community with a median household income in the $50,000s, not wealthy by any stretch, but not particularly poor either, and above the statewide median. Much of North Miami Beach is right around or slightly above the statewide average in terms of wealth and income. The lower income parts of the district are Golden Glades, parts of North Miami Beach and much of the southern part of the district that dips into the city of North Miami, an area where some Census tracts have median incomes in the $20,000s, well below the state median. The affluent parts of the district are in the northeast, particularly Ojus, where the median income is above $80,000.

Another group that lives in this district: the parents of professional football players. At the beginning of the 2013 NFL season, Norland High School was tied with Fort Lauderdale's St. Thomas Aquinas among all the schools in the nation for having the most former players on an NFL roster, with six graduates playing in the league.

The district has lots of young families, with 40 percent of households having children under 18 in them, and only 25 percent having someone over 65. The median age of the district is 35, well below the state median.

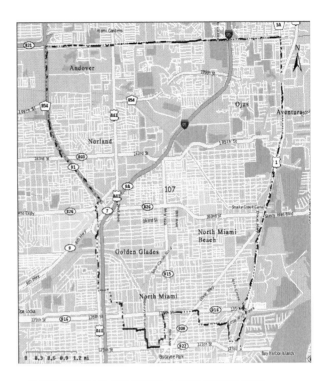

POLITICAL ISSUES AND TRENDS

This is a Super Democrat district where Republicans don't stand much chance. It has the third lowest percentage of registered Republicans (behind neighboring Districts 108 and 109) in the state, with just 9.9 percent of voters signed up with the GOP. Nearly 68 percent are registered Democrats. It was Barack Obama's fourth best performing district in the state in 2012, giving the president 86 percent of the vote in his re-election bid. That was even better than in Obama's first election year of 2008, when he got 84 percent of the votes here. Democratic gubernatorial candidate Alex Sink also got about 84 percent of the vote in the district, and Republicans didn't run a House candidate in 2012.

The general elections here aren't any contest, but for the district's representative, Barbara

Watson, the primaries have more than made up for any lack of suspense in November. Watson was first elected to the House in early 2011 in a special election to replace Oscar Braynon, who was elected in a special election to the Senate. Watson's race went to a recount, but she narrowly defeated Sharon Pritchett, who later was elected to a different House seat.

Then, in 2012, after redistricting forced several incumbents into primaries against other incumbents, Watson faced off against Rep. John Patrick Julien of North Miami Beach in the primary for District 107, a race she won by 13 votes. Julien challenged the result in court, alleging fraudulent absentee ballots were collected in nursing homes, but the challenge was rejected. Julien said he pushed the issue because, as a Haitian-American, he was fighting to continue to be able to represent his community in the House.

In 2013, Watson worked with the National Rifle Association to pass an NRA-backed bill to strengthen the ban on selling firearms to the mentally ill. The bill put restrictions on gun purchases for people who had voluntarily committed themselves for mental treatment, and passed overwhelmingly, but has been the only legislation Watson managed to pass in her first two sessions.

DISTRICT 107 STATS

Registration (Book closing, 2012)
Democrats 67.6 percent
NPA 21.4 percent
Republicans 9.9 percent

Voting Age Population (2010 Census): 117,446
Black 54.3 percent
Hispanic 26.4 percent
White (Non-Hispanic) 15.8 percent

Median Age: 35.3

Men: 47 percent
Women 53 percent

2012 PRESIDENT
Barack Obama 86 percent, Mitt Romney, 13.5
percent (Estimated)*

2012 STATE HOUSE
Democratic Primary: Rep. Barbara Watson, D-
Miami Gardens, 50.1 percent, Rep. John Patrick
Julien, D-North Miami, 49.9 percent. Watson
faced only write-in opposition in the general
election.

2010 GOVERNOR
Alex Sink 83.6 percent, Rick Scott 14.7 percent

2008 PRESIDENT
Barack Obama 83.9 percent, John McCain 15.6
percent

HOUSE DISTRICT 108
NORTH AND NW MIAMI, LITTLE HAITI

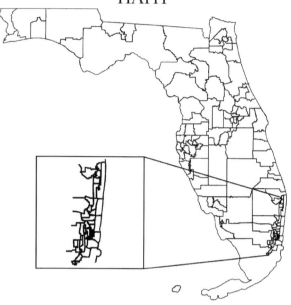

COUNTIES: Miami-Dade

RATING: Super Democrat

THE DISTRICT WITH THE HIGHEST PERCENTAGE OF BLACK RESIDENTS

Straddling Interstate 95 and Biscayne Boulevard, in the north end of the city of Miami is one of the state's most reliable Democratic areas. House District 108, which runs along Biscayne Bay, through the neighborhood of Little Haiti and north through the city of El Portal and into North Miami, is the House district where residents voted most lopsidedly for President Obama in both 2012 and 2008. Obama got just under 90 percent of the vote in the district in both elections. In

2010, Democrat Alex Sink got 86 percent of the vote in the governor's race from voters now in District 108. It's also the district with the highest percentage of black voters.

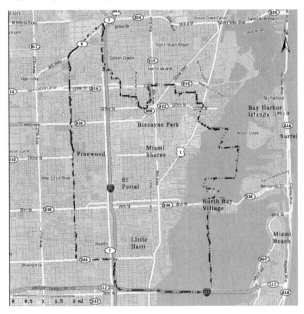

WHO LIVES HERE?

House District 108's 60 percent black voting age population is the highest of all 120 House districts. Many of those are Haitian-Americans: in fact, El Portal and North Miami were two of the three communities in America with the highest percentage of Haitian-Americans in the last decade, with nearly a third of residents claiming Haitian ancestry.

The most Haitian community in the entire United States is Golden Glades, next door to the north in House District 107, but the Haitian community straddles the two districts and the feel of the island nation's culture is hard to miss here - from the signs in Creole along NE 54th St. and NE 2nd Ave., to Toussaint Loverture

Elementary School, named for the man who led Haiti's revolutionary creation as a state, to restaurants like Chez Le Bébé, where patrons sip on goat's head soup in the morning. With Hispanics making up another 25 percent of the voting age population, HD 108 is also one of the least white areas of the state. Just under 13 percent of the voting age population is non-Hispanic white. Most of the Hispanics are of Cuban descent, though there is a small Puerto Rican population, about 4 percent of the district overall.

Though there are some pockets of upper middle class residents, around Miami Shores Country Club, in El Portal, and on the bayside of U.S. 1, most of this district is pretty poor. More than half the people in the district are renters rather than homeowners, and according to a 2005 Brookings Institution Report Haitians in the city of Miami (not just in this district, but largely in this general area) had a median household income of just $20,000, about $16,000 less than the county's median household income and almost $30,000 less than whites in Miami-Dade County at the time. The same survey found the poverty rate for Haitians living in the city of Miami - many of them in the current HD 108 - at nearly 38 percent. Levels of educational attainment in this immigrant community are also lower than average. Barry University, started in 1940 by the Adrian Dominican Sisters, is in the middle of the district. Miami Northwestern High School, with a student population that is more than 90 percent black, has long been an iconic institution in the Miami African-American community. It is also a football powerhouse, having produced numerous NFL stars.

POLITICAL ISSUES AND TRENDS

While Haitians have been coming to Miami in large numbers for several decades it was only in the late 1990s and early 2000s that the community began to flex some political muscle. Philip Brutus, a lawyer born in Port-Au-Prince who moved to the area in 1985 was elected in 2000 to represent much of this area in the House, becoming the first Haitian-American member of the Legislature. Since then, other Haitian-Americans have followed, including Yolly Roberson and Daphne Campbell, who now represents HD 108.

In addition to basic economic concerns that tend to be important to people struggling financially, issues related to immigration are obviously important in the area. Many Haitians have for several years wanted consideration of the special immigration status enjoyed by people coming from Cuba. Haitians have argued that they are equally deserving of automatic acceptance. Concerns about how the voting machinery works in Florida – or rather, whether it does work for everyone equally – are pronounced in poor, minority areas of Miami-Dade County, which has had serious problems with conducting elections and reporting the results. This district is home to Desiline Victor, the Haitian immigrant woman who in 2012 at age 102 stood in line to vote for hours at the North Miami Public Library, leading President Obama to mention her in the State of the Union address and to a Florida bill aimed at making it easier to vote being named for her.

Campbell, a Miami Democrat, remains one of just a few Haitian-Americans to have served in the Florida Legislature, and is a nurse. She is the ranking Democratic member on the Health Quality Subcommittee and on the Local and Federal Affairs Committee. She has pushed for legislation to allow physician assistants and advanced registered nurse practitioners to be able to initiate involuntary commitment under the Baker Act, and was one of the sponsors of a successful bill aimed at reducing cyber-bullying. Campbell has been controversial – feuding with other members of her own party over her joining Republicans on anti-abortion votes, and is outspoken, unafraid to court controversy with her remarks on the floor. Campbell was a sponsor of an effort to repeal the law allowing red light cameras, and the Miami Herald noted that her husband's van had been ticketed for red light violations after being caught on camera five times. Shown red light camera pictures of her husband's van, Campbell said it was a fabricated photo. She has also faced public scrutiny over tax liens and Medicaid fraud allegations at her family's health care business, and allegations of abuse at an assisted living facility her company owns. Campbell was elected to the House in 2010 and re-elected with no Republican opposition in 2012 after easily winning a three-way Democratic primary.

DISTRICT 108 STATS

Registration (Book closing, 2012)
Democrats 71.7 percent
NPA 18.2 percent
Republicans 8.9 percent

Voting Age Population (2010 Census) 118,792
Black 60 percent
Hispanic 25.4 percent
White (Non-Hispanic) 12.7 percent

Median Age: 35.5

Men: 48.6 percent
Women 51.4 percent

2012 PRESIDENT
Barack Obama 89.8 percent, Mitt Romney, 9.8 percent (Estimated*)

2012 STATE HOUSE (Democratic primary)
Daphne Campbell 60.1 percent, Alex Desulme 23.4 percent, Pat Santangelo 16.6 percent; No Republican opposition to primary winner

2010 GOVERNOR
Alex Sink 86 percent, Rick Scott 12.4 percent

2008 PRESIDENT
Barack Obama 88.6 percent, John McCain, 10.9 percent

HOUSE DISTRICT 109
MIAMI-DADE: OPA-LOCKA TO OVERTOWN

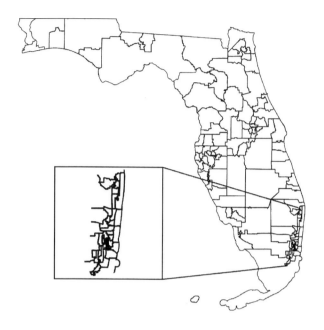

COUNTIES: Miami-Dade

RATING: Super Democrat

LOADED WITH FLORIDA BLACK HISTORY ... AND DEMOCRATS

Republicans don't bother much with running local candidates in this area of Miami-Dade County, and really, there's not much point. Republicans Mitt Romney, Rick Scott and John McCain got less than 12 percent of the vote – the lowest percentage for Scott in any House district during his 2010 governor's race. The district is stacked with Democrats, who make up 71 percent of voters here and no-party voters who make up another 18 percent. Just under 10 percent are Republicans. The district is a long, skinny one stretching from Bunche Park and Opa-locka in the north along a narrow stretch of central Miami-Dade County through West Little River and south to the Overtown neighborhood in inner city Miami itself.

House District 109 includes iconic African-American communities, including Moorish-themed Opa-locka, which is 70 percent African American, the Bunche Park neighborhood of Miami Gardens, which is more than 90 percent black, and Overtown, once the commercial and cultural center of black life in Miami.

Overtown began as the home for the mostly black railroad workers who were instrumental in the creation of Miami when Henry Flagler extended the railroad, opening up the southern part of the state. It became the black entertainment capital of South Florida – known as the "Harlem of the South" - when blacks were barred from staying on Miami Beach. The area was carved up by interstate construction, and fell on hard times in the 1960s, becoming a community of substandard housing and a haven for drug dealing and related crime. Overtown and neighboring Brownsville and Liberty City, also in House District 109, were the scene of some of the worst race-related rioting in the history of the United States. In 1980, after several police officers were acquitted in the beating death of black motorcyclist Arthur McDuffie, the area erupted into riots that left 18 people dead.

Also in the district is neighboring Wynwood, another area laced with poverty. Wynwood has long been home to Puerto Ricans – part of it for years was known as Little San Juan - and has recently seen some revitalization centered around an emerging arts and fashion scene. Another historically black neighborhood, Liberty City, is partly in House District 109, and partly in neighboring House District 108.

Miami-Dade College (formerly Miami-Dade Community College) is the largest institution of higher education in the United States, with 175,000 students on eight campuses. Two of its biggest campuses are in House District 109, including the original campus, in Westview, and the sprawling medical campus, adjacent to Jackson Memorial Hospital and the University of Miami medical school just north of downtown Miami. While enormously important to the community, the institution is a commuter school and doesn't have a major impact on the political demographics of the area the way a large university sometimes can.

WHO LIVES HERE?

Just under half of the residents of the district are black. There are concentrations of middle class African-Americans in parts of Opa-locka, and West Little River. The southern end of the district, including Overtown and Liberty City, is poorer. In the far north of the district is Bunche Park, which has one of the highest Bahamian-American populations in the United States. Other mostly black neighborhoods in the district include Westview and Gladeview. The district also includes part of Allapattah, which is heavily Hispanic, with large numbers of Dominican residents.

The median household income in the Opa-locka and Bunche Park areas is about $26,000, but moving south it jumps to around $35,000 in Westview and West Little River. In the part of the district that includes Overtown, the median household income drops back down to below $20,000 and one in four Overtown households has an annual income of less than $10,000.

POLITICAL ISSUES AND TRENDS

Race has always simmered just beneath the political landscape in Miami. Like other Southern cities with fairly large African-American populations, the city's blacks were second class citizens and forcefully segregated from the whites in its power structure, and even after the Civil Rights movement have been slow to claim economic success coming close to that in white Miami. And then, many blacks in Miami resented the rapid rise in political power in the Cuban community, watching as Spanish speaking newcomers – many of whom were from better educated, upper middle class and affluent families in Cuba - quickly passed blacks on the ladder of clout in the community.

It has taken court involvement, including judicially drawn political boundaries, to give South Florida blacks a place in the larger power structure, but in the last couple of decades they have at least become participants in the process. Carrie Meek was a pioneering state legislator from Miami's black community who went on to a long career in Congress, and saw her son Kendrick have his own career in the state House and Senate before he, too, went to Congress. Gwen Cherry, the first female black lawyer in Miami also became the first African-American woman in the Legislature in 1970. But while access to power has come, blacks in Miami as a whole have remained economically disadvantaged compared to whites and many Hispanics. Economic issues remain a major part of many political discussions in the black community, but a long-standing sense of being cheated and mistreated also remains an important current in urban black political discourse, as it is in much of black America. In South Florida, that notion has arisen in debates over whether lawmakers in Tallahassee have tried to make it harder for blacks to vote in recent years, to concerns over the fairness of the criminal sentencing system, to debates over standardized testing requirements in schools.

African-Americans in Miami are nearly universally Democrats, forming a coalition with some white northern transplants and retirees, many Jewish voters, and some new Latino and Haitian immigrants, while the large number of

Cuban-American Hispanics (more than half the population) for years have tended to vote Republican (though that is starting to change). In the last decade or so, black lawmakers have become a major part of the Democratic Party's presence in the state Legislature, along with women and Jewish legislators. On a few issues, some black lawmakers have split with Democrats, including some support for private school vouchers, prayer in schools and opposition to traffic safety measures that could lead to racial profiling. But generally, the black vote is solidly Democratic in Miami and elsewhere in Florida.

Rep. Cynthia Stafford, D-Miami, is the representative from House District 109. An attorney born and raised in Miami, Stafford was elected to the House in 2010 and re-elected after easily winning a primary in 2012 against Bernadine Bush, the wife of former Rep. James Bush, and facing no general election opposition in this Democratic-lock district. Stafford got her start in politics as an aide to former U.S. Rep. Carrie Meek, who represented many of the same neighborhoods when she was in the Legislature and later in Congress. In the House, Stafford has sponsored legislation that would make certain elderly prison inmates eligible for early release, and an unsuccessful measure that would have overturned a requirement that welfare recipients be drug tested. Before getting elected to the House, Stafford was a staff attorney for the Miami-Dade Bar Legal Aid Society. When she was campaigning she said promoting public education, increasing economic development in her district and promoting access to health care for the poor were among her priorities.

DISTRICT 109 STATS

Registration (Book closing, 2012)
Democrats 71.1 percent
NPA 18.3 percent
Republicans 9.7 percent

Voting Age Population (2010 Census) 118,409:
Black 46.1 percent
Hispanic 45.7 percent
White (Non-Hispanic) 6.9 percent

Median Age: 34.8

Men: 49.8 percent
Women 50.2 percent

2012 PRESIDENT (Estimated*)
Barack Obama 89.2 percent, Mitt Romney, 10.5 percent

2012 STATE HOUSE (Democratic primary)
Rep. Cynthia Stafford, D-Miami, defeated Bernadine Bush in the Democratic primary 63.5 percent to 36.5 percent and faced no general election opposition

2010 GOVERNOR
Alex Sink 86.8 percent, Rick Scott 11.5 percent

2008 PRESIDENT
Barack Obama 88.3 percent, John McCain, 11.5 percent

HOUSE DISTRICT 110
MIAMI LAKES, NW HIALEAH

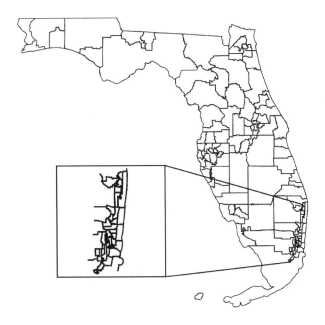

COUNTIES: Miami-Dade
RATING: Swing District

SOMETHING'S HAPPENING HERE.
WHAT IT IS, AIN'T EXACTLY CLEAR

Statistically, it could be argued that Miami won Florida for Barack Obama in 2012. Obviously there were many places where Obama did better than Romney, but in Miami the president improved over his 2008 run in a hard-to-believe fashion. The swing is striking. There were a few Florida House districts where John McCain would have won in 2008 (using the 2012 precincts) but Obama won in 2012, or where Rick Scott would have won in 2010, but Obama won in 2012. Nearly all of them were in Miami-Dade County. Zooming out and looking at larger geographic areas, there were only three Congressional districts in the entire country that McCain won in 2008, but Obama won in 2012. One was in Staten Island, New York. The other two were in Miami-Dade, Florida Congressional Districts 26 and 27.

And at the tip of that spear of new Democratic success in Miami is the overwhelmingly Hispanic House District 110. Obama won the precincts in this western Miami-Dade district ever so slightly - by less than a percentage point. For all intents and purposes, you could call it a tie. But consider this: Republican Rick Scott won in the precincts in this district by 20 points over Alex Sink in the 2010 governor's race. And McCain beat Obama in this area of the city by 13 points.

The district is a tall, narrow sliver running from the Country Club area north of Miami Gardens Dr., down through the heart of Miami

Lakes, to an area in the northwest corner of Hialeah.

WHO LIVES HERE?

This narrative of the 2012 election around the country and in Florida played heavily on new Hispanic voters siding with Obama over Romney and a Republican Party that, to many, seemed out of touch with working class Latinos, who have now been in the country long enough to register in increasing numbers. In Florida, while the degree of it is hotly disputed, another part of the narrative was also a shift in Cuban-American voting patterns, long locked into the GOP, but, recently, flirting with Democrats. This district was solidly part of those narratives. The voting age population of House District 110 is 89.5 percent Hispanic. Nearly 60 percent of those Hispanics here are of Cuban descent. There's no single non-Cuban group that comes anywhere close by itself to making up the other one-third or so of the population. There are more than 10,000 Colombians in the district, and while it's not clear how many are citizens and registered to vote, exit polling showed that Colombian-American voters played a role in Obama's win. Hialeah also has a growing number of residents from Nicaragua, and with the same caveats that many aren't yet citizens, they, too, told pollsters they liked Obama. This non-Cuban population has largely come in the last couple of decades, and those who are eligible to vote have only become so in recent years, likely explaining in part the increase in Democratic votes here.

POLITICAL ISSUES AND TRENDS

But with about 60 percent of voters here being Cuban-Americans, it is clear that some Cubans voted for Obama in this district, and exit polling gives the same indication - that Cuban-Americans in the Miami area may have given half their vote to Obama. [1] That's a stunning development for the Florida GOP. Jim Messina, Obama's campaign manager, said the results in the Cuban-American communities of Miami like this one marked a "dramatic realignment of politics in that state." It was a shift that had already started in 2008, when exit polling also showed young Cuban-Americans were beginning to sometimes vote for Democrats, and that made some of these areas close, but still Republican. Now, they're close, but leaning Democrat, at the top of the ticket. In most of them, including House District 110, however, the Democratic votes for the presidential candidate aren't yet translating to Democrats getting elected here farther down the ticket. Part of that is a natural lag time - Democrats have not run in these districts in several years because there was no chance to win. Now that it appears Democrats can get votes, candidates may step forward.

The influx of non-Cuban Latinos in Miami has produced very few high profile local political candidates. Former Rep. Juan Zapata, a Colombian-American, was for many years the face in the Legislature of that community, but

---

[1] John Fund, "Romney's Hispanic Disaster," *National Review Online* 1(Online, 9 November, 2012, http://www.nationalreview.com/corner/333072/romney s-hispanic-disaster-john-fund)

mostly the non-Cuban Hispanic communities of Miami are yet to gain a foothold in state politics. (Former Rep. Ana Rivas Logan was born in Nicaragua, but her parents were both Cuban.)

Rep. Jose Oliva, R-Miami Lakes, is the CEO of the Oliva Cigar Company, and was actually born in the other state with a huge Cuban community, New Jersey. Oliva defeated two other Republicans in a 2011 special election primary to fill the seat vacated by Esteban Bovo, who left the House to be a Miami-Dade commissioner. Oliva, who said coming in that reducing taxes and shrinking government were his top two priorities, quickly took up a popular tax break idea pushing through proposed constitutional amendments to give additional homestead exemptions to seniors. He also passed a 2012 bill that allowed additional money to be invested by the State Board of Administration in "alternative" investments. While Oliva has been a solid vote on most Republican issues, he's flown below the public radar, mostly, and hasn't pursued many high profile controversial issues. Behind the scenes, however, Oliva sought the future speakership, and is thought to have the commitments necessary to make him the presumptive speaker in 2018.

DISTRICT 110 STATS

Registration (Book closing, 2012)
Republicans 38.5 percent
Democrats 32.3 percent
NPA 27.7 percent

Voting Age Population (2010 Census)   122,622

Hispanic 89.5 percent
White (Non-Hispanic) 5.7 percent
Black 3.7 percent

Median Age: 39.5

Men: 47.1 percent
Women: 52.9 percent

2012 PRESIDENT
Barack Obama 50 percent, Mitt Romney, 49.5 percent (Estimated)*

2012 STATE HOUSE
Republican Primary: Rep. Jose Oliva, R-Miami Lakes, 85.7 percent, Ileana Abay, 14.3 percent. Oliva faced only write-in general election opposition.

2010 GOVERNOR
Rick Scott 59 percent, Alex Sink 39 percent

2008 PRESIDENT
John McCain 56.3 percent, Barack Obama 43.3 percent

HOUSE DISTRICT 111
HIALEAH, MIAMI SPRINGS:

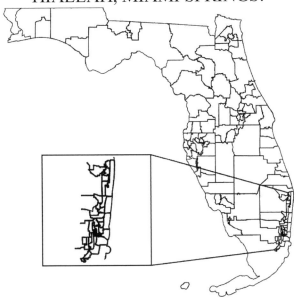

COUNTIES: Miami-Dade
RATING: Leans Republican

FLORIDA'S MOST HISPANIC DISTRICT

Florida's most Hispanic district is just to the west of Miami, taking in Miami International Airport, and the areas just north and east of the airport, and a little bit south of it. It juts north into the mostly Cuban-American city of Hialeah (the sixth largest city in Florida and about 95 percent Hispanic). It also includes the near-Miami suburbs of Miami Springs and Virginia Gardens, squeezed in between the airport and Hialeah along NW 36th St. as it runs out past the airport toward Doral. The district is L-shaped, with the top going north into Hialeah and the bottom leg of the L sticking east into the city of Miami itself in an area along the Miami River bordered on the north by NW 36th St., the south by NW 7th St. and just getting into the Allapattah neighborhood along the district's eastern border of NW 17th Ave.

The Hialeah part of the district includes the iconic and historic Hialeah Park racetrack, which now hosts live quarter horse racing, instead of thoroughbreds, but still has its famous flamingos living on an island in the track's infield. The track now is also home to a casino. Solidly Republican and overwhelmingly Cuban, Hialeah has in recent years gotten a tiny bit less of both, as other Hispanic immigrants have moved in. But Cuban families – some of whom have been in the Miami area for the full four post-Castro generations - still are the majority.

Much of the Miami Springs area was built by Glenn Hammond Curtiss, the aviation pioneer who is considered the founder of Hialeah and Miami Springs, and who designed the Miami Springs Golf Course that sits in the middle of the district and for years hosted the Miami Open. The major thoroughfare in Miami Springs remains Curtiss Parkway, which runs through the golf course, and connects NW 36th St. in Miami with South Okeechobee Rd. The town of Miami Springs actually started as the golf course itself, with the rest of the town being built around the course in the early 1920s. The course, partially desegregated in 1949 and fully open to African-Americans in 1957, was the first in Florida to allow blacks to play golf on the same course as whites.

Northwest 36th St., which runs through the heart of the district, is a major east-west thoroughfare running right up along the entire north side of Miami International Airport (stop at a red light along the street, put down the window, and smell the jet fuel). It is home to several businesses that service the airport like airline uniform and aviation hardware companies, but also a number of budget motels.

The street is the access point for much of the "working" part of the airport, dominated for blocks by buildings of companies like AAR Corp., and Aerothrust, which do aircraft maintenance and repair.

In the eastern part of the district, east of the airport, Allapattah is a mixed residential and commercial neighborhood, heavily working class, and while there are pockets of African-American residents in the neighborhood (who moved there in large numbers in the 1950s), the area is now largely Hispanic. It straddles the Miami River, which continues to be a working river, with industrial docks, and ship servicing companies. The major roads of Allapattah, like NW 27th Ave and NW 20th St., are bustling with commercial and light industrial businesses, clothing wholesale companies, and strip malls. The homes here are small and modest. Natives of the Dominican Republic have flocked to Allapattah – some call it "little D.R," or "Dominican Town."

WHO LIVES HERE?

The district's culture is distinctively Latin and its language mostly Spanish. School district officials say Miami Springs High School has one of the largest percentages of foreign-born students in the county, and the voting age population in the district is 93 percent Hispanic. Importantly from a political standpoint, it's not all Cuban-Americans. Just 64 percent of Hispanics in the district are of Cuban descent, according to the Census. Hialeah as a whole, is 72 percent Cuban-American, and while no other single Latino immigrant group exceeds 6 percent in that city, there are more than 10,000 Nicaraguans, and about 7,000 Colombians, two groups who voted overwhelmingly for President Obama in 2012. Non-Cuban Hispanics in House District 111, in addition to Nicaraguans and Colombians, also include significant numbers of Puerto Ricans, Hondurans and Dominicans. The distinction is important politically because while the Republican Party may have lessened its grip on Cubans as a voting bloc, they still tend to vote GOP and most of the Cubans in the Legislature remain Republicans. But non-Cubans are far less likely to vote Republican, according to exit polling in 2012.

POLITCAL ISSUES AND TRENDS

A decade ago, the central issue for Miami Cuban-Americans likely would have been Cuba, or more specifically Castro, and the U.S. position regarding the Castro regime. Polling and some political research show that is changing. Many Cubans in the Miami area once thought of themselves as exiles waiting to go back and not permanent immigrants to the United States. But each successive generation that's born here thinks of themselves less as Cubans and more as Cuban-Americans. And the farther time marches on from the 1959 revolution that put Castro in power, the less Castro and the communist regime are in the minds of the American Cuban community. Polling has also shown a shift in party allegiance, with exit polls showing more than half of Cuban-American voters under 30 in Miami-Dade County having voted for President Obama and some exit polls even showing Cuban-American voters of all ages nearly split during the 2012 election between Mitt Romney and Obama. And the embargo on Cuba, and its treatment of political dissidents may no longer be the main thing most people in this area care about.

All this means Republican domination in these precincts is lessening. President Obama got less than 40 percent of the vote here in 2008, and Republican Gov. Rick Scott beat Democrat Alex Sink by about 30 percentage points, but in 2012, Obama got 48 percent of the vote, losing to Mitt Romney by just 3 percentage points.

In the wake of the recent recession, the economy is the biggest concern in most of South Florida's working class areas, where construction jobs mostly disappeared in the late 2000s. Decent paying jobs are joined by the cost of property insurance as a major concern among South Florida residents, particularly those on fixed incomes. Immigration-related issues have never been an overwhelming concern in the Cuban-American community, mostly because Cubans enjoy special immigration status. But other Central American immigrants consistently say immigration policy is a major concern.

House District 111 is represented by Rep. Eddy Gonzalez, R-Hialeah, who is term-limited and can't seek re-election in 2014. He is the senior member of the Miami-Dade delegation, and in 2013 was its chairman. Gonzalez most recently pushed a controversial proposal being spearheaded by the Miami Dolphins that would have given the team tax rebates to pay for upgrades at Sun Life Stadium, but the measure failed. In 2011, Gonzalez had begun a campaign for mayor of Hialeah, but said the race was starting to focus too much on personalities of the candidates and personal agendas and decided to drop out and remain in the House. Gonzalez, who was born in Cuba, previously served as a Hialeah city councilman, and has been on the board of the Florida League of Cities since 1999. During the 2008 and 2009 House sessions, he served as deputy majority whip. In the summer of 2013,

Gonzalez was one of several lawmakers that were alleged to still be living in the districts they represented before redistricting. Gonzalez had said he would move into a house in the new district.

DISTRICT 111 STATS

Registration (Book closing, 2012)
Republicans 42 percent
Democrats 30.2 percent
NPA 26.3 percent

Voting Age Population (2010 Census): 127,389
Hispanic 93 percent
White (Non-Hispanic) 5.4 percent
Black 1.1 percent

Median Age: 42.2

Men 49.4 percent
Women 50.6 percent

2012 PRESIDENT
Mitt Romney 51.3 percent, Barack Obama 48.1 percent (Estimated)*

2012 STATE HOUSE:
Rep. Eddy Gonzalez, R-Hialeah, faced only write-in opposition.

2010 GOVERNOR
Rick Scott 64.4 percent, Alex Sink 33.6 percent

2008 PRESIDENT
John McCain 61.2 percent, Barack Obama 38.3 percent

HOUSE DISTRICT 112
DOWNTOWN MIAMI, CALLE OCHO, THE GROVE,

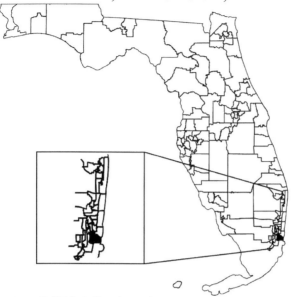

COUNTIES: Miami-Dade

RATING: Swing District

EL CENTRO FOR CUBAN EXILES

According to the owners of Versailles Cuban restaurant, the TV networks have all already reserved space there for the day Fidel Castro eventually dies. Of course they have. The restaurant with the walk-up window, where seemingly every Cuban exile goes each morning to get a cafecito and rail against Fidel, has been the go-to spot for decades for Cuban-American political talk. Versailles is one of those must-stop places for candidates. If you want the Cuban vote, you've got to show up sooner or later at Versailles.

The restaurant is in the heart of Little Havana, on Calle Ocho, or SW 8th St., officially known here as Felipe Valls Way. Valls opened the place in 1971, planning on it being a short-term money maker while he waited out Castro.

Just as Versailles has long been a focal point in exile politics, Little Havana could be considered the center, psychologically, of District 112. But whether Little Havana is these

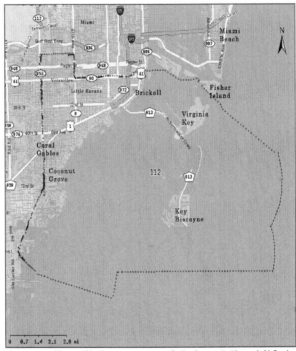

days really still the center of Cuban Miami life is in question. The politics and culture of the Cuban exiles has long-since grown well beyond Little Havana's borders and now dominates much of Miami-Dade County. One might argue that Hialeah, a city of nearly a quarter million people next door to Miami and more than 70 percent Cuban, is at least as much the center of Cuban-America as Little Havana. Little Havana remains, however, symbolically important to the Cuban-American experience, and to this district where about 40 percent of residents are of Cuban heritage.

WHO LIVES HERE?

The district as a whole is about 70 percent Hispanic, with many non-Cuban Latinos living in the neighborhood that takes its name from the capital of Cuba. As long ago as 1997 the New York Times wrote about the influx of non-Cubans, noting that the Cuban-born pastor at Little Havana's St. John Bosco Church was ministering to a congregation that was nearly 70 percent Nicaraguan, and that at the nearby La Esquina de Tejas restaurant the waitresses were from Honduras, Uruguay and Peru. [1]

POLITICAL ISSUES AND TRENDS

Miami's Cuban community is at the heart of what may be the biggest shift in Florida politics of the last decade, the transformation of the exile population from rock solid Republican voting bloc to one split between the two parties, with age as the primary fault line. Democrat Jose Javier Rodriguez surprised many by winning the House seat here in 2012, defeating former state Sen. Alex Diaz de la Portilla, a member of a well-known Miami Cuban political family.

With our secret ballot, of course, it's impossible to know exactly who gets Cuban-Americans' votes. For the most part, estimates of voting patterns of various groups rely on exit polling, but because many ethnic and national

---

[1] Mireya Navarro, "Other Hispanic Groups Growing in Miami," *The New York Times*, 6 April, 1997.

groups live clustered together in the same precincts, we can be fairly certain how the community votes based on results in the "most Cuban" neighborhoods. But after the 2012 election there was a heated debate among political scientists and others about whether the Cuban-American vote went to Barack Obama or Mitt Romney. A large pollster that focuses on Hispanic communities reported Obama won 51 percent of Cuban votes. But a university group said Romney may have gotten as much as 59 percent of the Cuban vote. The biggest exit polling group, the one working for the TV networks, said Cuban voters were split, with Romney getting about 50 percent of the vote and Obama 47 percent.

Wherever the exact truth is, one thing certain is that a large percentage of Cuban-Americans, definitely more than 40 percent, and maybe more than 50 percent, is now voting Democratic. That wasn't true a decade ago. Cuban-Americans have been one of the most solid GOP constituencies since the late 1960s. Republicans like Marco Rubio, Mel Martinez, the Diaz de la Portillas, the Diaz-Balart brothers and Ileana Ros-Lehtinen, have been the faces of the Cuban-American community. So the notion that Cuban-American voters are now split is a stunner, for many.

But watching the trend lines, it's been predictable for a while. Polling and Cuban precinct results showed about 75 percent of Florida Cubans voted for George W. Bush in 2000, but in 2004 Bush's support in the community dropped to 71 percent. And in 2008, only about 65 percent of Cuban-

American voters backed John McCain. But the degree to which Cuban-Americans may have moved to the Democratic party between 2008 and 2012, possibly shifting 15 points rather than the recently common 5 points per four-year-cycle, is hard to comprehend.

Some of it may be attributable to larger than realized numbers of non-Cuban Hispanics moving in to neighborhoods that have traditionally been mainly Cuban (though that is a problem with using vote totals, not with exit polling, which typically asks Latinos their country of origin.) But the bigger issues are likely just time and generational change. Exile voting patterns were rooted in the Cold War hard line against communism in general and the Castro regime in particular - a regime many original exiles knew well. They lost property to the Castro regime, some lost all they had. Some saw relatives killed or imprisoned. Anger and hatred over Castro's takeover of their island homeland drove their political beliefs and their worldview.

More than 50 years later, the grandchildren of the original exiles know little of Cuba, a land to which they have never been, or Castro. While a very real presence in daily life in Cuba, and to many with close relatives still there, to lots of younger Cubans in Miami, Castro is an abstract historic villain, and Miami is their homeland. These kids are fans of the Marlins, not Almendares or Cienfuegos. Their political-cultural references are George W. Bush, Barack Obama and other Americans, more than Batista and Castro. Most still care about Cuba and what goes on there, but unlike their grandparents, most don't harbor dreams (or plans) to return - they're Americans now.

House District 112 is now a swing district that may even be trending Democrat, having gone for Barack Obama in 2012 by about 8 points and elected Rodriguez over a well-known Republican, Diaz de la Portilla. But as recently as 2010, voters here went with a GOP candidate, giving Rick Scott a tiny margin of victory in the governor's race. John McCain and Obama basically tied in this district in 2008.

Cuban-Americans have not just been politically assimilated, their DNA is now mixed into the American stew as well. Cuban-Americans in Miami are still likely to marry other Cuban-Americans, mainly because they're so numerous here. But the likelihood of marrying a non-Cuban has increased. That gives their children a broader cultural background on which political leanings may be based.

That's the case with Jose Javier Rodriguez, the district's representative. He's a proud Cuban-American, whose father Guillermo was airlifted out of Cuba as part of Operation Pedro Pan, which brought thousands of Cuban children to Miami right after the revolution. But his mother Joyce is not Cuban, and originally from the Midwest. While rooted in the Cuban South Florida experience, Rodriguez, like many second and third generation Cuban-Americans, also has a broader cultural and political context in which he is forming his beliefs.

During his first session in the House, Rodriguez dealt with several technical pieces of legislation, including a measure that codified certain practices having to do with land trusts that was signed into law. He did carry one high profile bill, a measure that would have granted in-state college tuition to children who have no legal residency status because they were brought to the country illegally as children. The measure failed, but Rodriguez has filed the bill again.

DISTRICT 112 STATS
Registration (Book closing, 2012)
Republicans 35.3 percent
Democrats 33.9 percent
NPA 28.9 percent

Voting Age Population (2010 Census): 128,709
Hispanic 73 percent
White (Non-Hispanic) 21.9 percent
Black 3.1 percent

Median Age: 40

Men 48.2 percent
Women 51.8 percent

2012 PRESIDENT
Barack Obama 53.6 percent, Mitt Romney, 45.7 percent (Estimated)*

2012 STATE HOUSE:
Jose Javier Rodriguez, Democrat, 53.7 percent, Alex Diaz de la Portilla, Republican, 46.3 percent

2010 GOVERNOR
Rick Scott 49.3 percent, Alex Sink 48.8 percent

2008 PRESIDENT
John McCain 49.9 percent, Barack Obama 49.5 percent

HOUSE DISTRICT 113
MIAMI BEACH

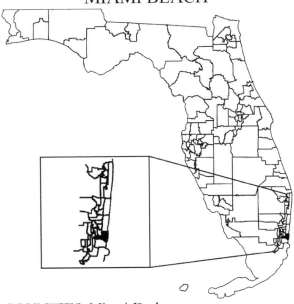

COUNTIES: Miami-Dade

RATING: Solid Democrat

TRENDY, SEXY, LATIN... AND DEMOCRATIC, MIAMI BEACH

When most people outside of South Florida think of Miami, they're actually often thinking of Miami Beach. The spit of sand that makes up the mostly man-made island sitting just off the coast of actual Miami is mostly made up of the separate city of Miami Beach. The most famous part of the island city is the South Beach neighborhood with its art deco architecture, and celebrities partying all night at exclusive night clubs, and eating at fancy restaurants. And of course, this is where the beach is. The island is more than South Beach. Miami Beach is a densely populated urban area, its coastline lined by residential high rises, and a neighborhood of high end single family homes around the middle of the island near La Gorce golf course. The northern end of the island is a little older, much less flashy, and includes some neighborhoods of apartments where lower income and working class people live.

In addition to Miami Beach itself, House District 113 includes the wealthiest neighborhood in Florida, on Fisher Island, just across Government Cut from South Beach. It also includes an iconic Miami image, seen in just about every video of the city, the cruise ship port on Dodge Island, as well as several small islands between Miami Beach and the mainland.

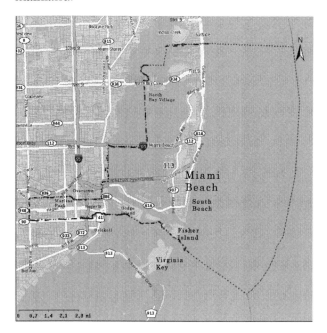

District 113 also reaches across Biscayne Bay on to the mainland, with a small sliver of the district going ashore in the heart of downtown Miami and extending in a narrow strip westward through Little Havana - though that neighborhood's heart, Calle Ocho, is one block south of the district boundary in District 112. This district, however, includes the new Marlins Park, where the baseball team plays, and American Airlines Arena, home to the Miami Heat of the NBA. The district includes most of the major government buildings in downtown Miami.

With Miami Beach being a popular tourist destination and the kind of place celebrities like to hang out, it's easy to find plenty of published descriptions. Some in a smattering of guidebooks and articles include "chic," "tragically hip," and the word "sexy," is almost always used. Eccentricity is another quality on the island, or as the Frommer's guide book puts it, "Individuality is as widely accepted on South beach as Visa and Mastercard."

WHO LIVES HERE?

The Latin vibe that comes with Miami and Miami Beach is no affect for the tourists - it is definitely genuine. House District 113 is no different, as the district is nearly 70 percent Hispanic, in part because it includes so much of Little Havana, but also because Miami Beach is heavily Latino, at 53 percent. While Little Havana remains mostly Cuban-American, in Miami Beach, "other" Hispanics - mostly South and Central Americans - now outnumber those of Cuban origin.

Aside from the older Cuban-Americans still living in Little Havana, many of them as stridently anti-Castro as they were in 1960, this district has four pillars of Democratic performance in Florida's recent elections: it has a large non-Cuban Hispanic population; it's relatively young, with pockets of 20 and 30-somethings who trend Democratic; it has a relatively small, but clustered-together Jewish population on Miami Beach; and it has a significant number of affluent, professional, gay residents (and the district's representative is one of two openly gay members of the House.) Those are some of the major Democratic voting blocs in Florida, with the only major missing Democratic groups being black voters, active union members and college students.

The district also includes the state's wealthiest zip code, though it only includes just a few hundred homes. It's Fisher Island, just off the south end of Miami Beach, accessible only by private boat or ferry. The island's 33109 zip code is not only the wealthiest in the state, but annually among the wealthiest few in the nation. In 2011, Forbes pegged the average net worth of the island's residents at $57.2 million. Once owned by the Vanderbilt family, in recent years it's been home mostly to wealthy celebrities wanting some privacy, including Oprah Winfrey and Andre Agassi, among others. The island doesn't have much influence on the vote in the district, however, because many of the residents are part-timers and about half of them are foreigners.

POLITICAL ISSUES AND TRENDS

As noted, this district has all the ingredients to put it firmly in the Democratic column and the party has done well here. Miami Beach was one of the first areas to send a Democratic Hispanic to Tallahassee in recent years, former Rep. Luis Garcia of Miami Beach. Barack Obama won here in 2012 by 28 percentage points, better than he did in 2008 when he won by just over 20 points. Democratic gubernatorial candidate Alex Sink won by 14 points in 2010, and Republicans didn't contest the area's House seat in 2012. The only thing keeping this from being a Super Democratic fortress district, like some others in South Florida, is the smattering of holdover Republican votes coming from the Little Havana part of the district. No party voters actually outnumber registered Republicans in the district.

Rep. David Richardson defeated three other candidates in the Democratic primary in August, 2012 to become the first openly gay man to be elected to the Florida House. (Rep. Joe Saunders of Orlando would be elected in the general election in November of that year to become the second.) An accountant, Richardson had never run for office before. During his first session, Richardson was probably most outspoken about efforts by professional sports teams to get government subsidies, which he has opposed. And in 2013 he filed a bill for his second session that would require legislative staff to produce an annual report listing economic development tax incentives and other measures that reduce business taxes. Richardson also was sponsoring a bill to ban "sexual orientation change therapy" to gay people under the age of 18. In Richardson's first session, he was backer of a successful measure to require an inspector general and internal auditing at state-created Citizens Property Insurance Co. Other legislation sponsored by Richardson, including a bill that would have required carbon monoxide alarms in public schools, and one that would have required hospitals to develop procedures for safely lifting and handling patients, died without becoming law.

DISTRICT 113 STATS
Registration (Book closing, 2012)
Democrats 41.7 percent
NPA 30.3 percent
Republicans 25.8 percent

Voting Age Population (2010 Census): 133,664
Hispanic 66.8 percent
White (Non-Hispanic) 27.3 percent
Black 3.6 percent

Median Age: 39.3

Men: 52.4 percent
Women 47.6 percent

2012 PRESIDENT
Barack Obama 63.5 percent, Mitt Romney, 35.7 percent (Estimated)*

2012 STATE HOUSE
Democratic Primary: Rep. David Richardson, D-Miami Beach, 33 percent; Mark Weithorn 26.4 percent; Adam Marc Kravitz, 24.4 percent; Waldo Faura, 16.2 percent. Richardson faced no general election opposition.

2010 GOVERNOR
Alex Sink 55.8 percent, Rick Scott 41.8 percent

2008 PRESIDENT
Barack Obama 60.4 percent, John McCain, 38.9 percent

HOUSE DISTRICT 114
CORAL GABLES TO CUTLER BAY

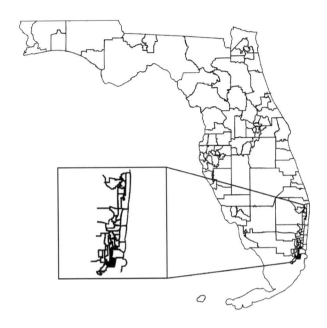

COUNTIES: Miami-Dade

RATING: Swing District

BY THE POOL AT THE BILTMORE; THE CITY BEAUTIFUL

"The future of the Republican Party is by the pool at the Biltmore." That was the headline atop a 2013 story on the BuzzFeed website that went on to detail how national Republicans put a lot of hope in both Marco Rubio and Jeb Bush for the future of the GOP. Rubio, when not in Washington, lives near the grand old hotel in Coral Gables, and sometimes uses its gym. He spent his wedding night there, and, according to the BuzzFeed article, used to drink on its golf course as a young man. Bush also lives in Coral Gables, known as "The City Beautiful," and he has an office at the Biltmore.

[1] So in the early 2010s, anyway, Coral Gables is central to the Florida, and maybe the national, Republican universe.

Even without the fact that several U.S. presidents and would-be presidents stay here when visiting the Miami area, Coral Gables is "serious" Miami, as opposed to the city at large, which has a reputation as more of a playground than a place for commerce and government (which it also is.) Coral Gables is where foreign policy is made by visiting diplomats. Blockbuster deals are made here by big time deal makers. Liquor giant Bacardi and Fresh Del Monte Produce have their headquarters in Coral Gables. Construction giant MasTech is based here. The Brazilian conglomerate Odebrecht, one of the biggest infrastructure companies in the world, has its American headquarters in Coral Gables. Many of the foreign nations that maintain a consulate in the Miami area have them in Coral Gables. The Miami area's movers and shakers, like Rubio and Bush, call Coral Gables home. Coral Gables is, as you would guess, also fairly affluent, with a median household income over $80,000, nearly double the statewide median. The broader House District 114 is similarly affluent, including most of a zip code south of Coral Gables that has the most expensive homes in Florida, and is on the list of the priciest neighborhoods in America. It's a Whole Foods district (South Dixie Highway in

[1] McKay Coppins, "The Future of the Republican Party is by the Pool at the Biltmore," BuzzFeed, 12, February, 2013.

Pinecrest.) The private University of Miami, in Coral Gables, is also in the district.

House District 114 is just to the west of Little Havana, and in addition to much of Coral Gables, includes the city of West Miami, just three-quarters of a square mile big. West Miami started in the 1940s with a secession of sorts by people who liked to drink late at night and gamble, after the rest of the county moved to ban gambling and curtail drinking hours. Now, however, it's a standard family-oriented suburban area. The district also takes in the area south of Coral Gables down through part of the affluent suburb of Pinecrest and, hugging the shore of Biscayne Bay, goes far enough south to include Cutler Bay.

WHO LIVES HERE?

The affluence of the area is the most distinguishing demographic characteristic of District 114, which may have the overall highest median income of all 120 House districts. Nearly every Census tract in the district has a median household income of at least $90,000, and some are well over $100,000. Miami-Dade County's Census tract 78.01, a triangular area not too far south of the University of Miami in the Pinecrest area has a median household income above $250,000. In that same Census tract, homes in the Snapper Creek neighborhood have an average listing price above $5 million. Forbes puts that area's 33156 zip code on its list of the priciest places to buy a home in the country, and most expensive in Florida. The southeastern corner of the district, the areas of Cutler Ridge and Cutler Bay, are the exceptions to the area's overall wealth, but median incomes there are still right around the state median, so the areas aren't poor.

The district is majority Hispanic, about 65 percent, with most of the Latino population, and about 42 percent of the overall district population of Cuban descent. Nearly all of the areas in the district, including Coral Gables, are majority Hispanic. West Miami is over 90 percent Hispanic. The exception is Pinecrest, which is about 40 percent Hispanic.

POLITICAL ISSUES AND TRENDS

This district is a political super storm, the equivalent of the influential tropical air mass from the Gulf of Mexico slamming into the cool mass of air coming down from the north for a battle royal that spawns a storm. Yes, the future of the Republican Party may be by the pool. The most wealthy neighborhoods in the state, the places where the "captains of industry," and moguls of high finance live, tend to vote Republican. These are Mitt Romney's business, social and political peers - guys like Jeb Bush. That produces a strong Republican current - one that gave John McCain, Rick Scott and Rep. Erik Fresen wins in recent elections here. But the Republican characteristics of the district bash right into two things that create votes for Democrats. The biggest is Latino voters. The other factor is Whole Foods. There's one in Pinecrest. The young, urban, highly educated, affluent people who frequent Whole Foods tend to vote for Democrats, unless they're very wealthy. So, in several recent elections, voters here have split nearly evenly. In 2012, Fresen won by just over 2 percentage points, while Barack Obama appears to have bested Romney by about half a point. Scott's win in 2010 was by less than 2 points. This is clearly a swing district.

Fresen has been a leader in the Legislature on early childhood education, advocating for higher standards for preschool programs, and has been prominently involved in education issues generally, including serving as chairman of the Education Appropriations Subcommittee. He also was one of the sponsors of a failed effort to get hotel tax money tossed toward the Miami Dolphins for stadium upgrades. Fresen, a land use consultant, was first elected to the House in 2008. He served as an aide in the House from 2000-2002.

DISTRICT 114 STATS

Registration (Book closing, 2012)

Republicans 37.8 percent
Democrats 34.9 percent
NPA 25.7 percent

Voting Age Population (2010 Census):123,590
Hispanic 66 percent
White (Non-Hispanic) 25.6 percent
Black 5.7 percent

Median Age: 40.2

Men: 47.9 percent
Women 52.1 percent

2012 PRESIDENT
Barack Obama 50 percent, Mitt Romney, 49.3
percent (Estimated)*

2012 STATE HOUSE
Rep. Erik Fresen, R-Miami, 51.2 percent, Ross
Hancock, Democrat, 48.8 percent

2010 GOVERNOR
Rick Scott 49.6 percent, Alex Sink 48.5 percent

2008 PRESIDENT
John McCain 51.4 percent, Barack Obama 47.9
percent

HOUSE DISTRICT 115
SW MIAMI-DADE:
WESTCHESTER, KENDALL,
CUTLER

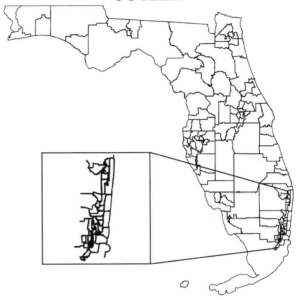

COUNTIES: Miami-Dade
RATING: Swing District

MIAMI'S BEDROOM COMMUNITY

District 115 is quintessential suburban Miami. It includes most of Kendall, which is probably the area most Miamians think of first when asked to think of a suburb. It's heavily Hispanic, like the area at large. And it is home to the Dadeland Mall, one of South Florida's first malls. (Though even the "quiet" suburbs follow the Miami script: in the 1970s as drug wars were beginning to give the city its Miami Vice image, the Dadeland Mall was the scene of an infamous drug gang hit in the parking lot.)

The district is narrow, but extremely long, running almost into Hialeah in the north, starting northwest of Miami International Airport and running past the airport going south, roughly following the Palmetto Expressway. It includes part of Westchester and then in the south, it widens to include most of what is generally thought of as Kendall (though Kendall doesn't have precisely defined borders.) Along the eastern edge of the district is the affluent suburb of Pinecrest. The district stops just short of Biscayne Bay in Perrine.

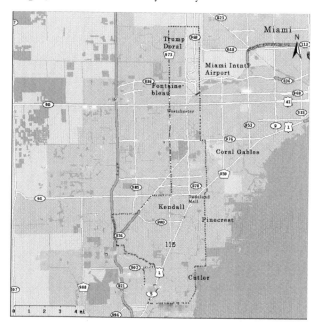

WHO LIVES HERE?

The urban demographer Richard Florida has ranked many of the nation's Census tracts by the jobs people do - whether they're in jobs classified as "working class," "service class," or the "creative class." A Census tract in Pinecrest is the one in Miami-Dade with the most number of people in the "creative class," which includes people who work in high-skill, usually high-pay jobs in science and technology, business, the arts, media, or entertainment. It also includes doctors and lawyers. More than 75 percent of the residents in the main Pinecrest tract are "creative class" members in a city where fewer than one in three people are defined by doing that type of work. The other Census tract that includes part of Pinecrest is also on the Top 10 list for Creative Class workers in the Miami metro area.

Overall this is an affluent district, with a number of upper middle class residents throughout. It's majority Hispanic, 65 percent, and about 27 percent non-Hispanic white. The district is young, with working families the dominant group, and a median age of about 41.

POLITICAL ISSUES AND TRENDS

House District 115 is split politically, with about 4 in 10 voters registered Republicans, more than 3 in 10 registered Democrats and just about a quarter of voters in neither party. The district was on the fence on Election Day 2012 as well, nearly splitting evenly between Mitt Romney and Barack Obama, giving Romney a razor-thin edge. Similarly, Democrat Alex Sink won by 1 percentage point in this district in the 2010 governor's race and the district's House member, Michael Bileca, had a fairly close race, too, beating Democrat Jeffrey Solomon in the 2012 election 53 percent to 47 percent.

Bileca was first elected to the House in 2010, when he was elected in the old House District 117, and beat Democrat Lisa Lesperance with 60 percent of the vote. Bileca was probably most noticed in the House for sponsoring a highly controversial school choice bill, and for being one of the Miami lawmakers who opposed legislation that would have allowed a local referendum in the city on increasing the hotel tax to improve the Miami Dolphins' Sun Life Stadium. After opposing the effort, Bileca is one of several area lawmakers now targeted for defeat by a political action committee linked to the Dolphins owner. Bileca has consistently been anti-tax, and also opposes a proposed Miami referendum on an increased local sales tax for higher education.

Bileca is the chairman of the House Choice and Innovation Subcommittee of the Education Committee which deals with school choice, and as such was the 2013 sponsor of a controversial bill on the role parents play in what happens to failing public schools. The measure would have allowed parents to vote to allow the school to be taken over by a private charter school company. Opponents fought the measure vigorously, saying it created an opening for the for-profit charter school companies to lobby parents to let them take over schools. The closely watched bill died on a 20-20 vote in the Senate.

DISTRICT 115 STATS

Registration (Book closing, 2012)
Republicans 38 percent
Democrats 34.8 percent
NPA 25.7 percent

Voting Age Population (2010 Census):123,590
Hispanic 65.5 percent
White (Non-Hispanic) 26.5 percent
Black 4.5 percent

Median Age: 40.7

Men: 48.2 percent
Women 51.8 percent

2012 PRESIDENT
Mitt Romney 50.2 percent, Barack Obama 49.1
percent (Estimated)*

2012 STATE HOUSE
Rep. Michael Bileca, R-Miami, 52.6 percent,
Jeffrey Solomon, Democrat, 47.4 percent

2010 GOVERNOR
Alex Sink 49.6 percent, Rick Scott 48.6 percent

2008 PRESIDENT
John McCain 52.4 percent, Barack Obama 47
percent

HOUSE DISTRICT 116
SW MIAMI-DADE: DORAL, SUNSET, FIU

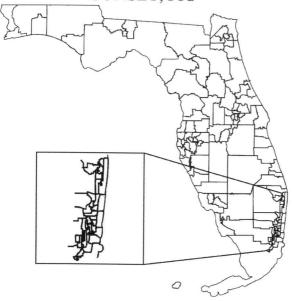

COUNTIES: Miami-Dade
RATING: Solid Republican

HEAVILY HISPANIC DISTRICT
INCLUDES 'DORALZUELA'

House District 116 is "out west" in the suburban Miami area west of the airport. It includes part of Doral (and the Trump National Doral, which has hosted PGA events since the 1960s and is currently home to the World Golf Championships-Cadillac Championship), the Fontainebleau neighborhood, Olympia Heights, Sunset and at its southern end just getting into Kendall. The area includes the main campus of Florida International University and the adjacent University Park area. It also includes

Miami-Dade College's Kendall campus. The area is sandwiched roughly in between the Florida Turnpike on the west and NW and SW 87th Ave. (Galloway Rd.) on the east, and the Don Shula Expressway on the southeast.

Doral, built by Doris and Alfred Kaskel, whose combined first names gave the place its name, is home to large numbers of import and export companies, in part because it is so close to Miami International Airport. The area, in addition to a number of businesses that rely on the airport, is also home to a number of corporate office parks.

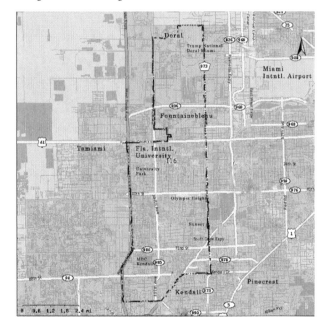

WHO LIVES HERE?

Nearly 8 out of 10 people of voting age in this district are Hispanic, and the majority are Cuban-Americans. While they're nowhere near as numerous as Cuban-Americans in the district as a whole, Venezuelans have made Doral their primary home in North America, leading some in Miami to refer to the area as Doralzuela. The city claims the largest expatriate Venezuelan community in the United States, between 10 and 20 percent of Doral's population. Luigi Boria, a millionaire computer executive who fled the Chavez regime in Venezuela, was elected mayor of Doral in late 2012, and is believed to be the first Venezuelan-born mayor of a Florida city. [1] With ongoing political turmoil in the South American nation, some expect the community to continue to grow in Doral. [2] The Miami Association of Realtors says since the beginning of the Chavez era in Venezuela in 1998, Venezuelans have bought more property in Miami - much of it in Doral and House District 116 - than any other national origin group from Latin America. Most of those who fled Venezuela and ended up living in Doral are fairly well-off financially, like Boria.

The district is mixed between young families - one in three households has a child under 18 - and retirees and empty nesters. Nearly 40 percent of households include adults over age 65. The largest segment of the population is people in their 40s, who make up 15 percent of district's population, and the median age is in

---

[1] For more, see: Phil Latzman, "Meet the New Mayor of Doralzuela....' WLRN (Online, 10 January, 2013, http://wlrn.org/post/meet-new-mayor-doralzuela-first-venezuelan-born-mayor-florida)

[2] Enrique Flor, "Doral Expects New Wave of Venezuelan Immigrants," *The Miami Herald,* 16 April, 2013.

the low 40s. It's mostly a white collar community, though many here also work in service industry jobs. The median household incomes in the district are generally below the state average, in the low $40,000s, though in some of the wealthier neighborhoods, primarily in the Sunset area, the median household income is closer to $70,000, well above the state median.

POLITICAL ISSUES AND TRENDS

The fact that the area that now makes up the district is over 50 percent Cuban-American, and has been for a while, is reflected in voting patterns. The area has been solidly Republican for years, with both John McCain in 2008 and Rick Scott in 2010 winning by roughly 20 percentage points in the area's precincts. However, as with elsewhere in the Cuban community, there appears to be a bit of a shift going on. In 2012, Mitt Romney won the district's precincts by only about half that amount, just under 10 percentage points. Several political observers have noted that with each succeeding generation, the Republican grip on Cuban-American politics has lessened. Exit polling done in 2012 by the Bendixen and Amandi firm showed that while Cuban-Americas still voted narrowly for Mitt Romney, President Obama may have gotten as much as 60 percent of the vote from Cuban-Americans who were born in the United States.

Venezuelans, even though many fled a leftist regime in their home country and might be expected to have Republican tendencies, didn't, at least in 2012. The same Bendixen exit polling data found Venezuelan-Americans voted for

Obama over Romney by a 76-24 percent margin. Some Cuban-Americans, and conservatives discount Bendixen's polling, in part because founding partner Sergio Bendixen has also been paid by Democrats, including the Obama campaign, to do polling and research. But exit polls from the Pew Hispanic Center and Edison Research (for the major TV networks and the AP) also showed a large shift in Cuban-American sentiment in the 2012 election.[3]

Democrats, however, still haven't been able to compete farther down the ticket with Republicans in most of the heavily Cuban neighborhoods of Miami-Dade County, in part because they don't have a lot of experienced Democratic candidates, owing mostly to the fact that the districts were so clearly unwinnable for so many years. The party often doesn't run candidates in many of these areas, and in 2012 didn't have a candidate for House District 116.

Rep. Jose Felix Diaz, a land use attorney, was chosen to be chairman of the Miami-Dade legislative delegation in 2011, despite having been just elected to the House in 2010. But often when Diaz' name appears in print, it is preceded by "rising star." And in addition to

---

[3] Bendixen Polling Election Results, (Online, 2012, http://bendixenandamandi.com/wp-content/uploads/2011/05/ElectionResults-ExitPoll.pdf

See Also, "John Fund, "Romney's Hispanic Disaster," National Review Online. (Online, 9 November, 2012.

http://www.nationalreview.com/corner/333072/rom neys-hispanic-disaster-john-fund) academic bona fides - he went to Columbia for law school - Diaz has some pop culture star appeal as well, having been a contestant on Donald Trump's "*The Apprentice*" TV show. Diaz has also convinced his colleagues and party officials that he's a winner, having beaten a well-financed Democratic candidate, Jeffrey Solomon, in the 2010 general election for what was then HD 115, and prevailed in what some said was one of the nastiest Republican primaries after redistricting. In that race, Diaz defeated fellow GOP Rep. Ana Rivas Logan after both were redistricted into HD 116 in a race marred by personal and political attacks.

In 2013 Diaz was the House sponsor of one of the session's major pieces of legislation, a bill to prevent utilities in the future from charging customers for yet-to-be-built nuclear plants. The bill, which was signed into law by Gov. Rick Scott, also put in place new benchmarks for companies already billing customers for un-built plants. But despite the bill taking on utility companies, Diaz was better known as one of three Miami-area House Republicans who opposed a bill that could have allowed public money to help the Miami Dolphins upgrade their stadium. That has reportedly made Diaz and the other two, Carlos Trujillo and Michael Bileca, targets of the team's billionaire owner Stephen Ross, whose political group was looking for candidates to oppose them, though late in 2013 none of the three had drawn an opponent for 2014. [4]

---

[4] Patricia Mazzei, "Dolphins Owner Recruiting Candidates..." The Miami Herald, 31 July, 2013

DISTRICT 116 STATS

Registration (Book closing, 2012)
Republicans 42.5 percent
Democrats 28.5 percent
NPA 27.5 percent

Voting Age Population (2010 Census): 127,582
Hispanic 84.4 percent
White (Non-Hispanic) 11.8 percent
Black 1.8 percent

Median Age: 41.5

Men 46.7 percent
Women 54.5 percent

2012 PRESIDENT
Mitt Romney 54.5 percent, Barack Obama 44.9
percent (Estimated)*

2012 STATE HOUSE
Republican Primary: Rep. Jose Felix Diaz, R-
Miami, 66 percent, Ana Rivas Logan, 34
percent; Diaz faced only write-in opposition in
general election

2010 GOVERNOR
Rick Scott 59.3 percent, Alex Sink 38.8 percent

2008 PRESIDENT
John McCain 59.7 percent, Barack Obama 39.7
percent

HOUSE DISTRICT 117
SOUTH DADE, RICHMOND
HEIGHTS TO FLORIDA CITY

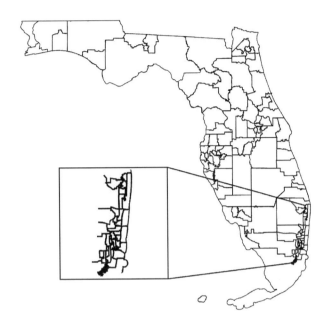

COUNTIES: Miami-Dade

RATING: Super Democrat

DIVERSE COMMUNITY OF
FARMWORKERS AND COMMUTERS;
DEMOCRATIC LOCK

House District 117 is a narrow sliver of a
district that mostly runs between U.S. 1, or
Dixie Highway, and the Florida Turnpike
Extension in south Miami-Dade County. It
starts in the north in Richmond Heights and
then includes all or parts of West Perrine,
Goulds, Naranja, and Leisure City and then in
the southern part of the district picks up part of
Homestead and most of Florida City.

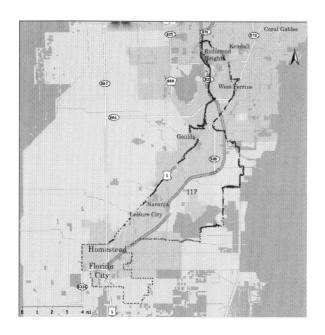

Richmond Heights has one of the more
interesting historical stories among Miami-area
communities. It may have been the first
planned community for African-Americans.
The neighborhood was built at the end of
World War II by Army Col. Frank C. Martin, a
white man who had led black troops during the
war and wanted to help returning African-
American veterans find needed housing options
in the segregated South. He consulted the black
community and then built the homes, and
donated land for parks and churches and the
area became a haven for middle class black
families at a time when their housing options
elsewhere in the Miami area were limited. Many
of the residents of the area are the second and
third generation descendants of those African-
American veterans who first bought here in the
late 1940s.

At its north end, the district is urban-
suburban, bumping up against the Miami

suburb of Kendall along South Dixie Highway. At its southern end, the district has a rural feel. The district also includes the former Homestead Air Force Base and the current Homestead Air Reserve Base. Much of this district was hit hard by Hurricane Andrew in 1992, and many of the homes here have been built or rebuilt since then. The Homestead area and the surrounding Redland area is the heart of Miami-Dade County's agriculture industry. Miami-Dade County is second in the state in terms of the value of agricultural products produced and nearly all of that produce is grown in the southern tip of the county around Homestead. Many of the farms themselves are outside of District 117, which mostly takes in the densely populated narrow strips along U.S. 1 and the Turnpike, but Homestead is where many of the farm workers live, do their shopping and take care of other business.

WHO LIVES HERE?

The district is diverse - a little over half of the residents are Hispanic, and about 35 percent are black, while just under 10 percent are non-Hispanic white. About 20 percent of residents are Cuban-American, but nearly 10 percent are Mexican-Americans, mostly working in agriculture. Farming employs thousands in South Dade - the nursery industry alone puts more than $600 million into the economy here each year. At the southern part of the district, where many of the farm workers live, the percentages of non-Cuban Hispanics is higher. "Other Hispanic or Latino people" mostly Central Americans, make up 23 percent of the population of Homestead, the largest group of Hispanics in that city, while Mexicans and Cubans make up 15 percent each. And just next to Homestead in Leisure City, the percentage of Mexicans increases to 22 percent, while Cubans make up 26 percent and other Latinos 17 percent.

The median family incomes in the southern part of the district are in the mid-to-high 30-thousand range, but at the north end of the district in middle class Richmond Heights, the median family income rises to over $50,000. Naranja - where the district's current representative, Kionne McGhee, grew up in public housing - is the one of the poorer parts of the district, with median family income barely making it to $30,000, and more than a third of the population living below the poverty level. Florida City, also at the southern end of the district, is even worse off, it's one of the poorest communities in the state. It has a per capita income of just $8,300, a median household income of only about $25,000 and more than 45 percent of its residents live below the poverty line.

POLITICAL ISSUES AND TRENDS

This district is lopsidedly Democratic, a super stronghold for the party that doesn't seem to have any chance of being competitive anytime soon. President Obama won the district by more than 60 percentage points in 2012, after Democratic gubernatorial candidate Alex Sink won the area in 2010 by just under 60 points. Obama also won in 2008 by nearly 60 points. Non-Cuban Hispanic growth is expected to continue in South Dade, and while Republicans have talked about courting the

Latino vote, there's no reason to expect they could make a strong showing here.

Top issues locally include growth and infrastructure, water and wastewater, and taxes and local services. Property insurance rates, availability of jobs, and traffic on U.S. 1 are also big issues in the community.

When he was in high school, McGhee could have been voted least likely to become a legislator. Or a lawyer, or a college graduate, or a success at all. McGhee was raised in public housing in Naranja and mostly on his own with his five siblings, roaming the neighborhood while his mother worked picking beans in the fields nearby. McGhee writes that he tested for an IQ of 78 labeling him mentally disabled, and was suspended from school more than 20 times, and arrested with the prospect of prison seeming likely. By the time he was a young man, his father and a brother had both been murdered.

Somehow, McGhee persevered and managed to get to Howard University, where he got a bachelor's degree in just two years, and then to the Thurgood Marshall School of Law in Houston, where he got his law degree. He wrote a memoir titled "A Mere 'I Can' is American," and returning to Miami got a job in the Miami-Dade County prosecutor's office. He later went into private legal practice, and started to get involved in Democratic politics. He ran for the House in 2010, challenging Democratic incumbent Rep. Dwight Bullard. McGhee lost the primary, but got 47 percent of the vote. In 2012, McGhee ran for the newly drawn District 117 and defeated two other Democrats,

Carmen Morris and Harold Ford in the primary, overcoming the Miami Herald's endorsement of Morris. McGhee has also been a motivational speaker since overcoming his bleak childhood prospects, and in the Legislature he quickly gained attention as willing to speak thoughtfully as a freshman on a number of issues in committee and on the floor. As a member of the minority party, passing legislation was a different matter, though - and McGhee failed to pass a single bill in his first session. But he also didn't shy away from big issues or take the easy road of carrying feel-good and easy-pass legislation. McGhee proposed a controversial bill to ban stores from using disposable plastic bags, a measure that went nowhere, and also pushed a new administrative fee - some would say tax - on the sale of guns and ammunition, another measure that had no chance in a gun-friendly House. Another bill sponsored by McGhee in 2013 would have created a civil cause of action for failure to provide notice to tenants of pending foreclosure of property, and another bill would have required electronic recording of statements made to police during interrogation and a presumption of inadmissibility for those statements not taped.

DISTRICT 117 STATS

Registration (Book closing, 2012)
Democrats 60 percent
NPA 24 percent
Republicans 15 percent

Voting Age Population (2010 Census): 108,393
Hispanic 55.2 percent

Black 34.2 percent
White (Non-Hispanic) 8.6 percent

Median Age: 30.4

Men 48.2 percent
Women 51.8 percent

2012 PRESIDENT
Barack Obama 81.6 percent, Mitt Romney, 18
percent (Estimated)*

2012 STATE HOUSE:
Kionne McGhee, Democrat, faced only write-
in opposition

2010 GOVERNOR
Alex Sink 77.9 percent, Rick Scott 20.4 percent

2008 PRESIDENT
Barack Obama 79.2 percent, John McCain 20.3
percent

HOUSE DISTRICT 118
SOUTHWEST MIAMI SUBURBS

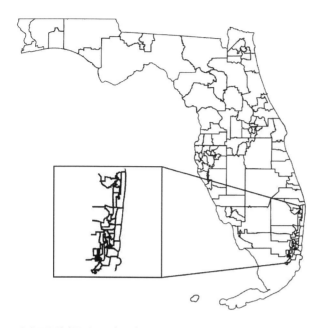

COUNTIES: Miami-Dade
RATING: Swing District

NICARAGUAN AND COLOMBIAN-AMERICANS, FUTURE OF THE DEMOCRATIC PARTY

Just as houses in the suburbs are the realization of the stereotypical American dream, these Hispanic suburbs southwest of Miami are a central part of the hopes and dreams of the Democratic party. Middle and upper middle class Hispanics, some just starting out on the immigrant American dream, some a generation or two removed from their original homeland, voted in neighborhoods like these just enough for Barack Obama in 2012 to give him a win in the state, and, most encouraging for Democrats, in larger numbers than they did in

2008 or any other recent top of the ticket election. In fact, the precincts in this district were won by John McCain in the 2008 presidential race, by about 7 percent, and by Republican Rick Scott in the 2010 governor's race by about the same amount. But in 2012, Obama narrowly defeated Mitt Romney here. Democratic strategists widely credited the Hispanic vote, and this district - one of six Miami-Dade House districts that is more than 80 percent Hispanic - was the epicenter of that shift.

The district is southwest of Miami, south of

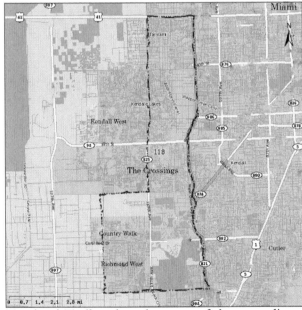

Tamiami Trail and to the west of the sprawling suburb of Kendall. It's a tall, narrow district that starts at its northern end right along Tamiami Trail in the Tamiami neighborhood, and goes south through Kendale Lakes. The district also includes the planned communities of "The Crossings," and Country Walk. Much of this area has been rebuilt and repopulated since 1992, when Hurricane Andrew ploughed through the area. The Country Walk subdivision, which lost 90 percent of its homes in the storm, and the Dadeland Mobile Home Park in Richmond West were two of the areas hardest hit by Andrew.

WHO LIVES HERE?

House District 118 is one of six Florida House districts - all in Miami Dade - where more than 80 percent of residents are Hispanic. But while most of the others are more heavily Cuban-American, HD 118, along with its southwest Dade neighbor District 119, has a large population of "other Hispanic or Latino" residents. The district is 45.5 percent Cuban-American and about 30 percent are "other." It's that "other" group, thought to be growing, that makes the districts in this part of the Miami area so tantalizing for Democrats.

While many Cubans, especially older ones, continue to vote for Republican candidates, that too is changing fairly dramatically, as the Cuban "exile" community gets farther and farther away in time and psychological focus from the 1959 revolution that sent its members packing for Florida. Latinos from Central and South America are more likely by far to vote for Democrats. But Cuban-Americans are now spread out all over South Florida - and they aren't coming to Florida in large numbers anymore. The "other Hispanics" are coming, though, and they're moving to the southwest suburbs of Miami. Many residents in this part of the county are Colombian, with Kendale Lakes and The Crossings both with Colombian-American populations nearing 10 percent. The Nicaraguan-American populations of Kendale

Lakes and Tamiami are both above 6 percent and those two communities are No. 7 and No. 8 on the list of largest Nicaraguan communities in the United States, according to the Census Bureau's American Community Survey. [1] Richmond West also has large numbers of Nicaraguans and Colombians. The district also includes smaller numbers of Mexicans, Puerto Ricans, Dominicans, Venezuelans, and Peruvians. While Cuban-Americans here are likely to be second and third generation Americans, most Central and South Americans in the area are immigrants or young second generation Americans.

The district is above the state median in terms of income, with families in Kendale Lakes having a median income in the mid-$50-thousands, although more than 13 percent there live below the poverty line. Family incomes are higher in The Crossings and very high in Richmond West at the south end of the district, where median household and family incomes are just shy of $70,000. Many of the people who live in this area are white collar professionals, including many of the immigrants. A 2010 analysis of Census data by the Fiscal Policy Institute found that more than half of Miami's immigrants, the majority of whom are Hispanic, are in white collar management or technical jobs. [2]

---

[1] United States Census, 2012 American Community Survey, 1-Year Estimate. Table B03001, Hispanic or Latino Origin by Specific Origin.

[2] Fiscal Policy Institute "Across the Spectrum, The Wide Range of Jobs Immigrants Do," (April, 2010.

The distinction between Cuban-American Hispanics and those from elsewhere in Latin America still matters - although less than it used to. Exit polling by the Bendixen and Amandi firm, which works for Democrats but is respected for reputable Hispanic voter research, showed in 2012 that Cuban-Americans voted for Mitt Romney in the presidential race by a 52 percent to 48 percent margin, while those of Central and South American origins gave Barack Obama closer to 75 to 80 percent of the vote. Colombians voted about 80 percent for Obama, according to the Bendixen exit polling, and Nicaraguans about 72 percent for Obama . With those two groups and other non-Cuban Hispanics making up nearly 30 percent of the total population of House District 118, it's easy to see how Obama managed to get just a shade over half the votes here. It's a recent phenomenon - the district, along with neighboring District 119, are among just a few in which the precincts voted for one party's presidential candidate in 2008 and for the other party's in 2012. It appears their ability to draw 50-plus-1 in districts like this one is so new that even Democrats weren't ready for it. They didn't put up a House candidate in District 118 in 2012, giving Republican Rep. Frank Artiles a free return pass.

Artiles, R-Miami, was elected to the House in 2010 in a race for an open seat in what was

---

Online:
http://www.fiscalpolicy.org/FPI_ImmigrantsAndOccupationalDiversity.pdf)

then District 119 against a candidate Democrats had hoped could turn the seat to their party. The seat had been vacated by term-limited Juan Zapata, a Colombian-American Republican, and seeing a chance to flip a seat, Democrats had pushed hard for Miami-Dade Farm Bureau head Katie Edwards. But Artiles defeated her in the 2010 GOP wave election, and then after redistricting, he was elected without opposition in 2012 to represent House District 118.

In 2013 Artiles sponsored a bill that would specify that students born in the United States who attend Florida high schools could get in-state tuition, even if their parents are in the country illegally, a measure that died in committee. Artiles has also been among the leaders of a push to repeal the state law allowing red-light cameras, which have been criticized by some as just being used by cities for raising revenue. In 2013 Artiles was also a major player in a bill to allow Miami Children's Hospital to open a labor and delivery unit. Artiles has also been a critic of efforts to allow Citizens Property Insurance to charge more money, saying that many in South Florida don't have a choice about their property insurance and can't afford rate hikes.

As with the insurance debate, Artiles can be independent-minded, and while he is in line with Republican talking points on taxes and regulatory issues, he also campaigns on seeking to bolster public education, while many Florida Republicans talk more about education in the context of offering alternatives to public education. Artiles has called for providing more money for music and art and higher pay for teachers in public schools. Artiles is Cuban-American, the son of immigrant parents, and was born and raised in Miami-Dade County. He went away to school at Florida State, and returned to Miami to get a law degree and to serve a stint in the U.S. Marine Corps, including a tour in Iraq. He now runs a business that helps people file insurance claims.

DISTRICT 118 STATS

Registration (Book closing, 2012)
Republicans 37.1 percent
Democrats 31.9 percent
NPA 29.6 percent

Voting Age Population (2010 Census): 121,790
Hispanic 81.2 percent
White (Non-Hispanic) 11.5 percent
Black 4.9 percent

Median Age: 39

Men 47.9 percent
Women 52.1 percent

2012 PRESIDENT
Barack Obama 50.9 percent, Mitt Romney, 48.6 percent (Estimated)*

2012 STATE HOUSE
Rep. Frank Artiles, R-Miami, faced only write-in opposition

2010 GOVERNOR
Rick Scott 52.4 percent, Alex Sink 45.8 percent

2008 PRESIDENT
John McCain 53.3 percent, Barack Obama 46.3 percent

HOUSE DISTRICT 119
WESTERN MIAMI SUBURBS, KENDALL WEST

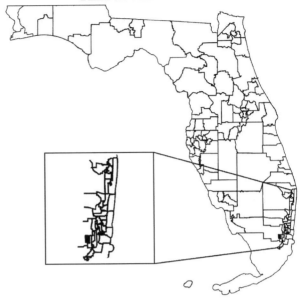

COUNTIES: Miami-Dade
RATING: Swing District

NO PARTYTOWN, FLORIDA

House District 119, out on the western edge of suburban Miami, where the city fades into the Everglades, is the district in Florida with the highest percentage of voters who aren't in one of the two major parties. Nearly one in three voters here, 31.9 percent, at the end of 2012, was registered with no party affiliation. But the most interesting thing about the district may be the degree to which voters here voted for President Obama in 2012. While Republican Rick Scott defeated Democrat Alex Sink here by a comfortable 10 percentage points in 2010, just two years later in 2012, Obama narrowly defeated Republican Mitt Romney in the district, by about a percentage point. That's also a big shift from the first time Obama was on the ballot - in 2008 Republican John McCain defeated Obama by nearly 10 points in those same precincts. The fairly dramatic shift means either many of those no-party voters are new to the area and likely to vote for a Democrat, which is the most likely scenario, or that the no-party voters switched from Republican to Democrat in their allegiance in the last few years, a less likely scenario. The number of NPA voters voting for Obama in 2012 had to be fairly high, assuming most party members vote for their candidate: 37 percent of voters here were Republicans during that election, to just 29.8 percent who were Democrats.

The district includes an area south of SW 8th St. west of SW 137th Ave. on the very

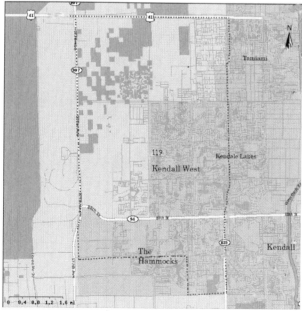

western edge of the Miami area, including the area known as Kendall West and part of The Hammocks. This district is quintessential suburbia (there's even an ice skating arena out here on the edge of the Everglades).

WHO LIVES HERE?

District 119 is heavily Hispanic – about 87 percent of the voting age population, but only about 45 percent Cuban-American. The Hammocks neighborhood, west of Kendall, split between HD 119 and neighboring HD 105, is home to a large number of Colombian immigrants, accounting for much of the non-Cuban Hispanic population. Peruvians, Venezuelans, Nicaraguans and Dominicans also live in the district. African-Americans make up about 2.5 percent of the district and non-Hispanic whites about 8.3 percent. The area is middle to upper middle class, with the median household income in The Hammocks about $60,000 and in Kendall West over $45,000.

POLITICAL ISSUES AND TRENDS

Just why the district has so many "no party" voters isn't totally clear, though voters like those here - with reasonably high levels of education and upper middle class incomes - are generally more likely to eschew the two parties than the very poor and the very wealthy. Heading into the 2012 general election, more Florida Hispanics – more than a half million – registered with no party affiliation than did with the Republican Party in the state. While Republicans acknowledged they turned off many Hispanics with a hard line on immigration, some observers have posited that many Latinos may have registered independent of the two major parties rather than identifying as Democrats because Catholic Hispanics tend to have more conservative social positions than the Democratic Party. Most of those Hispanic no party voters are believed to have supported Obama in 2012, however. Pew Center polling showed more than 90 percent of Romney voters were non-Hispanic whites. Also unclear is the degree to which the trend from Republican in the 2008 presidential and 2010 governor's race to Democrat (barely) in the 2012 presidential will stick. The district's Republican House member, Rep. Jeanette Nunez, is a moderate Republican, but wasn't on the ballot in 2012, so it also remains to be seen whether Democrats will be able to win in this district farther down the ballot, and when Barack Obama isn't on the ticket. As of late 2013, nobody had filed to challenge Nunez.

The area has all the concerns of any place where the comfortable middle class live on the edges of a big city. Among the issues here are just where the line should be between the progress of new development and preservation of a unique ecosystem next door; education; delivery of basic government services; and because it is an area with a large number of non-Cuban Hispanics, immigration policy.

Nunez was first elected to the House in 2010. She is a Miami native and has worked in government affairs for hospitals, including the Jackson Health System and Kendall Regional Medical Center. She started her career in politics working for then-state Sen. Alex Diaz de la Portilla. Nunez took what was likely a popular position in her district in sponsoring a bill to clarify that children born in the United States, even if their parents came to the country illegally, should qualify for in-state college tuition, though it wasn't a terribly difficult push with House leadership also behind the proposal. The bill did not cover, however, children born outside the United States and brought to the country illegally by their parents.

DISTRICT 119 STATS
Registration (Book closing, 2012)
Republicans 37 percent
NPA 31.9 percent
Democrats 29.8 percent

Voting Age Population (2010 Census): 119, 182
Hispanic 86.8 percent
White (Non-Hispanic) 8.3 percent
Black 2.5 percent

Median Age: 37.5

Men 47.2 percent
Women 52.8 percent

VOTING PERFORMANCE

2012 PRESIDENT
Barack Obama 50.1 percent, Mitt Romney, 49.3 percent (Estimated)*

2012 STATE HOUSE
Republican Primary: Jeanette Nunez, R-Miami, 72.6 percent, Libby Perez, 27.4 percent. Nunez faced only write-in opponent in general.

2010 GOVERNOR
Rick Scott 54.1 percent, Alex Sink 44 percent

2008 PRESIDENT
John McCain 54.6 percent, Barack Obama 45 percent

HOUSE DISTRICT 120
FAR SOUTHERN MIAMI-DADE
AND THE KEYS

COUNTIES: Miami-Dade, Monroe

RATING: Swing District

THE SOUTHERNMOST DISTRICT

The most recognizable part of House District 120 for most is the Florida Keys. The entire island chain - the only archipelago in the United States - stretching from Key Largo at the top, south and west down to Key West, the largest city in the Keys, is in the district. But it also includes communities at the bottom of the mainland peninsula, mostly unincorporated farming areas in South Miami-Dade County, surrounding Homestead and Florida City.

SOUTH DADE AND THE REDLAND

While farming doesn't come to mind when most people think of a modern metropolis like Miami, Miami-Dade County is second in the state only to Palm Beach County in the value of agricultural products produced and nearly all of that produce comes from the area at the far south end of the county. The nursery industry in the area is the second largest in the nation, and a major driver of Miami-Dade County's economy - with 1,500 nurseries and $660 million in annual production of ornamentals - accounting for thousands of jobs here. This is the only true tropical farming area in the country and farms here produce a number of tropical fruits, including many not grown anywhere else in the United States in any significant number. If you're buying American-grown starfruit or mamey sapote, they were almost certainly grown in South Dade, along with acres of lychee, bananas, plantains and passion fruit. Miami-Dade County is the top producer of mangoes in the United States and the 5th largest avocado producing county in the nation, and a huge supplier of winter vegetables to much of the country. Much of this semi-rural part of the Miami area is known as the Redland.

THE KEYS

People in lots of places claim their home is ifferent from everywhere else. Among those who are undoubtedly right about that are the often free-spirited people who live in this island chain that culminates in the continental United States' southernmost town, Key West, a place some call "the last resort." The most noticeable difference at first between the Keys and the mainland is the geography - this is a series of fairly narrow spits of gravel and sand jutting down off the continent to form the border between the Atlantic Ocean and the Gulf of

Mexico. But the real difference is the people. Many here came from somewhere else to start over - and the Keys are a place where slightly offbeat characters are not only accepted, but kind of expected. For a long time, the isolation of the area and its proximity to the Caribbean and Latin America, made it a drug and people smuggling haven and while not everyone in the Keys was involved, you never knew for sure who was and who wasn't. In 1984 the Key West Police Department - *the police department* - was declared a criminal enterprise by the U.S. Justice Department because it was helping cocaine smugglers operate. One guy testified his job was to deliver cocaine to the deputy chief's office. The fire chief - a guy named Bum Farto who wore red leisure suits and Elvis-style rose-tinted glasses - had been convicted of dealing drugs out of the fire house a decade earlier, and then disappeared, maybe a fugitive, maybe a murder victim.

In the 1970s, pushed mostly by outsiders like the feds, a clean-up of some of the criminality and corruption had begun, and as the economy grew and more and more wealthier people moved to the Keys and tourism in the islands boomed, it intensified. Now days the criminal part of Monroe County's identity is mostly a story about the past, part of the lore that goes along with Ernest Hemingway's bar-room brawls and the time in 1982 when Keys officials seceded from the United States and declared the creation of the Conch Republic. (The secession, in response to an unwanted federal roadblock checking for narcotics and illegal immigrants, was short-lived. The Republic declared war on the United States, quickly surrendered and applied for foreign aid.) While the big-time smuggling and drug dealing is now mostly gone, the spirit of not quite living by the same rules as the rest of the country continues. The Keys these days draw artists, contrarians, and lots of members of the gay community, rather than criminals on the run, but the original pirate mindset and refusing to be conventional remains at the center of the local ethic.

WHO LIVES HERE? MIAMI-DADE

The Miami-Dade part of the district is home to a large number of Hispanic farm workers, the backbone of the workforce in the agricultural area. Some are migrants, though many live in the area year-round. In the western parts of Homestead, the population is more than 50 percent Hispanic and mixed in origin. For example, in the 33030 zip code, which includes the western and northwestern parts of Homestead, about 22 percent of the population is of Mexican origin and about 14 percent of Cuban origin, while another 21 percent are other Latinos, mostly from Central America. Many of the non-Hispanic residents of the area are also closely tied to farming - some own or lease farmland, and some are working land that's been in their families for generations. New residents have moved in - and in some cases they're not particularly welcome. Many who have been here for a long time are against the building of new subdivisions that could portend the demise of the farming culture and economy in the area. Some of the newcomers, however, have moved to the area to be part of the agricultural economy. In the last quarter century, a few agro-tourism and boutique farm operations have sprung up, and there's even a winery that makes its wine from exotic tropical fruits like mango and lychee.

THE KEYS

Probably the most distinguishing factor about residents of the Keys is that most of them are from somewhere else. About half of the residents of the Keys were born in another state, and another roughly 20 percent or so were born in another country, with only about 30 percent born in Florida and a smaller percentage than that actually born and raised in the Keys. Take a look at the bios of the people on the websites of various businesses - whether it's the people who work at the local dive shops, teach in the local schools, work in the government agencies, or at the front desk of a hotel (or the local state representative). Almost all of them have some version of a sentence that says something like "she moved down to the Keys in 1996 to live her dream of being by the ocean," or "he escaped the cold northern winters to the Keys, to live at a slower pace, and do more fishing."

Most of the people in the Keys work in the service and hospitality industry, catering to tourists. In the 2010 Census recording of what jobs people do in Monroe County, the largest industry category by far was "arts, entertainment, recreation and accommodation and food services," which accounted for 1 in 5 workers here. Another 13 percent work in retail shops. Despite the fact that many here work in shops, restaurants and hotels, Monroe County's median household income is just under $54,000, above the $47,000 annual median household income in Florida as a whole. The per capita income is also a relatively high $35,000 a year - statewide it's just $26,733. The residents here are generally statistically well off mostly because if they're not - they can't afford to live here.

Four decades ago, Key West was a shady, low-cost place to which people escaped and melted into the ramshackle scenery. But the clean-up of the drug and "on-the-run" culture also spurred a change in that scenery. Now that it was cleaning up, "respectable people" with

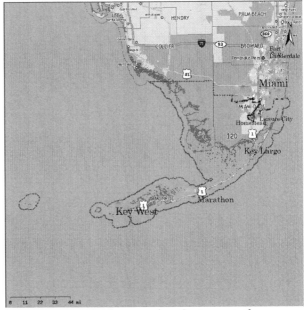

money wanted to move in. Out went the run-down places like Houseboat Row and in came the multimillion dollar condos and half-million dollar bungalows. By the late 2000s, it had become one of the most expensive real estate markets in the country. While it took a hit in the recession, the high values have returned and the median single family home sale price in Key

West in the first half of 2013 was right about a half million, just over $300,000 for the lower Keys as a whole. That's still not back to where it was at its peak, when homes were selling for around $800,000, typically, but the need to make good money (or bring it with you) to live in the Keys, especially the lower Keys, remains.

In part because it is so expensive to buy, nearly 40 percent of the population of Monroe County rent their housing, much higher than the state percentage of about 33 percent. Some who work in the service jobs don't actually even live in the islands, but commute from the mainland. Every morning, vans full of hotel housekeepers and other low-paid service industry workers leave Homestead and Florida City for the Keys because of a lack of low-cost housing on an island chain with few places to put new homes. Other service industry workers cram together in group houses full of people related only by the fact that they all wait on tables, or work on dive boats. Key West also has a large number of Eastern European guest workers who do many of the service industry jobs. Some find ways to stay for the long term - though as non-citizens they don't factor into the electoral demography. While there are wealthy people throughout the Keys, the invitation-only Ocean Reef Club, at the northern tip of Key Largo, is one of the wealthiest developments in the country, with pretty much all of its residents millionaires.

Monroe County is about 71 percent non-Hispanic white, 20 percent Hispanic, and 5 percent black. Most of the Hispanics who live here are of Cuban ancestry, with some of those, particularly in the upper Keys, having moved here from Miami. Some of Cuban ancestry in Key West are the descendants of early inhabitants of the city - some sources say there were nearly 10,000 Cubans living in Key West in the 19th Century, and one of its mayors in the 1870s was the son of Cuban Republic founder Carlos Manuel de Cespedes.

Key West's "live and let live" aura for years drew a relatively large gay community to the city, both as residents and vacationers, and it was the first city to openly recruit gay tourists. In the 1980s, Key West residents twice elected an openly gay mayor, Richard Heyman. In the 2010 Census, the first during which same-sex couples living together were encouraged to identify themselves as such for the purpose of being counted, about 34 couples per 1,000 in Key West identified themselves as gay, making the city fifth in the state on a percentage basis (Wilton Manors in Broward County is tops). But at just under 2 percent, Monroe County as a whole has the highest percentage of gay couples among Florida counties, and the third highest in the country. [3]

POLITICAL ISSUES AND TRENDS

The entire district has an independent, somewhat Libertarian current running through it - not surprising in the Keys where actual elected officials once "seceded" from the country, but it may be even stronger in South Dade. There's a strong tide of rural anti-

---

[3] The Williams Institute at the University of California Law School. *Analysis of Same-Sex Couples by Census Tract.* (2011) http://williamsinstitute.law.ucla.edu

establishment feeling in the Miami-Dade farming areas, with residents, most of whom hope to keep the area's agriculture viable, often fighting proposals by the county to allow more building. In 2013, they battled a proposed dump in the Redland, just as in the past they'd fought efforts to allow more housing, and even opposed a plan to build a fire station. "Redland Farm Area, Keep it Ag," can be seen on fliers and websites publicizing the effort to prevent suburban encroachment. The Keys have their own well-known tolerant, liberal social climate.

That combination of "leave us alone libertarianism" and "leave us alone social liberalism" mixes with a higher than average income population that includes a number of wealthy retirees and semi-retirees to produce a relatively high number of independent voters - about one in four - and otherwise a fairly competitive district. Registered Democrats narrowly outnumbered registered Republicans 37 percent to 34 percent in 2012 and it's a true swing district in recent elections where predictions are dicey.

President Obama won the precincts in the district in 2012 by just about 4 percentage points, and by about 7 percentage points in 2008. Democrat Alex Sink also won here in the 2010 governor's race, but barely, by just about 2 percentage points. And the district's House member, Rep. Holly Raschein is a Republican, but she previously worked for Democratic Rep. Ron Saunders, who represented the area before her. And before Saunders, Keys voters sent Republican Ken Sorensen to Tallahassee.

Most of the issues here come back to three

things - the high cost of windstorm insurance, providing infrastructure such as water and sewer, and balancing growth against environmental protection. Premiums on windstorm insurance charged by state-backed Citizens Property Insurance are always a big issue in the Keys - because in an island chain where few live more than a couple blocks from the water, private insurers don't write policies. The Keys were hit during Florida's back-to-back bad hurricane seasons of 2004 and 2005, getting brushed by Katrina before its infamous New Orleans hit, and hit fairly hard by Wilma in 2005. In the years after, property insurance rates skyrocketed and many in the Keys said they couldn't afford insurance. Lately, the affordability of flood insurance has also become a big issue. While property insurance takes up much of her time, the decidedly unglamorous and parochial issue of wastewater and storm-water management is often described by Raschein as her top priority in the Legislature. The area is under a state mandate to upgrade to a modern sewer system to alleviate environmental damage from septic tanks, but needs money for the upgrade.

Before she was elected to the House in 2012, Raschein worked as an aide to former Rep. Sorensen, a Key Largo Republican, and then to Saunders, a Key West Democrat. When she ran for the seat, Raschein played up that experience, saying she had already spent lots of time in Tallahassee building relationships and learning issues of importance to the Keys. In the GOP primary, Raschein defeated former Key West Mayor Morgan McPherson, and then beat Democrat Ian Whitney in the general election 52.4 percent to 47.6 percent, a result that again demonstrated the split-down-the-middle nature of the district politically. Raschein's focus has mostly been on trying to keep windstorm insurance rates low and securing money for sewer and stormwater infrastructure in the Keys. For Raschein, the insurance premium issue has been a difficult one, because many in her Republican Party see higher rates for Citizens as necessary to restoring a private insurance market - but Raschein has to work to keep rates low at the demand of her constituents. She's also been a top backer of Everglades restoration - the mainland part of Monroe County is in the Everglades - and seems to generally come down on the environmental protection side of decisions between preservation and unlimited growth.

As you might expect in such a district and from someone who spent six years as an aide to a Democratic lawmaker, Raschein works well across the partisan aisle and calls herself "fiscally conservative and socially moderate." In 2013, Raschein co-sponsored legislation adding sexual orientation and gender identity to the list of protections in the state's anti-discrimination law, a proposal that died in committee. Her major legislative victories in 2013 included passing a bill providing funding authority for the state to acquire certain land adjacent to military bases to keep it out of development, and a measure, co-sponsored with the area's Democratic senator, Dwight Bullard, that prohibits local government restrictions on agritourism, an issue important in the South Dade mainland part of the district where some boutique farmers are trying to draw tourists to their property. Her support for agriculture issues made her Florida Farm Bureau Legislator of the Year for 2013. Like so many others in the Keys, Raschein is a transplant, having moved to Florida in 1999. She was born and raised in Alaska.

DISTRICT 120 STATS
Registration (Book closing, 2012)
Democrats 37.2 percent
Republicans 34.4 percent
NPA 25.9 percent

Voting Age Population (2010 Census): 122,292
White (Non-Hispanic) 49.7 percent
Hispanic 40.1 percent
Black 7.9 percent

Median Age: 40

Men 52 percent
Women 48 percent

2012 PRESIDENT
Barack Obama 51.3 percent, Mitt Romney, 47.6 percent (Estimated)*

2012 STATE HOUSE
Holly Raschein, Republican, 52.4 percent, Ian Whitney, Democrat, 47.6 percent

2010 GOVERNOR
Alex Sink 49.5 percent, Rick Scott 47.2 percent

2008 PRESIDENT
Barack Obama 52.5 percent, John McCain, 46.4 percent

ABOUT THE AUTHOR

David Royse spent 17 years writing about Florida, 15 of them focusing on public policy, politics and the Legislature, first for The Associated Press and then as the founding executive editor of the News Service of Florida. During that time, he covered government, including more than 15 legislative sessions and the administrations of four governors, and political stories, including the deadlocked presidential election of 2000 and every legislative election for more than a decade. Royse has also worked for the AP in Miami and Louisville, Ky., as well as for newspapers and radio stations. A native of Louisville and a graduate of The College of Wooster in Ohio, he has a master's degree in journalism from The University of Missouri.

INDEX

This index is intended not to include every place, person or concept mentioned, rather only to help readers find districts based on House members, or places discussed at length.

Made in the USA
Charleston, SC
23 April 2014